NEVERENDING STORIES

NEVERENDING STORIES

TOWARD A CRITICAL NARRATOLOGY

Ann Fehn, Ingeborg Hoesterey,
and Maria Tatar, Editors

PRINCETON UNIVERSITY PRESS

PRINCETON, NEW JERSEY

COPYRIGHT © 1992 BY PRINCETON UNIVERSITY PRESS
PUBLISHED BY PRINCETON UNIVERSITY PRESS, 41 WILLIAM STREET,
PRINCETON, NEW JERSEY 08540
IN THE UNITED KINGDOM: PRINCETON UNIVERSITY PRESS, OXFORD

LIBRARY OF CONGRESS CATALOGING-IN-PUBLICATION DATA

NEVERENDING STORIES : TOWARD A CRITICAL NARRATOLOGY /
ANN FEHN, INGEBORG HOESTEREY, AND MARIA TATAR, EDITORS.

P. CM.

INCLUDES INDEX.

ISBN 0-691-06895-X (ALK. PAPER)

1. NARRATION (RHETORIC) 2. FICTION—TECHNIQUE. I. FEHN,
ANN CLARK. II. HOESTEREY, INGEBORG. III. TATAR, MARIA M., 1945–.
IV. TITLE: NEVERENDING STORIES.

PN3383.N35N4   1992   808.3—DC20   91-19460   CIP

THIS BOOK HAS BEEN COMPOSED IN LINOTRON GALLIARD

PRINCETON UNIVERSITY PRESS BOOKS ARE PRINTED
ON ACID-FREE PAPER, AND MEET THE GUIDELINES FOR
PERMANENCE AND DURABILITY OF THE COMMITTEE ON
PRODUCTION GUIDELINES FOR BOOK LONGEVITY
OF THE COUNCIL ON LIBRARY RESOURCES

PRINTED IN THE UNITED STATES OF AMERICA BY
PRINCETON UNIVERSITY PRESS, PRINCETON, NEW JERSEY

10 9 8 7 6 5 4 3 2 1

For Dorrit Cohn

IN MEMORIAM

Ann Clark Fehn, 1945–1989

CONTENTS

LIST OF CONTRIBUTORS   xi

Introduction   3
Ingeborg Hoesterey

PART ONE: HISTORY, FICTION, AND THE CLAIMS OF
WRITING: THE AUTO/BIOGRAPHICAL MODE   15

ONE
Between History and Fiction: On Dorrit Cohn's Poetics of Prose   17
Thomas Pavel

TWO
Fictionality in Historiography and the Novel   29
Paul Michael Lützeler

THREE
Fictionality, Historicity, and Textual Authority: Pater, Woolf,
Hildesheimer   45
Judith Ryan

FOUR
Mocking a Mock-Biography: Steven Millhauser's *Edwin Mullhouse* and
Thomas Mann's *Doctor Faustus*   62
Jens Rieckmann

FIVE
Habsburg Letters: The Disciplinary Dynamics of Epistolary Narrative in
the Correspondence of Maria Theresa and Marie Antoinette   70
Larry Wolff

SIX
Authenticity as Mask: Wolfgang Hildesheimer's *Marbot*   87
Käte Hamburger

PART TWO: THE SUBJECT IN QUESTION: THE NARRATION
OF CONSCIOUSNESS   99

SEVEN
Interpretive Strategies, Interior Monologues   101
Shlomith Rimmon-Kenan

EIGHT
Consonant and Dissonant Closure in *Death in Venice* and *The Dead* 112
Franz K. Stanzel

NINE
Identity by Metaphors: *A Portrait of the Artist* and *Tonio Kröger* 124
John Neubauer

TEN
Patterns of Justification in *Young Törless* 138
Stanley Corngold

PART THREE: GENDER, DIFFERENCE, AND
NARRATION 161

ELEVEN
Crossing the Gender Wall: Narrative Strategies in GDR Fictions of
Sexual Metamorphosis 163
Gail Finney

TWELVE
Feminist Intertextuality and the Laugh of the Mother: Leonora
Carrington's *Hearing Trumpet* 179
Susan Rubin Suleiman

THIRTEEN
Telling Differences: Parents vs. Children in "The Juniper Tree" 199
Maria Tatar

FOURTEEN
No No Nana: The Novel as Foreplay 216
David Mickelsen

PART FOUR: THE DISCOURSE OF NARRATOLOGY 235

FIFTEEN
Contingency 237
David E. Wellbery

SIXTEEN
A Narratological Exchange 258
Dorrit Cohn and Gérard Genette

INDEX 267

LIST OF CONTRIBUTORS

DORRIT COHN is a professor of German and comparative literature at Harvard University. She is the author of *Transparent Minds: Narrative Modes for Presenting Consciousness in Fiction*, and has published numerous articles on narrative poetics and twentieth-century fiction.

STANLEY CORNGOLD is a professor of German and comparative literature at Princeton University. He is the author of *The Fate of the Self: German Writers and French Theory* and *Franz Kafka: The Necessity of Form*. Two books are in press—*Borrowed Lives*, a metafictional narrative, and *Literary Tensions*, a study of German writers and thinkers from Lessing to Benjamin.

ANN CLARK FEHN (1945–1989) received her Ph.D. at Stanford and taught German literature and language at Harvard University from 1974 to 1982 before she joined the faculty of the University of Rochester. As dean, she was instrumental in reconstructing the undergraduate curriculum. Professor Fehn is the author of *Change and Performance: Gottfried Benn's Text for Paul Hindemith's Das Unaufhörliche* and editor of *Gottfried Benns Briefwechsel mit Paul Hindemith*. Her numerous articles address problems of the interrelation of music and literature, lieder, GDR literature, and cultural theory. Ann Fehn devoted most of her energy during the last two years of her life to the preparation of the collection at hand.

GAIL FINNEY is a professor of German and comparative literature at the University of California, Davis. She is the author of *The Counterfeit Idyll: The Garden Ideal and Social Reality in Nineteenth-Century Fiction* and *Women in Modern Drama: Freud, Feminism, and European Theater at the Turn of the Century*, as well as numerous articles on nineteenth-century European literature and postwar German fiction.

GÉRARD GENETTE is a professor of aesthetics and poetics at the Ecole des Hautes Etudes en Sciences Sociales in Paris. His most recent book are *Palimpsestes*, *Seuils*, and *Fiction et Diction*. He is the editor of *Poétique*.

KÄTE HAMBURGER is a professor emeritus of comparative literature at the Technical University, Stuttgart, Germany. Among her many books on German and world literature, it is the study *Die Logik der Dichtung*, first published in 1957, that established her as one of the foremost narratologists. The revised edition (1968) has been reprinted often and translated into many languages. The English version appeared in 1973 under the title *The Logic of Literature*.

INGEBORG HOESTEREY is an associate professor of Germanic studies at Indiana University. She is the author of *Verschlungene Schriftzeichen: Intertextualität von Literatur und Kunst in der Moderne/Postmoderne* and the editor of *Zeitgeist in Babel: The Postmodernist Controversy*. She has published numerous articles on twentieth-century German fiction, the interrelation of literature and visual art, and postmodernism in the arts.

PAUL MICHAEL LÜTZELER teaches German and comparative literature at Washington University in St. Louis. His articles on literary history and theory have appeared in European and American journals. His books include *Hermann Broch: A Biography*.

DAVID MICKELSEN is an associate professor of English at the University of Utah. His articles on nineteenth- and twentieth-century fiction range from Hamsun and Huysmans to Faulkner and Réage, and from the bildungsroman to spatial form.

JOHN NEUBAUER is a professor of comparative literature at the University of Amsterdam. His recent publications include *The Emancipation of Music from Language* and a large number of contributions to the Munich edition of Goethe's works.

THOMAS PAVEL teaches French and comparative literature at Princeton University. He is the author of *The Poetics of Plot: The Case of English Renaissance Drama*, *Fictional Worlds*, and *The Feud of Language: A Critical History of Structuralism*.

JENS RIECKMANN is a professor of German at the University of Washington. He is the author of *Aufbruch in die Moderne: Die Anfänge des Jungen Wien*, as well as articles on Thomas Mann, turn-of-the-century literature, and narrative theory.

SHLOMITH RIMMON-KENAN is a professor of English and comparative literature at the Hebrew University of Jerusalem. She is author of *The Concept of Ambiguity: The Example of James* and *Narrative Fiction: Contemporary Poetics*. She edited *Discourse in Literature and Psychoanalysis*, and has written many articles on narrative theory as well as on specific authors (James, Faulkner, Nabokov, Grass, Brooke-Rose).

JUDITH RYAN is the Robert K. and Dale J. Weary Professor of German and Comparative Literature at Harvard University. She is the author of a book on Rilke's poetry, *Umschlag und Verwandlung*, a book on the postwar German novel, *The Uncompleted Past*, and a forthcoming book on modernism, *The Vanishing Subject*. She has also published numerous articles on twentieth-century literature.

FRANZ K. STANZEL is a professor of English at the University of Graz, Austria. He is the author of several books on the novel, among them *A Theory of Narrative*, and numerous articles on English, Canadian, and German literature.

SUSAN RUBIN SULEIMAN is a professor of Romance and comparative literature at Harvard University. Her books include *Subversive Intent: Gender, Politics, and the Avant-Garde, Authoritarian Fictions: The Ideological Novel as a Literary Genre*, and the coedited volume *The Reader in the Text: Essays on Audience and Interpretation*.

MARIA TATAR is a professor of German at Harvard University. She is the author of *Spellbound: Studies on Mesmerism and Literature, The Hard Facts of the Grimms' Fairy Tales, Off with Their Heads! Fairy Tales and the Culture of Childhood*, and numerous articles in the fields of German Romanticism and Weimar culture.

DAVID E. WELLBERY is a professor of German at the Johns Hopkins University. He is the author of *Lessing's "Laocoon": Semiotics and Aesthetics in the Age of Reason* and *Goethe's "Harzreise im Winter": Eine Deutungskontroverse*. He has edited several volumes on criticism and interdisciplinary studies and published articles on literary theory and on German literature from the eighteenth century to the present.

LARRY WOLFF is an associate professor of history at Boston College. He is the author of *Postcards from the End of the World: Child Abuse in Freud's Vienna, The Vatican and Poland in the Age of the Partitions*, and the novel *The Boys and Their Baby*.

NEVERENDING STORIES

INTRODUCTION

Ingeborg Hoesterey

THE ANALYSIS of narrative technique in fiction has generally been considered something of a craft, practiced at times with painstaking descriptive precision and analytic power, and predominantly used in the service of interpretation. Narratology has often been mentioned in the same breath with structuralism, for both aspire to systematic comprehensiveness and attempt to identify and classify mechanisms and structures that generate, respectively, cultural and textual meaning. To be sure, "low structuralism" (as Robert Scholes was to call Genettean narratology) could not have matured in the sixties and seventies without the tradition of close textual analysis inaugurated by New Criticism.[1] Structuralist poetics crossed the Atlantic from France to an American scene open to form-oriented approaches. The reception of French structuralism in the United States also coincided with the introduction of Russian Formalism, and the two literary projects fueled a narratological enterprise already well launched by Percy Lubbock's *Craft of Fiction*, E. M. Forster's *Aspects of the Novel*, and Wayne C. Booth's *Rhetoric of Fiction*—to name just a few of the most influential titles.

From our fin de siècle vantage point, the seminal work of the text-oriented aesthetics of New Criticism marks what might be called the first, "archaic" phase of narratological scholarship. The structuralist-formalist paradigm, then, paved the way for "classical" narratology, the phase of maturation and peak of achievement for this branch of literary criticism. During the past decades, certain literary critics have moved away from narratology's almost exclusive focus on the question of what individual texts mean (a preoccupation grounded in implicit and explicit assumptions about the autonomy and privileged position of the literary text) to a heightened awareness of how texts ("texts" now used in a wider semiotic sense) mean, and for whom. Narratology, with its attention to the structures and conventions by which meaning is negotiated in fictional discourse, has played a prominent role in this shift. As critics have sought a clearer understanding of the discourses that constitute cultural and social institutions, and as they have moved toward a more complete understanding of the many ways in which readers' interpretations, including those of theorists, are caught up in the process of signification, narratology has provided paradigms and instruments of analysis, even as it has itself undergone critical scrutiny and development.

The attempt to come to grips with the state of affairs "beyond narratology" has prompted an invocation of the triadic sequence that divides Greek art into an archaic, a classical, and a Hellenistic era. Somewhat in jest, yet not entirely without a claim to typological stringency, one might conceive of "critical" narratology as a new Hellenism, a project merging impulses from critical theory and narratology proper into a hybrid form of critical discourse. Narratology's mingling with philosophical, political, and psychoanalytical positions in the past decade can be compared, structurally, to the exposure of Greek culture to foreign influences during what we now call the Hellenistic Age (Alexander the Great to Augustus).

The classical period of narratology begins in the 1970s. Franz K. Stanzel's typology of "narrative situations," first published in German in 1955, was introduced into Anglo-American critical discourse by Dorrit Cohn in the sixties and seventies, and a translation, *Narrative Situations in the Novel*, appeared in 1971.[2] Gérard Genette's structuralist analysis of narrative entered American literary criticism in the wake of "high structuralism," largely through the mediation of French literary scholars and comparatists, but also through the translation into English of his work in 1980. By using these and other narratological models to build her own theory concerning techniques of rendering consciousness in fiction, Dorrit Cohn fueled the debate with a certain synthesizing energy.

In the late seventies there emerged a group that would become an important integrative force in the increasingly international narratological scene. This was the circle of scholars connected with the Porter Institute for Poetics and Semiotics at Tel Aviv University—Meir Sternberg, Shlomith Rimmon-Kenan, Brian McHale, Tamar Yacobi, and others—who welcomed the concepts created by Russian Formalism and "low structuralism" and helped move narrative theory into a truly intercultural stage in the 1980s.[3]

This narratological upswing set in motion a lively debate, in large measure owing to the brilliant administration of *Poetics Today*, the journal published by the Porter Institute under the editorship of Benjamin Harshav and Brian McHale. For more than a decade the journal acted as a clearinghouse for the debate in narratology, featuring contributions from its most prominent participants. Certain issues would become discursive events; certain articles would mirror in specific terms a communality of narratological concern.

Dorrit Cohn's review of Stanzel's magnum opus, *A Theory of Narrative*, is a *mise en abîme* of the international debate.[4] Appearing in 1980, Cohn's "Encirclement of Narrative" puts the various structural approaches to the systematic study of narrative into historical perspective for the first time, drawing a striking parallel between narrative theory as developed by the *Poétique* group in Paris and by Stanzel in his early work. The sensational eighth issue of *Communications* (1966), with Barthes's essay "Introduction à l'analyse structurale des récits" and Genette's "Les frontières des récits," had come out without French knowledge of Stanzel's 1955 study and its popular sequel, *Typische Formen des Romans* of 1964 (now in its eleventh edition).[5] Nor did French low structuralists in the 1960s know of Käte Hamburger's *Logic of Literature* and its phenomenological structuralism.[6]

First and foremost, Cohn's *Poetics Today* piece is a brilliant staging not only of the visible similarities, but also of the essential differences in the French and German treatments of prose texts. Cohn endeavors to bring Stanzel's work—and thereby an older *Erzähltheorie* tradition in German— into the narratological mainstream dominated in Anglo-American, Israeli, and Dutch theory by the influence of Gérard Genette.[7] While both Stanzel and Genette are concerned with the exploration of narrative form in its relation to narrative content, their approaches differ in principle: according to Cohn, Genette's system is analytically constructed, whereas Stanzel's is phenomenologically informed and synthetic in its orientation.

Cohn's comparative operation in "The Encirclement of Narrative" serves as a guide through the classificatory maze, making it possible for students of narrative to employ the tools of both models. The dialogical quality of Cohn's text is a marker for the "classical" in the discourse formation of narratology. With Cohn's *Transparent Minds: Narrative Modes for Presenting Consciousness in Fiction* (1978), Stanzel's *Theorie des Erzählens* (1979), and Genette's *Narrative Discourse* (1980; a partial translation of *Figures III*, 1972), as well as his *Nouveau discours du récit* (1983),[8] a unique triangular constellation of minds productively obsessed with the analysis of form in fiction made narratological history. Theoretical refinement is at an all-time high, with intense dialogue marking differences even as it effaces them by conveying the sense of common narratological enterprise.

A fundamental and lively controversy arose in connection with the concept of "person" (in the grammatical sense of the term). In a 1987 article, Nilli Diengott analyzed the debate about "the validity of the 'person' distinction in the construction of typologies of narrators."[9] She distinguishes between theorists with a structural model of narrative—Genette, Bal, Rimmon-Kenan—and those with a "traditional" typology that sorts narrators according to the criterion of person. Since they sustain the first-person versus third-person opposition, Stanzel and Cohn are in the latter group, which Diengott sees as employing a "mimetic" approach that contrasts with Genette's structuralist orientation. For Genette, in Diengott's reading, the distinction between first person and third person is merely a function of narrative instance, with the basic first-person narration generating its opposite: a *récit* devoid of (first-person) narrator; Genette calls these two modes homodiegetic and heterodiegetic narration respectively.

While there are many instances of theoretical contact and overlap in the works of our trio of narratologists, the issue of person has proved a perennial point of disagreement. Whereas for Genette voice and focalization (what Stanzel and Cohn term person and mode) are independent issues, it is precisely their interdependence that is central to Cohn's theory of how consciousness is narrated in fictional texts. And while for Stanzel the decisive question hinges on the location of person (as grammatical designation) within or outside the fictional world of the characters in a novel,[10] Cohn has to radicalize the person distinction in order to generate a heuristic space for her study of hitherto unexplored modes of narrating fictional consciousness. Only by dramatizing the opposition of first-person and third-person narration could the manifold interior differentiations in the person/al realm be mapped out adequately. This has allowed Cohn to explore the spectrum of narrative situations from authorial to figural in virtuoso fashion.[11] Without a full awareness of the third-person voice as the conventional agency of narration, the transgressive nature of forms such as free indirect style (Cohn's "narrated monologue") would not come into focus. What may be perceived as mimetic language games (Diengott, using Moshe Ron's concept), and unfavorably contrasted with the turning away from grammatical classification by Genette, Rimmon-Kenan, and Bal, in fact functions as the solid base that makes the pursuit of the most intricate narrative structures possible.

On the question of transvocalization, Cohn and Genette diverge even more dramatically. Although Genette considers himself a formalist, he is not willing to concede that the choice of person by an author could be of great importance. For Cohn, when Kafka abandons the first-person narrative situation in *The Castle* and moves to a figural perspective in the third-person register, it means he is writing a different text. The indeterminate nature of the new text, wavering as it does between the narrator's voice and a figural perspective, inevitably affects the way in which we go about the task of interpretation. Genette's charge of a lingering "psychologism" is the price Cohn pays for having opted to describe so rigorously the forms that represent the inner lives of fictional characters.

The transvocalization issue is part of a highly spirited exchange of letters between Dorrit Cohn and Gérard Genette that first appeared in *Poétique* in 1985 and is presented in this volume in English translation. This correspondence attests to the cross-fertilization characteristic of the narratological enterprise at its zenith. And while this exchange of narratological propositions continues,[12] the practitioners of the new Hellenism are bent on—depending on the point of view—subverting classical narratology by calling into question its drive for systemic perfection, or enriching it by problematizing its premises. Critical narratology ventures beyond the highly codified discourse of classical narratology to selected areas of critical theory, though it retains that discourse as its working base.

Of the different theoretical programs that may be brought to bear on pure narratology, reader-response theory is perhaps the most congenial. A reader-oriented approach is in many ways inscribed in the text-oriented enterprise of narratology. It is the reader who must identify modulations of mode and perspective (or focalization), and it is the reader who has to make a choice about whether a sentence such as "But he was still free" (*Noch war er frei*) in Kafka's *Trial* represents the thoughts of the narrator or of K. The interpretation of the text, the question of K.'s (or "modern man's") guilt, hinges on that seemingly trivial decision by the reader. To be sure, Dorrit Cohn's work on narrated monologue (or free indirect style) has so sensitized her readers to this particular ambiguity in voice that our eyes are continually on the lookout for the subtle markers of *erlebte Rede*, to use the German term.

Textual indeterminacy, an issue central to reception theory as derived from Ingarden's phenomenology of the literary work of art and developed by Wolfgang Iser into a theory of the gap (*Leerstelle*), has been a concern of narratology, if in an untheorized fashion. The study of devices promoting indeterminacy inevitably directs itself to the formal appearance of the narrative, to questions and problems raised by contradictions that become evident through narratological analysis. Among the numerous types of structural and stylistic indeterminacies in narrative, two are isolated here as being of particular interest to the narratological reader: the identity and allegiances of the narrator in third-person fiction, and the challenges presented by texts situated on the borderline of historical and fictional biography and autobiography. In an essay on Thomas Mann's *Death in Venice*, Dorrit Cohn problematizes the narrator and draws new distinctions between narrator and author. Critics have traditionally looked on the narrative voice in that novella as identical with that of the author in many passages. Cohn uncovers the dramatic communication that develops between the now consonant, now dissonant narrator and his protagonist. This very relationship constructs its own textuality; it becomes evident that "the author *behind* the work is communicating a message that escapes the narrator he has placed *within* the work."[13] Stanley Corngold directs our attention to a similar narratological distinction by pointing out how the narrator of Musil's *Young Törless* must "fight clear of identity with Törless the sadist, voyeur, and collector of poisonous moods." He cannot expose himself as his character's accomplice, but to escape incrimination—potentially entailing the literal incrimination of the author Musil—he must be presented as a disembodied intelligence. Similarly, John Neubauer directs attention to autobiographical questions in third-person narratives from a discourse-analytical perspective when he suggests—in writing on Joyce's *Portrait of the Artist as a Young Man* and Mann's *Tonio Kröger*—that the metaphors used by the narrators invite closer scrutiny. Neubauer appeals to "the *reader's* historical perspective on language use" to concretize the exceedingly subtle relationship between narrator and character.

All these readers treat their texts as "writerly texts," in Barthes's sense of the term: "The writerly text is *ourselves* writing."[14] The mutual dependence of text- and reader-oriented approaches is perhaps most urgently felt in the current revival of the challenge to map the borderline between historiography and fiction. This task, performed laboriously by everyone except Aristotle, as Paul Michael Lützeler enviously states, is today fraught with additional epistemological doubt generated by discursive practices that read everything, including "reality," as a text. As Judith Ryan demonstrates in her "Fictionality, Historicity, and Textual Authority," the boundaries between the literary and the extraliterary are deliberately blurred by creative writers posing as historiographers, thus producing shifting but fertile ground for the narratologist.

Dorrit Cohn feels that those historical and novelistic genres that focus on a life story present the greatest potential for overlap of factual and fictional narratives.[15] Conversely, the generic juncture is likely to allow one to perceive theoretical borderlines more dramatically. That the major site of difference should be the narration of consciousness is not surprising. Biographers work within certain epistemological constraints when they deal with the inner lives of historical figures. This is so even when what Cohn terms "psychonarration"—the most distanced mode for presenting the thoughts of a figure—is used.[16] Käte Hamburger noted in *The Logic of Literature* (83) that the historian cannot see Napoleon "in the subjectivity, the I-originality of his inner, mental processes"; if such an interior perspective were given, one would be dealing either with a Napoleonic novel or a fictionalized biography.

Intensified attention to narrative technique reveals the fictional even where it poses militantly as nonfiction, as in the trompe l'oeil operations of Virginia Woolf and Wolfgang Hildesheimer. Hildesheimer's *Marbot: A Biography* (1981) figures as the most exciting borderline case for Dorrit Cohn, most conducive to testing the reader's willingness to negotiate the authenticity of genre.[17] By a certain genealogical logic, it makes sense that Cohn and Hamburger turned their attention almost simultaneously to *Marbot*, yet they were unaware of each other's interest in the work. Hamburger is less concerned with the pragmatic dimension of the text than with the turbulent contradictions implied in the act of classifying the purposely unclassifiable. Jens Rieckmann, in his treatment of an American mock-biography satirizing a German prototype, is able to point to a feature characteristic of most exemplars of the genre (except *Marbot*): greater emphasis on the supposed biographer stresses the act of mediation and thus points up problems inherent in all biographical narration. Thomas Pavel's thoughts on the relationship of history to fiction are consonant with Cohn's (and implicitly with Hamburger's) when he designates style as the major marker of the distinction between the two narrative genres. Yet after having argued convincingly against the segregation of fictional and historical autobiography, Pavel indicates that the distinction is not so "radical as style suggests." His piece is truly a specimen of "critical narratology"; coming from analytical philosophy, linguistics, and semiotics, this comparatist problematizes the autobiographical genre of confession in relation to the current critique of the Cartesian subject. In a syncretic move, Pavel recontextualizes the typological features proposed by Cohn on pragmatic grounds by pointing to their participation in cultural history.

Critical theory as a general discursive movement has pointedly questioned not only the convention of segregating fictional from nonfictional texts but also the claim to authenticity in the writing of history. Thus while the literary historian Lützeler tries to stem the tide begun by Hayden White's foregrounding of the narrative nature of documents, the historian Larry Wolff endorses that very approach. In examining the late eighteenth-century correspondence between the Austrian empress Maria Theresa and her daughter, the young Marie Antoinette, Wolff is concerned with the ideological values of letter writing in an age of absolutism, and in particular with the power relations implicit in first- and second-person epistolary discourse.

Visits to the toolshed of narratology are thus an advantage even to those making critical theory their primary residence. Questions central to a Foucauldian discourse analysis or to deconstructive operations such as "Who says so?" or "How did this meaning, this discourse, come about?" are well served by an awareness of classical narratological discussions of person, voice, and mode. The process of making meaning can be examined at different levels of inquiry. Narratologists in turn are invigorated by Bakhtin's conceptualization of a new type of word/culture relationship performed by the novel. To describe the "double-voiced" discourse of fictional characters as well as other "heteroglossia" requires a contextual perspective backed by the same close textual reading with attention to rhetorical strategies as is characteristic of narratology.

Such close, stringent inspections of the (fictional) text continue to be attacked as formalism, and frequently as monolithic formalism. The negative image bestowed by Marxist criticism on formalism survives today in new historicist circles.[18] For new historicism, with its fusion of neo-Marxist positions, Foucauldian discourse analysis, Bakhtinian concepts, and deconstructive practices, formalism is tainted by its participation in New Criticism and is thus automatically associated with the idealistic claims of that method. The need to dissociate oneself from form-oriented programs is therefore perhaps more strongly felt in American critical culture than in those scholarly regions that were not so visibly touched by New Criticism.

Is there some way to mediate between narratology and the critical avant-garde? As early as 1983, Shlomith Rimmon-Kenan pointed to the potentially shared interests of narratology and deconstruction. The latter project, "instead of abstracting a common, 'pre-medium,' aspect from various narratives . . . investigates narrative elements in the very rhetoric of historical, philosophical, and psychoanalytical texts."[19] For Rimmon-Kenan, literary narratives, because of their tendency to draw attention to their own rhetoricity qua fictionality, can furnish a paradigm for the investigation of those writings where narrative elements usually go unnoticed—for example, in historiography. Deconstruction itself, however, faces the charge of formalism in Frank Lentricchia's argument that deconstructive criticism has not done much more than provide New Criticism with a glorious "after."[20]

The specter of formalism so often associated with narratological pursuits is about to vanish into the fresh air of a cultural critique that synthesizes *Ideologiekritik*, psychoanalysis, and structuralist/poststructuralist positions. Film and media studies is an area where cultural analysis has drawn on narratological models, especially of French provenance, with a vengeance. "Perhaps narrative is a fundamental way that humans make sense of the world," argues a popular textbook on film in a chapter entitled "Narrative as a Formal System."[21] The terminology of the theory of narrative lends itself to the construction of a workable scaffolding for cultural arguments that might otherwise appear to be painted in the all-too-broad washes of ideological critique.

The formalist aspects of Lévi-Strauss's structuralism, which influenced the narratologies of the seventies and eighties, also helped shape a new cultural discourse affecting disciplines ranging from anthropology and sociology to religious studies and folklore. Folklore and other oral traditions, with their unstable "texts," may seem a singularly inappropriate field in which to apply the sophisticated distinctions drawn by narratologists, whose attention to detail is notoriously precise. Yet, as Maria Tatar's essay on "The Juniper Tree" suggests, questions about teller, audience, and mode of narration are critical for an understanding of oral traditions. Through analysis of such questions, along with issues of gender and generations, the Grimms' tale reveals itself to be a story that celebrates the rebellious and transgressive power of the child even as it produces a model of acculturation that assimilates and tames the dissenting child.

Having staked out its parameters as a critical theory and as a political program, the field of feminist studies has celebrated a syncretic mode for some time, borrowing from French poststructuralist writing, especially from Barthes and Lacan via Cixous and Irigaray, and adding semiotics and Bakhtinian concepts through the work of Julia Kristeva. This syncretism has facilitated the rise of a feminist narratology, by definition the conflation of an orientation toward form with a political agenda—an approach that has destabilized the formalism/antiformalism opposition that has so long been a staple of twentieth-century literary criticism.

In *Gendered Interventions: Narrative Discourse in the Victorian Novel* (1989), Robyn Warhol takes as her point of departure the obvious and yet unasked question why classical narratology has neglected the possibility of gender-based differences or patterns in narrative structures.[22] There have been certain studies—"preclassical" to be sure—such as William L. Courtney's *Feminine Note in Fiction* of 1904. "It seems to me to be a fact that a passion for detail is the distinguishing mark of nearly every female novelist. Such a limitation has its drawbacks, but one must accept the defects of one's qualities. Many female writers have done their best to escape beyond the bounds of illuminate detail, but very few have succeeded."[23] Obviously we are here in a presuffragette, not even archaic but "geometric" phase of narratology (the tenth to seventh centuries in Greek culture are also referred to as the Dark Ages)—we are inside a discourse far removed from the cultural sophistication of structuralist analysis. Not that *its* practitioners should be accused of being sexist, to return to Warhol's argument. But their model naturally led them to search for essential structures common to all narratives. Warhol is among those who are now attempting to modify the structuralist analysis of narrative by reordering its contextual priorities. Context, Warhol believes, had been reserved for the realm of *story* only, and not for *discourse*, to borrow Seymour Chatman's terms.[24] Taking advantage of narratology's desire to be comprehensive rather than exclusive, Warhol investigates the structure of direct address in Victorian novels by women writers as an example of a contextualized female discourse that evidences striking gender differences in narrative expression.

That narrative form can function as content (as "story") especially when it comes to shifts in person within one and the same perspective—first person to third person and vice versa—need no longer be a statement branded as "formalist." In her article on feminist stories of sexual metamorphosis, Gail Finney turns narrative situation into the principal carrier of a critique of stereotypical notions concerning gender differences. "Whereas *she* had previously aimed the shower spray at her belly . . . the water now hit *him* between his shoulders"—this type of shift in the regime of person in a short story by Sarah Kirsch effectively signals the split between a male consciousness and a female exterior.[25] Turning from the regime of person to the other end of the narratological spectrum and using reader-response theory as a point of departure, David Mickelsen draws on Barthesian and Derridian notions of textuality to produce a gender-oriented reading of Zola's *Nana*. His analysis attempts to detect the effects of gender on the appeal of literature, with the readers of the novel seen as identifying with the men looking in awe at the nude Nana and with the object of the (fe/

male) gaze shown as irretrievable for the sphere of the conventional and fixed. Lastly, Mickelsen's reading posits the figure of Nana as the continually deferred sign of the text itself: woman = text = *différance*.

Other critics, such as Susan S. Lanser, have worked to reveal how ideology can be reflected in and communicated through narrative technique. In examining several American novels written by women, Lanser is interested in showing that the extradiegetic-heterodiegetic narrator, usually thought of as a disembodied agency of narration, is able to have a female voice.[26]

In a first-person narrative, the voice of a woman can express a liberated, emphatically feminist existence, even in the 1930s, as Susan Rubin Suleiman demonstrates in her essay, "Feminist Intertextuality." Integrating the Bakhtinian notion of the carnivalesque as emancipatory strategy, Suleiman shows Leonora Carrington rewriting the exclusively male code of Surrealism, the movement that shaped the author. Her novel *The Hearing Trumpet* is constructed as a pastiche of intertexts of all kinds, ranging from the Bible through the Grail legend to classical mythology, and from fairy tales to Surrealist theories of collage, with much of the material reworked by a protofeminist pen. Less interested in micronarratology than in the larger textual pattern of Carrington's "maniac laughter," Suleiman identifies form as carnival, transgression, and affirmation of difference—politicized aesthetics in a new key.

Relocating the relationship of the aesthetic and the political in a discursive space beyond the oppositional mode of *l'art pour l'art* and the Marxist conflation of artistic and societal goals has been a concern of the postmodern movement. Reflecting on the ideological underpinnings of our critical strategies has, with and well beyond Gadamer, become imperative, for instance, for David E. Wellbery: "It is a matter of urgency that we get some conceptual hold on our own narrative constructions as literary historians." Wellbery challenges narratologists to face the phenomenon of contingency, the nonstructurable occurrence that, he claims, can never be narratively appropriated, but without which narrative would not exist. In a bold deconstructive operation, Wellbery investigates the significatory practices of the fictional text as well as those of its interpreters.

A poststructuralist perspective is part of a trend toward a new syncretism in criticism that productively avails itself of a full archive of theoretical options. Within this sometimes carnivalesque discursivity, an awareness of the existential intertextuality of the critic is crucial. As postmodern *bricoleurs*, we might pause in the perpetual movement of "theory" to ground our constructions in narratological foundations.[27]

NOTES

1. Robert Scholes, *Structuralism in Literature* (New Haven and London: Yale University Press, 1974), 157, coined the term in association and contrast to the "high structuralism" of Lévi-Straussian philosophical ethnography.

2. Franz K. Stanzel, *Die typischen Erzählsituationen im Roman* (Vienna: Braumüller, 1955); *Narrative Situations in the Novel*, trans. J. Pusack (Bloomington: Indiana University Press, 1971).

3. This introduction does not aim to provide a history of narratological evolution, nor can it claim to survey the discursive changes in the narratological debate. The work of Tzvetan Todorov was and is most seminal; the position of Aldiras Greimas proved very influential in certain circles concerned with semiotically and linguistically oriented analysis of prose—and there are others whose importance cannot be assessed here.

4. Franz K. Stanzel, *Theorie des Erzählens* (Göttingen: Vandenhoeck and Ruprecht, 1979), *Theory of Narrative*, trans. Charlotte Goedsche (Cambridge and New York: Cambridge University Press, 1984); Dorrit Cohn, "The Encirclement of Narrative," *Poetics Today* 2, no. 2 (1981): 157–82.

5. Franz K. Stanzel, *Typische Formen des Romans* (Göttingen: Vandenhoeck and Ruprecht, 1964).

6. Käte Hamburger, *Die Logik der Dichtung*, rev. ed. (Stuttgart: Klett, 1968); trans. Marilyn Rose, under the title *Logic of Literature* (Bloomington: Indiana University Press, 1973).

7. The tradition starts with Käte Friedemann, *Die Rolle des Erzählers in der Epik* (Leipzig: H. Haessel, 1910, repr. 1965), and blossoms in midcentury, with Eberhard Lämmert's *Bauformen des Erzählens* (Stuttgart: Metzler, 1955) as another milestone.

8. Gérard Genette, *Narrative Discourse Reconsidered*, trans. Jane E. Lewin (Ithaca: Cornell University Press, 1988). This study of Genette's is in many parts a debate with Cohn's position.

9. Nilli Diengott, "The Mimetic Language Game and Two Typologies of Narrators," *Modern Fiction Studies* 33, no. 3 (Autumn 1987): 523ff.

10. Stanzel, *Theory of Narrative*, 49.

11. Cohn has coined the terms "authorial" and "figural" narrative situation based on Stanzel's "auktoriale" and "personale Erzählsituation."

12. Stanzel, for example, profited from the theoretical discussion of *A Theory of Narrative* in Cohn's review of the work; see his "A Low-Structuralist at Bay? Further Thoughts on *A Theory of Narrative*," forthcoming in *Poetics Today*.

13. Dorrit Cohn, "The Second Author of 'Der Tod in Venedig,' " in *Probleme der Moderne*, ed. Benjamin Bennett, Anton Kaes, and William J. Lillyman (Tübingen: Niemeyer, 1983), 241.

14. Roland Barthes, *S/Z*, trans. R. Miller (New York: Hill and Wang, 1974), 5.

15. Dorrit Cohn, "Fictional *versus* Historical Lives: Borderlines and Borderline Cases," *Journal of Narrative Technique* 19, no. 1 (Winter 1989): 3–24.

16. Ibid., 9f.

17. Ibid., 11.

18. See, e.g., Carolyn Porter, "History and Literature: 'After the New Historicism,' " *New Literary History* 21, no. 2 (Winter 1990): 254ff.

19. Shlomith Rimmon-Kenan, *Narrative Fiction: Contemporary Poetics* (London and New York: Methuen, 1983), 131.

20. Frank Lentricchia, *After the New Criticism* (Chicago: University of Chicago Press, 1980). For the comparatist of academic discourse formations, it is interesting to note that Derridian close textual skepticism could flourish in outstanding literature departments in this country because their scholars were indeed working in a tradition of close textual analysis, in contrast, for instance, to the situation in recent German scholarship, where a specific variant of New Criticism in the 1950s, "werkimmanente Interpretation," was dismissed as apolitical. This in turn led to a very different reception of Derrida.

21. David Bordwell and Kristin Thompson, *Film Art: An Introduction* (New York: Knopf, 1986), is a popular textbook in film studies; Dudley Andrew devotes a chapter to "A Survey of Narratology" in his *Concepts in Film Theory* (Oxford and New York: Oxford University Press, 1984).

22. Robyn Warhol, *Gendered Interventions: Narrative Discourse in the Victorian Novel* (New Brunswick and London: Rutgers University Press, 1989), 4.

23. William L. Courtney, *The Feminine Note in Fiction* (London: Chapman and Hall, 1904), x–xi.

24. Warhol, *Gendered Interventions*, 5.

25. Shifts in person within the same narrative perspective, i.e., in a nonmimetic function, have been discussed in various contexts, most prominently by Stanzel, "The Alternation of First- and Third-Person Pronominal Reference," in *Theory of Narrative*, 99–110.

26. Susan Sniader Lanser, *The Narrative Act: Point of View in Prose Fiction* (Princeton: Princeton University Press, 1981).

27. I wish to express my gratitude to Shlomith Rimmon-Kenan, Susan Rubin Suleiman, Jane Lincoln Taylor, Judith Ryan, and Maria Tatar for a critical reading of my introductory remarks, and the latter two colleagues in particular for stylistically upgrading my non-native English.

PART ONE

HISTORY, FICTION, AND THE CLAIMS

OF WRITING:

THE AUTO/BIOGRAPHICAL MODE

ONE

BETWEEN HISTORY AND FICTION:

ON DORRIT COHN'S POETICS OF PROSE

Thomas Pavel

THE DISTINCTION between history and fiction is once again stir-ring the interest of critics.[1] The question seemed settled in premod-ern times, when history was assumed to narrate the particular and poetry the general. True, until the nineteenth century, history was counted among the belles lettres, but that was a matter of stylistic kinship rather than of epistemological classification. Later, the practitioners of modern historiography became confident that their trade was more scientific than literary; therefore, the attempts to find new criteria for distinguishing his-tory from poetry were welcomed. By then, fiction, or at least some of it, had ceased to aim at the general: its avowed purpose was, like that of his-tory, to narrate things "as they were." The general remained the object of science and philosophy, while history and fiction struggled with the partic-ular. In his foreword to the *Comédie humaine,* Balzac remarks that "reading these dry and disheartening lists of facts called *histories*, everyone can notice that the writers have always forgotten . . . to give us the history of cus-toms."[2] In other words, the realist project saw fiction as a complement to political history, comprising those aspects of the cultural texture that his-tory was bound to miss.

For Balzac, however, these were, above all, practical concerns. French realism felt the need to legitimize its incursions into the realm of everyday life not so much because it had to distinguish itself from history as because it had to justify a novel approach to fiction. It had to explain to its readers why, following the example of Walter Scott, novelists had begun to devote so much energy and space to the careful description of characters and their environment, and how the then-fashionable accumulation of details was designed to capture the history of customs truthfully. In order to describe the essence of the human condition, the classicists omitted as much detail as possible from their fiction. On the contrary, for both the Romantics and the realists, fiction had to map out human contingency. "Le hasard est le plus grand romancier du monde: pour être fécond, il n'y a qu'à l'étudier" ("Chance is the greatest novelist in the world: in order to be productive, it is enough to study it").[3]

and turns into fiction when its author claims to have direct access to a character's thoughts.

First-person narratives, by contrast, whether fictional narratives or genuine autobiographies, are all based on direct knowledge of the narrator's thoughts; hence the lack of formal marks to distinguish the genres. Acknowledging the difficulty, Cohn avoids reverting to truth-value semantic criteria. That Proust presumably narrated his own experiences in *Remembrance of Things Past* does not make the text a genuine autobiography. Conversely, it could be added, for all their exaggerations and distortions, Charles de Gaulle's memoirs do not qualify as a novel. There are no clear-cut textual marks of fictionality for first-person narratives. Turning to narratology for help, Cohn notices that the main difference between autobiography and fiction lies in the relationship between the author and the narrator: the author of an autobiography is identical with its narrator, while this is not the case for first-person fictional texts. Accordingly, these two families of texts also differ as to the potential reliability of their narrators. While fictional narrators (Michel in Gide's *Immoralist*) can be, and in our century are *expected* to be, unreliable, the narrator of a genuine autobiography is, in principle, reliable. Thus, a narratological feature allows Cohn to generalize for first-person narratives the clear-cut distinction between fiction and history that prevails in third-person narratives. Fictionality being a yes or no property, we read texts "in one key or the other." Fiction is never a matter of degree; it is a matter of kind.

One of the most interesting features of Cohn's argument is its unusual combination of various pragmatic features. The distinction between first-person and third-person narratives, which is here taken as primitive, is, of course, a pragmatic one, since it belongs to the deictic system that relates the message to the conditions of its production. Equally pragmatic is the selection of free indirect discourse as one of the marks of fictionality for third-person narratives. Free indirect discourse belongs, indeed, like verb tenses, pronouns, articles, and demonstratives, to the linguistic devices that offer information about the user and the context of the utterance. But since first-person discourse lacks definite linguistic marks of fictionality, here Cohn is interested in differentiating the *reading* of fiction from the *reading* of nonfiction. The distinction between reliable and unreliable narrators, while still belonging to the pragmatic sphere, is less related to observable linguistic features than it is to cultural behavior, in particular to its intentional aspects. Indeed, narratorial reliability is a notion that depends equally on the intention of the author and the suspicions of the reader. But the option to diagnose unreliability is, at best, *available* to the intelligent reader, without being compelling. In other words, we witness a switch from overt stylistic traits to covert narratological properties, and, accordingly, from the observational method proper to linguistics to a hermeneutical approach. Yet this switch does not affect Cohn's consistency, for when she opposes other intentional approaches (speech-act theories, for instance), it is less for their dependence on interpretative practice than for their narratological vagueness. As for semantic criteria, they remain resolutely excluded.

From here on, I will use the notion of "narratorial reliability" in a sense slightly more general than that of Dorrit Cohn. While in her work this notion simply indicates the difference between real-life autobiographers who write about themselves and fictional narrators, I would like to comment on reliability as a more general discursive property, shared by genuine autobiographers and imaginary first-person narrators. That first-person narratorial reliability, as a general discursive property, lies in the eye of the beholder is beautifully exemplified by Paul de Man's suspicious reading of Rousseau's *Confessions*,[6] an autobiography as genuine as any, which, nonetheless, the critic finds utterly unreliable, in spite of the author's professed transparency. A post-Freudian critic who understands something about self-deception cannot help mistrusting Rousseau's explicit intentions. In an age that assumes the subject to have lost the mastery of its speech and to share the responsibility for its language with uncontrollable forces (the unconscious, social background, perhaps gender and race), critics are only too eager to "debunk" their narrators, in fiction as in nonfictional discourse. But a disturbing anachronism is at work in such attempts. Clever as it may seem, critical debunking of Rousseau's sincerity depends, in fact, on twentieth-century standards of discourse scrutiny. For some of *us*, Rousseau sounds unreliable (in the Jamesian sense of "inconscient") insofar as our ears have been trained by writers and psychologists to detect every ruse and faltering of the ego's voice. It is not less true that, according to prevalent eighteenth-century standards, Rousseau was perfectly transparent. Even today, most readers find him quite reliable.

It is equally indisputable that the narrators of eighteenth-century *fictional* autobiographies are designed to sound reliable, at least in factual matters. Consider Defoe's *Moll Flanders*. The narrator may be confused as to the overall moral interpretation of her misdeeds, but as a witness of her own fall, she is meant to sound trustworthy. Details that might look suspicious to us had a different function in the eyes of the original audience. That Moll Flanders, for example, avoids mentioning the names of most other characters, and that she fails to narrate every little event of her adventurous life, is a sign of her discretion, and therefore of her reliability. Names and missing facts could have easily been filled in, but the narrator seems to hesitate before implicating other people. At no point does one need to suspect the dependability of her *deposition*, which, significantly, includes all the damaging facts about herself. And when, in *epistolary* novels, characters like Clarissa or Valmont (in *Les liaisons dangereuses*) do indeed, for a while, delude themselves about matters as simple as whether they are in love, in the end they always recognize the true nature of their feelings.

Until quite recently in history, the subject did not have trouble speaking about itself in the language of the community, nor did it hesitate to espouse the common moral values even when its own behavior contradicted them. For a long time, self-delusion was not assumed to be a pervasive feature of all discourse, and a tortured confession such as Dostoevsky's *Notes from the Underground* did not yet spell out the norms for self-narration. It is only when the self gradually gained a relative autonomy with respect to language and values that the subtle divergence between language and consciousness came to be noticed—first deplored, later exalted, and finally increasingly thematized.

Coincidence between (fictional or nonfictional) first-person discourse and reliability appears therefore to be a historical fact rather than a generic feature. Until late in the eighteenth century, first-person autobiographies, fictional or genuine, shared a set of assumptions about language and subjectivity. Modeled on the sacrament of confession and the legal institution of deposition, premodern first-person fictional narratives seem indeed to have partly imitated genuine speech acts. Spiritual autobiographies and personal diaries equally served as prototypes for early narratives, under the same assumption of reliability. Duplicity, irony, and self-deception have always existed, but since society believed that the self can, through confessions and depositions, be brought to tell the truth, the representation of duplicity was restricted to the characters' discourse in comedy, in third-person comic narratives, and in epistolary novels: the topos of *Miles gloriosus*, its sophisticated version, *Don Quixote*, and Clarissa's lack of awareness of her love for Lovelace are the best examples of such self-delusive discourse. Once the modern self, detached from its language, loses the ability ever to reach truth about itself, even in confessions and depositions, a new relationship of self and language takes hold of the social imagination. In both fictional and genuine autobiography, the parameter of unreliability becomes perceptible, involuntary in the case of real autobiography, and mimetic in such texts as *L'immoraliste* or *Felix Krull*. That the possibility of discursive unreliability should not be linked too firmly to fictional autobiography is shown by the fact that, in an age when *all* discourse becomes suspect, *third*-person narratives, from Kafka to the postmoderns, also make frequent use of narratorial unreliability.

This means that typological features such as those discovered by Cohn on pragmatic grounds have deep roots in cultural history. *Expressed* by stylistic and narratological properties, such shifts take place on a more general level, and are reflected in discursive practices as well as in other cultural manifestations. The tensions among subjectivity, language, and truth permeate the entire cultural space of the past two centuries. The unreliable narrator, like his or her model, the self-deluding autobiographer, can be enacted on the contemporary scene precisely insofar as the existence of these tensions makes the testimony of the self irreversibly hesitant and irreparably flawed.

Applying the same argument to third-person narratives, one can surmise that the use of free indirect style is itself a result of the rise of modern subjectivity, rather than a universal mark of fictional discourse. As many scholars have observed, free indirect discourse is not documented before the seventeenth century and starts to be extensively used only after the middle of the nineteenth century. Why should an essential phenomenological feature of third-person narration take so long to manifest itself? From an essentialist point of view, one can explain this anomaly by using a Hegelian argument: true free indirect discourse, which embodies the essence of epic fictionality, appeared late; its emergence means that epic fiction, after flourishing for so long, succeeded in revealing its true essence only in modern times. Unfortunately, such arguments are circular. Rather than postulate a stable essence and its belated revelation, it would be more relevant to notice that, since epic fiction must always tell stories that *interest* its public and do so in a language that closely reflects the public's interest, free indirect discourse, and more generally the representation of intimate thoughts of other minds, is *a symptom of these interests*, rather than a distinctive feature of epic fiction.

"But what *is* the right thing?" Tolstoy's Ivan Ilych asks himself just before dying—"and suddenly grew quiet."[7] Why have the last thoughts of Achilles in the *Iliad*, Turnus in the *Aeneid*, and, later, Quixote or M. de Clèves been left unrecorded? Why, for a very long time, did most fictional characters have almost *none* of their thoughts reported? The heroes of Homer and Virgil's epic poems only act and speak, and so do the characters of Greek, Roman, and medieval romance. Similarly, Thucydides and Plutarch report in the main only the *expressed* thoughts of their historic characters. Now and then, inferred emotions or thoughts are briefly alluded to, in close connection to the character's actions. When a seventeenth-century novelist like Mme de Lafayette writes about her character that "she again examined the reasons for which her duty opposed her happiness; she felt pain to find them so strong, and regretted having explained them so well to Mr. de Nemours,"[8] she reports intimate thoughts, but not in Flaubert's and Tolstoy's way. The quoted passage narrates not merely *incidental* thoughts, but inner *deliberations* related to action. The princess's silent soliloquy reminds us of the monologues spoken before or after making an important decision by heroines in the tragedies of Corneille and Racine. Like Hermione, Roxane, and Phèdre, the princess of Clèves ponders the consequences of her actions in the deliberative rhetorical mode of classicist morality. The premodern subject distinctly experiences the overpowering presence of normative values, which it describes in a language fully shared with the community. The author's access to the princess's thoughts is not problematic, since any woman endowed with a similar personality would have had them in a similar situation. In accordance with the Aristotelian dictum, fiction speaks about the universal; inner life, subject to universal rules, can effortlessly be made public. Thus, one can imagine a dramatic adaptation of *La princesse de Clèves* in which the main character, left alone on stage, would express the opposition between her duty and her happiness, and articulate her reasons for choosing duty.

To some extent, this is still true about the inner monologues of Julien Sorel in *Le rouge et le noir* by Stendhal. "Julien voulait à toute force être honnête homme jusqu'à la fin envers cette pauvre jeune fille qu'il avait si étrangement compromise; mais, à chaque instant, l'amour effréné qu'il avait pour madame de Rênal l'emportait" ("Julien intensely wanted to behave decently to the end toward this poor young woman whom he compromised in such strange circumstances; but on every occasion, the passionate love he felt for Madame de Renal would overcome him").[9] One can almost hear him speaking: "Je voudrais à toute force être honnête homme envers cette pauvre jeune fille que j'ai si étrangement compromise." The modern picaro still uses the intelligible language of shared morality, and the reasons for his hesitant behavior still can be limpidly explained at each point of his career. Just as first-person narratives resemble confessions and depositions, third-person reconstructions of inner lives are common in judicial discourse, in which the prosecution, like the defense, at length elaborates on the reasons—and the passions—that led the defendant to his or her acts. At the trial of Antoine Berthet (Julien Sorel's real-life model, 1827), in a typical outburst of judicial rhetoric, the defense counsel compared his speech with fiction: "Pourquoi ne représenterions-nous pas à des juges, et pour les nécessités de la défense, des tableaux d'amour, alors que sans nécessité et pour le stérile plaisir des spectateurs, tous les jours des scènes d'amour même incestueux remplissent d'horreur nos scènes tragiques?" ("Why wouldn't we represent to our judges, and in the interest of the defendant, love scenes, since every day, without any need, and only for the sterile pleasure of the spectators, love scenes, some even incestous, fill our tragic theaters with their horror?") (729). Berthet's heart is the object of unanimous attention: "Quel tableau s'offre à nos regards! L'innocence était dans le coeur de Berthet" ("What a picture offers itself to our gaze! Innocence reigned in Berthet's heart") (728), claims the defense. "Un amour adultère, méprisé . . . la soif de vengeance, telles furent . . . les causes de cette haine furieuse, de ce désespoir forcené, manifestés par l'assassinat, le sacrilège, le suicide" ("An adulterous love, despised . . . the thirst for revenge, these were . . . the causes of this furious hatred, this mad despair, manifested as crime, sacrilege, suicide") (718), accuses the prose-cution. The judicial reporter writes: "Ce jeune homme . . . s'était, en imag-ination, créé un avenir brillant d'autant plus glorieux qu'il n'était dû qu'à ses talents" ("This young man . . . had, in his imagination, created a bril-liant future for himself, all the more glorious as it was due only to his own talents") (728).

The point here is that so long as the self was understood as the locus of strategic and moral debates closely related to action and held in a language shared by an entire community, inner thoughts were taken to be as clearly articulated as public ones, and accordingly, the difference between them and overt speech was a matter of contingency. Any dramatic author could make his or her hero recite long soliloquies; likewise, any novelist, histo-rian, or court lawyer could reconstruct the thoughts of his or her characters or clients. That the three genres of discourse were so close in their treat-ment of other minds should not surprise us: they all focused on human action and its motivation, and, as such, were equally preoccupied with the links between visible deeds and inner deliberation based on moral and stra-tegic reasoning. Seen from outside, the "I" appeared thus analogous to a *deliberation chamber*, rather than to an absolute *origin* of solitary discourse.

The crucial shift alluded to earlier occurred during the nineteenth cen-tury, modifying the classical role of the "I" as the locus of strategic and moral reasoning. While judicial discourse has remained primarily inter-ested in individual motivation, history and fiction have each developed more specialized insights into the operations of the "I." Compared with earlier representations of inner thoughts, psychonarration, free indirect discourse, and the other techniques developed by Flaubert, Tolstoy, and later authors display two important features: the weakening of the links between thoughts and action and the representation of nondiscursive ele-ments through inner discourse.

The weakened links between thought and action fall in line with the diminished role of moral intention in many anti-Enlightenment views of the individual. These weak links are manifested, at the level of narrative construction, by the birth of the modern antihero, who cannot control nor understand himself (Adolphe, Benjamin Constant's character, being its first French occurrence), and by the rise of *chance*, as opposed to *reasoned strategy*, as the main plot device of the modern novel. Discursively, this weakened connection is responsible for self-deceptive or unreliable auto-biography, free indirect discourse, and the growing fragmentation of rep-resented inner speech. Affecting first-person as well as third-person narra-tives, the disappearance of the deliberating "I" is, indeed, a feature that, for a while, differentiates the objectives of fiction writing from history, making possible the rise of a modern rhetoric of fiction, so dissimilar from earlier novel techniques.

Second, the representation of nondiscursive elements through inner discourse is probably related to a new distribution of the roles within the "I." The moral strategist in perfect control of motivations and language gives way to a less articulated, yet more sensitive, ego. One of the reasons why the links between action and thought break down is that much more than just action and thought now takes place in the same inner space. The windows of the deliberation chamber open, letting in a world of sensations, memories, and diffuse desires over which the "I" has no effective linguistic command. Thus, what is quite novel in a sentence such as "Une immensité bleuâtre l'entourait, les sommets du sentiments étincelaient sous sa pensée" ("A bluish immensity surrounded her; the summits of feeling sparked under her thought"),[10] is less that the narrator has access to Emma's inner life than that he can write about it in terms *inaccessible* to *Emma herself*. How can we construe a speaker describing her moods in such terms: "Une immensité bleuâtre m'entoure, les sommets du sentiments étincellent sous ma pensée"! Later, the same will hold true for Virginia Woolf's and James Joyce's characters.

It is a fact of cultural history that the modern subject has less access to its own operations than other, better-informed people, and that these operations must be described from outside in a language that cannot be used by the subject qua subject. When the Viennese psychoanalyst tells his patient that he suffers from the Oedipus complex, does not this proposition describe something in principle outside the grasp of the conscious subject? And would the utterance of a sentence such as "I suffer from the Oedipus complex" not mean that the patient *accepted* the diagnosis rather than *discovered* it through introspection? How archaic a character like Edmund in *King Lear* sounds, with his unmediated access to his own wickedness. Modern fiction, therefore, writes about inner life the way it does, not so much because it is the essence of fiction to do so, as because our interest in the life of the subject is so differently shaped from that of our premodern ancestors.

As for the writing of history, given the growing specialization of discourse that prevails in our time, one should not expect it necessarily to follow suit and benefit from every discovery of literary art. As Cohn shows, there have been writers of historical biography who abused free indirect discourse, but their attempts have not been successful. But it should be made clear that, though fiction sensed the new role of the subject, earlier history did not let it go unnoticed. It might be that Hegelian and Marxist views of history, which deemphasize individual responsibility, provide a theoretical counterpart to the disappearance of the deliberation chamber from fictional discourse. It could be added that the representation of nondiscursive elements in the inner life of fictional characters recalls Dilthey's opposition to the Kantian disincarnated view of man, which he attempted to replace by a new conception of the human being as a whole, including will, feeling, and representation. Closer to our time, historians gradually discovered that reasoned action is only a shallow layer of human evolution, and that historical responsibility rests as well with many other factors: climate, technology, trade, social and symbolic arrangements. They started researching the history of feelings and perceptions, of smells and colors, the history of family, of birth, of childhood, of love and marriage, the history of time and death. To be sure, they do not use free indirect discourse. Yet they treat the human subject in a way quite similar to modern fiction. Style, as Dorrit Cohn beautifully shows, is indeed what, today, distinguishes history from fiction. But in the light of cultural history, one might surmise that the distinction between the two varieties of discourse is not so radical as style suggests.

NOTES

1. I must warn the reader from the outset that the present paper belongs to the genre of the essay, rather than to the scholarly genre of the footnoted article. My speculations owe a great deal to Dorrit Cohn's influential contributions to the poetics of fiction, to the work of historians of the novel, and to the ongoing discussion among philosophers and historians about the nature of modernity. My debts are too numerous to acknowledge, but I would like to mention Erich Kahler, *The Inward Turn of the Narrative* (Evanston: Northwestern University Press, 1987); Ian Watt, *The Rise of the Novel* (Berkeley and Los Angeles: University of California Press, 1957); G. A. Starr, *Defoe and the Spiritual Autobiography* (Princeton: Princeton University Press, 1965); Lorna Martens, *The Diary Novel* (Cambridge: Cambridge University Press, 1985); Herbert Schnädelbach, *Philosophy in Germany, 1831–1933* (Cambridge: Cambridge University Press, 1984); Lionel Gosman's articles on literature and history, now collected in *Between History and Literature* (Cambridge, Mass.: Harvard University Press, 1990); and Louis Dumont, *Essays on Individualism: Modern Ideology in Anthropological Perspective* (Chicago: University of Chicago Press, 1986). I was fortunate enough to have Dorrit Cohn read the first version of this paper; she made several important suggestions. I wish also to extend my thanks to Maria Tatar and the external readers for Princeton University Press, who formulated helpful criticisms.

2. H. de Balzac, *La comédie humaine*, ed. M. Bouteron (Paris: Gallimard, Bibliothèque de la Pléiade, 1951), 1:5.

3. Ibid., 7.

4. Dorrit Cohn, "Fictional *versus* Historical Lives: Borderlines and Borderline Cases," *Journal of Narrative Technique* 19 (1989): 3–24.

5. Quoted in ibid., 7–8.

6. Paul de Man, "Excuses (*Confessions*)," in *Allegories of Reading* (New Haven: Yale University Press, 1979), quoted in Cohn, "Fictional *versus* Historical Lives," 14.

7. Leo Tolstoy, *The Death of Ivan Ilytch and Other Stories*, trans. Aylmer Maude (New York: Signet Classics, 1960), 155, quoted in Cohn, "Fictional *versus* Historical Lives," 5.

8. Madame de Lafayette, *La princesse de Clèves*, in *Romanciers du XVIIe siècle* (Paris: Gallimard, Bibliothèque de la Pléiade, 1958), 1250 (my translation).

9. Stendhal, *Romans et nouvelles* (Paris: Gallimard, Bibliothèque de la Pléiade, 1952), 1:694.

10. Gustave Flaubert, *Oeuvres* (Paris: Gallimard, Bibliothèque de la Pléiade, 1951), 1:439.

TWO

FICTIONALITY IN HISTORIOGRAPHY
AND THE NOVEL

Paul Michael Lützeler

ARISTOTLE knew the answer. For him the matter of the division of labor between historiographer and poet was easily decided: the historiographer relates "what has happened," and the poet "what might happen."[1] In contrast to Plato's devastating criticism of literature, Aristotle considered poetry to be of high value. In Aristotle's eyes, literature dealt with problems of a more general and thus more significant nature, while the historian had to report about specific, and thus, *eo ipso*, less important matters. Aristotle's distinctions notwithstanding, one might assume that Calliope and Clio paid scant attention to whether they were called upon by rhapsodists or historiographers; apparently the two Muses generously offered their inspirational support—frequently together—in the one case as readily as in the other. For centuries one was not able to discern whether it was Calliope or Clio who was riding on Pegasus across the Helicon. Small wonder, since the two daughters of Zeus have always resembled each other, and their status symbols—the scroll and the stylus—never were useful in telling them apart. As if conspiring against their contemporary philosopher, the Muses upset Artistotle's tidy scheme; worse yet, they condemned it to oblivion. Witness the German homonym *Geschichte* ("story" or "history"), which signifies at the same time a form of fictional event and a real happening. Until approximately two hundred fifty years ago, historiography was considered a branch of literature. Since the eighteenth century (when Aristotle's distinctions were rediscovered), the differences between the two disciplines have been stressed, and it was only then that the term "literature" became synonymous with "poetry" and "fiction." Gottsched and Lessing still shared Aristotle's prejudice against history.[2] For them the field of history was merely a quarry from which they mined some of the raw material they used to build their preconceived literary plots. Of real importance to them was a moralistic story, and examples were taken from the repertoires in the areas of history, legend, and mythology. But the late eighteenth century is an important turning point. As Reinhart Koselleck has demonstrated, it is the time of the development of a genuinely new philosophical awareness about history.[3] The concept of a continuously progressing history as such replaces the traditional idea of history as a chaotic conglomerate of countless individual stories of a more or less exemplary nature. Through this philosophical development, literature is seen as part of history, and thus it loses its Aristotelian superiority.

Today the relationship between fiction and historiography poses a number of hermeneutic questions, and there is no modern Aristotle who might offer a simple and acceptable solution fitting for our time. I cannot offer a solution, only some reflections. First I will sketch the situation of narration in modern historiography, then the condition of the contemporary novel, and finally I will talk about the possible interrelations between historiography and literature.

Narration can be viewed as one of the primary tools of knowledge, and it determines the structure and aesthetic form in the presentation of a real or a fictional event. Narration discloses the dimension of historical reality as well as the sphere of poetic fiction. The logic of narration provides access to the logic of historiography and of fiction; it makes the structure of both historical consciousness and fantasy tangible. In every narrative, real or fictional events are supported by a structure through which happenings are accentuated, selected, or eliminated according to the law of relevance. Neither in historiographical nor in fictional narration are we dealing with a reproduction or duplication of events, but with a certain organization of actual or imaginary occurrences or experiences.

Both in literature and in historical writing, narration has fallen into a state of permanent crisis. Perhaps because it is so difficult to liberate it from its established forms, narration is constantly under attack. Writers of history feel even less comfortable with narration than do writers of fiction. In the discussion of modern historiography during the sixties and early seventies, it looked as if "narration" would be replaced by "description" and "explanation." "Historiography," Peter Szondi argued, must "divest itself increasingly of its narrative character"; narrative historiography must "turn into description if a new concept of history is to do justice to our knowledge of history as an anonymous process, as a sequence of events and changing systems."[4] The arguments of the antinarrativists can be summarized in the following way: the narrative recording of events in historicism was based on the belief that history was made by individuals. But this categorization did not adequately take into account the development of social processes. Processes and structures can only be described, not narrated. Thus the old "histoire événementielle" has to be replaced by the new "histoire structurale." The "nouvelle histoire" of French historians in particular, with their descriptions of structures underlying long periods of time, and their quantifying methods, forced the old paradigm of writing history by narrating events into a defensive position.[5]

However, according to some historiographers (Arno Borst, for example), history as a narration of events and history as a description of structures are not mutually exclusive. These historiographers concede that history as a narration of events is no longer the center of the historiographer's work and that it no longer provides the obvious support of historical writing. But they also concede that narration is allowed to stand as a possibility alongside the writing of history as a structural analysis of processes.[6] Other experts on history (such as Reinhart Koselleck) will have nothing to do with a strict separation of the two methods. "The fact that modern history is a series of processes," runs the argument, "can only be understood through the alternate explanation of events through structures and vice versa. . . . Narration and description are intertwined."[7] Although the structures become more accessible through description and events through narration, nevertheless in practice it would be impossible to maintain a demarcation between the two methods. The complementary characters of description and narration are increasingly emphasized, for example, by Lawrence Stone.[8] The defenders of the descriptive method like to confront the narrators among the historiographers with their lack of theory. They assert that the historiographer must not only narrate but also explain, and that this is only possible by means of a theoretical concept of the realities as it has long been practiced by the social scientists.

The proponents of the narrative method in writing history defend themselves vehemently against the charge of being antitheoretical. From their initially defensive position, they have turned to attack. Their most prominent representatives are Arthur C. Danto, Paul Ricoeur, and Jörn Rüsen. Danto has asserted that narration is vital for description and explanation, that the form of narration is at the same time a form of explanation. The narrative form always surpasses the given, and categorically uses all-encompassing concepts. Narrative structures influence our historical thinking in the same way theories do in the case of the sciences. Paul Ricoeur expresses the same idea in his phrase: "raconter, c'est déjà expliquer" (to tell a story means to explain it).[9] Danto's and Ricoeur's theses were received favorably. Jörn Rüsen agrees that narration is part of the logical structure of historiography and that consequently "description and explanation have a function subordinate to the narrative scheme."[10]

Is narration also an absolute necessity for the novel? The narrative crisis is just as prevalent in the area of fiction as it is in historiography. The renunciation of narration by the modern novelists of the twenties and thirties scared many a Germanist as late as the fifties. "The death of the narrator is the death of the novel," proclaimed one of the more prominent literary essays on the state of fiction, an article that read like a mixture of final judgment and lament. "The whole concept of the novel is in jeopardy when such forms as 'action' or 'story' . . . are denounced as invalid conventions,"

Wolfgang Kayser warned.[11] In connection with Gottfried Benn's poetics, Reinhold Grimm described a type of novel from which the narrator had disappeared. It was called "the novel of the phenotype" or "the inward directed novel," labels indicating a tendency toward lack of action and lack of characters.[12] The world and its events are banned here; significant for this novel is the reduction to the "I," the isolated subject: the "I" speaks only of itself. Consequently, one reads in Rilke's *Aufzeichnungen des Malte Laurids Brigge*: "It must have been before my time that stories were narrated, really narrated. I have never heard a person narrate a story."[13] Walter Benjamin's discussion of the decline of storytelling in his essay about the Russian writer Nikolai Lesskow, "The Storyteller," echoes Rilke's statement.[14] The aesthetic designation of the phenotype novel—exemplified in the novels of Virginia Woolf, Gottfried Benn, Carl Einstein, and Rainer Maria Rilke—is also appropriate for the writing of some contemporary authors; Botho Strauss and Peter Handke immediately come to mind. In the novel of the avant-garde (Joyce, Dos Passos, Gide, Döblin, Musil, Broch), narration was either complemented or largely replaced by montage techniques and cognitive means, by reflection or essayistic writing; here it was not so much a matter of narration of events, action, and mimesis as one of presentation of ideas and provision of knowledge. The same holds true for Peter Handke. Since 1979, when he published *Langsame Heimkehr*, he has emphasized a presented idea rather than a narrated fable. Even in an earlier phase he was influenced by the "nouveau roman" with its antinarrative tendencies. However, the traditional concept of the novel, with narration and action, is by no means so fragile as is often assumed, and its swan song was sung too early. Robbe-Grillet's thesis that narration had actually become impossible has not proved true.[15] The best-known postwar novelists of the German language (Böll, Johnson, Walser, Grass, Neutsch, Kant, and Wolf) uphold the traditional established narrative models. Even a postmodern novel that has no narrator—take *Commedia* (1980) by Gerold Späth—does not give up narration as such.[16] It only delegates narration to a whole complex of different narrative voices. One can write purely narrative novels; however, totally non-narrative epic fiction is nonexistent. Like historiography, the novel obviously cannot dispense entirely with narration, and thus it makes sense, now as ever, to adhere to the science of narrative technique. In the field of narrative technique, literary scholars are far ahead of the narratologists in the camp of the historiographers. The latter could learn a great deal from theoreticians like Dorrit Cohn, Gérard Genette, Käte Hamburger, Eberhard Lämmert, and Franz Stanzel.[17] For the writing of a novel Stanzel has worked out three typical narrative situations. Comparable, albeit not identical, narrative situations exist also in historiography. Historians could also learn from reader theories as developed by such literary theorists as Jonathan Culler ("the competent reader"), Umberto Eco ("the model reader"), Stanley Fish ("the informed reader"), Wolfgang Iser ("the implied reader"), Michael Riffaterre ("the superreader"), and Gerald Prince ("the narratee").[18]

In *Metahistory*, Hayden White draws interesting parallels between historiography and fiction, as did Peter Munz, under White's influence, four years later in his study *The Shapes of Time*. Hayden White strives for a poetics of historiography and attempts to describe the forms of historical presentation in order to compare them with literary forms.[19] He starts with the premise that no sequence of events—by itself—is a story; it is the task of the historiographer to transfer the events, the facts, to the narrative framework of a story. The connections between happenings do not occur spontaneously; they are the result of the historiographer's reflection. In each historiographical text White distinguishes between the "what" (the narrated events) and the "how" (the type of narration, the "emplotment").[20] White was not the only scholar to see that historiographical and fictional narration are related, but he was the first to make a systematic attempt to study the structure of historical consciousness—to show the fictional elements and their formal manifestations in historiography.[21] The situation in nineteenth-century historiography and philosophy of history serves as an example. Hayden White could have given his book the title *The Rhetoric of Historiography* as a parallel to Wayne C. Booth's study *The Rhetoric of Fiction*.[22] In *Metahistory* he concludes that the writing of history has little to do with such qualities as true or false, correct or incorrect, and that ultimately historical writing cannot be distinguished from fiction. In a second book, *Tropics of Discourse*, he maintains the same position and supports it with new findings. (In the introduction to this collection of essays he identifies—with reference to Kenneth Burke—four different tropes as the major categories of historical consciousness: metaphor, metonymy, synecdoche, and irony.)[23] The title of the German translation of this later study nicely sums up Hayden White's conviction: *Auch Klio dichtet oder Die Fiktion des Faktischen*.[24] The historian's style, White argues in *Metahistory*, depends on the combination of the following elements. First, there are three different strategies; he calls them "explanation by formal argument," "explanation by ideological implication," and "explanation by emplotment." Specific modes of articulation correspond to each strategy. In this context we are only interested in the strategy of "emplotment" (narration), with its four corresponding "poetic" modes of "romance," "comedy," "tragedy," and "satire."[25] Depending on the ideology and moral inclination of the historiographer, one of these "literary" narrative modes (or a combination thereof) would be selected in order to transform the *res gestae* into the *historia rerum gestarum*. White sees a fictionalizing process at work when he describes the transformation of the source material into a story of tragic, comic, satiric, or romantic character.[26] He points to Michelet's *Histoire de la Révolution française* (1847) as an example of "romantic" fictionalization; on the other hand he sees Tocqueville's treatment of the same topic in his work *L'Ancien Régime et la Révolution* (1856) as a case of "tragic" historiography. White's references to certain structural similarities between the unfolding of tragedies or comedies and that of historical representations are interesting, but these similarities should by no means be construed as an actual fictionalization of history. In his book *Metaphern für Geschichte*, Alexander Demandt has shown how thought-structures were mirrored in the poetic metaphors used by historiographers and how, in turn, the ideologies of the historiographers influenced their use of rhetorical figures.[27] But the use of metaphors does not signify a fictionalization of history. There exist basic narrative concepts that are equally valid for historical and for fictional narration. Without action, images, and metaphors, narration per se is unimaginable. Returning to White's example of the different depictions and interpretations of the French Revolution, it is evident that this is not a case of fictionalization because the historical process is not depicted as an "as if," but as something that actually did occur. No one will deny that "changing the language of historical sources into the language of historical description is a basic problem of utmost difficulty," and that the depiction of history is a creative process.[28] However, its qualitative difference from fictional narration remains, despite the use of literary interpretation patterns and flowery metaphors. While fiction has as its basis the so-called as-if structure, and thus proves to be pretense, illusion, and unreality, historiography always relates to actual events.[29] Käte Hamburger clarified the difference through the example of a historical report about Napoleon and a novel about Napoleon. The historiographer cannot see Napoleon "in the subjectivity, the ego-originality of his inner thoughts, of his very 'existence.' " If he does so, however, we "find ourselves in a novel about Napoleon, a piece of fiction."[30] The narrative techniques with which novelists depict the psyches of their characters have been most accurately analyzed by Dorrit Cohn. She differentiates between psychonarration, quoted monologue, and narrated monologue.[31] These are narrative techniques reserved for purely fictional narration, which cannot occur in historical writing. Just as the use of a literary (tragic or comic, for example) interpretive category cannot turn a historical narrative into a fictional one, a historical novel does not become a piece of historiography simply by including historical reality in the fictional field. Käte Hamburger validly defines the line between fiction and reality, "where there is no crossing over from one category to the other," when she discusses the different perceptions of mimesis in novel and historiography: whereas the historiographer is a mouthpiece telling of persons and things—while in historiography there is a definite relationship between the narrating process and the narrated material—the characters created by novelists are simply narrated persons. In fiction there is no relationship, only a functional context, between the narrating process and the narrated material. According to Hamburger, the fictionalization of the persons described consists in the fact that the characters are not presented as objects but as subjects, as "ego-origines."[32] This difference between historiography and fiction also becomes evident when we look at the results of more recent studies of the theory of fictionality. Aleida Assmann has shown that scholars in the fields of analytic language philosophy and of pragmatic communication theory insist on this distinction.[33] In the analytic philosophy of language the point is made that fiction has a very peculiar status as far as its logic of statements is concerned: the authors of fiction are not obliged to come up with any proof; their judgments are quasi, pseudo, or as-if statements. In communication theory, fictionality is studied with respect to its reception effects: it involves the elimination of the normal connection that exists between the participants of an act of communication. Dealing with fiction leads to a temporary liberation from thinking in terms of fixed institutions; it means the absence of social sanctions and a lack of verification pressure.

Hayden White's *Metahistory* has found a number of critics, among whom are William H. Dray, Eugene Golob, Dominick LaCapra, and Maurice Mandelbaum.[34] They all point out that there is a major difference between historiography and fiction, that White does not do justice to the tension existing between the historian's discourse and history as res gestae; also, they are opposed to what Golob calls White's "radical relativism." In a series of articles that appeared during the early eighties and in his latest book, *The Content of the Form*, White has tried to counter this charge of relativism by demanding that historians search for the truth, that they exercise a high degree of discipline when dealing with historical facts and sources.[35] Such an appeal, based on rhetoric, does not confront the question of relativism. Since White is not inclined to give up his basic assumptions about the poetic or fictional character of historiography, the attacks on his relativistic position will not cease.

"Historia vero testis temporum, lux veritas, vita memoriae, magistra vitae, nuntia vetustatis."[36] Cicero's classic definition of the function of historical writing is still valid today—with a few deviations and reservations. The modern formulations are somewhat less pretentious, but given such terms as "demand for truth," "imparting of meaning," "provision of identity," and "memory," the function of historiography is not defined so differently from Cicero's wording. Only the postulate "magistra vitae" is viewed more skeptically. Authors of novels are equally concerned with the pursuit of truth, the imparting of meaning, the provision of identity, and memory.

Friedrich Schlegel wrote in his introduction to the *Wissenschaft der europäischen Literatur*: "As history aims at recognition and truth it approaches science, but as it is also representation . . . it is related to art."[37] Here the double-faced aspect of historiography has been precisely formulated. No historiographer would be so arrogant as to assume that his or her report could encompass the whole truth of a historical event. Even Ranke's historicism was not marked by such arrogance. Ranke's intention to show "how it really was" ("wie es eigentlich gewesen") has often been misunderstood.[38] He simply wanted to distance himself from the poetic representation of history as it was practiced in the then-popular historical novel.[39] Historiography can claim with justification that its statements are "truthful" insofar as they have been gained "scientifically,"—insofar as they can be proven. And they can be proven because they can be proven wrong: the truth capacity of the narrative statements of historical writing is based on the fact that they can be falsified.[40] In this respect one can imagine no greater difference between historical writing and fiction. Since the statements of a novel are fictional to begin with, they cannot be falsified. While writers of fiction may embellish an event from the past with fantasy, historiographers must check the sources, which dictate what they cannot say. As early as 1946, R. G. Collingwood pointed out that "the historical imagination is not completely free but is bound to work from the evidence."[41] The truth of a poetic statement is not achieved by fiction imitating the principles of historiography. The propensity for truth and truthfulness itself are presented differently in the two narrative modes. The intent to provide the truth does exist in both literature and historical writing, but it is aimed in different directions. Historiographers attempt to achieve the most exact comprehension and representation of actual historical events; novelists have no such ambition.[42] On the contrary, their strength lies not in the realm of facts but in that of possibilities.

The aesthetics of the modern as well as of the postmodern novel are focused on the opening up of possibilities, of potentialities. Modernist literature aims to distance itself from the mimetic-realistic principle that dominated the novel of the second half of the nineteenth century. Robert Musil, for example, in *Der Mann ohne Eigenschaften*, plays with several types of utopias and arrives at the category of "possibility," in opposition to confidence in the power of history. Elias Canetti, in an early phase, attempts to work out the "increasing reality," a "reality of what is coming," and in *Die Blendung* succeeds in gaining an idea of the dangerous potential of the subseqent decades. Similar statements could be made about the novels of Hermann Broch. The continued effect of the principle of possibilities in contemporary literature cannot be overlooked. Such authors as Ingeborg Bachmann, Thomas Bernhard, Max Frisch, Peter Handke, Dieter Kühn, and Christa Wolf have made the concept of possibility an important part of their poetics.

In examining the truth-postulate in literature and in historiography, one must consider the premises on which historical and novelistic narration are based. In traditional narration the novelist, like the historiographer, is guided by ideas of totality as we know them, on the one hand from the aesthetics of Hegel to Lukács, and on the other hand from Hegel's and Marx's substantialist philosophy of history. In both cases the attempt is made to see events in such a way that they make sense within the context of a totality. Here the historical and artistic totalities are structurally identical. Danto has criticized as outdated the substantialist philosophy of history, with its concept of a teleological, continuous development. He states that this philosophy acts as if it knew of a "divine plan" of history, as if one could determine past and present from the perspective of the future. Danto wants to replace the speculative and dogmatic substantialist philosophy of history with an analytical (descriptive and coordinating) theory of history. In this theory the vantage would not be from a postulated future goal back to the present and past, but rather from the past to the present, with no certainties about the future.[43] The ancient trust, reaffirmed by Nietzsche, in the continuity of history is questioned, as are the Christian and Marxist tenets of the eschatological or utopian direction of history. Such beliefs once formed the foundation for the concept of continuity in history. Many contemporary historians shun these labels and are consequently faced with two choices: giving up the concept of continuity altogether, or adopting it from the tradition of historiography and perhaps developing it in their own fashion. Present-day historians are more aware than ever of the heuristic character of the concept of continuity; they see it merely as a "regulative idea" in historical narration.[44] Today the focus is more on discontinuity than on continuity. In this respect the impact of Michel Foucault as an outright anti-Hegelian thinker (especially with his study *L'archéologie du savoir* of 1969) is not to be underrated.[45]

The dismissal of the concepts of continuity and totality has also had an impact on the writing of the novel. The idea of the "self-contained" work of art that provides totality by way of typical characters is dead. Its place has been taken by the "open" novel with its open-endedness, as first envisioned by the early German Romantics. In his *Theorie des Romans* (1916), Georg Lukács declared that the modern novelist could outdo the historiographer if, after the loss of totality of meaning and being, he or she would counter the partial insights into the course of history with concern for a new, homogeneous cosmology. In contrast, however, the modern novel plays an important role as an instrument of cognition because such concepts of sytems are now distrusted. Not a new cosmology of being, but a view of the disparity of what is to be, of the diversity of the possibilities, is what this medium can provide.

Let me return to the controversy between Plato and Aristotle about the truth-value of fiction. In contemporary philosophy a similar discussion has been taking place. Theodor W. Adorno was convinced that, due to its autonomy, art—as a creative, nonalienated work—was the last vestige of freedom. According to him, art and literature alone can unveil what is hidden in reality, can destroy ideology and lies.[46] What Adorno criticized as a web of ideological deceptions is close to what Roland Barthes calls the "myth-icizing" of everyday life. Like Adorno, Barthes affirms that poetic language maintains direct contact with reality and, unlike historiography, escapes mystification.[47] In contrast to Adorno and Barthes, Eagleton and Jameson argue that the writing of literature is just another form of ideological production.[48] Jameson maintains the following position: "Ideology is not something which informs or invests symbolic production; rather the aesthetic act is itself ideological, and the production of aesthetic or narrative form is to be seen as an ideological act in its own right."[49] All four authors make extremely one-sided statements. The common ground of historiography and literature is narration. And when narration, through the eyes of Jameson, is seen as an ideological act per se, we cannot expect much truth in either historiography or fiction. But if, on the other hand, literature is able to destroy ideology and deception—to cite Adorno—this virtue should also be attributed to historiography. Narration can lead in both directions: it can help us approach truth, or it can produce ideological veils. Neither literature nor historiography is immune to the virus of error or the distortion of truth, but both are capable of making us see reality more clearly.

Among the functions of historiography and the novel are, along with the search for truth, the imparting of meaning and the provision of identity. The imparting of meaning (*Sinnbildung*) is far from the creation of meaning (*Sinnstiftung*).[50] Surely there were, and still are, historiographers and novelists who have declared themselves ideological creators of meaning, but neither modern novelists nor critical historiographers are interested in such ambitious goals. In historical narration the imparting of meaning is achieved through memory alone. And although novelistic narration cannot be reduced to memory, it plays an important role here as well. This is especially evident when historians fail to bring to mind certain aspects of historical experience through memory; then it is often the novelist who must assume this task. The fifties in West Germany provide a clear example of this phenomenon. With regard to the National Socialist past, repression rather than grief was prevalent. It was a novel that broke this taboo: *Die Blechtrommel*, by Günter Grass (1959). With the excursion into fantasy of this novel, Grass took over the task of the historiographer, namely to call to mind the historic events of the most recent past. Soon Rolf Hochhuth, Heinar Kipphardt, and Peter Weiss joined the preoccupation with the suppressed horror of those years. This literary breakthrough was followed by the works of the historiographers. George

Steiner listed a number of examples of this function of the "writer as re-membrancer."[51] It is particularly in cases of the conscious falsification of history by historians that the writer steps in.

Writers and historiographers can help define the identity of a generation, a nation, or a culture. Since the enlightenment and secularization, historiography and fiction (rather than religion) have been burdened increasingly with the function of providing an identity. By dealing with memories, the experiences of the present attain a coherent perspective that provides the reader with an orientation for the future. Repeatedly correlating experiences of the present with those of the past can bring about the dissolution of stagnant patterns of identity, with a critical view of ideological prejudices. The factual orientation of the historiographer as well as the novelist's interest in what is possible are part of the provision of identity. By means of memory, a potential of historical and literary meaning is activated that, along with the demonstration of actual limits and the allusion to yet untested possibilities, makes the provision of identity possible. Historical and literary consciousness is a complex construct of memory of the past, interpretation of the present, and expectation of the future, a construct in which memory is the prerequisite for interpretation and expectation. To structure an identity means, first of all, to identify with stories. During an identity crisis society may show greater interest in historical remembering (as was the case in Europe in the nineteenth century) or demand a more fictional provision of identity (as is presently the case in Latin America). The weaker the link with the historical past and the more suspect it appears, the stronger will be the desire for fictional patterns of identity.

The question has been asked whether a novel (or a work of art in general) can be understood as a historical event. Jauss has pointed out that both the publication of a novel and a political event have something in common: neither possesses a fixed or static meaning, and each is surrounded by a horizon of potential meaning that changes with time. Historiographers rewrite their reports whenever they have a new understanding of the consequences of a political event, and the reception of novels varies with literary and societal conditions.[52] The meaning of both historical events and of novels is open-ended, since it hinges on changing interpretations. Here the analogy ends. While a novel continues to live through constantly renewed readings, historical events, in the narrow sense of the word (the election of a government, the outbreak of a revolution), continue to have an effect on society even if they are forgotten by everyone.

Finally, it should be pointed out that narration plays a role in fiction and historiography in a less concrete, somewhat mystical sense as well. It is narration that changes neutral, static time into human time with the dimensions of past, present, and future. Volker Klotz has spoken of the death-effacing effect of narration, in the sense that it is a last attempt to overcome death (exemplified in the narrative situation of Scheherazade in *The Arabian Nights*).[53] Death lurks at that constantly changing border in time where future becomes present and present turns into past. The farther our consciousness reaches back from this point into the past by means of historical memory or forward into the future by means of poetic imagination, and the more we know of the life actually experienced and the life potentially to be experienced, the smaller in our consciousness looms the threat of death in the present.[54]

NOTES

1. Aristotle, *On Poetics*, chap. 9.

2. Horst Steinmetz, *Literatur und Geschichte: Vier Versuche* (Munich: Iudicum, 1988), 12, 62.

3. Reinhart Koselleck, "Wozu noch Historie?" in *Seminar: Geschichte und Theorie*, ed. Hans Michael Baumgartner and Jörn Rüsen (Frankfurt: Suhrkamp, 1976), 23.

4. Peter Szondi, "Für eine nicht mehr narrative Historie," in *Geschichte—Ereignis und Erzählung*, ed. Reinhart Koselleck and Wolf Dieter Stempel (Munich: Fink, 1973), 540–41.

5. See the more recent theoretical works by Georges Duby and Guy Lardreau, *Dialogues* (Paris: Flammarion, 1980); François Furet, *L'atelier de l'histoire* (Paris: Flammarion, 1982); Jacques LeGoff and Pierre Nora, *Faire de l'histoire* (Paris: Gallimard, 1974); and Paul Veyne, *Comment on écrit l'histoire: Essai d'épistémologie* (Paris: Seuil, 1971).

6. Christian Meier, "Narrativität, Geschichte und die Sorgen des Historikers," 580, and Arno Borst, "Das historische Ereignis," in Baumgartner and Rüsen, *Seminar*, 538.

7. Reinhart Koselleck, "Ereignis und Struktur," in Baumgartner and Rüsen, *Seminar*, 554, 521. Similar ideas regarding theory and narration are expressed in the introduction to *Theorie und Erzählung in der Geschichte*, ed. Jürgen Kocka and Thomas Nipperdey (Munich: Deutscher Taschenbuch-Verlag, 1979), 7–13.

8. Hans Robert Jauss, "Versuch einer Ehrenrettung des Ereignisbegriffs," and Harald Weinrich, "Narrative Strukturen in der Geschichtsschreibung," in Baumgartner and Rüsen, *Seminar*, 521, 554; Lawrence Stone, "The Revival of Narrative: Reflections on a New Old History," *Past and Present* 85 (1979): 3–24. Stone interprets the revival of narrative as a defeat of those dogmatic Marxist and Annalist historians who thought they could write history in a purely descriptive and analytical manner.

9. Arthur C. Danto, *Analytical Philosophy of History* (Cambridge: Cambridge University Press, 1965) and Danto, *Narration and Knowledge* (New York: Columbia University Press, 1985). See also Werner Schiffer, *Theorien der Geschichtsschreibung und ihre erzähltheoretische Relevanz: Danto, Habermas, Baumgartner, Droysen* (Stuttgart: Metzler, 1980), 27ff., and Paul Ricoeur, *Temps et récit* (Paris: Seuil, 1983), 1:251.

10. Hans Michael Baumgartner and Jörn Rüsen, "Erträge der Diskussion," in *Erzählforschung: Ein Symposium*, ed. Eberhard Lämmert (Stuttgart: Metzler, 1982), 697.

11. Wolfgang Kayser, *Entstehung und Krise des modernen Romans* (Stuttgart: Metzler, 1955), 34, 29.

12. Reinhold Grimm, "Romane des Phänotyp," in his *Strukturen. Essays zur deutschen Literatur* (Göttingen: Sachse and Pohl, 1963), 74–94.

13. Rainer Maria Rilke, *Die Aufzeichnungen des Malte Laurids Brigge* (Leipzig: Insel, 1910), 23.

14. Walter Benjamin, "Der Erzähler," in his *Gesammelte Schriften*, ed. Rolf Tiedemann and Hermann Schweppenhauser (Frankfurt: Suhrkamp, 1972), 2:438–65.

15. Alain Robbe-Grillet, *Pour un nouveau roman* (Paris: Minuit, 1963).

16. Hanns-Joseph Ortheil, "Das Lesen—ein Spiel: Postmoderne Literatur? Die Literatur der Zukunft!" in *Deutsche Literatur, 1986: Jahresüberblick*, ed. Volker Hage and Adolf Fink (Stuttgart: Reclam, 1987), 313–22. Ortheil describes Späth's *Commedia* as one of the recent postmodern novels written in German.

17. Dorrit Cohn, *Transparent Minds: Narrative Modes for Presenting Consciousness in Fiction* (Princeton: Princeton University Press, 1978); Gérard Genette, *Figures III* (Paris: Seuil, 1972) and *Nouveau discours du récit* (Paris: Seuil, 1983); Käte Hamburger, *Die Logik der Dichtung*, rev. ed. (Stuttgart: Klett, 1968); Eberhard Lämmert, *Bauformen des Erzählens* (Göttingen: Vandenhoeck and Ruprecht, 1979).

18. Jonathan Culler, *Structuralist Poetics: Structuralism, Linguistics, and the Study of Literature* (London: Routledge and Kegan Paul, 1975); Umberto Eco, *The Role of the Reader: Explorations in the Semiotics of Texts* (Bloomington: Indiana University Press, 1979); Stanley Fish, "Literature in the Reader: Affective Stylistics," *New Literary History* 2 (1970): 123–62; Wolfgang Iser, *The Implied Reader: Patterns of Communication in Prose Fiction from Bunyan to Beckett* (Baltimore: Johns Hopkins University Press, 1974); Michael Riffaterre, *Essais de stylistique structurale* (Paris: Flammarion, 1971); Gerald Prince, *Narratology: The Form and Function of Narrative* (Berlin: Mouton, 1982).

19. Hayden White, *Metahistory: The Historical Imagination in Nineteenth-Century Europe* (Baltimore: Johns Hopkins University Press, 1973), and Peter Munz, *The Shapes of Time* (Middleton: Wesleyan University Press, 1977). Munz argues that since we cannot get a glimpse of history (res gestae) directly, and since stories can be evaluated only by looking at other stories, it becomes difficult to distinguish between history writing and fiction, between myth and the philosophy of history. See also Peter Gay, *Style in History* (New York: Basic Books, 1974). Gay does not go so far in his conclusions as do White and Munz.

20. A few years later the structuralist Seymour Chatman distinguished in a similar way between the "what" ("story") and the "how" ("discourse") in his *Story and Discourse: Narrative Structures in Fiction and Film* (Ithaca: Cornell University Press, 1978).

21. Louis O. Mink, "Narrative Form as a Cognitive Instrument," in *The Writing of History: Literary Form and Historical Understanding*, ed. Robert H. Canary and Henry Kozicki (Madison: University of Wisconsin Press, 1978), 143. At the end of his article, Mink maintains that the difference between historiography and fiction should be upheld and that its disappearance would result in myth, an option unacceptable to him. The question of how the difference between the two should be conceptualized remains unanswered. The article concludes with a weak appeal to "the commonsense belief that history is true in a sense in which fiction is not" (148).

22. Wayne C. Booth, *The Rhetoric of Fiction* (Chicago: University of Chicago Press, 1961).

23. Kenneth Burke, *A Grammar of Motives* (Berkeley and Los Angeles: University of California Press, 1969), 503–17.

24. Hayden White, *Auch Klio dichtet oder die Fiktion des Faktischen: Studien zur Tropologie des historischen Diskurses*, introd. by Reinhart Koselleck, trans. Brigitte Brinkmann-Siepmann and Thomas Siepmann (Stuttgart: Klett-Cotta, 1986).

25. White borrowed these categories from Northrop Frye, *Fables of Identity* (New York: Harcourt, Brace, and World, 1963), 52ff.

26. Hayden White, "The Historical Text as Literary Artifact," in Mink, *The Writing of History*, 46–47.

27. Alexander Demandt, *Metaphern für Geschichte: Sprachbilder und Gleichnisse im historisch-politischen Denken* (Munich: Beck, 1978).

28. Theodor Schieder, "Die Darstellungsformen der Geschichtswissenschaft," in Schieder, *Geschichte als Wissenschaft* (Munich: Oldenbourg, 1965), 114.

29. Hamburger, *Die Logik der Dichtung*, 84.

30. Ibid., 73. E. M. Forster also stressed that an author should write a novel about Queen Victoria only if he could tell us more about the queen than a historiographer could—if he could acquaint us with her hidden psychic feelings and motives. On the other hand, we are then presented with a Queen Victoria who cannot be identical with the one described by historiographers. See E. M. Forster, *Aspects of the Novel* (Harmondsworth: Penguin, 1966), 52–53. Similar ideas were expressed by R. G. Collingwood, *The Idea of History* (Oxford: Clarendon, 1946), 65.

31. Cohn, *Transparent Minds*.

32. Hamburger, *Die Logik der Dichtung*, 113, 114.

33. Aleida Assmann, *Die Legitimität der Fiktion* (Munich: Fink, 1980), 10ff.

34. William H. Dray, "The Politics of Contemporary Philosophy of History," *Clio* 3 (1973): 35–53, 55–75; Eugene Golob, "The Irony of Nihilism," *History and Theory* 19 (1980): 55–66; Dominick LaCapra, "A Poetics of Historiography: Hayden White's Tropics of Discourse," in *Rethinking Intellectual History: Texts, Contexts, Language*, ed. Dominick LaCapra (Ithaca: Cornell University Press, 1983); Maurice Mandelbaum, "The Presuppositions of *Metahistory*," *History and Theory* 19 (1980): 39–54.

35. Hayden White, "The Value of Narrativity in the Representation of Reality," *Critical Inquiry* 7 (1980): 5–28; "The Politics of Historical Interpretation: Discipline and De-Sublimation," *Critical Inquiry* 9 (1982): 113–37; "The Question of Narrative in Contemporary Historical Theory," *History and Theory* 23 (1984): 1–33; *The Content of the Form* (Baltimore: Johns Hopkins University Press, 1987).

36. Quoted in Reinhart Koselleck, "Historia Magistra Vitae: Über die Auflösung des Topos im Horizont neuzeitlich bewegter Geschichte," in Koselleck, *Vergangene Zukunft: Zur Semantik geschichtlicher Zeiten* (Frankfurt: Suhrkamp, 1984), 41.

37. Friedrich Schlegel, *Wissenschaft der europäischen Literatur*, ed. Ernst Behler, *Kritische Friedrich Schlegel-Ausgabe*, vol. 11 (Munich: Schöningh, 1958), 10.

38. Leopold von Ranke, "Vorrede der ersten Ausgabe Oktober 1824," in von

Ranke, *Geschichten der romanischen und germanischen Völker von 1494 bis 1514* (Leipzig: Duncker and Humblot, 1874), vii.

39. Schieder, *Geschichte als Wissenschaft*, 113.

40. Hans-Jörg Porath, "Narrative Paradigma, Theorieproblem und historische Objektivität," in Lämmert, *Erzählforschung: Ein Symposium*, 662.

41. Collingwood, *Idea of History*, 246.

42. John Lukacs, "Facts and Fictions, or Describing the Past," in Lukacs, *Historical Consciousness, or the Remembered Past* (New York: Harper and Row, 1968), 98–127.

43. Danto, *Analytical Philosophy of History*.

44. Jörn Rüsen, "Die vier Typen des historischen Erzählens," in *Formen der Geschichtsschreibung*, ed. Reinhart Koselleck et al. (Munich: Deutscher Taschenbuch-Verlag, 1982), 531.

45. Michel Foucault, *The Archeology of Knowledge* (New York, 1972), 12: "The problem is no longer of tradition, of tracing a line, but one of divisions, of limits, it is no longer one of lasting foundations, but one of transformations, that serve as new foundations."

46. Theodor W. Adorno, *Ästhetische Theorie* (Frankfurt: Suhrkamp, 1970).

47. Roland Barthes, *Mythologies* (Paris: Seuil, 1957).

48. Terry Eagleton, *Criticism and Ideology* (Atlantic Highlands, N.J.: Humanities Press, 1976).

49. Frederic Jameson, *The Political Unconscious: Narrative as a Socially Symbolic Act* (Ithaca: Cornell University Press, 1981).

50. Rüsen, "Die vier Typen des historischen Erzählens," 520.

51. George Steiner, "The Writer as Remembrancer: A Note on *Poetics* 9," *Yearbook of Comparative and General Literature* 22 (1973): 51–57.

52. Jauss, "Versuch einer Ehrenrettung des Ereignisbegriffs," 535. See also Hinrich C. Seeba, "Literatur und Geschichte: Hermeneutische Ansätze zu einer Poetik der Geschichtsschreibung," in *Akten des VI. Internationalen Germanisten-Kongresses Basel, 1980* (Bern: Lang, 1980), 201–8.

53. Volker Klotz, "Erzählen als Enttöten," in Lämmert, *Erzählforschung*, 319–34.

54. This study is a heavily revised version of the introductory article "Geschichtsschreibung und Roman: Interdependenzen und Differenzen" in my book *Zeitgeschichte in Geschichten der Zeit: Deutschsprachige Romane im 20. Jahrhundert* (Bonn: Bouvier, 1986), 2–25.

THREE

FICTIONALITY, HISTORICITY, AND
TEXTUAL AUTHORITY:

PATER, WOOLF, HILDESHEIMER

Judith Ryan

L ET IT BE FICTION, one feels, or let it be fact. The imagination will not serve under two masters simultaneously."[1] Dorrit Cohn quotes this dictum of Virginia Woolf in her paper "Fictional *versus* Historical Lives," in which she studies—among other things—such borderline cases as "biographies that act like novels" and one extraordinary "novel that acts like a biography."[2] As far as I can see, Dorrit Cohn is quite correct to regard the latter, Wolfgang Hildesheimer's *Marbot: Eine Biographie*,[3] as generically unique; nonetheless, it has its predecessors, not least in Virginia Woolf's own work. Indeed, Woolf is by no means as dogmatic about the mingling of fact and fiction as this seemingly prescriptive statement suggests. Her comment, which occurs toward the end of her essay "The New Biography,"[4] is immediately followed by some remarks that make it clear how very much she was, in fact, attracted—as well as troubled—by the biographies of the 1920s that tended markedly to "act like novels." The peg on which her essay hangs is one of these, Harold Nicolson's *Some People*, in which, following in the footsteps of the quintessential "new biographer," Lytton Strachey, Nicolson "devised a method of writing about people and about himself as though they were at once real and imaginary."[5] Far from rejecting the new fashion, Woolf regards it as a signpost to a turning that needed to be taken. The concluding paragraphs of her essay show her wrestling with this problem: "And here again we approach the difficulty which, for all his ingenuity, the biographer still has to face. Truth of fact and truth of fiction are incompatible; yet he is now more than ever urged to combine them. For it would seem that the life which is increasingly real to us is the fictitious life; it dwells in the personality rather than in the act."[6] Announcing that "the days of Victorian biography are over," Woolf continues by noting how those aspects of the contemporary sense of life that seem "most real" would have "slipped through [the] fingers" of Nicolson's Victorian predecessors: "Nor can we name the biographer whose art is subtle and bold enough to present that queer amalgamation of dream and reality, that perpetual marriage of granite and rainbow. His method still remains to be discovered. But Mr. Nicolson, with his mixture of biography and autobiography, of fact and fiction, of Lord Curzon's trousers and Miss Plimsoll's nose, waves his hand airily in a possible direction."[7]

This view of Nicolson, whose book *Some People* in fact takes a distinct step beyond the "new biography," as one who points the way, who "waves . . . in a possible direction," is not what it might first seem: a gesture of politeness by a reviewer toward an otherwise somewhat lightweight new publication. On the contrary: Woolf's judgment of Nicolson should be taken entirely seriously. During the period in which she wrote this essay, Woolf had come increasingly to think of biography as an important genre. Not that this is really surprising from the daughter of Leslie Stephen, editor of the *National Dictionary of Biography*. To be sure, she never gives biography priority over fiction, but she had already come to regard it as more than just a lower form of literature. In her essay "The Art of Biography,"[8] she presents the biographer as an important explorer in the no-man's land where fact and fiction overlap: "Thus the biographer must go ahead of the rest of us, like the miner's canary, testing the atmosphere, detecting falsity, unreality, and the presence of obsolete conventions."[9] But even as she was writing these two essays on biography, she herself was moving ahead of the miner's canary through the perilous mineshaft, creating her own curious mixture of fact and fiction, *Orlando: A Biography* (1928). In this astonishing work, to which I shall return only after a considerable detour, Woolf was to prove that it certainly was possible for the imagination to "serve under two masters simultaneously."

In drawing attention to Nicolson's airily waving hand, Woolf was preparing the ground for her own *Orlando* to be seen as the crucial step that had yet to be taken. At the same time, however, she was assiduously erasing the traces of a more illustrious predecessor who had planted his flag on the ridge between fact and fiction long before. This was Walter Pater, whose *Studies in the History of the Renaissance* (1873) and *Imaginary Portraits* (1887) underlie the ingenious pastiche that is *Orlando*. To these two works of Pater we need to add a third, *Marius the Epicurean: His Sensations and Ideas* (1885), since it is here that Pater works the borderland of fact and fiction—in generic terms: history, autobiography, and novel— most assiduously. Indeed, he calls this work an "imaginary portrait," just as he was later to title his semiautobiographical tale "The Child in the House" (1878) *An Imaginary Portrait* when it was reprinted in 1894. Clearly, a great deal of Pater's writing falls within the genre "imaginary portrait," even, as I shall show, his *Renaissance*; he appears, furthermore, to have projected a trilogy of works that would have included *Marius the Epicurean*, the existing *Imaginary Portraits*, and a third volume of related portraits containing his tale "Emerald Uthwart" (1892) and a number of other pieces that remained unfinished at his death.[10]

Pater's "imaginary portraits" have been designated by Harold Bloom as "an almost indescribable genre,"[11] neither essays nor veiled confessions, neither short stories nor romance-fragments. After much hesitation, Bloom decides to call them "reveries," since he sees them as attempts to escape, through the creation of fictive selves, "the subjective confession that wells up in his 'Leonardo da Vinci' and 'Conclusion' to the *Renaissance*."[12] Though he recognizes the imaginary portraits as "crucial to our understanding of Pater," Bloom sees them nonetheless as "equivocal achievements, noble but divided against themselves."[13] They take on an entirely new aspect, however, when we see them as precursors of Woolf's *Orlando* and Hildesheimer's *Marbot*.

I shall begin by looking at one of the most representative examples of the genre, "Sebastian van Storck." The piece is an extraordinary trompe l'oeil in which the imagined figure, Sebastian van Storck, is seamlessly blended into a historical panorama filled with such real figures as the Dutch painters Adrian van de Velde, Isaac van Ostade, Albert Cuyp, Thomas de Keyser, Peter de Keyser, Jan van der Heyde, Jan Weenix, Gerard Terburgh, and Jacob Ruysdael. William the Silent, prince of Orange, and his son Frederick Henry make their appearance along with a number of Dutch political leaders, and Sebastian van Storck is said to have been present at the signing of the Westphalian Peace Treaty of 1648. The modern reader, who knows many of these figures but would have to look up at least some of them in an art handbook or encyclopedia, might well be tempted to look up Sebastian van Storck as well—were it not for the cautionary title *Imaginary Portraits*. The readers of *Macmillan's Magazine*, however, where "Sebastian van Storck" first appeared in 1886, the year preceding publication of *Imaginary Portraits*, would not have been so forewarned. For them, after all, Pater was the author of *Studies in the Renaissance*, the chapters of which bore similar titles ("Sandro Botticelli," "Leonardo da Vinci," "The School of Giorgione") and took the form of what Pater was later to call "appreciations," mostly of individual figures. "Sebastian van Storck" resembles, chameleonlike, these earlier portraits of real painters. Chameleonlike because, if one looks closely, one can dimly discern the outlines of the fictive creature disguising itself as part of its real surroundings. On the one hand, the writer claims the support of certain evidence of the type we would today call "documentary": he mentions a portrait of Sebastian van Storck by Isaac van Ostade "from a sketch taken at one of those skating parties"; he cites at length the testimony of young Sebastian's tutor to the youth's "intellectual rectitude and candour" as well as that of a slightly later writer who congratulates the Dutch on the luck which "hath disposed them to so thriving a genius"; and he finally quotes various writings of Sebastian van Storck's in which he appears to "anticipate Spinoza."[14] Nor does the literary portraitist fear to reveal his presence as our guide to the study of Sebastian van Storck: "I pause just here," he writes, "to indicate in outline the kind of reasoning through which, making the 'Infinite' his beginning and his end, Sebastian had come to think . . . ," and so forth (103). On the other hand, the portrait, though seemingly documented, is also curiously fictionalized: we are told that the summer "seemed wellnigh to suffocate" our protagonist (82), and we even enter at times—through the preeminently fictionalizing form of quoted thought—the mind of Sebastian van Storck: "Was it the music of the duets? he asked himself next morning" (92). Pater achieves here the very blend of fact and fiction that Woolf was later to argue (if only so she could later disprove her own argument) was by nature impossible. In fact, Pater's portrait of Sebastian van Storck is more than simply a homogeneous blending: it is an ironic commentary of fact and fiction on each other. However fictive the "testimony" of Sebastian's tutor or the anonymous Dutch historian cited in the portrait, the writings of the fictive Sebastian that are also cited by the portraitist are not fictive at all. They are, in fact, quotations from Spinoza's *Ethics*, in what I assume to be Pater's own translation. Thus at the very moment when Sebastian van Storck is said to be "anticipating Spinoza," the famous philosopher's own words are placed in his mouth.[15] Why does Pater need to postulate a fictive figure if the writings of this figure are, in fact, Spinoza's? Wouldn't an essay on Spinoza along the lines of the "studies" in the *Renaissance* have done as well, if not better?

To understand the reasons for this curious decision to blend fact and fiction rather than to serve one master or the other, we need to look back at *Marius the Epicurean*, the work whose completion was so important to Pater that he felt compelled to resign his position at Brasenose College, Oxford, in order to facilitate it.[16] Though it is commonly regarded as a novel, Pater himself called his *Marius* an "imaginary portrait." From a narratological point of view, it is important to identify those features of *Marius the Epicurean* that link it with Pater's *Imaginary Portraits*, on the one hand, and that distinguish it from historical novels of the Rosemary Sutcliff variety, on the other. Unlike "Sebastian van Storck," which vacillates between a documenting and an empathizing narrator, the modality of *Marius the Epicurean* is thoroughly fictional. In the form of a generalized "you," the reader enters the world and mind of Marius with the narrator: "Nothing, you felt, as you first caught sight of that coy, retired place—surely nothing could happen there, without its full accompaniment of thought, or reverie."[17] "If you can imagine" a certain kind of "inward mystic intimation," you, the reader, are told, "you conceive aright the mind of Marius" (10). The narrator knows this mind in all its nooks and crannies, never complaining—as the narrator of Hildesheimer's *Marbot* will later constantly do—of incomplete documentation or of any gulf that might separate him from the subject of his narration. Only very occasionally is there any suggestion that this empathy among narrator, reader, and the mind of Marius is actually a supposition, as in the following piece of interrupted interior monologue: "Let me be sure then—might he not plausibly say?—that I miss no detail of this life of realized consciousness in the present!" (85). In general, the narration takes forms familiar to us from fiction, including, from time to time, those hallmarks of fiction identified by Käte Hamburger, those combinations of present-time adverbs and past-tense verbs that enable the reader partially to enter the consciousness of the character: "Today was his own birthday" (143) and "It was the anniversary of (Christ's) birth as a little child they celebrated today" (217).[18] By the same token, there are frequent passages in free indirect discourse, of which these key formulations in Käte Hamburger's theory are in fact a special variation. Many of these, in *Marius*, take the form of questions, a particular modalization of free indirect discourse that holds our identification of the speaker—is it the narrator or the figure?—even more in suspense than does free indirect discourse in the statement form. Thus we find passages like the following, in which a question that might simply be posed in the mind of the narrator is revealed, through words like "surely" and "must," also to exist in the mind of his protagonist:

> And was not this precisely the condition, the attitude of mind, to which something higher than he, yet akin to him, would be likely to reveal itself; to which that influence he had felt now and again, like a friendly hand upon his shoulder amid the actual obscurities of the world, would be likely to make a further explanation? Surely, the aim of a true philosophy must lie, not in futile efforts towards the complete accommodation of man to the circumstances in which he chances to find himself, but in the maintenance of a kind of candid discontent, in the face of the very highest achievement. (264–65)

The shift that appears to take place here from the mind of the narrator to the mind of the figure is scarcely discernible in the context from which this passage is taken: a complex, free-flowing meditation extending over several pages and modulating through a variety of different techniques for presenting consciousness. Quoted thought, free indirect discourse, and narrative commentary are freely interwoven as we follow Marius's philosophical reflections, sometimes entering into his mind completely, sometimes moving partially outside it. Passages of this kind observe the distinction between narrator and protagonist while simultaneously dissolving it: technically speaking, syntactic markers differentiate the two, but Marius's thoughts and the narrating voice are stylistically identical and participate in a single, unbroken line of argument. More often, however, the mode of

Marius the Epicurean is that of omniscient narration, the voice of a speaker who knows Marius so intimately that he can say without a shadow of doubt "Marius felt" (258), "thought Marius" (124), "to him [it] seemed" (4), "so the story composed itself in the mind of Marius" (53); he is a speaker who knows even things that cannot be known by Marius: "he was not aware, of course . . ." (27).

Yet this almost overdetermined fictionalization is at odds with certain other features of the narrative, however seamlessly it blends with the tone of the whole. *Marius the Epicurean* opens, for example, with an extended section—almost the entire first chapter—cast in the mode of a historical essay, not so dry, to be sure, as such a study might be today, but imbued with the same combination of stylistic charm and factual accuracy that characterizes Pater's own more overtly historical pieces. Here, for example, is the second sentence of Pater's opening: "While, in Rome, new religions had arisen with bewildering complexity around the dying old one, the earlier and simpler patriarchal religion, 'the religion of Numa,' as people loved to fancy, lingered on with little change amid the pastoral life, out of the habits and sentiment of which so much of it had grown" (3). Pater goes on to support this contention by a quotation from Tibullus in the original Latin and to weave together an entire cultural picture through a variety of learned (though engagingly presented) references to second-century Roman literature, religion, and culture. This essayist-narrator, as opposed to the frankly fictional narrator, reappears at frequent intervals throughout the book. This essayist does not hesitate to indicate his own temporal origin: on the second page he refers to Wordsworth, for example (4). But the essayist-narrator's precise location in time does not invalidate in any way our sense that there is no gap between us and Marius. On the contrary, the narrator argues repeatedly that the two eras, second-century Rome and nineteenth-century England, are essentially identical. Again and again, he intrudes into the narrative to draw our attention to a variety of parallels: between Marius's apprehension of the world as illusion and "the *Neu-zeit* of the German enthusiasts at the beginning of our own century" (29), between Marius's Rome and the Rome of his own day (100), between Marius's "register of the movements of his own private thoughts and humours" and the modern habit of journal keeping (238). This narrator is intrusive because such parallels are a crucial part of the book's larger structure and ultimate significance: "That age and our own [he comments] have much in common, many difficulties and hopes. Let the reader pardon me if here and there I seem to be passing from Marius to his modern representatives—from Rome, to Paris or London" (149). Indeed, as the subtitle suggests, Marius is viewed throughout as a precursor of Pater's contemporaries, with their fascination for "sensations and ideas" as opposed to actions. Second-century Rome, caught in a complex transition from older to newer beliefs, is the ideal correlative for the equally transitional age of the 1880s. Small wonder that the emphasis of *Marius the Epicurean* is on culture, religion, and philosophy. Marius's passage from Epicureanism through Cyrenaicism, Platonism, and Stoicism to early Christianity resembles the succession of philosophies that characterized Pater's own age from aestheticism to a new mysticism. The narrator's description of Heraclitean philosophy can equally well be read as an account of nineteenth-century empiricism: "The negative doctrine, then, that the objects of our ordinary experience, fixed as they seem, are really in perpetual change, had been as originally conceived but the preliminary step towards a large positive system of almost religious philosophy" (75).[19] Marius concerns himself with such quintessentially late nineteenth-century problems as "a languid, enervating, consumptive nihilism" (78), "the doctrine . . . of what is termed 'the subjectivity of knowledge' " (79), and an epiphanic experience that seemed "to gather into one central act of vision all the deeper impressions his mind had ever received" (185). Marius is not only a fictional representative of second-century Rome, but also the spirit of Pater's own age and a fictional surrogate for himself. The fictional biography of Marius the Epicurean is, like many fictional biographies, also in some sense an autobiography of its author.

To recognize these parallels is not, however, by any means fully to identify the generic peculiarity of *Marius the Epicurean*. Its most genuinely experimental nature lies in its complex intertextuality. Unlike those historical novels for children that place a fictional character into the middle of a carefully researched recreation of the ancient world, its culture and history, Pater's *Marius* is in fact an early form of montage. Just as, in "Sebastian van Storck," he was later to place Spinoza's words in the mouth of his fictional subject, so here Pater inserts into *Marius the Epicurean* numerous passages cribbed verbatim, but without acknowledgment, from various classical sources. The method is especially confusing since it is combined with profuse citation from acknowledged sources of precisely the same kind: Tibullus, Martial, Virgil, Ovid, Homer, Plato, and many others. The most significant unnamed source is that of chapter 24, the better part of which is translated and adapted from Lucian's *Hermotimus, or the Rival Philosophies*. The chapter title, "A Conversation Not Imaginary" (221), gives a subtle hint of the quasi-documentary nature of the dialogue it contains, while at the same time referring to Pater's precursor in the art of combining the real and the imaginary, Walter Savage Landor's *Imaginary Conversations* (1824–29). But Pater also takes over other texts without indicating that he is doing so: Apuleius's version of Cupid and Psyche, passages from Aurelius's *Meditations,* a letter by Cornelius Fronto, a church epistle quoted by Eusebius, and another dialogue attributed in Pater's time to Lucian.[20] Yet we would search in vain for a classical source for Marius's journal-record of his "private thoughts and humours," which makes up virtually the entirety of chapter 25. Thus chapter 24, the dialogue from Lucian's *Hermotimus*, contrasts strangely with chapter 25, Marius's fictive diary, at least in terms of its documentary status; from the point of view of style, the unsuspecting reader would be hard put to tell the one from the other. Both are embedded in a narrative that also employs conscientious attribution of sources in the manner of the late nineteenth century.

In his perceptive introduction to the new Oxford text of *Marius the Epicurean*, Ian Small demonstrates how this unusual combination of various levels of discourse contributes to a "constant erosion of textual authority": "By the end of the novel," Small comments, "we have lost what had hitherto been considered a crucial critical privilege: the ability to organize the discourses in a text into a pattern that discriminates truth and fictionality through the attribution of textual authority" (xvii). This deliberate undermining of textual authority is also at stake in "Sebastian van Storck," when the quotation from Spinoza attributed to the pen of the fictional Sebastian is claimed to "anticipate Spinoza." Indeed, it underlies the whole genre of "imaginary portrait" as conceived by Pater. Unlike Landor, who simply does what many of us might wish to—imagine conversations with eminent statesmen to whom we cannot actually speak—Pater explicitly plays with the borderline between fact and fiction, documented and fabricated text.

In beginning her *Orlando: A Biography* in the Renaissance, Virginia Woolf deliberately establishes a relation between her own enterprise and that of Pater. Like Pater, she is a marvelous imitator of period styles; like Pater, too, she believes in a kind of chronology that is at once historical and simultaneous. Though the title page clearly marks *Orlando* as a biography, it is usually thought of as a novel; yet there is still some confusion about its status. The Harcourt Brace Jovanovich paperback[21] designates it "fiction" and describes it on the back cover as Virginia Woolf's "most exuberant, most fanciful novel"; but the front cover cites Nigel Nicolson, who knows that it is also "the longest and most charming love letter in literature"—a letter, in fact, to the novelist Vita Sackville-West, to whom *Orlando* is dedicated. Leon Edel and Daniel Madelénat, following Edel's argument closely,[22] discuss *Orlando* in their respective studies on biography. Edel calls the work "a fantasy in the form of a biography," a "livre à clé" that recounts the life of Vita Sackville-West, and a "fable" for biographers.[23] "The plot thickens considerably," as Edel puts it,[24] when we recall that Vita Sackville-West was married to Harold Nicolson, author of the mixed-genre studies entitled *Some People* that Woolf had taken for a signpost to something yet to come in her 1927 essay "The New Biography." This marks *Orlando* as the solution, or one attempt at a solution, of the problem she had set in that essay. I shall show in a moment how *Orlando* adapts Paterian techniques while taking them an important step further and transforming them into something entirely her own.

But first, let us look, with the hindsight of readers who already know Hildesheimer's *Marbot: Eine Biographie,* at the external form of Woolf's creation. Like *Marbot, Orlando* comes equipped with all the trappings of a conventional biography: portraits of the central figures, an index of proper names that includes a multitude of historical figures, and acknowledgments of those who have helped in its creation. Where Hildesheimer includes a chalk lithography by Delacroix supposedly representing the young Andrew Marbot, Woolf produces a Renaissance painting of "Orlando as a Boy" (only in retrospect do we recognize the irony of this title, since the final photograph in the series of portraits, "Orlando at the Present Time," shows Orlando as a woman). Woolf's index, unlike Hildesheimer's, includes not only the names of historical personages, but an analytical listing of important events in her protagonist's life, beginning "Orlando, appearance as a boy, 15; writes his first play, 16; visits Queen at Whitehall, 24" and so on up to "birth of her first son, 295."[25] The two references to Shakespeare in the index include the appearance of an unnamed, poetry-writing gentleman in a dirty ruff on page 21. Woolf's preface is particularly amusing. Besides thanking, in the traditional manner, those who have saved her from "some lamentable blunders," she also acknowledges her debt to a number of dead writers: "Defoe, Sir Thomas Browne, Sterne, Sir Walter Scott, Lord Macaulay, Emily Bronte, DeQuincey, and Walter Pater—to name the first that come to mind" (vii). With fine irony, Woolf states in addition that she has "had the advantage—how great I alone can estimate—of Mr. Arthur Waley's knowledge of Chinese" (ibid.). Before launching into an extended list of distinguished friends who have helped her "in ways too various to specify," she notes that "Miss M. K. Snowdon's indefatigable researches in the archives of Harrogate and Cheltenham were none the less arduous for being vain" (ibid.). Her preface, in short, is a skillful spoof of the usual author's acknowledgments.

We would expect, then, in keeping with this parodic beginning and with the benefit of our hindsight derived from Hildesheimer, that *Orlando* would turn out to be a parody of academic biography. But despite its quasi-scholarly trappings, *Orlando: A Biography* is usually thought of as a novel. When Virginia Woolf was writing *To the Lighthouse,* she noted in her diary that there was no word in the English language to designate this experimental work: "A new———by Virginia Woolf," she writes, imitating a putative reviewer's headline.[26] But how much more is *Orlando* a "new———" than its more clearly fictional predecessor. Woolf marks the peculiar status of *Orlando* on the borderline between a novel and a biography by moving almost imperceptibly between two different narrative modes, that of the distancing biographer and that of the empathizing novelist.

This oscillation is set in motion at the very beginning of the first chapter. The opening sentence articulates the problem of omniscience or lack thereof that distinguishes the writer of fictional lives from the writer of real lives, and simultaneously locates the narrative as set in a historical period preceding the time of narration: "He—for there could be no doubt of his sex, though the fashion of the time did something to disguise it—was in the act of slicing at the head of a Moor which swung from the rafters" (13). Setting us in medias res after the manner of a novelist, the narrator claims unequivocal knowledge ("there could be no doubt") about an important aspect of the protagonist. The second sentence gives us a painstakingly detailed description of the Moor's head that also suggests complete access to the narrated "reality": "It was the colour of an old football, and more or less the shape of one, save for the sunken cheeks and a strand or two of coarse, dry hair, like the hair on a cocoanut." The third sentence, however, revokes this semblance of omniscience: "Orlando's father, or perhaps his grandfather, has struck it from the shoulders of a vast Pagan." Who is this narrator, who both knows and does not know, who stands at once outside and inside his (or her) protagonist?

The position of the narrator is increasingly problematized as the text proceeds. "Happy the mother who bears, happier still the biographer who records the life of such a one! Never need she vex, nor he invoke the help of novelist or poet," exclaims the narrative voice. One mode of *Orlando* is a fictional one. Frequently, it moves into the mind of the protagonist, as in the skating scene where Orlando first catches sight of the Russian princess (a portrait of whom as a child forms part of the pictorial "documentation"): "When the boy, for alas, a boy it must be—no woman could skate with such speed and vigour" (38). The narrator knows, at least a good deal of the time, what Orlando feels and thinks: "Whom had he loved, what had he loved, he asked himself in a tumult of emotion, until now?" (40). Much later, once Orlando has become a woman, we have passages of interior monologue like the following thoughts as she continues to write her long poem "The Oak Tree": "Life? Literature? One to be made into the other? But how monstrously difficult!" (285). The same passage rapidly modulates into indirect discourse. "They made one feel, she continued, that one must always, always write like somebody else" (ibid.), and finally into direct speech: "For really, she thought . . . , I don't think I could? (285–86).

But despite its superficial appearance of fictionalized narration, the better part of *Orlando* takes place in what the narrator calls, toward the end of the text, "the region of 'perhaps' and 'appears' " (310). As the extraordinary plot gets underway, the narrator intrudes with increasing frequency and the narrative becomes increasingly modalized. One of the chief appeals, for Orlando, of his romantic interludes with the Russian princess is her enchanting conversation, but this takes place "unfortunately always in French, which notoriously loses its flavour in translation" (46). Orlando's desperate horseback ride to the sea at the conclusion of their affair is modalized in such a thoroughly ambiguous manner that it is impossible to tell whether what we have is authorial commentary or free indirect discourse: "Some blind instinct, for he was past reasoning, must have driven him to take the river bank in the direction of the sea" (61). Whose conjecture is this "must have": the narrator's or Orlando's? Although the conjecture might seem, on the face of it, to originate in the mind of the narrator, it is in fact part of a lengthy passage that reproduces Orlando's perceptions, knowledge, and feelings by frequent incursions into his consciousness. It is difficult to tell whether the narrator is speculating about Orlando from the outside or expressing in words Orlando's own inarticulate struggle to comprehend his subconscious motivation. Be that as it may, this passage closely precedes the first significant intrusion of the narrator to comment on the problems of writing biography: "The biographer is now faced with a difficulty which it is better perhaps to confess than to gloss over. Up to this point in telling the story of Orlando's life, documents, both private and historical, have made it possible to fulfil the first duty of a biographer, which is to plod, without looking to right or left, in the indelible footprints of truth" (65). In the face of this "dark, mysterious, and undocumented" episode, the narrator decides to "state the facts as far as they are known, and so let the reader make of them what he may" (ibid.). The episode is, of course, the change in sex that overcomes Orlando. The sex change is preceded by a trancelike sleep that recalls the transforming sleep Faust undergoes at the beginning of part 2 of Goethe's dramatic poem. Its form is thus overtly that of a Renaissance masque in which our sleeping hero is attended by the allegorical figures of Purity, Chastity, and Modesty before finally awaking as a woman. Thus a quintessentially literary, because allegorical, rendering of events is set side by side with a skeptical, essentially academic one. Surrounding the allegorical masque (complete with such items of Renaissance vocabulary as "avaunt," 135) are reflections on the limitations of the biographer and the difficulties of constructing a narrative from incomplete documentation that threaten to overwhelm the poetic interlude. The biographer's pseudo-scholarship had already begun with a listing from Orlando's "ledgers" documenting furnishings procured by him for the royal bedchambers (109), a list of unutterable boredom that starts to put the reader to sleep even before Orlando himself has entered his mysterious trance. Soon thereafter we hear, however, at the beginning of chapter 3, that the phase of Orlando's life in which the trance occurs is the one where "we have the least information to go on" (119). To be sure, "treaties in the vault of the Record Office bear testimony" to some external matters, but even these papers are "so damaged or destroyed . . . that what we can give is lamentably incomplete" (119). "It is with such fragments as these," continues the narrator, after a considerable amount of narrative conjecture, "that we must do our best to make up a picture of Orlando's life and character at this time" (124). Even the diary of John Fenner Brigge, an English naval officer, which provides a certain amount of testimony, "is full of burns and holes, some sentences being quite illegible" (127). As the narrator embarks upon the fateful night of Orlando's transformation, he comments: "So far, we are on the firm, if rather narrow, ground of ascertained truth" (131). But as Orlando passes into the seventh day of his trance, the complaints about the inadequacy of available records give way to their inverse: "And now again osbcurity descends, and would indeed that it were deeper!" (133). The "austere Gods" of biography, "Truth, Candour, and Honesty" (134), have nothing to seek here, nor can the narrator in any way enter Orlando's consciousness as she emerges from the trance other than through the distancing mode of the "must have" biographer: "Some slight haziness there may have been" as the woman Orlando links her memories with those of her former self, the man Orlando (138). The episode concludes with a final thrust at the biographer's art: "It is enough for us to state the simple fact: Orlando was a man till the age of thirty; when he became a woman and has remained so ever since" (139).

This ingenious combination of a preeminently literary form, the masque, with a surrounding narrative that mimics the most cautious of biographies is not the only way in which Virginia Woolf's *Orlando* crosses generic boundaries at the pivotal moment of its plot. Käte Hamburger's touchstone for the fictional mode was the presence of such sentences as "Tomorrow was Thursday." But Woolf invents another model of transgressive grammar that is equally indicative of her text's fictional status: "He was a woman" (137).

After this fictional utterance cast in the laconic tone of fact, *Orlando* moves, not into the "must have" school of biography, but into the realm of "it would seem" (for example, 158). Increasingly reality is put in question; indeed, the narrator comments that "to give a truthful account of London society at that or indeed any other time, is beyond the powers of the biographer or the historian. Only those who have little need of the truth, and no respect for it—the poets and novelists—can be trusted to do it, for this is one of the cases where truth does not exist. Nothing exists. The whole is a miasma—a mirage" (192). As we approach the nineteenth century, it becomes "more and more out of the question" to give "an exact and particular account of Orlando's life" (220). Even social history can only be given in parodistic form: "Then a change of diet became essential. The muffin was invented and the crumpet" (228). Thinking takes prece-

dence over action, and literature over life. The biographer resorts to recit-
ing the months of the calendar (266) or avoiding narration by breaking off
just before arriving at the crux of Orlando's reflections (291). Orlando's
final epiphany consists in the terrifying revelation that it is "the present
moment," 11 October 1928 (298), the date on which the narrative concludes.

Not only is the "present moment" dizzying in itself; the narrator's arrival
at this point creates an entirely new relation between narrative time and
narrated time at the end of *Orlando*. Whereas the first five chapters had
covered a time span of over three centuries, chapter 6 narrates the events
of only about two years, and its second half (approximately thirty pages),
following the epiphany in which Orlando recognizes the "present moment," traces fourteen hours of Orlando's experiences on the final day. This
discrepancy in the temporal relation of the narrative and the events narrated is yet another marker of the text's deliberately fictional status, for
although biographers can and do expand and contract time at will, they
tend to think of this method as a technique borrowed from fiction.[27]

Orlando ends neither with the protagonist's death, like *Marius the Epicurean*, nor with his mysterious disappearance and probable death, like
Hildesheimer's *Marbot*. It ends, rather, with a concerted attack on biography altogether, especially as practiced by the father of its author: "The true
length of a person's life, whatever the *Dictionary of National Biography* may
say, is always a matter of dispute" (306–7). *Orlando* thus remains resolutely and programmatically open-ended, but even more important, it
ceases simply to oscillate between biography and fiction by eliminating
these categories altogether. If a life has no fixed end, how can a biography
be written? If a book ends in "the present moment," how can it possibly be
fiction? *Orlando* effectively subverts the very categories with which it has
been playing all along.

These problems are transposed onto a broader plane when we come to
consider the referent of Virginia Woolf's *Orlando*. On one level, of course,
the referent is the history of England from the Renaissance to 1928, but it
is also—since Orlando is writing her poem "The Oak Tree" throughout
the book—the history of English literature over the same period. At the
same time, it is the story of Vita Sackville-West, beginning with her ances-
tor Sir Thomas Sackville and proceeding through his descendants to
Woolf's friend herself.[28] It was also, finally, in some sense an autobiography, the story of Virginia Woolf's stylistic and philosophical ancestors and
her gradual discovery that there was really no such thing as "a single self, a
real self" (314).[29] It is the story of a search for self that is doomed to fail, a
search epitomized by the unromantic bird that appears above the head of
Orlando's last love, Shelmerdine, at the end of the novel: " 'It is the goose!'
Orlando cried. 'The wild goose' " (329). To try to assign a genre to this

curious conflation, as much as to attempt to identify the ever-changing Orlando, is indeed vain.

In this sense, *Orlando* straddles the borderline between several of the domains identified by Dorrit Cohn: it is an autobiography, a biography, and a fictional biography; a historicized fictional biography and a fictionalized historical biography. In other words: an autobiography of Virginia Woolf, a biography of Vita Sackville-West, a fictional biography of Orlando; a historicized fictional biography of Orlando, a fictionalized historical biography of the Sackville family. Unlike Hildesheimer's *Marbot*, which stays firmly in its pigeonhole, Woolf's *Orlando*, like Pater's *Marius*, refuses to be so neatly filed.

Nonetheless, there are many suggestions in *Marbot* that it rests quite consciously on the shoulders of these giants. I have already shown how its external shape—its index, acknowledgments, and collection of pictorial documents—closely imitates Woolf's *Orlando*. But it also contains references, discreetly hidden in its vast and complicated montage, to its forerunner of the 1880s. Like Pater, Sir Andrew Marbot is an English art critic: his principal work is *Art and Life*—a title more appropriate for the time around 1900 than for the time around 1800, when Marbot is said to have lived and when the formulation would more likely have been "art and nature." The paintings reproduced in the illustrations to the "biography" include examples of Pater's favorite artists: Botticelli and Giorgione (recalling Pater's *Renaissance*), Andrea Mantegna (mentioned at length in *Marius the Epicurean*, 252–53), Antoine Watteau (who figures largely in one of the *Imaginary Portraits*, "A Prince of Court Painters"), and Jan van Eyck (recalling "Sebastian van Storck"). Pater is even mentioned in *Marbot* (along with Ruskin) as a later art critic who was familiar with *Art and Life* but did not actually learn from it: "Later John Ruskin and Walter Pater referred repeatedly to the book, but never made it part of their own theoretical apparatus, since it did not actually touch upon the areas of aesthetics they treated."[30]

Be that as it may, the question of textual authority that underlies Pater's unsettling montage and is explicitly articulated in Woolf's generic hybrid becomes the very backbone of Hildesheimer's historicized fictional biography. Not only is the problem constantly addressed by a narrator who can do no more than conjecture, filling in the gaps of incomplete documentation, it is reflected in a kind of *mise en abîme* in the discussion of the German translation of Marbot's magnum opus, *Die Kunst und das Leben*: "Here it was Carl Friedrich von Rumohr who—as a friend of the adult Marbot—cast doubt on the authenticity of the text."[31] Although the work's apparent authenticity is, in the last analysis, laid to the charge of a stiff, academic, and unironic translation by our judiciously weighing narrator, the theme of textual authority has clearly been sounded, and this at a relatively early point in the "biography." Hildesheimer's fictive biographer is a thoroughly skeptical one.

But as Dorrit Cohn also points out, not all biographies are written in this tone. It is much more the tone of a biography submitted as a dissertation than that of the hundreds of biographies that make their way every year into bookstores and lending libraries. While the best of these—biographies by Leon Edel or Richard Ellmann, for example—do not heavily fictionalize, they know that a "good read" demands avoidance of too much hedging, too much distancing, too much discussion of sources and their reliability. The only exceptions are the "debunking" biographies initiated by Lytton Strachey and exemplified in our day by Peter Ackroyd's *T. S. Eliot*;[32] even here, though, the narrating voice exudes confidence, not the "we can never know" of Hildesheimer's *Marbot*. Indeed, one might say that in the very consistency with which it foregrounds its nonomniscient posture, *Marbot* reveals itself as a quintessentially fictional "historicized fictional biography."

However brilliantly sustained, and unique as it may be in certain respects, *Marbot* should not be seen as a "perfected" example of something toward which Pater and Woolf were only groping. It only seems this way from the perspective of the present day, especially that of present-day academia. In fact, both *Marius* and *Orlando* are successfully realized chameleons: Pater's book a brilliant imitation of his own "appreciations," Woolf's a more parodistic mimic of contemporary "new biography." The differences among the three have more to do with changing fashions in the writing of lives than with their authors' ability to achieve the desired trompe l'oeil effects.

"The greatest realism is the greatest fakery," says a character in Peter Ackroyd's *Chatterton,* which, unlike his *Eliot,* is a novel, not a biography.[33] It is the tale of a modern biographer who decides to write a life of the "marvellous boy," a poet "so sure of his own genius that he allowed it to flourish under other names" (126). Writing his preface, the biographer finds himself increasingly uncertain "whether all this information came from the documents themselves, or from the biographies which Philip had lent him. In any case he noticed that each biography described quite a different poet" (127). Annoyed at first by these differences, he soon becomes exhilarated, "for it meant that anything became possible. If there were no truths, everything was true" (ibid.). This is of course the attitude not of a biographer but of a writer of fiction, and it is an attitude that underlies Pater's *Marius*, Woolf's *Orlando*, and Hildesheimer's *Marbot*, each in its own way. By undermining textual authority, they create new realms in which, paradoxically, "everything is true" and the mind can serve "under two masters simultaneously," constantly oscillating between fact and fiction.

Notes

1. Virginia Woolf, *Collected Essays* (New York: Harcourt, Brace, and World, 1953), 4:234.

2. Dorrit Cohn, "Fictional *versus* Historical Lives: Borderlines and Borderline Cases," *Journal of Narrative Technique* 19 (1989): 3–24. In a diagram offered by Dorrit Cohn when she presented a version of this paper to the Harvard Germanic Circle, she set out the principal categories with which I shall be working in this paper. I use this diagram here since it is more immediately accessible than the subtler and more complex diagram given on page 4 of the published essay:

Protagonist / Discourse	Historical	Fictional
historical	historical biography (*Mozart*)	historicized fictional biography (*Marbot*)
fictional	fictionalized historical biography (*Lenz*)	fictional biography (*Tonio Kröger*)

3. Wolfgang Hildesheimer, *Marbot: Eine Biographie* (Frankfurt: Suhrkamp, 1981).

4. Virginia Woolf, "The New Biography," *New York Herald Tribune*, 30 October 1927.

5. Woolf, *Collected Essays* 4:234.

6. Ibid.

7. Ibid., 234–35.

8. Ibid., 221–28.

9. Ibid., 226.

10. See Eugene J. Brzenk, ed., *Imaginary Portraits by Walter Pater: A New Collection* (New York: Harper and Row, 1964), esp. 1–15.

11. Harold Bloom, introduction to *Selected Writings of Walter Pater*, ed. Harold Bloom (New York: Columbia University Press, 1974), xxii.

12. Ibid., xxiii. Iain Fletcher calls them "experiments in ruminative fiction" in *Walter Pater* (London: Longmans Green, 1959), 10.

13. Bloom, introduction to *Selected Writings of Walter Pater*, xxiii.

14. Walter Pater, *Imaginary Portraits*, 4th ed. (London: Macmillan, 1901; reprint, 1914), 82, 83, 95, 105. Page references in the text below are to this edition.

15. See Harold Bloom's notes to *Selected Writings of Walter Pater*, 84–85.

16. He began *Marius* in 1882, resigned from Brasenose in 1883, and published *Marius* in 1885.

17. Walter Pater, *Marius the Epicurean: His Sensations and Ideas,* ed. with an introduction by Ian Small (Oxford: Oxford University Press, 1985; reprint, World's Classics Paperback, 1986), 9. Page references in the text below are to the reprint edition.

18. Käte Hamburger, *Die Logik der Dichtung* (Stuttgart: Klett, 1957), 33.

19. See my study, *The Vanishing Subject: Early Psychology and Literary Modernism* (Chicago: University of Chicago Press, 1991).

20. See Ian Small, introduction to Pater, *Marius the Epicurean,* xv–xvi.

21. Virginia Woolf, *Orlando* (San Diego: Harcourt Brace Jovanovich, n.d.). Page references in the text below are to this edition.

22. Leon Edel, *Writing Lives: Principia Biographia* (New York: Norton, 1984), and Daniel Madelénat, *La Biographie* (Paris: Presses universitaires de France, 1984).

23. Edel, *Writing Lives,* 186, 190, 196.

24. Ibid., 191.

25. Woolf, *Orlando,* index.

26. Virginia Woolf, *The Diary of Virginia Woolf,* ed. Anne Olivier Bell, 5 vols. (New York: Harcourt Brace Jovanovich, 1977–84), 34 (27 June 1925).

27. See Leon Edel's discussion of temporal structuring in biography in *Writing Lives,* 30–31, 196–97.

28. See Edel, *Writing Lives,* 190–91.

29. Makiko Minow-Pinkney gives a careful analysis of this aspect of *Orlando* in her *Virginia Woolf and the Problem of the Subject: Feminine Writing in the Major Novels* (New Brunswick: Rutgers University Press, 1987), 117–51.

30. "Später haben sich John Ruskin und Walter Pater wiederholt auf das Buch bezogen, es zitiert und diskutiert, haben es jedoch niemals zu ihrem theoretischen Handwerkszeug gemacht, da es die von ihnen behandelten Gebiete der Kunstästhetik nicht eigentlich berührte." Hildesheimer, *Marbot,* quoted from the Suhrkamp Taschenbuch edition of 1984, 97. The translation is mine.

31. "Hier war es Carl Friedrich von Rumohr, der—als Freund des erwachsenen Marbot—die Authentizität des Textes anzweifelte." Ibid., 90. The translation is mine.

32. Peter Ackroyd, *T. S. Eliot* (London: Hamish Hamilton, 1984).

33. Peter Ackroyd, *Chatterton* (London: Hamish Hamilton, 1987; reprint, Sphere Books, 1988), 139. Page numbers in the text below refer to the reprint edition.

FOUR

MOCKING A MOCK-BIOGRAPHY:

STEVEN MILLHAUSER'S *EDWIN MULLHOUSE*

AND THOMAS MANN'S *DOCTOR FAUSTUS*

Jens Rieckmann

WHEN STEVEN MILLHAUSER'S first novel, *Edwin Mull-house: The Life and Death of an American Writer (1943–1954), by Jeffrey Cartwright* was published in 1972, several reviewers remarked on its Nabokovian qualities and pointed to *Pale Fire* as the most likely model for Millhauser's mock-biography.[1] The very title of Millhauser's novel, however, seems to point to another possible model: Thomas Mann's *Doctor Faustus: The Life of the German Composer Adrian Leverkühn, as Told by a Friend*. In fact, a comparison of these two fictional witness biographies leads this reader to conclude that Millhauser's novel, in some of its themes and motives as well as in the person of its fictional biographer and in its parody of the conventions of biographical writing, bears more of a mockingly distorted resemblance to Mann's text than to that of Nabokov.

Millhauser's novel, which won the Prix Medicis Etranger, is ostensibly the biography of the prodigious writer Edwin Mullhouse, who meets a premature death at the age of eleven. Millhauser's novel focuses as much on Edwin's life as on the efforts of his biographer, Jeffrey Cartwright, Mullhouse's eleven-and-a-half-year-old friend, to shape Edwin's life into a meaningful whole. As Edwin's next-door neighbor, Cartwright is a privileged observer of his friend's life, and his desire to write his biography becomes an all-consuming passion. Compared to his "zealous sense of purpose, his industrious concentration on his subject's infinite variety and plenitude of sameness," Pearl Bell wrote in a review of the novel, "James Boswell seems inattentive, Richard Ellman's *Joyce* slipshod, Leon Edel's *James* cursory."[2]

The subjects of Mann's and Millhauser's mock-biographies, the modernist composer Adrian Leverkühn and the eleven-year-old writer Edwin Mullhouse, represent in the eyes of their fictional biographers the artist as genius. They give occasion for reflection on the nature of genius and the proximity of disease and creativity. Both novels are what Hoberman terms "mediated biographies"; Mann and Millhauser put particular emphasis on their fictional biographers' perception of their subjects. "It is as if these narrators were standing in front of a slide projector: they are themselves immediately present to the viewer, and thus experienced dramatically, unmediatedly, but the slides themselves [Leverkühn and Mullhouse in our case] are now visible only in relation to [the narrators]."[3] Hoberman's comparison very aptly captures the peculiar stance of narrators in mock-biographies. On the one hand, they are aware of their subservient role; on the other hand, their marked presence provides the opportunity for self-dramatization.

Edwin Mullhouse's brief life, culminating in the writing of his "immortal novel" *Cartoons*,[4] is told by his friend Jeffrey Cartwright. For him as for Zeitblom, the narrator in *Doctor Faustus*, the writing of the biography becomes a "mission" that gives "meaning" to his life (EM, 246). This sense of mission awakens early in both biographers. When Leverkühn chooses the University of Halle as his alma mater, Zeitblom follows him there "to keep a constant eye" on his friend, motivated by personal solicitude but even more by "something like a premonition of the fact that it would one day be my task to set down an account of the impressions that moulded his [Leverkühn's] early life."[5] Similarly, yet carrying the parody of the biographer's sense of mission further, Millhauser has Cartwright observe his subject "from the beginning"—from the day Mullhouse is eight days and Cartwright six months old, "with the fond solicitude of an older brother and the scrupulous fascination of a budding biographer" (EM, 17).

The biographer's mission thus becomes all-consuming and virtually takes over his life. "It should be said once more," Zeitblom confesses, implicitly boasting of the sacrifice of self involved in the biographer's task, "that I led my own life, without precisely neglecting it, only as if it were an aside, with half my attention, with my left hand; that my real concern and anxiety were centered upon the existence of my childhood friend" (DF, 312). Again, in *Edwin Mullhouse* the biographer's vicarious existence is carried to its extreme. When Mullhouse withdraws from the world to write his "immortal novel," Cartwright's own life is reduced to a void. His many "attempts to escape into sham hobbies" are futile (EM, 245), and the biographer's obsessive watchfulness, which is the content of his life, is hilariously spoofed when Cartwright attempts to witness his novelist friend's progress: "Often at night, unable to sleep, I would creep into my kitchen and watch Edwin's light until it went out: at 1:26, at 2:03, at 2:55. I even made a game of it, thrilling each time he broke a record. Once I watched from 3:27 (his previous record) to 5:06 . . . before I had to crawl back to bed, exhausted, though his light still burned; but that morning Edwin looked surprisingly well-rested, and I realized that he had fallen asleep with his light on" (EM, 247).

Both narrators, then, emphasize their subservient roles. Zeitblom, the self-styled "simple man," feels privileged to be the witness of the "life of an artist . . . this unique specimen of humanity" (DF, 24), just as Cartwright seems to be imbued with the sense that his subject is "the special one," and not he, although he is "an unusually bright child" (EM, 23). Ostensibly they know that for the biographer it is only fitting to assume "a place in the background of these memoirs," as Zeitblom puts it (DF, 353), or to "huddle modestly in the background," which is Cartwright's declared policy (EM, 236). An inkling of the biographer's desire to be emancipated from a subservient role is provided by Cartwright's observations on the relationship between biographer and subject:

> Edwin looked up to me as a prince looks up to a trusty servant; there was never any question of a clash of privileges. In bitter loneliness the prince asks his man to decide a subtle question of policy, and so the unseen man has a hand in the affairs of state. Then perhaps the prince forgets the existence of his man for a week or weeks or months at a time, until suddenly he needs him again. But the man never forgets his prince, and in the servant's chamber, which the prince never enters, who can tell what strange midnight thoughts flit through a skull? (EM, 24)

The extended metaphor reveals the tendency on the part of most narrators in mock-biographies to assert themselves, despite their protestations to the contrary. Although Zeitblom assures the reader in the opening sentence of his account of Leverkühn's life "that it is by no means out of any wish to bring my own personality into the foreground that I preface with a few words about myself and my own affairs this report on the life of the departed Adrian Leverkühn" (DF, 3), he does bring himself into the foreground to a degree that no narrator in a factual biography ever would. In this respect Cartwright is modeled directly on Zeitblom. Recalling his first meeting with the eight-day-old Mullhouse, he observes: "It is with no desire of thrusting myself forward, but only of presenting the pertinent details of a noteworthy occasion, that I thus intrude my personal history into these pages" (EM, 13). Yet intrude he does, and, as we shall see, not only "into these pages." The prominent role biographers assume in mock-biographies ultimately leads the reader to question the narrator's reliability and disinterestedness to such an extent that the focus tends to shift away from the account of the subject's life to its narrator.[6]

In psychological terms, the biographer's need to assert himself can be seen as part of a compensation syndrome. Zeitblom and Cartwright both claim the same motivation for writing their respective biographies: the desire to preserve for posterity the details of their friends' lives. Ultimately, however, both Zeitblom's and Cartwright's motives for rendering an account of their friends' lives stem from unrequited love. Zeitblom can barely hide his hurt feelings occasioned by the "friendly" and "objective" mention of himself in the note with which Leverkühn assigns his sketches and journals to him; neither can he deceive the reader about the intensity of the jealousy aroused in him by Leverkühn's homosexual relationship with Rudi Schwerdtfeger. Similarly, Cartwright cannot disguise his jealous disapproval of Mullhouse's two loves, Rose Dorn and Arnold Hasselstrom, and his feeling of rejection when Mullhouse includes him only as an afterthought among those who had influenced his life. It is this rejection that motivates Cartwright's most extreme statement of the biographer's need for self-assertion, made on behalf of all witness biographers who are tied to their subjects by a "burdensome friendship" (EM, 245). In his response to Mullhouse's critical comments on the fictionality of biography he notes: "But I take this opportunity to ask . . . : isn't it true that the biographer performs a function nearly as great as, or precisely as great as, or actually greater by far than the function performed by the artist himself? For the artist creates the work of art, but the biographer, so to speak, creates the artist. Which is to say: without me, would you exist at all, Edwin?" (EM, 101–2).

The rhetorical question of course reveals the very fictionality of biography it is intended to refute, and at the same time it draws attention to the chief characteristic of all mock biographies: through placing a greater emphasis on the supposed biographer than factual or "straight" fictional biographies do, they stress the act of mediation and reveal to the reader, as Petrie has pointed out, the problems inherent in all biographical narration.[7] Mann's comments on his choice of Zeitblom as narrator reveal his consciousness that this choice foregrounded the act of mediation and determined the hybrid character of his work. In *The Story of a Novel: The Genesis of Doctor Faustus* he writes: "My diary of the period does not record exactly when I made the decision to interpose the medium of the 'friend' between myself and my subject; in other words, not to tell the life of Adrian Leverkühn directly but to have it told, and therefore not to write a novel but a biography with all its trappings."[8] And rereading the fourteenth chapter of *Doctor Faustus*, he was struck by the degree to which he had realized his goal. In his diary, he noted: "Read in the evening the discussions among the students in the novel. The unnovelistic, strangely real biographical [sonderbar real Biographische] that nevertheless is fiction."[9] He did not anticipate, however, that some readers might be duped by the "sonderbar real Biographische," among them Arnold Schönberg, who feared that future generations of musicologists would read Mann's novel as a factual biography and assume that Leverkühn and not Schönberg was the actual creator of the twelve-tone system.[10] What Schönberg failed to see was the "mimicking of the biographer [Biographen-Mimik],"[11] the parody of the conventions of biographical writing. This among other features of *Doctor Faustus* establishes its fictionality and in its turn casts doubts on the nonfictional quality of factual biographies.

It is exactly this point that is made in Mullhouse's critical comments on the art of writing lives. In a conversation with his biographer, Mullhouse claims that

> the very notion of biography was hopelessly fictional, since unlike real life, which presents us with question marks, censored passages, blank spaces, rows of asterisks, omitted paragraphs, and numberless sequences of three dots trailing into whiteness, biography provides an illusion of completeness, a vast pattern of details organized by an omniscient biographer whose occasional assertions of ignorance or uncertainty deceive us no more than the polite protestations of a hostess who, during the sixth course of an elaborate feast, assures us that really, it was no trouble at all. (EM, 101)

Cartwright, anxious to protect the dignity of his trade, dismisses these comments as the "typical mixture of subtlety and inanity" characteristic of the thought processes of creative people (ibid.), but Mullhouse has of course put his finger on a problem that has received much attention in the critical discourse of the recent past.

The validity of Mullhouse's questioning of the biographer's trade is ironically confirmed by Cartwright's critical reflections on the methodological problems he encounters in the reconstruction of his subject's life, and once again these reflections mirror in a mockingly distorted fashion those of his predecessor Zeitblom. As we have seen, the weakest chinks in the biographer's armor are, according to Mullhouse, his imposition of a meaningful pattern on his subject's life, his desire to shape the life into an aesthetic whole, and his concealed claim to omniscience. As biographers, Zeitblom and, to a larger extent, Cartwright are guilty on all three counts. Zeitblom assures the reader that the account of his friend's life is necessarily limited to those parts of it he could witness (DF, 28). He ostentatiously renounces the novelist's omniscience and skillfully tries to disarm any doubts the reader may harbor concerning the extent of his *Zeugenschaft* by raising the issue himself: "May not my readers ask whence comes the detail in my narrative, so precisely known to me, even though I could not have been always present, not always at the side of the departed hero of this biography?" (DF, 149). Zeitblom tries to meet such possible objections by an array of statements interspersed throughout the text, such as frequent references to his excellent memory, the notes he took on conversations, and Leverkühn's "priceless sketches," letters, and diary pages that are in his possession (DF, 5). Yet when it serves his purposes, he oversteps the bounds of the witness biographer, though he himself had established them in a kind of contract with the reader. Although Zeitblom exclaims at one point that he is not writing a novel "in whose composition the author reveals the hearts of his characters indirectly, through scenic presentation" (DF, 295; my translation), this fictional technique abounds in *Doctor Faustus*. Significantly, it is not only employed for the presentation of scenes Zeitblom witnessed, but also for those he admittedly did not. In the latter instances the disavowed omniscience of the novelist is embraced by the witness biographer apparently because of a *horror vacui* shared by most biographers, and justified on the basis of the witness biographer's "frightful intimacy," which "makes him an eye- and ear-witness even to [the story's] hidden phases" (DF, 434).

There is, however, yet another kind of omniscience that novelists and biographers share, and it is this kind of omniscience Cartwright alludes to when he enumerates the preoccupations of Mullhouse's early childhood: "Comic books, cameras, photographs, Viewmaster reels—such were his simple games, but what omens for the omniscient biographer!" (EM, 62). The biographer's relationship to the life he narrates is a retrospective one, and this puts him perilously close to the novelist's omniscience, as Cartwright puts it in one of his many futile attempts to draw a clear distinction between the biographer's art and that of the novelist (EM, 54). It is this retrospective omniscience that accounts for a dual perspective in both historical (biographical) and fictional narration. The narrator, as Paul Hernadi points out, sustains a delicate balance between a retrospective point of view and the point of view of one immersed in the events as they occur. The two perspectives correspond to what Hernadi calls logos and mythos: the narration of events in terms of causality versus their narration in terms of intention or teleology.[12] No matter how much Zeitblom and Cartwright protest that they are writing biographies and not novels, they are caught up in the quandary created by this dual perspective. For the witness biographer, the quandary is exacerbated by the treacherous tricks memory is wont to play on the biographer's recollections. This added predicament is reflected in Cartwright's self-admonishing statement: "The true course of events must always be carefully distinguished from memory's false fusion, lest biography degenerate into fiction" (EM, 172).

The tensions created by this dual perspective are reflected in the oppositional directions in which Zeitblom and Cartwright feel themselves pulled as biographers. On the one hand, they labor under the obligation to narrate their subjects' lives chronologically, hence Zeitblom's misgivings at "jumping the gun" in the opening pages of the novel through his premature revelation of Leverkühn's pact with the devil. In a lengthy disquisition on the advantages of biographical writing as compared to fictional writing, Cartwright observes:

> God pity the poor novelist. Standing on his omniscient cliff, with painful ingenuity he must contrive to drop bits of important information into the

swift current of his allpowerful plot. . . . The modest biographer, fortunately, is under no such obligation. Calmly and methodically, in one fell swoop, in a way impossible for the harried novelist who is always trying to do a hundred things at once, he can simply say what he has to say, ticking off each item with his right hand on the successively raised fingers of his left. (EM, 54)

On the other hand, to adhere to the chronological straitjacket conflicts with the biographer's desire to impose a pattern on what Cartwright equates with "the stupid wretched pretense that one thing follows from another thing, as if on Saturday a man should hang himself because on Friday he was melancholy" (EM, 78). What Hernadi calls mythos is super-imposed on logos, and this superimposition ultimately causes the degen-eration of historical "truth" into fiction. Again, it is Cartwright, the more self-conscious of the two biographers, who, in the course of writing his life of Edwin Mullhouse, is forced to confirm the verdict of biography's ene-mies, "its helpless conformity to the laws of fiction" (EM, 100). This truth is brought home to him when he realizes that the "curse of chronology" threatens the biographer's ultimate goal: to write the life of his subject in such a way that "each date, each incident, each casual remark contributes to an elaborate plot that slowly and cunningly builds to a foreknown cli-max: the hero's celebrated deed" (EM, 100).

Closely connected to the interplay between logos and myth is the biog-rapher's desire to subsume the "question marks, censored passages, blank spaces, rows of asterisks, omitted paragraphs, and numberless sequences of three dots trailing into whiteness" of real life into an aesthetic whole. Cart-wright's endeavor in this respect represents the ultimate, mockingly dis-torted reflection of Zeitblom's labor of love and at the same time the slighted biographer's revenge on his subject. Whereas Zeitblom as biog-rapher is motivated by, among other things, his hope that Leverkühn may find grace, if not in the eyes of God, then in the eyes of posterity once an account of his friend's life has been rendered, Cartwright, increasingly troubled that the "design" of his biography is "marred somewhat by Ed-win's indefinitely continued existence" (EM, 246), conceives and carries out the ingenious plan of killing off his subject, thus providing an aesthet-ically pleasing end to this "throbbing book" (EM, 257). At the same time he fulfills his labor of love, for had not Mullhouse told him shortly before his death that Cartwright had "saved his soul . . . by making him think of his life as biography, that is, a design with a beginning, middle, and end" (EM, 102)? As mock-biographies both *Doctor Faustus* and to a larger extent *Edwin Mullhouse* should be read, as I have tried to show, at least on one level as Cartwright would have us read Mullhouse's "immortal novel" *Car-toons:* "By the method of scrupulous distortion, Edwin draws attention to things that have been rendered invisible to us by overmuch familiarity" (EM, 265).

NOTES

1. For sample reviews, see Sharon R. Gunton and Gerard J. Senick, eds., *Contemporary Literary Criticism* 21 (1982): 215–21. For a discussion of *Edwin Mullhouse* as a mock-biography, see Timothy Dow Adams, "The Mock-Biography of Edwin Mullhouse," *Biography* 5 (1982): 205–14.

2. Pearl Bell, "A Wise Child," *New Leader*, 16 October 1972, 15.

3. Ruth Hoberman, *Modernizing Lives: Experiments in English Biography, 1918–1939* (Carbondale and Edwardsville: Southern Illinois University Press, 1987), 103.

4. Steven Millhauser, *Edwin Mullhouse: The Life of an American Writer (1943–1954), by Jeffrey Cartwright* (New York: Penguin Books, 1985), 6. All further references to this edition in the text are noted by EM followed by the page number.

5. Thomas Mann, *Doctor Faustus: The Life of the German Composer Adrian Leverkühn as Told by a Friend,* trans. Helen Lowe-Porter (New York: Vintage Books, 1971), 111. All further references to this edition in the text are noted by DF followed by the page number.

6. Witness the proliferation of articles on Zeitblom's reliability and motivations as a narrator—for example, Hermann Weigand, "Zu Thomas Manns Anteil an Serenus Zeitbloms Biographie von Adrian Leverkühn," *Deutsche Vierteljahrsschrift für Literatur and Geistesgeschichte* 51 (1977): 476–96; Osman Durrani, "The Tearful Teacher: The Role of Serenus Zeitblom in Thomas Mann's *Doktor Faustus*," *Modern Language Review* 80 (1985): 652–58; Philip Carroll, "The Paranoid Narrator of *Doktor Faustus*" (manuscript).

7. Dennis W. Petrie, *Ultimately Fiction: Design in Modern American Biography* (West Lafayette, In.: Purdue University Press, 1981), 32.

8. Thomas Mann, *The Story of a Novel: The Genesis of Doctor Faustus*, trans. Richard and Clara Winston (New York: Alfred A. Knopf, 1961), 30.

9. Thomas Mann, *Tagebücher 1944–1.4.1946,* ed. Inge Jens (Frankfurt: Fischer, 1986), 260. The translation is mine.

10. See the exchange of letters between Mann and Schönberg in the *Saturday Review of Literature,* 1 January 1949.

11. Mann, *Story of a Novel*, 29.

12. Paul Hernadi, "Clio's Cousins: Historiography Considered as Translation, Fiction, and Criticism," *New Literary History* 7 (1976): 249–50. See also Hoberman, *Modernizing Lives*, 63.

FIVE

HABSBURG LETTERS:

THE DISCIPLINARY DYNAMICS OF

EPISTOLARY NARRATIVE IN THE

CORRESPONDENCE OF MARIA THERESA AND

MARIE ANTOINETTE

Larry Wolff

O
N APRIL 19, 1770, the fourteen-year-old Habsburg archduch-
ess, Marie Antoinette, was married in Vienna by proxy to the faraway Bourbon dauphin, the future Louis XVI. Two days later,
Marie Antoinette left Vienna forever, setting off to join her new husband
in France, and taking leave of her mother, the Empress Maria Theresa,
whom she would never see again. That date—"21 April, the day of departure"—headed the first letter in the ten-year correspondence that then en-
sued between mother and daughter. It is a correspondence that has exercised a certain historical fascination since its first publication in 1864,
especially inasmuch as the empress addressed herself to her daughter's "frivolity" and "dissipation," precisely the qualities that were making Marie
Antoinette into an emblem of decadence for the ancien régime on the brink
of the French Revolution. The unmitigated separation of the two correspondents leaves their letters as the substance of their direct relations during these ten years until the death of the empress, no personal encounter
intervening. This integrity of the epistolary relation offers a model for analysis of correspondence as a narrative form, since in this case it need never
be interpreted as a secondary and subordinate epiphenomenon of a more
immediate personal relation. This condition, furthermore, encourages the
application of literary and textual techniques to the historical correspondence, inasmuch as the historical actors, Maria Theresa and Marie Antoinette, could come to exist for each other as narrative constructs, more and
more with each passing year of separation.

Theoretical approaches to epistolary issues are largely based on epistolary fiction of the eighteenth century, in which correspondents are, by def-

inition, the literary constructs of the author, while any personal encounter between corresponding characters must be read as a secondary construct of the fictional letters themselves, located within the crevices of the correspondence. Historical letters, on the other hand, may be read in terms of a literary relation subordinate to an authentic connection, serving the historian as a textual means of trying to achieve historical truth. The historian must penetrate and pass through such letters, while the reader of epistolary fiction must find literary meaning, however deeply embedded, in the text itself. Historical and fictional letters suggest reciprocal perspectives on the relation between correspondence and encounter: the primary "authenticity" of history mirrored in the secondary "artifice" of fiction. This opposition rests on the historian's professional faith that history itself is something more than a scholarly construct. In fact, from a purely formal point of view, epistolary fiction and nonfiction are very close indeed, and it is telling that some of the most famous correspondences have not been definitively categorized as one or the other. The seventeenth-century *Lettres portugaises*, the love letters of a Portuguese nun, remain to this day of ambiguous historical authenticity, while even the twelfth-century letters of Abelard and Heloise have been called into question under the hypothesis that Abelard fictionally wrote her side of the correspondence as well as his own. The eighteenth century was unquestionably the golden age of letters, both fictional and nonfictional, and in examining the letters of Maria Theresa and Marie Antoinette, the application of literary methods to historical texts may suggest some of the particular significances of epistolary narrative in both history and literature.

The first publication of these letters in 1864 was the work of Alfred von Arneth, the great nineteenth-century archivist and historian.[1] He was director of the Habsburg archives in Vienna, and the author of a ten-volume work on Maria Theresa. Arneth and M. A. Geffroy published in 1874 a new edition that presented the letters of Maria Theresa and Marie Antoinette together with the even longer and highly relevant correspondence between the Habsburg empress and her ambassador to France, Florimond Mercy-Argenteau. Arneth and Geffroy, though they filled three volumes, nevertheless edited with very particular Victorian discretion all material in the letters that referred to the unfortunate sex life of Marie Antoinette and Louis XVI. This important aspect of the correspondence became known in 1932, when Stefan Zweig published his biography of Marie Antoinette, and Georges Girard edited an unexpurgated edition of the letters in 1933.[2] By that time, the sexual details of the correspondence could not only be frankly included, but could even form the Freudian foundation for Zweig's historical argument: he argued that Marie Antoinette's notorious frivolity grew out of the sexual frustration of her unconsummated marriage. In 1951, G. P. Gooch published a long biographical essay that focused on

Marie Antoinette, "to depict her fortunes during the first decade of her public life with the aid of a series of letters unique in historical literature."[3] In 1985 Olivier Bernier published an English edition of the correspondence as *Secrets of Marie Antoinette*.[4]

The "secrets" of that title need not refer to the letters' unerotic sexual details, for every correspondence, fictional or nonfictional, whatever its thematic concerns, forces its readers into voyeurism by allowing them to read letters addressed to someone else. That same perspective, however, allows the reader the most direct observation of the forces and relations at play in epistolary narrative. Though the letters of Maria Theresa and Marie Antoinette may indeed, in certain respects, be "unique in historical literature," they are letters nevertheless, and the text holds as yet unappreciated secrets that may emerge in formal epistolary analysis.

Maria Theresa's first letter of 21 April was, strictly speaking, neither a letter nor simply sequentially the first item of the correspondence. In fact, it was probably presented to Marie Antoinette on her departure from Vienna, rather than posted to her in France. Lacking both salutation and formal closing, the document described itself in the heading: "Regulation [*Règlement*] to read every month."[5] Stripped of the personal salutation that signals a letter as a letter, this self-styled "regulation" revealed all the more clearly the very nature of epistolary writing as the narrative of power—that is, the literary articulation of the relation of power existing between two subjects. The regulation here prescribed for Marie Antoinette, while nominally concealing its epistolary nature, in fact suggests the essential characterization of a narrative form that reaches out from within its own text to affect (to entertain, to engage, to inform, to enlighten, to regulate) its designated reader. This capacity for designation is in itself one of the principal powers of the letter. Every narrative, of course, must affect its readers, but it is only the letter that specifically names its reader and focuses its narrative forces on that chosen object. For this reason, every reader except Marie Antoinette—the "nondesignated" readers who have examined Maria Theresa's letters with historical interest since their first publication in 1864— is placed in an illicit triangular relation with the two correspondents. This triangle is essential to epistolary fiction, in which the nondesignated readers are taken for granted as the text's conventional audience.

The historian's false reading relation to Maria Theresa's *Règlement* is immediately indicated in the stipulation "to read every month." No editor will reprint this regulation one hundred twenty times over the ten years' collected correspondence, and no historian will refer constantly back to the opening document for a fresh reading. Indeed, it seems hardly likely that Marie Antoinette herself dutifully cooperated for many months, but a letter, as a textual expression of power, exists independent of its consequences, of whether it "fails" or "succeeds" outside the world of the text. Though the *Règlement* may be the first letter Maria Theresa wrote, and the first Marie Antoinette read, the historian who accepts it as simply "the first letter" will have failed to appreciate the way that power was expressed here in epistolary form. This letter designated not only its reader but its time of reading, and became not an introduction but the recurrent key to the entire correspondence, governing its style, structure, and purpose as a coherent literary entity. Maria Theresa may have had second thoughts about the imprecision of that heading, for in the next letter, dated 4 May 1770, she specified that the *Règlement* was to be read regularly on the twenty-first day of each month.[6] The heading "Regulation to read every month" suggests that one of the principal powers of the letter as a narrative form is its revision, reordering, and regulation of time itself.

It is obviously fundamental to the nature of a letter that it breaks down geographical space, functioning economically as a postal commodity that may be produced in one place (Vienna, for instance) and then carried across Europe to be consumed in another place (Versailles, perhaps). The space between collapses as the correspondents send and receive their letters. The gap, however, is both temporal and geographical, and the letter breaks down time as well as space. The text must be written at one time and read at another—thus bringing those two times together as surely as it does the two associated places. Indeed, the text may be read any number of times (every month, for instance), each time bringing the past moment of writing into immediate conjunction with the present moment of reading. The temporality of the letter is so essential to its nature that the letter generally dates itself, usually recording its time of origin just before designating its reader in the salutation.

For the historian, this dating of the document is of the greatest importance for interpretation, so much so that the time of reception and reading, often more difficult to pinpoint, may not be so carefully considered. Similarly, in epistolary fiction, less strict standards of dating may make it still harder to bear in mind that each letter joins two points in time. It is, however, precisely this dual temporality, this capacity to take hold of time at more than one point, that enables the letter to compress time or stretch it, to order or deform, to liberate or regulate. Maria Theresa began her *Règlement* thus:

> When you wake up, you will immediately upon arising go through your morning prayers on your knees and read some religious text, even if it is only for six or seven minutes [ne fût-ce même que d'un seul demi-quart d'heure] without concerning yourself about anything else or speaking to anyone. All depends on the right beginning for the day and the intention with which you begin it, for it may change even indifferent actions into praiseworthy ones.

You must be very strict [très exacte] about this, for it depends on you alone, and your temporal and spiritual happiness [votre bonheur spirituel et temporel] may depend upon it.[7]

The conventional figurative linking of "temporal and spiritual" seems exceptionally apt, inasmuch as the spirit of Marie Antoinette was treated as a problem of time and temporality. Clearly, however, that linkage was far less an issue of her happiness than an aspect of her mother's power, while that power, at once spiritual and temporal, found appropriate expression in epistolary form.

It was not simply that the letter of the empress crossed time and space to address her daughter at each reading, but also that the narrative form allowed the writer an imperialistic assault on broader domains of future time that are mapped out and colonized from afar and before. The future tense was boldly employed from the first sentence, and the prescribed monthly readings of the letter were revealed as a mere framework for the prescription of daily readings and prayers. This breaking down of time into months and days did not preclude an interest in still smaller units, as evidenced in the empress's recommended minimum for morning devotions: "un seul demi-quart d'heure." The concept of the "half-quarter hour" does not exist in English, but the more graceful translation of "six or seven minutes," though arithmetically plausible, loses the very essence of Maria Theresa's epistolary approach to time. The function of her letter was to exercise power over her daughter's spiritual life by analyzing it into its fractional temporal components: years into months into days, hours into quarters into half-quarters.

Michel Foucault attributes to the Age of Enlightenment a "microphysics of power" based on "techniques of discipline."[8] Maria Theresa, an enlightened absolutist who exercised power both as an empress and as a mother, found in her correspondence with her daughter a narrative form ideally suited to weaving a disciplinary web across time and space. The fractional analysis of time, and indeed the very notion of the "half-quarter hour," revealed a mind attuned to the refinements of "microphysics." Foucault particularly cites "the time-table" as a disciplinary mechanism, and Marie Antoinette, after all, was expected to be "très exacte."[9] In one of her first letters to her mother from France, dated 12 July 1770, she elaborately responded to her mother's request for a daily schedule, including hairdressing at eleven, mass at noon, harpsichord and singing at five, cards at six, supper at nine. She promised that in a future letter she would account for Sundays and holidays.[10]

Six years later, on 31 October 1776, concerned about her daughter's "life of constant dissipation," Maria Theresa took her own name day, the feast of St. Theresa, as an occasion to state explicitly the terms of her temporal analysis: "Your excuses about forgetting my name day are accepted without rancor; but, my dear daughter, it is not once a year that I wish you to think of me, but every month, every week, and every day [tous les mois, semaines et jours], so that you forget neither my love nor my advice and the examples I give you."[11] The name day could serve as an annual marker, but in the *Règlement* of 1770, the empress was even bolder in her claims on the empire of time, reaching beyond her own death without letting go of her daughter's future: "Never forget the anniversary of your late dear father's death, and mine in its time: in the meantime you can use my birthday as the date on which to pray for me."[12] Her birthday and name day were both useful markers, but already, ten years before her death, Maria Theresa was putting the anniversary of that future date on the calendar of Marie Antoinette.

The prescribed monthly reading of the *Règlement* provided the perfect temporal framework for what was to become the most urgent occasion on the calendar cycle in the whole correspondence: the monthly menstrual period of Marie Antoinette, initially designated in the letters as "la générale." This aspect of the correspondence remained generally unknown before the twentieth century. When Arneth first published the correspondence in 1864, the letter of 12 July 1770, addressed to Maria Theresa in the formal third person, showed Marie Antoinette responding thus to the temporal monitoring of her religious life: "Regarding what you asked about my devotions, I will say that I have only taken communion one time."[13] Arneth had neatly and discreetly edited out half the agenda, as history discovered when Girard published his edition in 1933: "Regarding what you asked about my devotions and my period [la générale], I will say that I have only taken communion one time. . . . As for my period, this is the fourth month that it has not come, without there being any good reason."[14] The absence of "good reason" reflected the absence of consummation in the marriage and the impossibility of pregnancy. If the fourteen-year-old girl did not have her period for four months, it might be attributed to the stress of royal marriage and leaving home, but it definitely did not mean she was pregnant.

The unexpurgated passage indicates the dual religious and gynecological monitoring imposed by maternal discipline in the correspondence, a supervisory interest in devotions and periods, envisioning a future of regular communion and intercourse. The continued postponement of the latter (for seven years) was distressing to Maria Theresa, perhaps as much as to Marie Antoinette. The empress naturally wanted her daughter's marriage to be consummated in order to produce an heir to the French throne. Furthermore, Maria Theresa saw in the sexual union of the young couple, after 1774 the king and queen of France, the guarantee of the Bourbon-Habsburg alliance, as well as a key to Habsburg influence on Louis XVI. The correspondence followed the monthly menstrual cycle, ultimately because sex was an issue of public and political power for both France and Austria, but also because through sexual supervision the empress could express her personal power over her daughter's private life.

Even with the marriage unconsummated, gynecological monitoring remained important, for menstruation could serve as an indicator of the young woman's general physical and spiritual condition. After a year in France, on 16 April 1771, Marie Antoinette began a letter to her mother with a careful account of herself: "Madame my very dear mother, I am delighted that Lent has not damaged your health. Mine is still rather good—I have the générale quite regularly [assez régulièrement]; this time it was nine days early."[15] Here the menstrual cycle was superimposed on the Lenten calendar, and Maria Theresa was informed very exactly that the cycle was nine days early. The phrase "assez régulièrement" showed how well Marie Antoinette understood the nature of her mother's disciplinary concerns. Those concerns may also be interpreted in the light of Foucault's discussion of the "docile body" as an eighteenth-century disciplinary object. Foucault identifies the "analyzable" body with the "manipulable" body, and argues that this was the age that "discovered the body as an object and target of power."[16]

After the long-delayed consummation of the marriage in 1777, the delicate subject of menstruation acquired a fresh urgency in the correspondence. On 15 January 1778, Marie Antoinette began her letter by writing, "I am quite ashamed and distressed to be obliged to inform my dear maman that my period [mes règles] came yesterday morning."[17] Marie Theresa immediately registered this information with displeasure, and began her reply of 1 February with the following remark: "Your letter of the 15th gave me no pleasure because of the return of your period."[18] The sense of being "obliged to inform my dear maman" summed up the disciplinary dynamic of the whole correspondence, while the juxtaposition of the daughter's shame with the mother's displeasure clearly represented the emotional relation that Maria Theresa had sought to cultivate in her letters as an aspect of that dynamic. The substitution of the more conventional expression "règles" for "générale" was also convenient in its suggestion of gynecological discipline, and the attention to the monthly "règles" of Marie Antoinette, now queen of France, may still have called to mind the Règlement—to be read every month—that she had received eight years before when she first went to France as the dauphine.

The immediacy with which epistolary writing juxtaposes separate points in time and space is a function of its particular narrative nature. Just as a letter may be simply said to join two people, an epistolary narrative may be said, theoretically, to join two narrative persons: the first person and the second person. In the Règlement of 1770, Maria Theresa introduced the second person from the very beginning, with four instances in the opening phrase: "When *you* wake up, *you* will immediately upon arising go through *your* morning prayers on *your* knees" ("A *votre* réveil *vous* ferez tout de suite, en *vous* levant, *vos* prières du matin à genoux").[19] One could say that the employment of the second person here brought Marie Antoinette to her knees, for it was that narrative construction that made the document a letter, and at the same time made the letter an expression of power. The presence of the second person identifies an epistolary narrative—or rather the combination of first and second persons, for the "you" implies an "I" who is writing, even when, as above, it does not immediately advertise itself. The second person, of course, also existed in eighteenth-century writing outside letters: "It is enough to tell you, that as some of my worst comrades . . . knew me by the name of Moll Flanders, so you may give me leave to speak of myself under that name." The "you" to whom Moll Flanders addresses herself is all of us who read her story, whereas the distinction of the epistolary "you" is its exclusion of all of us by the singling out of the designated reader. Yet, paradoxically, though its narrative form emphatically excludes us, the letter also allows us the most immediate observation of the balance between the two narrative persons, for the narrator who ignores us can not authorially mediate our reading of the text.

"You" and "I"—locked into their own relationship—offer the nondesignated reader a narratively unmediated field for observing and analyzing the microphysics of power. The *Règlement* of Maria Theresa, opening with the second person alone, very quickly goes on to choreograph the relation between the narrative persons:

> You will always write me and tell me which book you are using. [Vous me marquerez toujours de quel livre vous vous servez.] You will pray [vous vous recueillerez] during the day as often as you can, especially during the celebration of Holy Mass. I hope you will attend it [j'espère que vous l'entendrez] every day in the proper spirit, and twice on Sunday and holidays.[20]

The most obvious concern was still temporal calendar discipline, mass every day, twice on Sundays. The pronouns of person, however, embedded in the epistolary text, reveal a more subtly conceived disciplinary strategy. In the first sentence, the "you" deceptively proclaims itself the subject, though the intent is clearly to subordinate it to the second-person object— "vous me marquerez"—so that the grammatical subject becomes an object of disciplinary surveillance. It is always the writer of the epistolary narrative who defines the relation of power between its two persons, reserving the option of assuming either subject or object status. In the second sentence Maria Theresa allows the "you" to enjoy both statuses in reflexive relation—"vous vous recueillerez"—so that surveillance gives way to self-discipline. Again, the discipline is only deceptively self-imposed by the second person (as it is only deceptively self-proclaimed in the first sentence), for the writer is always present in the epistolary text even without the advertisement of her own pronoun. On the other hand, to translate this sentence without the reflexive—"you will pray during the day as often as you can"— is to miss the self-disciplinary implications of the narrative strategy. For that, one must more awkwardly and less religiously render "vous vous recueillerez" as "you will collect yourself." It is not until the third sentence that the pronouns honestly proclaim their true epistolary relation—"j'espère que vous l'entendrez"—with the "I" as a hoping subject and the "you" itself the subject of a subordinate clause. Here the subordination in grammar perfectly reflects the formulated balance of power between the narrative persons.

These grammatical and narratological relations correspond to important issues of eighteenth-century cultural history. Both surveillance and self-discipline are crucial concepts in Foucault's formulation of the disciplinary revolution of the Enlightenment, which he traces from the spectacle of naked power and royal authority in public execution, to the enclosed and unostentatious disciplinary surveillance in Bentham's vision of the Panopticon.[21] Maria Theresa's employment of the reflexive may be placed in the context of an eighteenth-century cultural trajectory. Already in 1693 Locke heralded a revolutionary rethinking of child-rearing and education, deploring the brutality of excessive corporal punishment and advocating instead the disciplinary inculcation of feelings of shame and disgrace. Locke explained his preference in reflexive terms: "Every man must some time or other be trusted to himself."[22] One century later, Tuke could consummate this development and revolutionize mental health care by allowing self-discipline even to the insane at his York Retreat asylum. The madman too could be controlled reflexively: "He promised to restrain himself."[23] The echo of Locke's educational precepts in Maria Theresa's reflexive verbs reminds one that the correspondence (and balance of power) was between mother and daughter. Maria Theresa, one of the most powerful people in the world in 1770, was far from unversed in the articulation of authority, and she could assume the expressions and techniques of an enlightened mother as well as an enlightened empress. The letters reveal precisely how little she felt that the fourteen-year-old Marie Antoinette could, in fact, be trusted to herself, but the transition to reflexive formulation, like the previewing of calendar anniversaries beyond her own death, recognizes the regrettable inevitability of independence. Just as epistolary narrative, by joining points in time, allows the writer to reach out beyond the moment of reception to broader temporal horizons, so the relation between "I" and "you," joining two persons, allows the writer boldly to manipulate the reflexive relation of the second person to herself.

In the most audacious line in the *Règlement*, Maria Theresa effaced herself completely, the better to warn her daughter that people will be watching her when she goes to church: "All eyes will be fixed on you [tous les yeux seront fixés sur vous], so do not give any cause for scandal."[24] The absent mother (pronominally absent from the sentence, as well as geographically distant in Vienna) could conjure up guardian eyes of surveillance lest Marie Antoinette too fully embrace her independence. It was a sort of inverted Panopticon: instead of one eye on all the prisoners, all eyes on the one dauphine. In fact, Maria Theresa, keeping herself fully informed about her daughter through the dispatches of Mercy, the Austrian ambassador to Versailles, always tried to imply to her daughter that reports reached her in Vienna by way of general European gossip—the witnessed testimony of all those eyes. Thus, the warning was both cunningly false and at the same time politically prophetic. Already during her mother's lifetime, Marie Antoinette would begin to cause scandal and would start on the path to being a public emblem of royal decadence.[25] Eyes would remain fixed on her with an ever-growing intensity until the ultimate moment when she ascended the guillotine in 1793. Thus, the narrative strategy of eighteenth-century discipline shows itself to be structurally related to the cultural strategy of eighteenth-century political mythology; the eyes that stand in for the concerned mother and empress meet the eyes of the outraged pornographers, philosophers, and revolutionaries.

In 1776, thirteen years before the revolution, nine years before the diamond-necklace scandal that would ruin the reputation of Marie Antoinette beyond repair, Maria Theresa was already elaborating epistolary constructs that called into play the formal and thematic elements of revolutionary mythology. She wrote on 2 September, supposedly in response to the anonymous eyes and tongues that constituted "the news from Paris."

> All the news from Paris announces [toutes les nouvelles de Paris annoncent] that you have made a purchase of bracelets for 250,000 livres, that to that effect you have upset your finances and gone into debt, and that to remedy this you have given up some of your diamonds at a very low price, and that it is supposed [qu'on suppose] now that you lead the king astray [que vous entraînez le roi] into so many useless profusions, which have been mounting again for some time and putting the state in the distress where it finds itself. I believe [je crois] these articles to be exaggerated, but, loving you so tenderly, I believed it was necessary that you be informed of the rumors [des bruits qui courent]. These kinds of anecdotes pierce my heart, especially for the future.[26]

One sees immediately that the thematic concerns anticipated the coming of the revolution with startling clairvoyance, especially the mythological association of the queen's extravagance with the state's financial crisis. On closer examination, one sees that Maria Theresa organized her concerns within a particular narrative strategy that isolated Marie Antoinette as the object of anonymous critical surveillance. In the whole first sentence the second person stands alone, acting in subordinate clauses that are governed anonymously by "all the news from Paris." In the second half of the sentence the "you" is even more punishingly isolated by the interposition of an intermediary subordinate clause—"qu'on suppose"—between the news of Paris and the culpable "you" who is leading the king astray. That is: "Les nouvelles de Paris annoncent / qu'on suppose / que vous entraînez le roi."

Not until the following sentence did Maria Theresa permit herself to enter the narrative in the first person with a self-effacing "je crois." Then, she subtly cast herself as the twin victim of the same anonymous forces of rumor—"des bruits qui courent"—that were assaulting Marie Antoinette. That is: "These kinds of anecdotes pierce my heart." It was a narrative performance of strategic concealment, first, because Maria Theresa received full reports on her daughter from Mercy, and second, because, as the letter-writer, she always controlled completely the formal construction of the text. Interestingly, the enlightened absolutism of the empress seemed to announce itself in the further juxtaposition of her own victimized position—pierced to the heart—and that of "the state," not even her own, in "distress."

In the letters, as the purely grammatical relation between the "I" and the "you" moves toward the construction of the more culturally interpretable relation between the "eye" and the "you," epistolary narrative yields historical meaning. Paradoxically it is the most formal aspects of the narrative that illustrate the most historically complex issues of power, authority, and discipline. For this reason the theoretical treatment of epistolary form, though usually devoted to fiction, points the way toward a convergence of historical analysis and literary criticism. In 1962, Jean Rousset wrote about the epistolary novel as a literary form, and observed that such novels could resemble journals in their intimacy (as in *Pamela* or *Werther*), or alternatively could resemble works of theater in their immediacy, offering speech, action, and relation to the unmediated observation of the audience.[27] Rousset stresses the importance of a letter's recipient, even in the Portuguese letters, where the officer's actual absence and unresponsiveness make him no less an urgent presence in the nun's narrative.[28] In discussing *Les liaisons dangereuses*, which critics of the genre tend to find most fascinating and most rewarding of analysis, Rousset remarks that "each letter is so well addressed to someone, so much composed according to the measure of its addressee [*destinataire*], that this addressee is in the letter he receives as much as in that which he writes."[29] This consciousness of the narrative balance points to a conclusion about the world of the epistolary novel that would carry equal validity for letters in the historical world: "The world is a tissue of relations that diversify and intermingle."[30]

François Jost, writing in 1966 about narrative technique and the eigh-

teenth-century epistolary novel, emphasized the distinction between a passive, static, confidential correspondence and an active, dynamic, dramatic
correspondence.[31] *Les liaisons dangereuses* provides Jost with his finest specimen of the latter, and again the critical vocabulary indicates those issues
of power that might interest the historian. In 1967, Tzvetan Todorov published a study of *Les liaisons dangereuses*, exploring "the signification of letters in general, and not only as a novelistic procedure."[32] Todorov observes
the "temporal deformations" that may emerge from the epistolary form,
and also identifies the "two opposite poles" of that form as the chronicle
of impersonal events versus the drama of corresponding characters. The
marquise de Merteuil serves as Todorov's "formal" heroine, insofar as her
letters realize more than anyone else's the dramatic potential of the form.
Just as she instructs Cécile that "when you write to someone, it is for him
and not for you," so in her own letter writing the marquise is unique
among the characters: according to Todorov, "she is the only one to aim
[*viser*], in all her letters, at the reaction of her interlocutor."[33] It is she who
appreciates, as Maria Theresa did, the special potential of the epistolary
form for the microphysics of power, and the letters of the fictional eighteenth-century marquise, like those of the historical empress, offer a model
for the maximal manipulation and exploitation of epistolary narrative.
Both women are mistresses of epistolary discipline—for discipline, as Foucault defines it, is "a type of power, a modality for its exercise, comprising
a whole set of instruments, techniques, procedures, levels of application,
targets."[34]

In 1982 Janet Altman published a book, *Epistolarity*, whose title underlines the importance of defining the unique qualities of the form. Altman
notes the special literary triangle created by the letter-writer, its internal
reader or recipient, and the external reader or audience.[35] She stresses the
designation of the reader as a "particularity of the I-you." She emphasizes
the immediacy of the present tense, and points to the "temporal polyva-
lence" whereby "any given epistolary statement is relative to innumerable
moments."[36] Altman identifies the "paradox of epistolarity" in its naviga-
tion of "polar consistencies."[37] The polar dimensions of the form include,
for instance, "I/you, here/there, now/then," the specifications of person,
place, and time.[38] She finally proposes three "registers" of epistolarity: one
of reported events, one of the letter-writer, and one of the recipient
reader.[39]

The scrupulousness of Altman's formal approach makes her observations
on epistolarity as relevant to historical as to fictional letters. At the same
time, her thoroughness in cataloguing the competing "polarities" of the
form tends to avoid any highlighting of extreme, emphatic, essential epistolarity, the ideal type, as implied in Todorov's special fascination with the
marquise de Merteuil. For while letters may vary tremendously and occupy

a diversity of points on any graph of polar dimensions, it is precisely those letters that exploit the fullest combination of polarities that illustrate the fullest qualities of epistolarity. Plenty of letters, for instance, do not trespass far beyond the home turf of the first-person writer and the present time of writing. These are letters nonetheless, but one might argue that they demonstrate a less emphatic epistolarity than those that break out boldly from the circumscription of their origin. The marquise de Merteuil or the empress Maria Theresa, as they simultaneously embrace and assault the second person, the correspondent, the *destinataire*, exhibit a whole other level of epistolarity. Thus for Rousset, epistolary narrative may resemble either journal or theater; for Jost it may exhibit either static passivity or active dynamism; for Todorov it may rise from chronicle to drama. It is these latter qualities of extreme epistolarity that invite the historian to analyze and interpret letters as "instruments, techniques, procedures" in the evolving forms of disciplinary power.

Altman's triple register offers an approach not only to analyzing the letters as literary texts, but also to understanding the different ways historians make use of letters as historical documents. Any letter may involve all three registers—reported events, the sentiments of the writer, and the "aim" at the recipient—and these registers also generally correspond to the employment of three different narrative persons: third, first, and second. Todorov observes that the letter may resemble a third-person chronicle, and Rousset that it may resemble a first-person journal; for the historian, both chronicles and journals are valuable documents, and letters are often exploited just as if they were one or the other. For instance, the correspondence of Madame de Sévigné is an invaluable source of reported information about elite society in Paris and at Versailles in the age of Louis XIV. Consider the following reports:

> M. de Langlée has given Mme de Montespan a dress of gold on gold, all embroidered with gold, all edged with gold, and on top of that a sort of gold pile stitched with gold mixed with a certain gold, which makes the most divine stuff ever imagined. (6 November 1676)[40]

> The King wants to go to Versailles on Saturday, but it seems that God is not willing because it will be impossible for the buildings to be in a fit state to receive him and because of the enormous mortality of workmen of whom, as from the Hospital, they take away cartloads of dead every night. (12 October 1678)[41]

Such reports find their place in various historical treatments of the age, but it is important to observe that, taken thus as useful fragments, they exhibit no epistolary qualities, and may be employed by the historian without reference to their occurrence in letters. The correspondence of Madame de Sévigné may be treated as if it were, for all intents and purposes, the same sort of source as the memoirs of the duc de Saint-Simon.

Although the literary theory of epistolarity has especially focused on the eighteenth century, when the epistolary novel became such an important literary form, the formal analysis of letters is certainly also relevant to other centuries. Madame de Sévigné, the great epistolary genius of the seventeenth century, may inspire this sort of attention from scholars of French history and literature alike. On the other hand, looking forward to the correspondences of the nineteenth and twentieth centuries, when letters may assume a less self-consciously literary form, one sometimes further underestimates the significance of their formal epistolary qualities. For instance, the Freud-Fliess correspondence, which is so fundamental for modern intellectual historians, offers up as its most spectacular treasures the sentiments of the letter-writer, Sigmund Freud himself.

> For the last four days my self-analysis, which I consider indispensable for the clarification of the whole problem, has continued in dreams and has presented me with the most valuable elucidations and clues. (3 October 1897)[42]

> I have found, in my own case too, being in love with my mother and jealous of my father, and I now consider it a universal event in early childhood. (15 October 1897)[43]

Here again the nuggets of gold may be mined without reference to their epistolary context. Just as Madame de Sévigné is invaluable for her third-person reports, so Sigmund Freud is for his first-person sentiments. The Freud-Fliess correspondence, in spite of its special narrative form, may be handled historically as if it were formally little different from the autobiography of John Stuart Mill or the diaries of Virginia Woolf.

At the same time, historians cannot help recognizing that the letters of Madame de Sévigné to Madame de Grignan reveal something important about relations between mother and daughter in the seventeenth century, and that the Freud-Fliess correspondence illustrates the odd collaborative origin of a cultural revolution. The second person cannot be ignored in these examples of correspondence, any more than in that of Maria Theresa and Marie Antoinette.

> And what do you think I am doing, my poor dear? Loving you, thinking of you, giving way to emotion at every turn more than I would like, concerning myself with your affairs, worrying about what you think, feeling your sufferings and pains, wanting to suffer them for you if possible, removing anything unpleasant from your heart as I used to clear your room of any tiresome people. (1 April 1671)[44]

Your happiness can vanish all too fast, and you may be plunged, by your own doing, into the greatest calamities. That is the result of your terrible dissipation, which prevents your being assiduous about anything serious. What have you read? (30 July 1775)[45]

You said nothing about my interpretation of Oedipus Rex and Hamlet. Since I have not told it to anyone else, because I can well imagine in advance the bewildered rejection, I should like to have a short comment on it from you. (5 November 1897)[46]

The historian's challenge must be to remain always aware of the narrative nature of the documents, to analyze them in their epistolary context. Literary theory offers an approach to epistolary form that may be used to historical advantage. Thus, the historian who appreciates the importance of the second person, the correspondent, in the letters of Madame de Sévigné, Maria Theresa, or Sigmund Freud, will discover in their relations and liaisons the fundamental dynamics of social, political, and cultural history. It is Maria Theresa herself who reminds us that our critical eyes must be fixed on the "you."

NOTES

1. Alfred von Arneth, ed., *Maria Theresa und Marie Antoinette: Ihr Briefwechsel* (Paris and Vienna, 1865); A. Arneth and M. A. Geffroy, eds., *Correspondance secrète entre Marie Thérèse et le comte de Mercy-Argenteau* (Paris, 1874).

2. Georges Girard, ed., *Correspondance entre Marie-Thérèse et Marie Antoinette* (Paris: Editions Bernard Grasset, 1933); Stefan Zweig, *Marie Antoinette* (Leipzig: Insel Verlag, 1932).

3. G. P. Gooch, "Maria Theresa and Marie Antoinette," in Gooch, *Maria Theresa and Other Studies* (1951; reprint, Archon Books, 1965), 119.

4. Olivier Bernier, ed., *Secrets of Marie Antoinette: A Collection of Letters* (1985; reprint, New York: Fromm, 1986).

5. Girard, *Correspondence*, letter of Maria Theresa, 21 April 1770, 21. All translations are mine except as otherwise noted.

6. Ibid., letter of Maria Theresa, 4 May 1770, 26.

7. Ibid., letter of Maria Theresa, 21 April 1770, 21; the translation is from Bernier, *Secrets*, 31.

8. Michel Foucault, *Discipline and Punish*, trans. Alan Sheridan (1975; reprint, New York: Vintage, 1979), 139.

9. Ibid., 149.

10. Girard, *Correspondence*, letter of Marie Antoinette, 12 July 1770, 30.

11. Ibid., letter of Maria Theresa, 31 October 1776, 192; the translation is from Bernier, *Secrets*, 203.

12. Girard, *Correspondence*, letter of Maria Theresa, 21 April 1770, 23; the translation is from Bernier, *Secrets*, 32.

13. Arneth, *Maria Theresa*, letter of Marie Antoinette, 12 July 1770, 5.

14. Girard, *Correspondence*, letter of Marie Antoinette, 12 July 1770, 29.

15. Ibid., letter of Marie Antoinette, 16 April 1771, 40; the translation is from Bernier, *Secrets*, 61.

16. Foucault, *Discipline and Punish*, 136.

17. Girard, *Correspondence*, letter of Marie Antoinette, 15 January 1778, 229.

18. Ibid., letter of Maria Theresa, 1 February 1778, 231.

19. Ibid., letter of Maria Theresa, 21 April 1770, 21; the translation is from Bernier, *Secrets*, 31 (emphasis added).

20. Girard, *Correspondence*, letter of Maria Theresa, 21 April 1770, 21; the translation is from Bernier, *Secrets* 31.

21. Foucault, *Discipline and Punish*, part 3, chap. 3, "Panopticism," 195–228.

22. John Locke, "Some Thoughts Concerning Education" (1693), in Peter Gay, ed., *The Enlightenment: A Comprehensive Anthology* (New York: Touchstone, 1973), 91.

23. Michel Foucault, *Madness and Civilization* (1961; reprint, New York: Vintage, 1973), 246.

24. Girard, *Correspondence*, letter of Maria Theresa, 21 April 1770, 22.

25. Simon Schama, *Citizens: A Chronicle of the French Revolution* (New York:

Knopf, 1989); on Marie Antoinette, see chap. 6, "Body Politics," section (i), "Uterine Furies and Dynastic Obstructions," 203–27.

26. Girard, *Correspondence*, letter of Maria Theresa, 2 September 1776, 185–86.

27. Jean Rousset, "Une forme litteraire: Le roman par les lettres," in Rousset, *Forme et signification* (Paris: Librairie José Corti, 1962), 67.

28. Ibid., 72.

29. Ibid., 95.

30. Ibid., 85.

31. François Jost, "L'evolution d'un genre: Le roman épistolaire dans les lettres occidentales," in Jost, *Essais de littérature comparée*, vol. 2, Europaeana, first series (Urbana: University of Illinois Press and Fribourg: Editions Universitaires Fribourg Suisse, 1968), 124.

32. Tzvetan Todorov, *Littérature et signification* (Paris: Librairie Larousse, 1967), 13.

33. Ibid., 36–37.

34. Foucault, *Discipline and Punish*, 215.

35. Janet Gurkin Altman, *Epistolarity: Approaches to a Form* (Columbus: Ohio State University Press, 1982), 111.

36. Ibid., 117–18.

37. Ibid., 190.

38. Ibid., 186–87.

39. Ibid., 207–8.

40. Madame de Sévigné, letter of 6 November 1676, in Sévigné, *Selected Letters*, ed. and trans. Leonard Tancock (New York: Penguin, 1982), 215.

41. Ibid., letter of 12 October 1678, 226.

42. Sigmund Freud, letter of 3 October 1897, in *The Complete Letters of Sigmund Freud to Wilhelm Fliess*, trans. Jeffrey Moussaieff Masson (Cambridge, Mass.: Harvard University Press, 1985), 268.

43. Ibid., letter of 15 October 1897, 272.

44. Madame de Sévigné, *Selected Letters*, letter of 1 April 1671, 84.

45. Girard, *Correspondence*, letter of Maria Theresa, 30 July 1775, 156; the translation is from Bernier, *Secrets*, 172.

46. Freud, *Complete Letters*, letter of 5 November 1897, 277.

SIX

AUTHENTICITY AS MASK:

WOLFGANG HILDESHEIMER'S *MARBOT*

Käte Hamburger

WOLFGANG HILDESHEIMER'S latest book, *Marbot: A Bi-ography*, invites us to consider questions quite different from those that every literary work, in one way or another, provokes.[1] This is also an indication of how unusual, indeed extraordinary, this book is. But its unconventionality is not without pitfalls, and thus it presents us with a difficult case for interpretation and evaluation. This only becomes completely clear if we put ourselves in the position of a reader fifty or one hundred years hence, when it is no longer possible to set up television interviews with the author, or indeed to ask him any questions at all. (Here we also exclude the possibility of gaining access to authorial comments in the future.)

The hero of this biography is the young Sir Andrew Marbot, born on 4 April 1801 at Marbot Hall in Northumberland, son of Sir Francis Marbot (1773–1822) and Lady Catherine (1781–1832), the beautiful daughter of the third Viscount Claverton of Redmond Manor in Westmorland. Sir Andrew's portrait, a chalk lithograph executed by Delacroix in 1827, adorns the book's jacket and frontispiece, and a portrait of his parents by Henry Raeburn, as well as one by Anton Graff of his maternal grandfather, Claverton, are to be found among the plates, along with illustrations of Marbot Hall and Redmond Manor. The boy's tutor is Father Gerard van Rossum (the family is Catholic), great-uncle of Willem van Rossum (1854–1932), a cardinal of the Curia. Until Marbot's suicide at an early age, in 1830, Father Gerard is, along with the boy's mother, one of the people closest to him.

From an early age, young Andrew's chief passion in life is fine art, an interest sparked by the precious collection of paintings owned by his grandfather, Claverton. We should already note that the heart of this biography, its real focus, is Marbot's aesthetics and psychology of art. Certain writings by Marbot are mentioned: these were published posthumously in 1834 under the title *Art and Life* and appeared in German translation in 1839. There are also numerous references to, and quotations from, the 1888 monograph on Marbot by the American art historian Fredric Hadley-Chase. In addition, a critical new edition of *Art and Life*, with commentary, is announced, as well as an edition of Marbot's letters.

Marbot embarks on his grand tour in the autumn of 1820, is summoned to Marbot Hall in 1822 on the death of his father, and after three years in England leaves his country forever. After spending some time in Hamburg, Braunschweig, Weimar, and Kassel, he travels to Italy and settles in Urbino. In late February 1830, he sets off on horseback into the mountains, never to return. His body is never found. In England and on his travels, he comes into contact, for shorter or longer periods, with the following individuals (listed in alphabetical order): William Blake, Karl Blechen, Sulpice Boisserée, Eugène Delacroix, Thomas De Quincey, Goethe, Ottilie von Goethe, Countess Teresa of Guiccioli, Giacomo Leopardi, Count August von Platen, Henry Crabb Robinson, Freiherr Carl von Rumohr, Arthur Schopenhauer, Joseph W. Turner, and William Wordsworth.

The summary of the circumstances of Sir Andrew Marbot's life, as laid out by the biography, is not to be read as the synopsis of a novel: it is merely a summary of what the book itself reports. Nor do the numerous references to Marbot's letters or quotations from his writings in any way detract from this documentary style, a style appropriate for a biography and thus for any historical work. Needless to say, this is part of any biography, when the author is fortunate enough to have a rich fund of material at his or her disposal. The author's reflections and commentaries on the motivation, personality traits, and so forth of his hero are also, to a certain point, legitimate biographical methods. He quotes, for example, from one of Marbot's letters: "Why, when I see something beautiful, do I always have the feeling that I am seeing it for the last time, not for the first time? Do others have the same feeling? By others I mean of course those who are at all capable of experiencing something that goes beyond their physical needs and their satisfaction, that is if one can even find that something." The author comments: "Here an element of misanthropy is added to melancholia. And yet it is not true to say that Marbot hated other human beings; he lamented their lot, rather, and their powerlessness, they were an object of his sympathy, indeed often he suffered with them" (103). Here the author does not go beyond what he can glean objectively from the letters concerning the character of his hero.

What about other aspects of the Marbot biography, in which Hildesheimer adheres so strictly to the style of biographical reportage? It has already been noted that the biography never deviates from its precise chronology. The index also strengthens the biography's claims to historical and scholarly accuracy: in addition to the names and dates of those individuals listed above, who were personally known to Marbot, it also includes artists, poets, philosophers, and others who had influenced him: Botticelli,

Tintoretto, Dante, Shakespeare, and so on. But it is significant that precisely those names most likely to be found in the index are missing: not
only Sir Andrew's own name, but also those of his parents, of his grandfather Viscount Claverton, and of Father von Rossum. Even if this may be
a justifiable omission in the case of the biography's hero (and Hildesheimer
followed the same convention in his Mozart biography), surely in the case
of the other individuals it is not. Could the author justify these lacunas by
saying that the dates of these people are already given in the index? Here
we should sit up and take notice: we should note that dates given in a
narrative text serve a different function from those in an index—especially
when it is an index of authentic historical figures. Years and dates of birth
and death may appear in any novel, both the dates of the fictitious characters in the novel and of historical figures who may appear in the work. But
invented, fictitious names may not be included in a scholarly index. Here
the crafty author tips off a perceptive and expert reader (the reader is assumed to be of this type). He drops a hint that there might be something
suspicious about the hero's supposed historical existence: the oft-cited author of the 1888 Marbot monograph, the American art historian Fredric
Hadley-Chase, does not appear in the index either.

Let us turn from the index to the text itself. I have already listed those
contemporaries of Marbot—artists, writers, and so on—whom he had met
or with whom he had corresponded. Here we arrive at the heart of the
book's problematics, not only in terms of literary criticism but also in terms
of literary theory. Let us leave aside for the moment Marbot's visit to Goethe in July 1825, the point of departure for the first chapter of the biography, which is loosely constructed and in a sense introductory. (Only from
the second chapter does the work proceed chronologically.) Hildesheimer
reports that at the age of seventeen, Marbot met, at the house of his grandfather Claverton, the author of the famous *Confessions of an English Opium
Eater* (1821), Thomas De Quincey. De Quincey's "opium excesses had
reached their peak at that time and made a powerful and lasting impression
on the seventeen-year-old" (66). There follows a longer account of a visit
to De Quincey, quoted in the form of an extract from Marbot's writings.
It is reported that De Quincey was also the first to review Marbot's book
Art and Life, and that this was in fact in *Blackwood's Magazine* (89). In a
letter to him Marbot describes the peculiar goings-on in Byron's household in Pisa, where he had spent the winter of 1821–22 (123). And it
should be noted that Marbot later had a brief affair with the beautiful
Countess Teresa of Guiccioli, who had in real life been the mistress of Byron. (She too is listed in the index.) Another acquaintance of Marbot,
whom he met in Siena, was Freiherr Carl von Rumohr, connoisseur of the
visual and culinary arts (*The Culinary Spirit*, 1823), who later expressed

some criticism of the editors who posthumously published Marbot's *Art and Life* in 1839 (90).

These are merely a few examples for the time being. Let us now examine Marbot's visit to Goethe, mentioned above. With this visit, the biography opens in medias res, in mid-scene, which, if not forbidden territory for biography, is at least unusual. "If I am to believe the myth, Your Excellency, said the twenty-four-year-old Sir Andrew Marbot to Goethe, who had inquired after his last name. . . ." In order to avoid having to reproduce the exchange in its entirety, let us sum it up: Goethe responds with an observation on mythology and tradition and continues the conversation with questions concerning the young man's aristocratic family name. This conversation of 4 July 1825 is quoted as having been recorded in a letter from Councillor of State Schultz, who was present at the time, to his wife (7ff.). Next are Marbot's reports of the visit and his impressions of Goethe, addressed to Father van Rossum and to his mother, as well as later remarks of Goethe about Marbot, among others those to Eckermann in December 1825. "One does not wish to be hollow and generalizing, but rather one wishes to say something fitting to each individual. But now I am gradually becoming freer, and I feel more inclined to conversation. One which gave me particular pleasure was the conversation with that young Englishman. What a strange person! He spoke so earnestly, as if he were weighing every word" (17). As far as the words "inclined to conversation," these words are indeed recorded by Eckermann on 25 December 1825. But there Goethe continues in quite a different vein, and after further general observations—"Everything that we do has consequences"—he discusses mistakes he has made in negotiations with booksellers and which turned out to his advantage. Neither here nor elsewhere does he mention a young Englishman. As far as Schultz is concerned, the Prussian councillor of state from Berlin who corresponded with Goethe and occasionally visited him, there exist in published form no letters to his wife. The author must be aware that these facts, especially the Eckermann quotation, are easily verifiable. And the montage he has undertaken could be interpreted as a further hint to the reader not to rely absolutely on the biographical authenticity and truth of the text. Since no sources are given, it would require extensive research to verify the authenticity of remarks attributed to the other figures, or indeed even their relationship with Marbot—figures such as Rumohr, De Quincey, Herman Grimm, Henry Crabb Robinson (an English writer, 1775–1865), Turner, Boisserée, Leopardi, and so on. However, the Goethe montage should suffice to render such research superfluous.[2]

The main substance of the biography is provided by Marbot's writings and letters, or rather by frequent quotations from them. In the first third of the book, the source of the information is not made clear. It would seem that the description of Marbot's childhood and adolescence at Marbot Hall is based on these writings, yet for the most part what we are given from Marbot's writings are only general observations reflecting his experience of art and poetry. The portrayal of the main events seems to the reader as independent of biographical sources as that of any work of fiction. An important part of this, to which we must now turn our attention, is the story of the "monstrous" occurrence that, as we shall see, constitutes the very nucleus of the book's central theme, the psychology of art and of the artist. This nucleus is the incestuous relationship between the son and his beautiful mother. How did the biographer gain knowledge of these most intimate and secret events? What kind of unimaginable source would enable him to report the following? "For it was here in London, at the Clavertons' townhouse on Curzon Street, in one of the rooms on the upper story—two came into play as possibilities—that this monstrous thing occurred. . . . It overcame them suddenly and violently, when they realized during one of many nights that no obstacles of time, place, or person stood in the way of their actions" (73). It is only after this passage that the biographer admits to the fertile powers of his imagination: "I picture it in this way: it is nighttime, a party at the Clavertons has just come to an end, the last guests leave the hall, drowsy servants extinguish the lights in the rooms and corridors. . . . Andrew and Lady Catherine climb the stairs, he holds out his arm to her, she presses it against her . . . the ordinary goodnight kiss becomes extraordinary" (74).

If, then, this novelistic scene is, as he admits, the product of his imagination, where has he found his factual information, the time and location of the events? Here we should note the author's later remarks about the fate of Marbot's posthumous writings. Among those who played a role in Andrew's life was Anna Maria Baiardi, the owner of the house in Urbino that he had rented. A young and sensitive widow, she became his companion through life. She too, like Father van Rossum, is missing from the index. Yet she and Father van Rossum are portrayed at great length in their roles as guardians and custodians of the writings and letters. At the end of 1830, Anna Maria had sent them to Lady Catherine. She in turn passed them on to Father van Rossum (to whom she had confessed the monstrous deed), "along with her letters" (Marbot's letters to her) "after she had destroyed the intimate letters and thought she had rendered any other suggestions of personal details illegible" (94). Everything has been carefully laid out; the history of the manuscripts has been rendered plausible. Those passages she had made illegible were later chemically restored. After Father van Rossum's death in 1847, the estate initially fell into the hands of his nephew Adrian van Rossum, who reportedly "singled out the fragments of the letters to the mother and placed them under lock and key separately from the others, because he realized himself that the sin had to be kept secret." This was until "Frans van Rossum, the last heir to all the family papers, placed them all, including these documents, at my [Hildesheimer's] disposal, and thus made the book possible" (96). (These letters do not document the secret events either, as they are portrayed, nor are they used as supporting evidence.)

Frans van Rossum, then, who appears in the index as a Dutch musicologist born in 1940, might be able to provide some information about Marbot's existence. Since one could just as well ask Hildesheimer himself, and consulting van Rossum behind his back would be construed as double-dealing, I have refrained from doing so. But that was not the only reason for the decision. This book, as I noted at the start, should be judged from the perspective of a future reader, fifty or one hundred years from now. I also pointed out that my account of this biography's technique of representation aims neither at a verification of sources nor at an analysis of its contents.

The book is presented as a genuine biography of a previously unknown individual. His reality is concretized, indeed constituted, by his relationships with famous historical personages. Random checks have shown that the quotations from conversations, notes, and letters do not stand up to the test of authenticity. We can therefore conclude that the hero of the biography is an invented character, a suspicion strengthened by the absence of his closest friends and family from the index, if not quite as convincingly as by the absence of his own name. The inexactness of references to sources, correspondence, diaries—indeed, their nonexistence—may be regarded as a further clue, though it is as inconspicuous as ever. For a literary and generic evaluation of the book, such as the one we are undertaking, our point of departure must be that the hero is a fictitious character, in the sense that he is an artistic creation.

Every writer is of course free to dispose of poetry and truth, fiction and reality, as he pleases. It would be superfluous even to point to the historical novel, were it not for the fact that precisely this genre might yield the criteria for evaluating a work like *Marbot*. What happens to historical figures when they appear in novels? When Napoleon talks to Alexander I or Field Marshal Kutusov talks to Prince Bolkonsky (a fictitious character) in Tolstoy's *War and Peace*? Or when Hofrätin Charlotte Kestner, née Buff, has long conversations with F. W. Riemer, August von Goethe, and Adele Schopenhauer in Thomas Mann's *Lotte in Weimar*, and when even Goethe himself, in the book's famous interior monologue, reflects on Goethean problems, artistic works, and concerns? These are only some random examples, and they hardly need to be marshaled in order for us to see what happens to historical figures in the novel. It is just this: they become novelistic, fictional characters, who only differ from the other, invented characters in our awareness that they represent historical, and therefore real, individuals (though of course this is not clear in all situations for all readers). The writer here has complete poetic license. The freedom is absolute, since the historical novel, as a novel, can never function as a historical source, even if it is based on the most impeccable documentary material. The integration of this material, along with historical figures, into the fiction (and that implies its fictionalization, as we shall see below), means that it cannot be used in the service of reality or in the establishment of reality.

The reverse is true in the case of *Marbot*, and thus it is problematic. As far as I can see, *Marbot* constitutes a new literary form. Here, a fictitious figure—or let us be more cautious and call him a figure whose fictionality or reality is not clearly discernible—is presented as real. This is established with all the conventional biographical methods, and, as we should stress, in an authentic biographical style—that is, in the tone of a nonfictional, informative report. Fictional narrative is not invented narrative, but rather, in a theoretical sense, the production of a fiction. Fiction in this sense means appearance (*Schein*), the appearance of life: this is created when the characters are not only described as objects, but as if they were alive in the here and now; speaking, thinking, silent subjects or selves. The characters of novels (and dramas) are fictional because they are created as fictional subjects, so real historical figures also become fictional characters in a novel.[3]

At no point in the Marbot biography does Hildesheimer fall prey to the temptation of fictionalization—through dialogues or monologues, for example—nor is he even tempted by the *biographie romancée*, which might permit that approach. Even the imaginative fabrication of the incest scene deviates only from the conventions of biographical documentation, not from biographical narrative style. We have already noted that only quotations from letters, diaries, and so on enter this narrative, the documented and therefore legitimized utterances of the biographical hero. If we still feel compelled, on the basis of the evidence already mentioned, to regard Sir Andrew as a fictitious character, then we can only claim this to the extent that he is invented; but he is not created, as a fictitious novel hero. Here is where the book becomes problematic, and several different aspects and interpretive possibilities open up.

If the biography of a fictitious character claims to be that of a real person, then so long as that fact remains undetected, it can justifiably be regarded and used as a historical document or source. That the Marbot biography may be interpreted in this way is the result of a "trick"—Marbot has, so to speak, been integrated seamlessly into a circle of real people (and here we will not go into the artistry and expertise with which this has been accomplished, and which give the book its charm). Seen in this way, it can be described as a deception, even as a hoax, and this is perhaps even proclaimed by the Delacroix portrait that bears the title *Marbot*. But what is the purpose of this hoax perpetrated by the author? In order to get to the bottom of it, we have to go beyond the biographical contents of the book to its real essence, to what is at stake in it.

Marbot is an art lover and aesthetician. The spiritual and intellectual substance of the book lies in his analyses of paintings, quoted from his notebooks and letters: of Watteau's "Gilles," van Eyck's "Arnolfinis," Giorgione's "Self-Portrait," and many others. The psychology of art and of the artist evident in these analyses is, however, perceived and described as a precursor of the psychoanalytic school of art interpretation, and the author's interest in Marbot's personality largely derives from it. Of course there is also a suggestion that we should not take this interest too seriously—we read, for example, in the tour guide to Marbot Hall, published (supposedly) by the National Trust, that he was "the first to explore the artist's workings of the mind" (154), a conscientious citation from the original English text.[4] Obviously the central incest fiction suggests that what is meant by the inner workings of the artist has more to do with libido than anything else, and I see it as possible that the biographer is smiling in amusement, even if enigmatically, when he reports: "This does not mean, of course, that on a guided tour of Marbot Hall the sinful room will be pointed out as having provided the psychic preparation for this individual to understand the artistic spirit" (155). It is clearly stressed that it is not only the unconscious libidinous urges of the artist that must be explored, but also those of the aesthetician and of the viewer of art. Otherwise Marbot's writings would be robbed of "depth," "namely of that element that enables the viewer to empathize with the artist by revealing a deeper dimension within the artist, more precisely through the viewer's attempt to explore the libido of the artist" (153). If we are to take this somewhat abstruse prerequisite for art appreciation seriously, it is surely a piece of audacity to make not only the Oedipus complex, but its resolution, the incest itself, the precondition for the achievements of this aesthetician—for the author would surely not want to claim its universal validity.

But it is impossible to be sure whether one should take this seriously. It seems to me that one can hear the author's quiet laugh behind his presentation of the origins of Marbot's "anomaly," its first embers: the painting "The Origin of the Milky Way," supposedly by Tintoretto (fig. 6), in which Jupiter places his infant son Hercules, whom he fathered with Alcmene, on the breast of his wife Juno, who lies outstretched and naked. As we read on, we see how the six-year-old Andrew, who sees the painting in his grandfather's gallery and who questions his mother about it, is Oedipally predetermined.

What is the meaning and intention of this story, so confusing to the knowledgeable reader? Using all the legitimate techniques of the biographical account, not only does it mix fictional and real elements, but it thereby actually presents the fictional as real. It may be true that the libidinal theory of art interpretation is being parodied or ironized, but this can be no more than a suspicion, for parody is not made recognizable by parodistical or satirical elements of style. It also cannot be forgotten that Marbot's short life, ending in suicide, is perceived as tragic, not only because of the monstrous love entanglement but also because of his suffering, which is repeatedly stressed, and which is caused by the fact that fate led him to art criticism but not to the creation of art itself. This is one of the main reasons for our confusion when judging the biography as biography. A glance at Hildesheimer's biography of Mozart (1977) might lead us to conclude that the entire biographical genre is being parodied in *Marbot*, indeed taken ad absurdum, and that this is an attempt to demonstrate how a biographical myth is created. The Mozart biography attacks traditional biography, the "norms of mythologizing biography,"[5] and the cavalier attitude of biographers toward "the boundary between fact and conjecture,"[6] along with the way in which they present their subjective interpretations as objective observations. But in this respect, too, an interpretation of *Marbot* remains on the level of conjecture.

The (largely panegyric) press criticism[7] demonstrated that in fact *Marbot* provides no secure criteria for evaluation. On the one hand, for example, the biography was termed a "perfect satire and parody,"[8] but it was also praised for exactly the opposite reasons, as "the truth about an artistic figure."[9] Günter Blöcker, who used that last phrase as the title for his review, quotes an observation by Hildesheimer from his essay "The End of Fiction":[10] the writer's task is not to transform reality into fiction, but to transform fiction into reality. The latter, Blöcker thinks, can only be realized fully in a fictional biography.

Hildesheimer's aphorism can be put to good use to describe his fictional Marbot biography. Precisely what this work does is to turn reality into fiction rather than fiction into reality. Here truth is not to be understood in the vague sense of some inward, higher, deeper, or artistic truth, but rather, in Goethe's words, as "the truth of reality."[11] The problem with this work of fiction masquerading as a genuine biography is that the real individuals do not, as in the historical novel, become fictional, but that they consciously remain real. This is also the case for Sir Andrew Marbot, as long as the reader believes that he is a historical figure and that the biographer is following "the tracks of a forgotten man."[12] If its fictionality comes to light, however, then the fiction does not become truth; rather, it acquires a hint of illusion, of deception. The invented character Marbot does not, as has been claimed,[13] become an artistic figure in the sense of Thomas Mann's Doctor Faustus, the composer Adrian Leverkühn. In Mann's work another fictional character, the Leverkühn biographer Serenus Zeitblom, steps between the author and his creation; *Doktor Faustus* is a first-person narrative. When in 1929 Leverkühn composes the cantata

"Dr. Fausti Weheklag" using the twelve-tone technique of his contemporary Schönberg, this account by Zeitblom, himself a character in the novel,
does not perplex us in the same way as does the pronouncement by the
biographer Hildesheimer that Marbot anticipated libidinal theory. As soon
as we recognize Marbot as a fictional (that is, invented) character, such a
claim, in my opinion, dissolves into thin air, and what remains are only the
author's views of art and the art of interpretation—whether intended seriously or parodistically, or both at once—incarnated in a fictional figure.
The point is that this is a fictional character who is not portrayed as fictional, recognizable as such; he is instead presented as a real person. Herein
lie the problematics and stumbling blocks of the book *Marbot: A Biography*,
a book one might also term a theoretical paradox.

NOTES

This essay was translated by Catriona MacLeod.

1. Wolfgang Hildesheimer, *Marbot: A Biography* (Frankfurt: Suhrkamp, 1981). Page references in the text are to this edition. Translations are by Catriona Mac-Leod.

2. Another element of the Goethe montage is that Marbot figures as one of those young Englishmen who had courted Ottilie von Goethe, yet he does not correspond to any of these historical figures (Sterling, Taylor, Wymess, and so on).

3. For the concept of literary fiction, I refer readers to my book *Die Logik der Dichtung*, rev. ed. (Stuttgart: Klett, 1968), trans. Marilyn Rose, under the title *The Logic of Literature* (Bloomington: Indiana University Press, 1973).

4. An integral part of the presentation of a credible historical reality is the inclusion here and there, in parentheses, of individual sentences and passages from the letters and notebooks in the English "original."

5. Wolfgang Hildesheimer, *Mozart* (Frankfurt: Suhrkamp, 1977), 9.

6. Ibid.

7. The press was aware of the fictional nature of the biography, probably because of a television interview with Hildesheimer.

8. Uwe Schultz, *Stuttgarter Zeitung*, 14 October 1981.

9. *Frankfurter Allgemeine Zeitung*, 31 October 1981.

10. Wolfgang Hildesheimer, "The End of Fiction," *Merkur* 30, no. 1 (1976): 57–70.

11. "There are only a few human beings who possess the imagination to perceive the truth of reality." Letter to Eckermann, 25 December 1825. Ironically, this is from the same conversation Hildesheimer uses for his Goethe montage, with little regard for the truth of reality.

12. "A Sinful English Aristocrat: Wolfgang Hildesheimer on the Tracks of a Forgotten Man," *Die Welt*, 14 October 1981. Some have expressed amusement that this reviewer fell for the "trompe l'oeil" (François Bondy, *Weltwoche*, 13 January 1982). But it seems to me that precisely this review is the most subtle and that the reviewer (of whom we have no proof that he was not aware of the fictionality), Johannes Kleinstück, professor of English in Hamburg and author of the book *Die Erfindung der Realität* (Stuttgart: Klett-Cotta, 1980), has ironically accepted the invention of Marbot's reality as reality and now pretends to take it seriously.

13. Bondy, *Weltwoche*, 13 January 1982.

PART TWO

THE SUBJECT IN QUESTION:

THE NARRATION OF CONSCIOUSNESS

SEVEN

INTERPRETIVE STRATEGIES, INTERIOR

MONOLOGUES

Shlomith Rimmon-Kenan

T HE BROADEST conceptual framework for this paper is my belated realization that interpretation permeates many more analytic
activities than was usually believed in the heyday of structuralist
narratology. Todorov's 1966 distinction between the "sense" of an element, "its capacity to enter into correlation with other elements of the
same work and with the work as a whole," and the "interpretation" of an
element, its inclusion "in a system which is not that of the work but that
of the critic,"[1] seems to me now to be much more problematic than it did
when it was initially proposed. It seems problematic precisely because an
element does not "enter into correlation" by itself; it is the reader, the
critic, the theoretician who perceives (and sometimes creates) a correlation, and such a perception (or creation) is already an interpretation of
sorts. Culler's poststructuralist declaration that "to engage in the study of
literature is not to produce yet another interpretation of *King Lear* but to
advance one's understanding of the conventions and operations of an institution, a mode of discourse"[2] appears equally problematic, if only because the conventions and operations now seem to me not merely properties of a mode of discourse (literature, in Culler's statement) but also
characteristics of a mode or modes of interpretation (which is itself another
discourse). Put differently, the institution concerned is to a large extent an
institution of interpretation, regulating both the conventions of the discourse of literature proper and the strategies used in discourse about literature. (Deconstructionists will forgive me for maintaining the distinction
between the two.)

The infiltration of interpretation into what had seemed a separate activity, often called "description," is (for me) both distressing, because of the
doubt it raises as to the "objectivity" or "scientific nature" of narratological
research, and liberating, because it opens a new area for research, namely
the relations between narrative phenomena and interpretive strategies.
However, since the centrality of interpretation has already been forcefully
argued for by hermeneuticists, deconstructionists, and reader-oriented the-

oreticians, this paper will not attempt another head-on confrontation with
the issue at its most general level, but rather will select one of its aspects
for close examination. I would like to inquire into the interaction between
interpretive strategies and the interior monologue—a narrative phenomenon (and narratological concept) dear to Dorrit Cohn[3]—and I hope this
relatively limited inquiry will bear on some more general issues of description and interpretation. In order to make my discussion as concrete as possible, I have chosen to draw on Faulkner's *As I Lay Dying*,[4] a text consisting
of fifty-nine monologues by fifteen characters, each identified by name as a
section heading.

My argument is twofold: First, I argue that the conventions governing
interior monologues are informed by an interpretive stance about the
world and the relations between world and text. To support my argument
I shall use examples from Vardaman's first monologue—a discourse convenient for this purpose, since it adheres to most of the conventions of
interior monologues. Second, I argue that interpretive strategies inform
our understanding, or even our identification and labeling, of interior
monologues. This part of the argument will be illustrated by two monologues—one inwardly spoken by Darl, the other by Addie—both of which
deviate from some of the conventions underlying the form. My choice of
"deviant" monologues is not meant to suggest that interpretive strategies
are not at play when the conventions of interior monologue are adhered
to, but only that the instances of departure from conventions make the
need for interpretation more pressing, and hence foreground the whole
question more explicitly.

A brief recapitulation of some of the basic points in Cohn's masterful
Transparent Minds is a convenient starting point. First, let us remember
that she distinguishes between the interior monologue as an autonomous
form or genre and the interior monologue as a technique. As a form or
genre, the interior monologue is "a variant—or better, a limit-case—of
first-person narration."[5] *As I Lay Dying* seems to be in this category, consisting not of a single autonomous monologue but of a succession of such
monologues. However, as we shall see later, even this preliminary classification of Faulkner's text can be questioned when a different set of interpretive strategies is applied to it.

As a technique, the interior monologue can appear within the context of
either a third-person or a first-person narrative. Cohn enumerates three
modes for rendering consciousness within the context of third-person narratives: (1) psychonarration: the narrator's discourse about a character's
consciousness, (2) quoted monologue: a character's mental discourse, and
(3) narrated monologue: a character's mental discourse in the guise of the
narrator's discourse (*erlebte Rede, style indirect libre,* free indirect discourse).[6] It is the second of these techniques that is usually called "interior

monologue." Three parallel techniques can be found within the context of first-person narratives, and only a prefix is needed to signal the modified relationship of the narrator to the subject of his or her narration: (1) self-narration, (2) self-quoted monologue, and (3) self-narrated monologue. Again, it is the second technique that is most readily labeled "interior monologue."

According to Cohn, interior monologues create an effect of verisimilitude, which is itself based on a paradox typical of narrative fiction: "But this means that the special life-likeness of narrative fiction—as compared to dramatic and cinematic fictions—depends on what writers and readers know least in life: how another mind thinks, another body feels."[7]

It is the convention of psychological verisimilitude that underlies most of the narrative and stylistic features of interior monologues. This can be shown by listing the main features Cohn detects in autonomous interior monologues, accompanying them by examples from Vardaman's first monologue in *As I Lay Dying*. The list will be confined to features characteristic of autonomous monologues, because this is the category most relevant to Faulkner's text, but readers familiar with Cohn's book will no doubt remember that quite a few of them also characterize quoted and self-quoted interior monologues. In anticipation of my discussion of the interpretive stance informing the various features and conventions, I would like to divide the list into two related sets. Some narrative and stylistic features, it seems to me, reflect the assumption that interior monologues are a "mimesis of an unheard language."[8] Since unheard language is taken to be less-governed by chronological and logical constraints than audible language (language used for communication with others), its looser organization is usually conveyed by features like:

1. Temporal oscillations, moving freely among present thoughts, past memories, and future projections.[9] Thus, in Vardaman's first monologue there is a shift from "Then I begin to run" to past memories, rendered in the present tense—"I can hear the bed and her [his mother's] face and them and I can feel the floor shake when he [the doctor] walks on it that came and did it"—and then to thoughts about the near future: "If I jump I can go through it like the pink lady in the circus, into the warm smelling, without having to wait" (45).

2. Abbreviated or incomplete syntax,[10] as in the truncated sentence conveying Vardaman's suspicion that the doctor is responsible for his mother's death: "That came and did it when she was all right but he came and did it" (45).

3. An abundance of exclamations, invocations, invectives, curses;[11] for example, "The fat son of a bitch" (45), "You kilt my maw! . . . You kilt her!" (46).

4. Idiosyncratic vocabulary, or lexical opaqueness.[12] Vardaman's similes and metaphors clearly belong to this category; for example, "The trees look

like chickens when they ruffle out the cool dust on the hot days" (45), or the metaphor that recurs in many of his sections: "My mother is a fish" (67 and elsewhere). His synesthesias, near-synesthesias, and oxymorons are equally id-iosyncratic: "the warm smelling" (45), "then I vomit the crying" (45), "I can hear wood, silence" (47).

Whereas the foregoing set of features reflects a view of interior mono-logue as a mimesis of unheard language, the second set is governed by the assumption that interior monologue is language addressed to no one, or language in which speaker and listener coincide.[13] To preserve plausibility, speakers do not tell themselves things they already know. The result is two-fold:

1. An absence of expositional information, often coinciding with an avoid-ance of narrative and reportive tenses.[14] Thus, as we have seen earlier, Varda-man does not narrate his suspicion that the doctor is responsible for his moth-er's death, but refers to it as a given. Similarly, the text offers no expositional information about Vardaman's age, letting the reader infer it from the former's childish style.

2. A lack of explicitness in pronominal reference.[15] Since the speaker knows who he has in mind, he often refrains from specifying the designation of pro-nouns, for example "And now she [his mother] is getting so far ahead I cannot catch her" (45), "The life in him [the horse] runs under the skin, under my hand" (45).

My purpose in presenting this list is to point out the interpretive stance informing it. The assumptions underlying the first set of features can be enumerated somewhat pedantically as follows: (a) there is such a thing as inaudible language (although this assumption seems to some to be con-firmed by introspection, it is still an assumption, nor is introspection free of interpretation); (b) inaudible language is less coherent than audible speech; (c) the special quality of unheard language can be translated into audible speech (or writing); and (d) such a translation is best effected by the use of abbreviated syntax, lexical opaqueness, and so forth. Since in-audible language (if it exists) is something we do not hear in reality, the techniques used to convey it are based on interpretive assumptions, not on empirical observation. To quote Cohn once again: "Everyday reality offers both writers and readers an almost unlimited empirical basis for assessing the verisimilitude of dialogues in fiction. But how can a writer know, or a reader judge, the plausibility of a language for which no audible models exist in his non-literary experience?"[16] As this quotation shows, and as I have suggested earlier, verisimilitude is the key to most of the features gov-erning interior monologues. But verisimilitude is itself an interpretive stance, assuming that literature can (and does) represent reality and that it does so by translating certain lived phenomena by certain verbal character-istics.

Underlying the second set of features is the assumption that language can be addressed to the self, and behind it the more basic assumptions (a) that there is a correlation between voice (whether heard or unheard) and person—which is why the "I" in monologues is taken to refer to the speaker, and (b) that there is such a thing as self. Clearly, these are inter-pretations concerning both the state of affairs in the world and its manifes-tations in literature.

With the hope that I have sufficiently argued for the role of interpreta-tion in the conventions underlying interior monologues themselves, I now wish to pass to its centrality in discourse about interior monologues by readers, critics, and theoreticians. Obviously, interpretive strategies are at play both when talking about interior monologues which adhere to the conventions and in discussing those that depart from them. Nevertheless, as I have already suggested, the question of interpretation is foregrounded when dealing with the second type of monologue. I have therefore chosen one monologue which departs from a central linguistic norm and another which departs from the convention of psychological realism. The first is Darl's last monologue, unexpectedly cast in the third person, with strange reversions to the first. The second is Addie's only discourse in the novel, a monologue properly cast in the first person, but "improperly" spoken (or thought) by a non-person, a corpse. What interpretive strategies can be summoned to explain these departures from accepted norms, or to explain them away? And how are these texts to be described?

Darl

Being accustomed at this point to first-person monologues, the reader is startled when Darl's last section begins as follows: "Darl has gone to Jack-son. They put him on the train, laughing, down the long car laughing, the heads turning like the heads of owls when he passed" (202). Who speaks (or thinks) these lines? Can it be Darl, as in the other sections? But why would he speak (or think) about himself in the third person? Is the section a monologue by its title character, as the other sections are, or is it not? If not, who speaks the lines I quoted? Perhaps an extradiegetic (omniscient) narrator is talking here *about* Darl. This interpretation has its attractions, partly because it can anchor in a common source expressions that recur in various monologues. Thus, in the section preceding Darl's, Vardaman thinks: "Darl he went to Jackson is my brother Darl is my brother . . . Darl went to Jackson . . . He went to Jackson on the train" (199–200). Since images, motifs, and expressions get repeated in the discourses of the different characters, the reader infers the presence of an omniscient narrator be-hind the characters' monologues.[17] But if so, can the novel be described as a series of autonomous monologues, as I have done thus far, or is it rather a succession of *quoted* monologues, the narrator's presence being gathered not only through the repetitions but also through the very act of quotation and the name preceding each monologue? "A multiple point of view," says Richard Chase, "if it is multiple enough, of necessity becomes the point of view of the omniscient author."[18] And Bleikasten asks "Is the extreme mul-tiplicity of points of view not, in the end, omniscience in disguise?"[19]

Attractive though this possibility may be, it is insufficient to solve the problem of Darl's last section. Immediately after the opening third-person passage we find: " 'What are you laughing at?' I said" (202). Who is this "I"? Is he the extradiegetic narrator? And would an omniscient narrator speak *to* Darl, addressing him first as "you" and later by his name: "Is that why you are laughing, Darl?" (202)? Would Darl then answer the narrator, saying "Yes yes yes yes yes yes" (202)? If so, does this not make the narrator almost a character within the represented world (intradiegetic)? Or are these unexpected metalepses? To what end?

The reader's perplexity increases on reaching the end of Darl's section: "Darl is our brother, our brother Darl. Our brother Darl in a cage in Jack-son where, his grimed hands lying light in the quiet interstices, looking out he foams. 'Yes yes yes yes yes yes yes yes' " (203). Can this still be attrib-uted to an extradiegetic narrator? Is the narrator one of Darl's brothers? If so, he cannot be extradiegetic (or omniscient). And is the whole section consequently attributable to one of the brothers, not to a narrator outside the represented world? If this is the case, however, why is the section headed "Darl," rather than "Cash" or "Vardaman" or "Jewel" or all of them together? Moreover, if the speaker at the end is one of the brothers, or all the brothers together, how do they know what Darl does in Jackson? Surely they are not there with him.

It seems to me that instead of trying to justify the departure from the linguistic convention habitual in autonomous interior monologues by pos-iting an extradiegetic narrator or a brother-narrator, it may be more fruitful to accept the departure as such. Further interpretation is then needed to account for the aim or effect of this departure. Why does the novel deviate from its own convention by heading a section "Darl" and then letting him speak (or think) in the third person? Why the shift to the first person, and how is "our brother" to be understood? In my opinion, the departure from the linguistic norm enhances the other convention, that of psychological verisimilitude. The section renders the consciousness of a person gone mad, and it is therefore quite plausible to show him sometimes thinking of himself as another person ("he"), sometimes quoting an inner dialogue between two parts of his split self (" 'What are you laughing at?' I said" /

"Yes yes yes yes yes"), and sometimes experiencing his condition as his brothers would.

Whereas Darl's monologue departs from the linguistic convention in order to preserve psychological verisimilitude, it is precisely the latter that is rendered problematic by Addie's discourse.

Addie

A text entitled *As I Lay Dying* leads the reader to expect a first-person monologue by the "I" of the title. What the reader encounters, however, is a series of monologues by other characters and only one by the character assumed to be the main speaker/focalizer/actor. Moreover, Addie's discourse is located at a point in the text when she is no longer dying, as the title would have us think, but already dead. The initial effect of such an autobiographical account, spoken (or inwardly spoken) by a corpse is nonrealistic and strange. According to Cohn, "These concerns with psychological credibility stand in striking contrast to Faulkner's autonomous monologues: the self-address of a speechless idiot (Benjy in *The Sound and the Fury*) or of a dead woman (Addie in *As I Lay Dying*) are radical departures from monologic verisimilitude that are difficult to imagine in the context of a third-person novel, where we expect figural language to be as real as its fictional speaker."[20]

How are such radical departures to be treated? How can they be interpreted, described, or even classified? The various available strategies seem (perhaps superficially) to fall into two categories: those that help preserve the realism of the "deviant" monologue and those that do not (or not so overtly). In an attempt to preserve the realism of Addie's monologue, one may, for example, summon the narrative convention of anachrony (or temporal dislocation). Thus, the argument would run, although Addie's monologue appears in the text at a point posterior to her death, its status is that of an analepsis (flashback), and its chronological place in the story (as distinct from the text) precedes her death. Addie's discourse is thereby made to issue from a live character, it can be classified as a "normal" first-person interior monologue, and its psychological realism is preserved. This, of course, is a possible strategy, though its plausibility is somewhat limited in a text where the various monologues follow the chronological order of the story. It is perhaps for this reason that Cohn describes Addie's discourse as a radical departure from "monologic verisimilitude" rather than an adherence to it. In fact, by labeling Addie's discourse and its likes "unreal" or "anti-monologues,"[21] Cohn shows her desire to emphasize the psychological realism of the technique in general, though not in the specific monologues in question. The rule of "monologic verisimilitude," she argues, "is most convincingly proved by its exceptions."[22]

The attempt to make Addie's monologue comply with the norm of psychological realism and the attempt to confirm that norm by treating Addie's monologue as an exception seem opposed to each other. Nevertheless, underlying both is the concern with a correspondence between the text and reality-models. Sharper is the opposition between those interpretive strategies based predominantly on a correspondence between the text and "reality" and those that lean more heavily on congruence (or coherence) within the text itself. From this point of view, one can discern thematic or symbolic harmony between Addie's views of the relations between words and experience, and the very fact of her postmortem discourse.

Central to Addie's monologue is the emergent distinction between words and deeds. When she is pregnant with Cash, she realizes "that words are no good: that words don't ever fit even what they are trying to say at" (136). Feeling the difference between her immediate blood intimacy with Cash and her intercourse with Anse in the nights, she concludes that words are not only inadequate to express experience, but are also a poor substitute for it: "He [Anse] had a word, too. Love, he called it. But I had been used to words for a long time. I knew that that word was like the others: just a shape to fill a lack" (136). It is a lack, an absence of experience, that gives rise to words: "Sin and love and fear are just sounds that people who never sinned nor loved nor feared have for what they never had and cannot have until they forget the words" (133). Being so insignificant, words "go straight up in a thin line, quick and harmless" whereas "doing goes along the earth, clinging to it" (137). Deeds are characterized by presence and plenitude, whereas words are absences, just shapes to fill a lack.

There are, however, words that approach the fullness of deeds. In "the dark voicelessness" words become deeds (138), and it is to "the dark land talking the voiceless speech" that Addie often listens in the night. These voiceless words do not function as mediation, nor do they act as substitution; they are themselves deeds, performatives, and are thus opposed to "the other words that are not deeds, that are just gaps in people's lacks" (138). Full, voiceless words stand against empty, voiced frames for absences.

The very fact of Addie's monologue is in perfect agreement with her "theory." Words coming from a dead, absent source are a confirmation of the view that language is a substitute for lived reality. Addie's monologue thus shows, not only says, that words are merely shapes to fill a lack (the lack here being a literal lack of life). Thus, whereas Cohn's view implies that Addie speaks *although* she is dead, the present interpretation suggests that she speaks precisely *because* she is dead.

I have said above that the opposition between those interpretive strategies based predominantly on a correspondence with reality-models and those that lean more heavily on intratextual coherence is sharper than the contrast between the two strategies employed to preserve psychological realism. But even the sharper opposition can be attenuated when one realizes that on a higher level of abstraction its alternatives can both be seen as activating the same principle of congruence. Thus, the "higher" opposition is between the principle of congruence (whether in the form of iconicity or in that of internal coherence or unity) and the principle of incongruity (whether in terms of a representational rift between text and world or in terms of incoherences, contradictions, and nonunity within the text itself).

Looking at Addie's monologue with the principle of incongruity in mind, the correspondence between her view of words as mere frames for absences and the fact that she herself speaks only when she becomes a (present) absence can be subverted. Paradoxically, however, the subversion becomes a confirmation of another aspect of Addie's "theory." Thus if—as I suggested earlier—Addie speaks *because* she is dead and if her monologue actually does what it says, then it becomes characteristic of full voiceless words rather than of mere frames for absences. In other words, the performative status of Addie's monologue in relation to its content can be taken not only to confirm what she says about the vacuity of language, but also to undermine it, thus paradoxically exemplifying the plenitude of language through the conjunction of word and deed. Such a possibility also emerges—behind Addie's back, as it were—from the connotations of some of the words she uses in her derogatory statements about language: "I would think about his [Anse's] name until after a while I could see the word as a shape, a vessel, and I would watch him liquefy and flow into it like cold molasses flowing out of the darkness into the vessel, until the jar stood full and motionless: a significant shape profoundly without life like an empty door frame and then I would find that I had forgotten the name of the jar" (137). The overall tone is certainly negative, but note that the "vessel," the "jar," stands "full" and that the "shape," though "profoundly without life," is still "significant." Note also that "an empty door frame" usually opens onto a room or some other inhabited space, so that its emptiness can be said to signal the fullness of something beyond it. Similarly, Addie characterizes words as "quick and harmless," whereas "doing goes along the earth, clinging to it" (137). On the face of it, "harmless" emphasizes the ineffectiveness of words, especially in comparison to deeds. But in a context where Addie's main deed—an extramarital affair resulting in an illegitimate child—has harmful consequences, at least in some respects, harmlessness can become an unintended compliment. From a different, less conventional point of view, however, Addie's sin is her salvation, and the undermining view can itself be undermined.

If by unveiling such inconsistencies, the interpreter saves language (at least partly) from Addie's scathing criticism, and if by insisting on the performative nature of Addie's own monologue, the interpreter joins in her glorification of words-become-deeds, one has to remember that these words are enunciated by a corpse, so that their glorified voicelessness can also be "seen as pernicious, because it is the very image of deathliness and meaninglessness."[23] Thus the deconstructive reading that "saved" Addie's view of language can in turn be further deconstructed by another that condemns it.

But what does this deconstructive process do to the very status of Addie's discourse as interior monologue? Some may see in the self-subversion of Addie's language an indication of the presence of an additional voice: that of the extradiegetic narrator. Such an interpretation changes the status of Addie's section from that of an autonomous monologue to that of a quoted one—a possibility that also came up in an earlier stage of my discussion in connection with Darl's last discourse. On the other hand, the self-subversion detectable in Addie's monologue may be attributed to language as such, not to a specific voice undermining her behind her back. Indeed, Addie's monologue can be said to problematize the very notions of origin, mimetic voice, and so forth. According to Stephen M. Ross:

> *As I Lay Dying* both enhances and challenges mimetic voice by disrupting the expected correlations between voice and person. The features of the discourse that lead the reader to identify and to characterize speakers operate ambiguously for some utterances, so that we may be unable to specify an appropriate speaker, or we may be forced to acknowledge two or more possible speakers (usually on different discursive levels) for a single utterance. In this way the problematical status of verbal representation in general and of mimetic voice in particular becomes a crucial part of what this novel signifies.[24]

Such an approach challenges some of the basic interpretive assumptions I outlined earlier. Clearly, a questioning of mimetic voice leads to a questioning of the very notion of interior monologue,[25] thereby rendering unnecessary a discussion of the various interpretive strategies used to explain departures from the norms which govern it. This, however, is a subject for another paper.

NOTES

1. Tzvetan Todorov, "Les catégories du récit littéraire," *Communications* 8 (1966): 125–51 (my translation).

2. Jonathan Culler, *The Pursuit of Signs: Semiotics, Literature, Deconstruction* (London and Henley: Routledge and Kegan Paul, 1981), 5.

3. Dorrit Cohn, *Transparent Minds: Narrative Modes for Presenting Consciousness in Fiction* (Princeton: Princeton University Press, 1978). In fact, Cohn has valuable reservations concerning the term itself (see, for example, 13, 15), but decides to use it nevertheless (sometimes with qualifying adjectives, as in "quoted interior monologue") because it has become "solidly entrenched in theoretical discourse."

4. William Faulkner, *As I Lay Dying* (Harmondsworth: Penguin, 1972). All references in the text are to this edition.

5. Cohn, *Transparent Minds*, 15.

6. Ibid., 14.

7. Ibid., 5–6.

8. Ibid., 90. Note that Cohn objects to the view of interior monologues as presenting preverbal mental states (77–78, 86).

9. Ibid., 219.

10. Ibid., 94, 250.

11. Ibid., 92, 223.

12. Ibid., 94, 250.

13. Ibid., 225, 226.

14. Ibid., 221, 223, 226.

15. Ibid., 223.

16. Ibid., 89.

17. Pauline E. Degenfelder, "Yoknapatawphan Baroque: A Stylistic Analysis of *As I Lay Dying*," *Style* 8, no. 2 (1973): 134, 145–46. Degenfelder gives several examples of motifs and expressions that recur in various monologues.

18. Richard Chase, *The American Novel and Its Tradition* (Garden City, New York: Doubleday and Company). Quoted by Degenfelder, "Yoknapatawphan Baroque," 131.

19. André Bleikasten, *Faulkner's "As I Lay Dying"* (Bloomington: Indiana University Press, 1973), 63.

20. Cohn, *Transparent Minds*, 77.

21. Ibid., 77.

22. Ibid., 76.

23. John T. Matthews, *The Play of Faulkner's Language* (Ithaca and London: Cornell University Press, 1982), 42.

24. Stephen M. Ross, " 'Voice' in Narrative Texts: The Example of *As I Lay Dying*," *PMLA* 94 (1979): 305.

25. This, indeed, is the direction in which Ross's article develops.

EIGHT

CONSONANT AND DISSONANT CLOSURE IN
DEATH IN VENICE AND *THE DEAD*

Franz K. Stanzel

A S SO OFTEN, Lewis Carroll pinpointed the problem long before literary theory became concerned with it: "Begin with the beginning," the King said, very gravely, "and go on till you come to the end: then stop."[1]

It is, of course, the king's nonchalant presupposition that "the end" requires no further definition that encapsulates one of the most intractable problems of narrative theory: what is a proper ending of a story, and what does it do to the reader? Since Frank Kermode's *Sense of an Ending* (1967), the study of endings in novels and short stories has steadily grown in importance; it is still flourishing.[2] That the shorter forms of fiction, the tale and the short story, have thereby also received their full share of attention reflects a recognition of the structural connection between the brevity of the narrative and its specific kind of closure.[3] In the shorter narratives the ending is more obviously tied to the beginning since the story usually passes rapidly from the beginning to the middle, with its crisis and peripeteia, and on to the ending. Gertrude Stein, in her inimitable way, has chiseled this observation into the following block of language. Sherwood Anderson's short story "Hands" has, she says, "a beginning an ending an ending and an ending."[4] That was meant as a criticism. For once we find Stein on the side not of the innovators but of the traditionalists, insisting on a story having a proper beginning, a middle, and an ending. However, this does not diminish the aptness of her formula as a definition of a specific structural element of the short story, in particular of the short short story.

In 1966 Alan Friedman described *The Turn of the Novel* as marking the transition from the traditional novel, in which experience is closed, to the new novel, represented for Friedman by Hardy, Conrad, Forster, and D. H. Lawrence, where experience is shown to be essentially unlimited, whereas the traditional novel "leans toward a well-closed final chapter."[5] It is interesting to note that Friedman finds it difficult to define the openness of the new novel. He finally has to resort to metaphor: "Battered by experience, compelled toward a wider and wider moral experience, central selves in the modern novel achieve no restricting moral integration. The openness is unrelieved."[6] In this Friedman goes further than Robert M. Adams, who in *Strains of Discord: Studies in Literary Openness* (1958) defined literary openness as the form of a novel that leaves at least one conflict unresolved.[7] From now on "open" and "closed" become critical terms widely used in narrative theory and criticism, with "openness" remaining by far the more recalcitrant concept requiring ever-new definition, a characteristic the concept evidently has inherited from the discussion in the fine arts, where it made its first appearance in Heinrich Wölfflin's *Kunstgeschichtliche Grundbegriffe* (1915) as one element in the opposition "geschlossen/offen."[8]

Since Alan Friedman, the discussion of the ending of a novel or a story has centered more and more on the effect it has on the reader's expectation to see the artistic structure of a work rounded off at the end, an expectation that ultimately derives from a deep-seated desire in man to find order, coherence, and sense where the world seems to offer disorder, incoherence, and contingency. Frank Kermode's *Sense of an Ending*, which takes Jean-Paul Sartre and his novel *La nausée* as its point of departure, has explored this subject in depth from a largely philosophical perspective.

Almost simultaneously with Kermode's book, Barbara Herrnstein Smith's *Poetic Closure: A Study of How Poems End* (1968) appeared. Whereas Kermode's approach is philosophical, Smith's is psychological: to be more exact, it is indebted to the psychology or physiology of perception. This makes her general considerations, even though her main concern is closure in poems, also relevant to our study. One general point of her thesis in particular deserves to be mentioned here. The reader's sense of the closure of a poem or story is largely a function of the perception of the structure of the *whole* poem or story.[9] Its effect, therefore, also depends on the individual reader's experience of the whole poem or story. Most of Smith's study is concerned with sixteenth- and seventeenth-century poetry. But there are two concluding chapters on "Closure and Anti-Closure in Modern Poetry" and a "Coda: Beyond Closure." In much modern poetry, as Smith notices, there is an apparent tendency toward "anticlosure,"[10] which on first sight appears to present an analogy to the open endings in stories by Chekhov, Joyce, Katherine Mansfield, Anderson, Hemingway, and others. Many of these stories do not conclude properly, but seem merely to stop. To apply to the ending of these stories the term "anticlosure" could, however, be misleading, because it would suggest that this kind of abrupt ending is not so tightly integrated into the whole structure of the story as when the ending is formed by an event traditionally used to mark finality, such as, for instance, the death of the main character, or by a proper denouement of the plot. I shall, therefore, continue to use the traditional distinction between closed and open endings of stories. It will soon become apparent how problematic these designations, and in particular the concept of an open ending, in fact are.

I shall concentrate on some of those narrative devices that integrate the ending of a story into its overall structure. They can be found both in stories with a closed ending and in ones with an open ending. My treatment of the example of a story with a firmly closed ending, Thomas Mann's "Death in Venice," will be rather brief since here I can rely for the main part of my argument on Dorrit Cohn's essay "The Second Author of 'Der Tod in Venedig.' "[11] This will leave space for a more detailed examination of "The Dead" by Joyce as an example of a story with an apparently open ending.

Of the many narrative devices that contribute to the integration of the ending into the total structure of a story, I should like to consider one that has been neglected because of its almost subliminal way of affecting the reader: the relationship of complicity or antagonism between narrator and protagonist. This relationship is likely to be ignored particularly in stories from which the figure of the narrator has virtually disappeared or where the narrator has merged with the main character to such an extent that only a very close analysis of the narrative situation can reveal any discrepancies between the views and values of the two. The fact that this relationship is rarely of a static, and more often of a dynamic, nature further complicates matters. Change in that relationship, except where it is wholly erratic, making description practically impossible, can take place along either divergent or convergent lines. My thesis is that the lines of divergence or convergence between the views of narrator and protagonist structurally connect the ending with the main part of a story. Such an observation will probably reveal less in a story like "Death in Venice," with its firmly closed ending, than in a story with an open ending. The reference to "Death in Venice" will, however, serve an important comparative purpose. The comparison with "The Dead" will highlight two crucial aspects of that story: the function of the narrator in evaluating the behavior of the main character, and the meaning of the apparently open ending.

In *Transparent Minds: Narrative Modes for Presenting Consciousness in Fiction* (1978), Dorrit Cohn distinguishes between "consonant and dissonant" relations between narrators and their protagonists, a distinction seminal here:

> In psychological novels, where fictional consciousness holds center stage, there is considerable variation in the manner of narrating this consciousness. These variations range between two principal types: one is dominated by a prominent narrator who, even as he focuses intently on an individual psyche, remains emphatically distanced from the consciousness he narrates; the other is

mediated by a narrator who remains effaced and who readily fuses with the consciousness he narrates.[12]

Cohn goes on to illustrate "dissonant psychonarration" with reference to "Death in Venice" and "consonant psychonarration" using the example of *A Portrait of the Artist as a Young Man*. The distinction here introduced is mainly a typological one, as becomes evident from Cohn's comparison of her terms with those of other typologies of narrative.[13] The whole potentiality of this opposition for the description of the dynamics of the narrator-protagonist relationship was revealed in Cohn's later article, "The Second Author of 'Der Tod in Venedig.'" Here she can show how the dissonant type of psychonarration used by Mann offers the narrator room for maneuvers by which he manages to extricate himself gradually from the initial fascination exerted on him by the artist-protagonist Aschenbach. The process of increasing dissonance between the mind of the narrator and that of Aschenbach is punctiliously traced in the comments, most of them explicit but some of them implicit, with which the narrator marks Aschenbach's aesthetic and moral "progress" during the Venetian adventure that terminates in his death. At the beginning, the narrator's attitude to Aschenbach is, as Cohn points out, "eventually sympathetic, respectful, even reverent."[14] Consonance dominates this part of the tale, including the report of the first stirrings of homoerotic feeling in Aschenbach for the boy Tadzio and Aschenbach's creative endeavor to transmute this affection of mind and body creatively with the assistance of Plato's theory of beauty. Much of this (end of chapter 3 and beginning of chapter 4) is, as Cohn says, narrated significantly in free indirect style,[15] the form of presenting consciousness that allows a wider range of oscillation in the attitude of the narrator to his protagonist than any other narrative mode. Here, free indirect style is used to offer narratorial support to Aschenbach's eroto-aesthetic ruminations without, however, giving them unreserved approval, or as Cohn puts it with slightly different emphasis, "The employment of free indirect style, in the absence of other distancing devices, points rather to a momentary "sharing" of Aschenbach's inner experience by the narrator—as though he were himself temporarily on vacation from his post as moral preceptor."[16] This temporary vacation by the narrator of his post as moral preceptor is one of the first signs indicating that the so far predominantly consonant attitude of the narrator to the protagonist is gradually becoming modulated into dissonance. This happens about halfway through Aschenbach's Venetian experience, when the Apollonian phase of his enthrallment by the boyish charms of Tadzio begins to descend into Dionysian excess. From here to the end, dissonance prevails. The narrator, who now clearly stands for "discipline, dignity, decorum, achievement and sobriety,"[17] seems to move further and further away from his protagonist, who is bent on an impassioned course toward self-destruction. Closure in "Death in Venice" is marked in two ways: on the story level by the death of the protagonist and on the discourse level by the ultimate divergence of the lines of inner development of narrator and protagonist.

This summary cannot do justice to the many subtle qualifications Cohn brings to bear on her reading of the story, questioning, among other things, how far the reader will be prepared to follow the narrator's harsh judgment of Aschenbach's Venetian progress, or, an even more complex matter, to what extent we can equate the narrator's judgment with that of the author.[18]

Dorrit Cohn's example of consonance between narrator and protagonist is Joyce's *Portrait of the Artist as a Young Man*:

> Joyce's *Portrait* shares a number of features with Mann's *Death in Venice*. Both protagonists are artists—one on the rise, the other on the wane—whose intense mental lives range from high rationality to surreal vision. Both works are focused on these central figures, invariably adopting their angle of vision in the presentation of the world surrounding them. Yet the narration of the protagonists' consciousness differs in the two works: in sharpest contrast to Mann's narrator, Joyce's cannot be grasped as a separate entity within the text. His most striking characteristic is, in fact, that he is ungraspably chameleonic. He persistently adapts his style to the age and mood of his hero, coloring it with baby-talk in the beginning section, with the bathos of the budding artist-in-revolt at the end, and in between with a spectrum of psychological states and developmental stages.[19]

The narrator's stance of "chameleonic" noninterference is, however, not maintained throughout the novel. Joyceans have in fact been divided, as Cohn realizes,[20] about the amount and the degree of narratorial interference in this novel. The discussion as a rule focuses chiefly on whether certain stylistic and tonal qualities of the text, in themselves difficult to evaluate, are to be regarded as devices used by the narrator in his inclination to distance himself from the protagonist's adolescent moods and judgments. It is curious that the one objectively verifiable fact signaling the author-narrator's distance from Stephen's self-assessment, the shift from figural third-person narration to first-person narration in the final diary section, has not been given the consideration it deserves. For the final diary section with which *Portrait* closes, the distinction between consonance and dissonance becomes irrelevant. The shift from third to first person reveals a refusal on the part of the narrator to be in any way, even in the most covert manner, implicated in Stephen's grandiloquent manifesto with which he announces the rebel-artist's departure into exile. This shift in the narrative mode from third to first person brings about a closure of the novel from which the narrator of the main part has absconded altogether. The shift of the narrative situation at the end of *Portrait* must be interpreted as the definitive parting of ways between the main narrator and the protagonist.

Joyce's story "The Dead," from *Dubliners*, seems better suited than *Portrait* to illustrate a narrative in which the ultimate consonance of narrator and protagonist determines the ending of the story. "The Dead" in its later parts is also focused mainly on one character. The narrative situation, which in the earlier sections occasionally still reveals the presence of an authorial narrator (nowhere, however, so obviously as in "Death in Venice"), later tends to become figural, focusing more and more on Gabriel Conroy's thoughts and observations. Here the narrator keeps in the background, from where he intrudes into the story only rarely and inconspicuously. However discreet these intrusions by the narrator may be, taken together they reveal the development of his attitude to Gabriel. In the opening and in the main part of the story, a mildly dissonant note is often to be heard. The ending, on the other hand, containing Gabriel's great epiphany ("The time had come for him to set out on his great journey westward")[21] brings total consonance, a consonance that reveals its significance only if it is regarded also in its closural function. With closure thus being determined by consonance, "The Dead" forms an illuminating contrast to "Death in Venice," with its dissonant ending.

Before I turn to the much-discussed ending of "The Dead," let me review some instances from the earlier parts of the story that suggest a difference between the narrator's and Gabriel's evaluations of the Morkan party. Nowhere is the dissonance shrill, yet it cannot be missed. Gabriel, who is shown to be much occupied with the notes he has jotted down for his dinner speech, asks himself, for instance, whether a quotation from Robert Browning he had intended to use would not be "above the heads of his hearers," and he finally concludes that "their grade of culture differed from his" (179). The narrator, it is clear, wants to make the reader see the streak of cultural arrogance that runs through much of what Gabriel thinks and says during the evening. Gabriel's retort to the nationalist taunts of Miss Ivors also sounds disproportionately ill-humored: "I'm sick of my own country, sick of it!" (189). The echo of this gives to his later praise of Irish hospitality, as represented by his hostesses, the Morkan sisters, a somewhat rhetorical ring: it sounds too artfully contrived to be entirely convincing. In this context the careful reader will also notice a very subtle trick of Joyce's narrative strategy: he reserves the one substantial proof of the hospitality praised, the description of the richly laden dinner table, for the narrator, thus denying it to Gabriel, who, presiding at one end of the table, would occupy the natural vantage point from which to perform such an act of silent homage to the hostesses. That we are in fact given the authorial narrator's view of the sisters' cornucopia is evident. Gabriel's mind would not have bothered to give us such a detailed enumeration of all the good things assembled there: "two little minsters of jelly, red and yellow bunches of purple raisins and peeled almonds . . . a solid rectangle of Smyrna figs," and so forth (196–97).

The narrative situation of the main part of the story is, indeed, characterized by frequent, unobtrusive shifts between authorial and figural presentation, the external perspective of the narrator passing imperceptibly into that of Gabriel and back again to the authorial narrator's point of view. Such a narrative mode greatly facilitates variations of tone, signaling either distance or empathy between protagonist and narrator.

At the end of the party, in the "Distant Music" scene (209–10), for the first time the focus of presentation is firmly fixed on Gabriel, when in the general bustle of leave-taking he suddenly sees his wife Gretta in an emotionally intensified aura of beauty, and with sensuous anticipation of further "moments of their secret life together" (213). These feelings still dominate Gabriel's mood when he and Gretta arrive in their room at the Gresham Hotel. Here attention must be drawn to two seemingly trivial details. The first is Gabriel's condescending way of talking to the porter: " 'And I say' . . . pointing to the candle, 'you might remove that handsome article, like a good man' " (216). The second is when Gabriel, crossing the room to comfort his wife, who has just recalled the "Liebestod" of a youthful lover of hers many years ago with such intensity that she has suffered an emotional breakdown, takes time in passing in front of the mirror to catch a glimpse of himself as reflected in the cheval-glass, noticing with approval "in full length, his broad, well-filled shirt front . . . and his glimmering gilt-rimmed eyeglasses" (218). These two occasions are last echoes of the earlier dissonance between narrator and protagonist. From here on to the end of the story, the lines along which the two consciousnesses (the narratorial and the figural) move converge, achieving the complete consonance of the two minds that is the distinctive mark of the closure of this story.

Let us look more closely at this process in the final part of "The Dead." It is the section that contains Joyce's most famous epiphany. Gabriel's eyes pass from Gretta, who after her breakdown has fallen asleep on the bed, to her clothes, thrown carelessly over a chair and on the floor. It is clearly Gabriel's perception that turns this tumble of Gretta's clothes into a metonymic image of the riot of sensual emotions in him a moment earlier and of his disengagement from this emotion now:

> She was fast asleep. Gabriel, leaning on his elbow, looked for a few moments unresentfully on her tangled hair and half-open mouth, listening to her deep-drawn breath. . . .
> His eyes moved to the chair over which she had thrown some of her clothes. A petticoat string dangled to the floor. One boot stood upright, its limp upper

fallen down: the fellow of it lay upon its side. He wondered at his riot of emotions of an hour before. (222)

In this passage the narratorial voice has totally merged with the figural voice. The consonance attained here, in which both minds seem to be perfectly tuned to each other, prepares the reader for the final paragraph with the description of the snow falling all over Ireland. In the very last sentences, the voice of the narrator begins gradually to dominate the unison of the two voices, finally giving to the epiphanous all-over-Ireland snowfall a significance transcending Gabriel's capacity to understand the meaning of the wintry scene:

> A few light taps upon the pane made him turn to the window. It had begun to snow again. He watched sleepily the flakes, silver and dark, falling obliquely against the lamplight. The time had come for him to set out on his journey westward. Yes, the newspapers were right: snow was general all over Ireland. It was falling on every part of the dark central plain, on the treeless hills, falling softly upon the Bog of Allen and, farther westward, softly falling into the dark mutinous Shannon waves. It was falling, too, upon every part of the lonely churchyard on the hill where Michael Furey lay buried. It lay thickly drifted on the crooked crosses and headstones, on the spears of the little gate, on the barren thorns. His soul swooned slowly as he heard the snow falling faintly through the universe and faintly falling, like the descent of their last end, upon all the living and the dead. (223)

This last passage of "The Dead" at first continues the unmarked narrative tone of the preceding paragraphs. After a few sentences, however, its style is modulated toward a more poetic level. The poetics of alliteration, repetition, and variation in the words "falling softly" and "faintly falling" gives to these lines an authorial validity that reinforces and underlines the heightened significance of this much-discussed ending. Were we to read it only as a presentation of Gabriel's personal awareness of the moment, comparable to his perception of the tumble of Gretta's clothes, our understanding of the epiphany would have to be bound by Gabriel's limited horizon of awareness. Such a reading would leave us confronted with the traditional dilemma: what does the all-over-Ireland snowfall symbolize? Death, which takes survey of all the world, or a rebirth, a new beginning, an awakening to a new life of social responsibility, of an enlarged sense of humanity? If, however, we can hear the authorial voice becoming audible over Gabriel's inner voice, which became silent when his "soul swooned slowly," then it will be easier for us to accept the mysterious paradox that the snowfall is a symbol at once of death and of rebirth. The final epiphany, which would have been a static glimpse if confined to Gabriel's consciousness, turns into a dramatic disclosure of the ambivalence of Gabriel's situation. In such a reading of the final epiphany of "The Dead," consonant closure figuratively takes the deathly coldness away from the snow falling all over Ireland and makes snow a symbol of warmth and protection covering the still raw parts of Gabriel's newly expanded consciousness as well as the last traces of the old Adam in him.

A similar case where a character's epiphany is heightened by a consonant narrative voice occurs at another much-discussed ending. In Kafka's *Trial*, as Dorrit Cohn has shown,[22] Josef K.'s thoughts only moments before his "execution" are temporarily superseded by those of the narrator, who in full consonance with Josef K. develops his sense of helplessness into a broader realization of the plight of human existence than is possible for Josef K. in these last moments of his life. The one sentence in which this becomes most clearly evident, "Logic is doubtless unshakable, but it cannot withstand a man who wants to go on living," is firmly embedded in a syntactic context characterized by free indirect style or narrated monologue:

> His glance fell on the top storey of the house adjoining the quarry. With a flicker as of a light going up, the casements of a window there suddenly flew open, a human figure, faint and insubstantial at that distance and that height, leaned abruptly far forward and stretched both arms still farther. Who was it? A friend? A good man? Someone who sympathized? Someone who wanted to help? Was it one person only? Or was it mankind? Was help at hand? Were there arguments in his favour that one had overlooked? Of course there must be. Logic is doubtless unshakable, but it cannot withstand a man who wants to go on living. Where was the Judge whom he had never seen? Where was the High Court, to which he had never penetrated? He raised his hands and spread out all his fingers.[23]

Cohn comments on this passage: "This is the moment of his novel where Kafka perhaps comes closest to 'giving away' the existential implications of *The Trial*, or at least the fact that the work *has* existential implications. And it is not coincidental that this moment takes the form of a narrated monologue: had it been quoted directly, signaled as K.'s mental language, fenced off from the surrounding narration, it could not have implicated the narrator (and the reader) in K.'s anguish to nearly the same degree."[24]

Had these thoughts in extremis of Josef K. been quoted directly (that is, rendered in the fist-person form of the interior monologue), they could not have implicated the narrator in the same way. That is exactly what we found with regard to Gabriel's thoughts that conclude "The Dead." The significance of such a closural procedure is unexpectedly highlighted by the presentation of the last scene in John Huston's film version of "The Dead." At the end of the film we hear Gabriel recite a rewritten first-person form of the story's final paragraph, with the epiphany. The first person is heard as voice-over while a series of snow-covered landscapes is projected onto the screen. This shift from third to first person reduces the dimension of meaning from near-universal validity to Gabriel's subjectively limited personal view. Such a procedure, probably induced by the necessities of the camera art, throws light on the difficulty, if not the impossibility, of rendering in the medium of film the precarious equilibrium between figural and narrative voices achieved in the story through free indirect style. Consonance and dissonance as corollaries of free indirect style in a predominantly figural narrative situation thus stand revealed as features of presentation specific to the narrative genre in literature.

Once again, free indirect style has proved to be perhaps the most supple of all the elements of narrative grammar. It offers the author a wider scale of choices between various degrees of consonance (or dissonance) between narrator and protagonist than any other form for presenting thought or consciousness. It facilitates the transitions between narratorial and figural thoughts, often profoundly affecting in particular our reading of so structurally crucial a part as the ending of a story. The traditional distinction between closed and open endings, which so often proves unsatisfactory when applied to the Chekhov-Mansfield-Joyce-Hemingway type of story, can be given a new critical edge if it is amplified by the consonance/dissonance distinction. Our reading of "Death in Venice" would have to be revised drastically if the death of Aschenbach were presented by a consonant narrative voice, and our understanding of the final epiphany of "The Dead" would require a similarly drastic revision if it were presented by a dissonant narrative voice.

NOTES

1. Lewis Carroll, *Alice's Adventures in Wonderland* and *Through the Looking Glass* (Toronto: Bantam, 1981), 93.

2. For a comprehensive bibliography the reader is referred to the most recent study of endings in the novel: Barbara Korte, *Techniken der Schlußbildung im Roman: Eine Untersuchung englisch- und deutschsprachiger Romane*, Europäische Hochschulschriften, Reihe 14, Angelsächsische Sprache und Literatur 148 (Frankfurt: Lang, 1985).

3. Cf. John Gerlach, *Toward the End: Closure and Structure in the American Short Story* (Tuscaloosa: University of Alabama Press, 1985), and Helmut Bonheim, *The Narrative Modes: Techniques of the Short Story* (Cambridge, England: D. S. Brewer, 1982), which contains two chapters on "How Stories End" (118–64). Nearly all studies of the specific character of the short story since Edgar Allan Poe have discussed the endings of short stories.

4. Gerlach, *Toward the End*, 99.

5. Alan Friedman, *The Turn of the Novel: The Transition to Modern Fiction* (London: Oxford University Press, 1966), 36.

6. Ibid., 34

7. Cf. Robert M. Adams, *Strains of Discord: Studies in Literary Openness* (Ithaca: Cornell University Press, 1958), 13.

8. Oskar Walzel first applied Wölfflin's concepts of "offene Form" and "geschlossene Form" to literary texts in his *Wechselseitige Erhellung der Künste: Ein Beitrag zur Würdigung kunstgeschichtlicher Begriffe* (Berlin: Reuther and Reichard, 1917). See also Ulrich Weisstein, "Literature and the Visual Arts," in *Interrelations of Literature*, ed. Jean-Pierre Barricelli and Joseph Gibaldi (New York: Modern Language Association of America, 1982), 251–77, 256.

9. Cf. Barbara Herrnstein Smith, *Poetic Closure: A Study of How Poems End* (Chicago: University of Chicago Press, 1968), 4.

10. Ibid., 237.

11. Dorrit Cohn, "The Second Author of 'Der Tod in Venedig'," in: *Probleme der Moderne: Studien zur deutschen Literatur von Nietzsche bis Brecht: Festschrift für Walter Sokel*, ed. Benjamin Bennett et al. (Tübingen: W. Niemeyer, 1983), 223–45.

12. Dorrit Cohn, *Transparent Minds: Narrative Modes for Presenting Consciousness in Fiction* (Princeton: Princeton University Press, 1978), 26.

13. Cf. ibid., 275, n. 10.

14. Cohn, "Second Author," 226.

15. Dorrit Cohn has suggested calling this stylistic phenomenon, which has become so important a form of modern narrative discourse, "narrated monologue." Unfortunately, this has not succeeded in replacing the traditional "free indirect style," a term as opaque as the corresponding German term "erlebte Rede." Cohn introduced the term "narrated monologue" in what Helmut Bonheim recently called the "now classic essay" on free indirect style. Dorrit Cohn, "Narrated Mono-

logue: Definition of a Fictional Style," *Comparative Literature* 18 (1966): 97–112.

16. Cohn, "Second Author," 231–32.

17. Ibid., 227.

18. Ibid., 234, 242–43.

19. Cohn, *Transparent Minds*, 30.

20. See Cohn's notes, *Transparent Minds*, 276.

21. James Joyce, *Dubliners: Text, Criticism, and Notes*, ed. Robert Scholes and A. Walton Litz (New York: Viking, 1969), 223. The quotations that follow are from this edition.

22. Cf. Cohn, *Transparent Minds*, 122–23.

23. Franz Kafka, *The Trial*, quoted in Cohn, *Transparent Minds*, 122–23.

24. Cohn, *Transparent Minds*, 122–23.

NINE

IDENTITY BY METAPHORS:

A PORTRAIT OF THE ARTIST AND

TONIO KRÖGER

John Neubauer

ONCE UPON A TIME, fictional narrators freely dispensed moral, aesthetic, and philosophical insights for readers who readily attributed these to the authors. But Henry James, Virginia Woolf, James Joyce, and other modernist followers of Flaubert muzzled their narrators and dissociated themselves from the narrative voice.

What are we to do, then, with highly autobiographical narratives that are told in the third person? If we resist reading them as autobiographies, the knowledge that they incorporate experiences of the author exerts a continued (and seldom acknowledged) pressure to read the story as the *narrator's* autobiographical reflection, even if the protagonist is addressed in the third person. Though we no longer read the story as the *author's* life, we may be led to another sort of reductive reading in which the narrator is merged with the protagonist, at the cost of overlooking the interplay between them.

Joyce's *Portrait of the Artist as a Young Man* and Thomas Mann's *Tonio Kröger* are third-person narratives of this kind—narratives that start with the author's personal experiences but elaborate on them in terms of an interplay between the narrator and the protagonist.[1] They do so, however, in very different ways, for they employ altogether different narrators and they resolve the protagonists' adolescent crises in diametrically opposed ways. I suggest that these different narrators and their differing kinds of interplay with their respective protagonists may be profitably read in terms of the metaphors that the narrators and the protagonists employ in their discourses, for this way we can establish their identity internally, without reference to authorial biography and intention. I conclude, however, that the notorious problems of narrative perspective and irony may be resolved only if we transgress the boundaries of the text—not by appealing to *authorial* biography and intention, but by using the *readers'* historical perspective on language use.

Third-person narratives may foreground the protagonist's or the narrator's discourse. In eighteenth- and nineteenth-century narratives like Fielding's *Tom Jones*, the minds of fictional characters were totally "transparent" to their narrators. Modernist narratives tend to restrict and narrow the narrator's insights. In the new narrative genre about adolescents, for instance, insight is usually offered only into the adolescent mind (frequently only into that of the protagonist); adult minds remain closed books. Nevertheless, such narratives seldom follow the modernist demand that the narrator totally refrain from commentary and judgments. In Mann's *Tonio Kröger* or Musil's *Törless*, the narrators freely comment, both directly and indirectly, on their protagonists, and this is what constitutes the heart of narrative tension and irony. Joyce's *Portrait* is told, to be sure, by a faceless, "chameleonic" narrator who blends with the protagonist, but even he is deprived of the luxury of the dramatic writer, who "pares his fingernails" (215) while dialogue and action occur onstage.[2]

While such narrators assume a position of intellectual superiority with respect to their adolescent protagonists, their superiority cannot compare with Fielding's narrator in *Tom Jones*. Irony and retrospective nostalgia intermingle in their discourse so ambiguously that their balance becomes, as in the case of *A Portrait*, a matter of interpretive dispute. The adolescent protagonist is naive and confused but more intense and authentic than the adult narrator, and if he matures to gain wisdom and insight, it is at the cost of authenticity and freedom. The "superior" narrator may blend into the protagonist's discourse or sentimentally portray an adolescent freedom that is no longer attainable by him. The fluctuating mood in turn-of-the-century narratives about adolescents builds on the interplay between narrator and protagonist.

II

Critics concerned with "aesthetic distance" in *Portrait* have traditionally asked what Joyce thought of his adolescent protagonist, Stephen Dedalus. Anderson finds three types of answers: (1) Stephen is "an autobiographical hero who triumphs over his tawdry environment. . . . There is little 'distance' between the painter and his portrait" (447); (2) "Joyce sees Stephen as an autobiographical representation of the author, a 'portrait of the artist' drawn 'as a young man' by an older man. Joyce asks the reader to join him in seeing Stephen as a priggish, narcissistic young egoist" (448–49); (3) "Joyce's view of his own past in Stephen is mixed, both ironic and romantic or sympathetic" (451).[3]

Yet such intertextual evidence is no more decisive than authorial commentary: if authorial comments cannot simply be attributed to the narrator, neither can we assume that the narrators and the Stephen-figures of the three texts are coherently interrelated. How could the narrator's perspective on Stephen in *Ulysses* of *Stephen Hero* shed light on the Stephen in the *Portrait* if, as critics frequently claim, the narrative perspective of the protagonist undergoes radical transformations even within the confines of the *Portrait*?

In fact, such approaches to Stephen are hardly "intertextual" in the contemporary critical sense, for they tacitly postulate a teleological development from early to "mature" works. Such a metaphysics of development is incompatible with Joyce's own notion of temporality, and excludes the possibility of radical breaks, inversions, and the simultaneity of mutually exclusive perspectives.[4]

Wayne Booth acknowledges the tenuousness of such intertextual evidence, yet falls back on it to avoid ambiguity: "Unless we are willing to retreat into babbling and incommunicable relativism, we cannot believe that it is *both* a portrait of the prisoner freed *and* a portrait of the soul placing itself in chains."[5] Though he regards the *Portrait* as "a better work because the immature author has been effaced," he turns to the "immature commentary" of *Stephen Hero* in order to decipher "the ironies of the later, purer work."[6] But surely "effacing" the narrator must also have meant shifting his relation to the protagonist.

The tenuousness of such extratextual evidence led John Paul Riquelme to focus on the "text itself." But the resultant text-internal approach imposes another unwarranted identity on the narrator, for Riquelme regards the narrator as the older, mature Stephen, now engaged in writing his autobiographical retrospective.[7]

Since the narrator never literally identifies himself with Stephen, Riquelme can merely suggest that by the end of the book Stephen is an artist who *could* write the novel: the closing pages, passages from Stephen's diary, signify that he has become a narrator, ready to retell his childhood and adolescence. The writing of the *Portrait* begins where the action of the story ends, Stephen-the-protagonist matures into Stephen-the-narrator. Better yet, the protagonist fathers the narrator who will recreate him as a fictional protagonist: in a truly Joycean manner the identities of father and son, Dedalus and Icarus are hopelessly intertwined.

Such transformations from protagonist into narrator do occur in first-person narratives like Hölderlin's *Hyperion*, which end with the protagonists' decisions to recollect and record their experiences.[8] But Joyce's novel is not told in the first person, and Stephen's loose, "metaphoric" link to the narrator should not be hardened into a literal identity, for the third-person form allows a shifting, oscillating perspective on the protagonist that first-person narratives cannot easily achieve.

Riquelme speaks of an "oscillating perspective" in the subtitle of his book, but his intention is to stabilize the meaning of *A Portrait*. To be sure, he regards the "subtle intermingling of third- and first-person perspectives" in *A Portrait* as "the most significant change in the style of his [Joyce's] autobiographical work, one that differentiates it clearly from *Stephen Hero*."[9] Riquelme devotes considerable attention to the most prominent stylistic marker of this intermingling, the "narrated monologue" (*erlebte Rede, style indirect libre*).[10] In contrast to "psycho-narration," where narrators integrate the thoughts of fictional characters into their own (third-person) discourse, and "quoted monologues," which are introduced with marking phrases (for example, "he thought") and told in the first person, "narrated monologues" continue the third-person discourse without quotation marks, but indicate (by means of style and content) that we are in fact privy to the thoughts of a character. Witness, for instance, Stephen's ecstatic vision and his annointment as a poet that concludes chapter 4 of *Portrait*:

> His soul had arisen from the grave of boyhood, spurning her graveclothes. Yes! Yes! Yes! He would create proudly out of the freedom and power of his soul, as the great artificer whose name he bore, a living thing, new and soaring and beautiful, impalpable, imperishable. (170)

> A girl stood before him in midstream, alone and still, gazing out to sea. She seemed like one whom magic had changed into the likeness of a strange and beautiful seabird. Her long slender bare legs were delicate as a crane's . . . Her bosom was as a bird's soft and slight, slight and soft as the breast of some darkplumaged dove. (171)

> A wild angel had appeared to him, the angel of mortal youth and beauty, an envoy from the fair courts of life, to throw open before him in an instant of ecstasy the gates of all the ways of error and glory. On and on and on and on! (172)

While "His soul had arisen from the grave of boyhood" and "A girl stood before him in midstream" are obviously narratorial, ecstatic words like "Yes! Yes! Yes!" must be attributed to Stephen even though they are spoken in the third person. We are urged to this attribution by the style, the content, and the conditional "he would," although the ecstatic words are not literally spoken by Stephen. We read them "as if" he spoke them, just as Stephen sees the girl "as if" she were an angel: "by leaving the relationship between words and thoughts latent, the narrated monologue casts a peculiarly penumbral light on the figural consciousness, suspending it on the threshold of verbalization in a manner that cannot be achieved by direct quotation."[11]

Riquelme observes that in *A Portrait*, "the style shifts from psycho-narration narrowly conceived toward narrated monologue," and he sees in this a rapprochement between the protagonist's and the narrator's mind, which culminates in the concluding diary segments, Stephen's emergence as a narrator.[12] The growth of narrated monologues would thus prepare for the final merging of narrator and protagonist.

Although narrated monologues interlink narrators and fictional figures, their ties to the former and the latter differ, and this is what gives the link its unique, "hovering" quality.[13] Riquelme acknowledges them as *temporary* alignments and complex mixes,[14] but uses them to combat "hovering" ambiguity, to stabilize the novel's meaning, and to polemicize against readings "that dwell on the problem of irony, or aesthetic distance, and on the impersonality of the narration": if Stephen is the narrator he cannot be portrayed with irony.[15]

But surely autobiographical reflections often recall the former self from a distance and with irony. The narrated monologues of the novel actually have a double function: they link but also distance the narrator from the protagonist; they are vehicles to indicate both affinity and distance between two different selves, whether they are meant to be different people or merely temporal stages of the same self. Consider a narrated monologue from the seaside scene against the closing direct discourse in Stephen's diary:

> He would create proudly out of the freedom and power of his soul, as the great artificer whose name he bore, a living thing, new and soaring and beautiful, impalpable, imperishable. (170)

> I go to encounter for the millionth time the reality of experience and to forge in the smithy of my soul the uncreated conscience of my race. (252–23)

The "hovering" indirection of the first passage sharply contrasts with the determinate thrust of the second, where the narrator is no longer present. The third-person form in the first passage indicates the narrator's presence and his separateness from Stephen. Does he share the verbal extravagances of his adolescent protagonist or does he merely smile at them? Many think that we get no internal "processing instruction," that the narrator does not show his hand. He adjusts to "the age and mood of his hero," and is barely perceptible as a "separate entity within the text."[16]

Still, the "barely perceptible narrator" does not fully blend into Stephen, for this scene of poetic initiation becomes credible only if we consider the similes "seabird" and "wild angel" as being written by Stephen. In this narrative, becoming a poet means envisioning the world by means of similes. Standing in the water, Stephen is baptized as an artist, and the logic of his new identity requires that he not *receive* a name but manifest his "profane" creative force by *endowing* things with metaphoric names. If, as Kenner writes, "it is through their names that things have power over Stephen,"[17] in scenes like this it is Stephen who acquires power over things and people by "rebaptizing" them with metaphors: his consecration implies that henceforth he himself will baptize girls to become "seabirds" and "wild angels." Stephen can now endow his dim and inarticulate perceptions with ecstatic metaphors the narrator would never use. The gradual dominance of Stephen's public and private thoughts in the latter parts of *Portrait* indicates that he is overcoming his adolescence by learning to verbalize his perceptions and experiences.

Stephen's growing verbal sophistication affects the identity of the narrator. At the beginning both Stephen and the narrator used mimetic language, but that of Stephen undergoes a transformation while that of the narrator remains mimetic. It is the narrator's continued mimicry that allows the later efflorescence of Stephen's creative discourse. In the later narrated monologues, the narrator *mimetically* adopts Stephen's *creative* discourse, which is emancipated because it reaches the reader without paternalistic narratorial intrusions.

III

Thomas Mann's *Tonio Kröger* shows some evident analogies to the *Portrait*: both narratives are heavily autobiographical accounts of adolescent crises by postadolescent authors, both tell how the resolution of those crises leads to the birth of artists, both use narrated monologues to portray the protagonist's (and only his) thoughts. Stephen's concluding diary entry corresponds to Tonio's concluding letter.

Yet Tonio is suspicious of the aesthetics Stephen embraces, and he finds a fragile modus vivendi with the bourgeois-civic world that his uncompromising fellow writer rejects. The differences are evident at the outset. Whereas the *Portrait* opens with the narrator's self-effacing presentation of Stephen's infantile memories, *Tonio Kröger* starts with a more traditional indication of setting: "The winter sun stood only as a poor reflection [*Schein*], milky and wan behind layers of cloud above the confined spaces of the city. It was wet and windy in the gabled streets, and a sort of soft hail, neither ice nor snow, drizzled occasionally."[18] The scene is a well-crafted metaphor of the protagonist's adolescent state of mind: the faint sun, the misty air, the interim state of slush, the street that is a mere conduit between home and school—all these vague images of transition and diffusion anticipate Tonio, who enters the scene with a hesitant gait: Tonio "walked carelessly and unevenly, whereas Hans's slender legs in their black stockings marched along elastically and rhythmically."[19]

Tonio's arhythmical, offbeat gait—so clearly different from Hans's self-assured march within the civic order—becomes a leitmotif. In the dancing

lesson of the second scene, the sixteen-year-old Tonio is to imitate the in-
imitably "elastic, swinging, weaving, royal"[20] steps of the grotesque danc-
ing-master, but loses his way and lands amidst the girls. The hesitant movements in the street and the blunder on the dance floor reveal Tonio's
disorientation, which was the seed-idea of the story, as Mann's first notebook entry for the novella from 1899 indicates: "Tonio Kröger. Some stray
with a sense that it is necessary, because a right path does not exist for
them."[21] Appropriately, the narrator's concluding commentary to the adolescent sections of the story laces this notebook entry with the predicates
of Tonio's gait ("carelessly and unevenly"):

> He went the way he had to go, a bit carelessly and unevenly, whistling to
> himself, gazing into the distance with head tilted, and if he went astray this
> happened only because for some there is no right way. Asked what in the
> world he thought to become, he provided various answers for he used to say
> (and he had already noted it in writing) that he carried in himself possibilities
> for thousands of different forms of existence, together with the secret knowl-
> edge that they were basically all impossibilities.[22]

This summary, like the story's opening passage, shows the superior insight
and perspective of Mann's narrator. Tonio's habit of recording self-obser-
vations indicates the growth of his mind, the deepening of his self-knowl-
edge, and his sharpening ability to verbalize it, but his observations and
metaphors have been anticipated in the narrator's discourse. In the last
sections of the story a sequence of events replicates Tonio's adolescent experiences, save that now he observes them happening to others and reflec-
tively evaluates them. When in the penultimate scene he watches a group
of young dancers that includes replicas of his adolescent infatuations, he
too can articulate the story's core idea: "For some go necessarily astray
because there is no right path for them."[23] Thus, when a girl of "his type"
slips during dancing, he helps her up and suggests that she stop dancing.

Consider next to the motif of "aimless gait" the "heart" metaphor as a
second index of the trajectory of Tonio's growth, his gradual appropriation
of narrative insight. At the conclusion of the Hans Hansen episode the
narrator comments: "His heart was alive then; there was longing in it, and
melancholy, a faint disdain and an altogether chaste bliss."[24] At the conclusion of the next episode, that of the dancing lesson, this develops into an
elaborate simile representing the cooling of Tonio's adolescent ardour:
"And he cautiously circled the sacrificial altar upon which the pure, chaste
flame of his love was glowing; he knelt before it, tended and nourished it
in every way because he wanted to be faithful. And after a while, imperceptibly, without stir and noise it went out nevertheless."[25] During the following period of professional success as a writer, Tonio's "dead and loveless
heart" oscillates between "icy intellect and consuming sensual fire,"[26] but

rekindling his adolescent fire at the end, he becomes conscious of his position and masters the narrator's metaphors in order to reaffirm his love for the Hanses and Inges: "There is yearning in it and melancholy envy; a tiny bit of disdain and an altogether chaste bliss."[27]

Both motifs show, then, that the end of the story appropriately shifts from the narrator's discourse to a letter from Tonio that outlines a permanent, though precarious, "hovering" position. Like Stephen, Tonio gradually masters his initial confusion by means of language, so that by the end he can articulate his identity. The acquired identities differ totally, however. Stephen defiantly departs from the Ireland of his childhood and adolescence, whereas Tonio, at thirty, reconsiders his departure and metaphorically returns, not to childhood but to an adolescent state of mind that is more open and hospitable to others than Stephen's departing aesthetic egotism: "[I am] a bourgeois who strayed into art, a bohemian with a nostalgia for proper upbringing, an artist with a bad conscience. . . . I stand between two worlds without being at home in either, and have it somewhat difficult therefore."[28]

Traditional critical preoccupation with the moral and aesthetic questions of Tonio's double homelessness has seldom given attention to the narrative presentation of these questions, which is not merely a formal matter but one that deeply affects their meaning. The initial difference between the narrator's and the protagonist's knowledge, and the gradually changing relation between them, is at the heart of the shifting irony in the novella. A good illustration may be found in this passage, which follows Tonio's bungling of the dance, where distancing irony and interlinking narrated monologue quickly follow each other:

> Tonio Kröger stole away, went unnoticed out into the corridor and stationed himself there, with hands behind his back, in front of a window with the blind down, without realizing that one could see nothing through this blind and that it was ridiculous to stand in front of it as if one were looking out.
>
> But he was looking inward, where there was so much pain and longing. Why, why was he here? Why was he not sitting by the window of his own room? . . . No, no, after all, his place was here, where he felt close to Inge, even though he stood lonely and aside, trying to recognize her voice that carried notes of warm life amidst the buzzing, clattering, and laughter in there. Your narrow, laughing blue eyes, you blond Inge![29]

Tonio's standing in front of a blind (no pun in German!) provides one of the rare passages in the story where the narrator's paternalistic benevolence tips over into direct irony. This distance is indicated not only by the ridicule but also by the very fact that the narrator tells us something of which Tonio is unaware. Yet the ridicule is immediately followed by a narrated monologue, in which the narrator's renewed sympathy for his hero is marked by his adoption of Tonio's familiar form of address ("du blonde Inge") to the girl. The emotional empathy of this scene will be replaced at the end of the story by an association through shared intellectual insight, which will reconfigure Tonio's relation to the narrator: by then, Tonio will have as much insight into the narrator's mind as the narrator now has by means of a narrated monologue into Tonio's heart. The shift constitutes an index of Tonio's growth.

IV

Not only are Stephen and Tonio different artists, but they develop in different ways and acquire different modes of identity. Stephen gained an *autonomous* voice in the baptismal scene by inventing metaphors to name things. By adopting the narrator's metaphors, Tonio internalizes prior knowledge and perceives already existing connections. He is no autonomous creator. The difference in use of metaphor anticipates the incremental difference between Stephen's and Tonio's final emancipations. Stephen, the sovereign creator of metaphors, cuts his ties with family, church, and country, whereas Tonio, an "adaptor" of metaphors, reassumes older emotional ties with the bourgeois order. Would Tonio's adoption of the narrator's language offer a better communicative position to narrate than Stephen's striving for an autonomous personal language?

The contrast is all too neat, and it forces me to reconsider a matter I have passed over until now in my discussion of *A Portrait*. We know, of course, that Joyce went on to write about his fellow citizens, just as Tonio promises to do in his closing letter to Lisabeta. But we need not turn to Joyce's biography and other questionable extratextual evidence to develop resistance against Stephen's rhetoric, which stylizes the closing of *A Portrait* as his glorious emancipation. If we perform the reading with a historical perspective we shall find the evidence inscribed, paradoxically, in the text itself.

Stephen's symbolist aesthetics speaks of an original creation, of forging "in the smithy" of his soul the "uncreated conscience" of his race (253)—as if his language contained no mimesis and represented an absolutely new departure. Yet Stephen's language is by no means original. When in the final chapter he struggles to emancipate himself from the domination of British English, he seeks to find a native dialect rather than a private idiolect. His discussion with the dean (185–90) and his subsequent reflections on language reveal the dilemma. When he finally understands that the dean's "funnel" means "tundish" in the native dialect of Lower Drumcondra familiar to him, he concedes with wounded pride: "The language in which we are speaking is his before it is mine. . . . His language, so familiar and so foreign, will always be for me an acquired speech. I have not made or accepted its words. My voice holds them at bay. My soul frets in the shadow of his language" (189). The final diary entries record Stephen's delight at having discovered in the dictionary that "tundish" was "good old blunt English too" (251)—but this merely shows that having emancipated himself from the dean's language, he is content to forge the "uncreated conscience" of his race with the "blunt" English of Lower Drumcondra. His rhetoric of creativity masks his debt to the native linguistic tradition.

Furthermore, Stephen's "poetic" language—the language of his epiphanies, his villanelle, and his concluding diary—is dependent on *poetic* conventions. Kenner is undoubtedly right in claiming that Stephen writes "purple prose" and that the language of his seaside ecstasy beats "again and again the tambours of a fin-de-siècle ecstasy."[30] Whether Joyce shared Stephen's ecstatic language or merely mimicked it smilingly, or whether we readers can appreciate that "purple prose," is not at issue here. It suffices to note that readers familiar with fin de siècle discourses will recognize that Stephen's originality is forged out of certain turn-of-the-century conventions in representing ecstasy and writing poetry: his rhetoric of "free" creation is undercut by his reliance on "prepatterned" language. Such conformity is inevitable because language always preexists. At best, it can be enriched in adoption for personal use, be transferred from alien spheres by means of metaphors. Since the "uncreated conscience" of the race, pace Stephen, always preexists, what he forges in the smithy of his soul is ultimately always also "forgery."

We can thus unmask Stephen's rhetoric and recognize that he, no less than Tonio, internalizes prior language. To be sure, the metaphors of Stephen's Irish forefathers and the "poetic" conventions of his age function as *silent* subtexts to his utterances, whereas Tonio's subtext is made explicit by the narrator. The difference in articulating the subtexts affects the protagonists' modes of self-consciousness: Tonio is conscious of and satisfied with the mimeticism of his ethics and aesthetics, whereas Stephen rebelliously tries to shake it off. It is the reader's task to recognize that Stephen's rebellious credo is negated by his practice, that his self-image as absolute creator is undermined by his adoptive rather than purely creative use of language.

It may be suggested in conclusion that the identity of fictional figures does not depend only on their own discourses and that of the narrator, but also on the various embedding discourses outside the text. The figures of language compel us to sacrifice part of the text's autonomy and to seek the

subtexts beyond its boundaries. To supplement the absent subtexts, to recognize that in spite of his rhetoric Stephen is no more emancipated than
Tonio, is the task of the reader. It is a legitimate transgression of textual
boundaries, the shaping contribution that readers must bring to the
"fuzzy" identity of *texts* and a corrective they must provide in contemplat-
ing the identity of *protagonists*.

NOTES

1. James Joyce, *A Portrait of the Artist as a Young Man*, ed. Chester G. Anderson (Harmondsworth: Penguin, 1977); Thomas Mann, *Tonio Kröger*, in *Gesammelte Werke in Einzelbänden: Frühe Erzählungen*, ed. Peter de Mendelssohn (Frankfurt: Fischer, 1981), 273–341. References to these texts are cited parenthetically.

2. Dorrit Cohn, *Transparent Minds: Narrative Modes for Presenting Consciousness in Fiction* (Princeton: Princeton University Press, 1978), 30.

3. Chester G. Anderson, "Controversy: The Question of Esthetic Distance. Editor's Introduction," in Joyce, *Portrait*, 446–55. Anderson places David Daiches and Hugh Kenner in the first category, adding that Daiches approves of Stephen's attitude (David Daiches, *The Novel and the Modern World* [Chicago: University of Chicago Press, 1939]). Since, however, Kenner calls *Portrait* "a meticulous pastiche of immaturity" and finds the last forty pages "painful reading," he should be included rather among those in the second category (Hugh Kenner, "The 'Portrait' in Perspective," in Joyce, *Portrait*, pp. 416–39).

Representatives of the second group maintain that Joyce takes an ironic view of Stephen's purple prose, his anticipated fall as Icarus, his "dry," "abstract," and "humorless" style in the last chapter, his romanticism, and the weakness of his only divulged poem (William York Tindall, *James Joyce: His Way of Interpreting the Modern World* [New York: Scribners, 1950]; Mark Schorer, "Technique as Discovery," *Hudson Review* [1948]: 67–68). Some actually find the villanelle good (Robert Scholes, "Stephen Dedalus, Poet or Esthete?" *PMLA* 89 [1964]: 484–89; John Paul Riquelme, *Teller and Tale in Joyce's Fiction* [Baltimore: Johns Hopkins University Press, 1983]).

Anderson's third category includes Kenneth Burke, Richard Ellmann, and, by virtue of Joyce's presumed "compassion" for Stephen, William York Tindall (Kenneth Burke, "Three Definitions," *Kenyon Review* 13 [1951]: 181–92; Richard Ellmann, *James Joyce* [New York: Oxford University Press, 1959]).

4. James Joyce, *Stephen Hero* (London: Granada, 1977).

5. Wayne Booth, *The Rhetoric of Fiction* (Chicago: University of Chicago Press, 1961), 328.

6. Ibid., 333.

7. In fact, Riquelme reads *Portrait* as a double autobiography, "the author's autobiographical fiction and the autobiography of the fictional character" (51).

8. Friedrich Hölderlin, *Hyperion*, vol. 3 of *Sämtliche Werke*, ed. Friedrich Beissner (Stuttgart: Kohlhammer, 1958).

9. Riquelme, *Teller and Tale*, 48.

10. Cohn, *Transparent Minds*, 104–5.

11. Ibid., 103.

12. Riquelme, *Teller and Tale*, 14.

13. In contrast to Virginia Woolf's *Mrs. Dalloway* and other modernist narratives, where the narrator shares narrated monologues with several fictional charac-

ters, the narrators of *Portrait* and *Tonio Kröger* read only the minds of their protagonists. This creates a special relationship between them.

14. Riquelme, *Teller and Tale*, 58.

15. Ibid., 51.

16. Cohn, *Transparent Minds*, 30–31. The *Portrait* is perhaps the most frequently cited narrative with a "vanishing narrator." Its opening, in particular, is often described as the narrator's "chameleonic" disappearance behind the language of childhood: "Once upon a time and a very good time it was there was moocow coming down along the road and the moocow that was coming down along the road met a nicens little boy named baby tuckoo" (7).

17. Kenner, " 'Portrait' in Perspective," 421.

18. "Die Wintersonne stand nur als armer Schein, milchig und matt hinter Wolkenschichten über der engen Stadt. Naß und zugig war's in den giebeligen Gassen, und manchmal fiel eine Art von weichem Hagel, nicht Eis, nicht Schnee" (273). In preparing the English translation of this and the following passages in the text I have consulted that of H. T. Lowe-Porter: Thomas Mann, *Tonio Kröger*, trans. H. T. Lowe-Porter (New York: Knopf, 1941).

19. Tonio "ging nachlässig und ungleichmäßig während Hansens schlanke Beine in den schwarzen Strümpfen so elastisch und taktfest einherschritten" (274).

20. "Elastisch, wogend, wiegend, königlich" (285).

21. "Tonio Kröger. Manche gehen mit bewußter Nothwendigkeit in die Irre, weil es einen richtigen Weg für sie überhaupt nicht giebt" (Hans Wysling, "Dokumente zur Entstehung des 'Tonio Kröger,' " in *Quellenkritische Studien zum Werk Thomas Manns*, ed. Paul Scherrer and Hans Wysling [Bern: Francke, 1967], 48–63, esp. 49).

22. "Er ging den Weg, den er gehen mußte, ein wenig nachlässig und ungleichmäßig, vor sich hin pfeifend, mit seitwärts geneigtem Kopfe ins Weite blickend, und wenn er irreging, so geschah es, weil es für etliche einen richtigen Weg überhaupt nicht gibt. Fragt man ihn, was in aller Welt er zu werden gedachte, so erteilte er wechselnde Auskunft, denn er pflegte zu sagen (und hatte es auch bereits aufgeschrieben), daß er die Möglichkeiten zu tausend Daseinsformen in sich trage, zusammen mit dem heimlichen Bewußtsein, daß es im Grunde lauter Unmöglichkeiten seien" (Thomas Mann, *Tonio Kröger*, in *Gesammelte Werke*, 290–91).

23. "Denn etliche gehen mit Notwendigkeit in die Irre, weil es einen rechten Weg für sie überhaupt nicht gibt" (335).

24. "Damals lebte sein Herz; Sehnsucht war darin und schwermütiger Neid und ein klein wenig Verachtung und eine ganze keusche Seligkeit" (283).

25. "Und er umkreiste behutsam den Opferaltar, auf dem die lautere und keusche Flamme seiner Liebe loderte, kniete davor und schürte und nährte sie auf alle Weise, weil er treu sein wollte. Und über eine Weile, unmerklich, ohne Aufsehen und Geräusch, war sie dennoch erloschen" (290).

26. "Eisiger Geistigkeit und verzehrender Sinnenglut" (292).

27. "Sehnsucht ist darin und schwermütiger Neid und ein klein wenig Verachtung und eine ganze keusche Seligkeit" (341). The heart metaphor shows that Tonio's story is both incremental and circular, for it entails a return to a more genuine

self after assuming a false identity: the story chronicles the faulty resolution of an adolescent crisis. Tonio temporarily resolves his confusions by accepting the professional-bohemian artistic conventions, but in the end he regains his adolescent "intermediacy." The final identity is paradoxically one of indeterminacy and hovering, a kind of permanent adolescence.

28. "[Ich bin] ein Bürger, der sich in die Kunst verirrte, ein Bohemien mit Heimweh nach der guten Kinderstube, ein Künstler mit schlechtem Gewissen. . . . Ich stehe zwischen zwei Welten, bin in keiner daheim und habe es infolgedessen ein wenig schwer" (340).

29. "Tonio Kröger stahl sich fort, ging heimlich auf den Korridor hinaus und stellte sich dort, die Hände auf dem Rücken, vor ein Fenster mit herabgelassener Jalousie, ohne zu bedenken, daß man durch diese Jalousie gar nichts sehen konnte, und daß es also lächerlich sei, davorzustehen und zu tun, als blicke man hinaus.

"Er blickte aber in sich hinein, wo so viel Gram und Sehnsucht war. Warum, warum war er hier? . . . Nein, nein, sein Platz war dennoch hier, wo er sich in Inges Nähe wußte, wenn er auch nur einsam von ferne stand und versuchte, in dem Summen, Klirren und Lachen dort drinnen ihre Stimme zu unterscheiden, in welcher es klang von warmem Leben. Deine länglich geschnittenen, blauen, lachenden Augen, du blonde Inge!" (288).

30. Kenner, " 'Portrait' in Perspective," 437.

TEN

PATTERNS OF JUSTIFICATION IN *YOUNG TÖRLESS*

Stanley Corngold

The bad conscience of the novel—the bad conscience of love.
(& of the hero. Hence the more or less worm-eaten hero).
—Musil, "Aus einem Rapial"

I AM CONCERNED with the logic of justification informing Robert Musil's first novel, *Young Törless* (1906).[1] The novel appears to do everything in its power to ward off moral criticism. It is doubly, triply insulated against it. I shall discuss the various strategies of narrative and persuasion by which the novel achieves a certain dandylike countenance of impassiveness and superiority. I do not believe that Musil consciously set about constructing fortifications around his work in order to defend against scandal, yet it is as if *Young Törless* had in fact been constructed that way. Pursuing its defensive design might throw new light on some of its well-known psychological and narratological salients. One of the reasons for giving importance to its defensive work, its *resistance*, is a certain effect the novel produces—to my mind, less an effect of truth in narration than of a subject matter that has been bled of life and given artificial strength through excessive protection.

The narrative mode of *Young Törless* shapes and is shaped by the matter it conveys—Törless's risqué experiments on the mind and body of his fellow pupil Basini.[2] The narrative mode—its situation-cum-perspective—is anomalous, no doubt. In order to get hold of it, we could proceed by trying to approximate it to a model of real speaking. So I shall identify the basic narrative situations the novel at times assumes, but from which it then systematically and significantly departs.

Let us consider a narrative mode the novel describes and evokes while never assuming as its own. This is the situation of the *direct report*: Törless, as author, would state his present confusions directly to a reader. He would describe his preoccupations while involved in them, and we would read them with the anxious sense that even as we were reading them, these sadistic adventures were going on.

The novel gives us a close approximation of this model when Törless's thoughts about Basini are literally reproduced: " 'I feel something in me,' he wrote, 'and don't quite know what it is. . . . I must be ill—insane!' "³ At this point, somewhat like Törless's parents, we are receiving an immediate report of his acts and moods at school. In a letter to his parents, for example, he had written "all about . . . [Basini's disgrace]; the only thing he passed over in silence was what he himself had felt at the time" (69; 51). Significantly, on receiving a temperate reply advising charity to Basini, Törless had "torn the letter into shreds and burned it" (71; 52): his parents' failure to acknowledge Basini's outlandishness threatens to disqualify him as a potential object of fascination. In a later letter, we learn that Törless had actually written to his parents "about his peculiar states of mind, though this was before he had been drawn into the sexual adventure." Perhaps because of this omission, the reply is equally "boring" and "prosaic," advising him "to get Basini to give himself up and thus put an end to the undignified and dangerous state of subservience he was in" (196; 128). We do not hear further of any letter Törless wrote, so he has presumably failed to spell out details of his acceptance of Basini's lovemaking, his inquisition of Basini in the attic, and the contempt with which he has then discarded him, having no further experimental interest in him. Such reports, especially as they might seem to be composed by a real person, would be bound to provoke concerned criticism and—if one were not parentally complaisant—dismay. This is a truth that Törless himself registers at a time when he is most fascinated with Basini. Glad that his parents will not spend the holidays with him, "he knew . . . that it would have been almost an interruption—at least it would have embarrassed him considerably [*es hätte ihn arg verwirrt*]—if he had had to face . . . [them] just at this stage" (142; 94).

He is right. For anyone for whom the existence of Törless matters, his stance of voyeuristic superiority is bound to invite reproof, because, at the very least, it falsifies his experience: it blinds him to his felt but repressed feelings of affinity with his victim.⁴ His superior stance conceals a certain truth of sympathy—"this secret sympathy for Basini" for which, for a time, he allegedly "suffers ceaselessly" (165; 108). But his actual behavior is revolting. Törless capitalizes on the anguish and confusions of Basini, who makes his body available for sadistic abuse. In the narrative situation of the direct report, we would have a mode almost completely bare of the mediations of elapsed time (between the events and the reporting of them) and of differences of personality (between the moral personality of the doer and his deeds and that of their narrator). *Young Törless*, I conclude, cannot be cast in such a mode, because the author of such confessions would be implicated in his story (if a legal personality, he would be incriminated in the legal sense). And few readers, I think, would bring to such a story the obligatory suspension of disbelief except at the price of an impulse to intervene. They would be inclined to shout at such a narrator: "Break off your story and save Basini instead! . . . And I will help you simply by breaking off sympathy with your story." This is exactly the effect that the novel needs to defend against, but it is an effect that, whatever its complications of form, it tends to produce because of its peculiarly horrible subject matter.

Young Törless, however, is never a direct report of experiences, since even Törless's literal report of his reflections is bracketed as a citation (132–34; 88–89). I hope that bothering to consider it, if only in a hypothetical mode—and if only to discard it—still serves to highlight the real complications of the narrative. *Young Törless* is told by an authorial intelligence vastly more articulate than the adolescent pupil at the boarding school, W. This is the intelligence of a considerably older person; the full range of narrative differences mentioned above are in play.[5] As I proceed to construct the narrative mode of the novel, I shall be putting forward not founded descriptions, not definitive identifications, but constitutive surmises—the stratified succession of profiles on narrative perspective that every reader will have to make.

To grasp this narrative intelligence on the model of a real speaking situation, we could imagine it as that of the adult Musil, the author of this novel. This is a hypothesis no longer obviously contrary to fact: it is a way of formulating the narrative situation bound to be an important part of any reader's response.

We are not now considering that Musil only "lends his authority" to a fictive narrator who is his representative—as, for example, the grown-up Törless or a confidant of his. This assumption makes more of a claim on an immediate authorial reality than one for which the fictive narrator incarnates aspects of the sensibility of an empirical author.[6]

As the hypothetically real, empirical narrator of *Young Törless*, Musil would then be reporting on either (1) a fictional episode, (2) an episode from the youth of someone known to him, or indeed (3) an episode from his own youth. Hypothesis (2) actually merges with hypothesis (1), because if the subject matter of the novel is the sensibility of someone other than the pupil Musil, then, considering the degree of its refinement and intricacy and the fact that it cannot be remembered, it cannot have been reproduced as original experience. It would have to have been imagined. But I believe it is correct to assume that for most readers, the adventures recounted in *Young Törless* have an undeniably personal character. They seem to constitute an "acquist of true experience" that has then been subsequently embellished.[7]

According to the hypothesis of the real autobiographical narrator, then, "Törless" is only a disguised name for the sinisterly adventuresome pupil Musil was. In the English-language version I am using, there is at least one plain textual fact to justify this surmise: the note "About the Author" preceding the novel declares that "Musil . . . attended military academy at Mahrisch [sic]-Weisskirchen in Moravia" (emphasis added) (ii). Readers will draw the obvious conclusion when they read, on page 2, that "in this town there was a celebrated boarding school . . . ; it was a particular advantage to have been educated at *W*" (emphasis added).[8] Furthermore, the boarding school W.—it is at least suggested—has "a military bias" as well,[9] since "it was here that the sons of the best families in the country received their education"—some of them then going on into the army (2; 8). The school library consists importantly of "drearily humorous tales of army life" (10; 13). As Törless begins his dismal walk with Beineberg to the prostitute Bozena's hovel, his "sword," we read, "clattered on the stones" (31; 26). Finally, Beineberg, in whom "the image of his eccentric father [the general] lived on in a kind of distorted magnification" and in whom "every feature [of the general] was preserved," would presumably have gone on to a military academy (20; 20). But this identification is only a hovering suggestion; that league of critics and cover illustrators who depict the boarding school at W. as a military academy[10] must have been bedazzled by Volker Schlöndorff's film.[11]

The note "About the Author" additionally contributes the impression that the narrative intelligence is Musil's personal best, since Musil, we learn, went on "to study experimental psychology in Berlin" (ii). The words "experiment" and "psychology" easily function as predicates linking the behavior and attitude of Törless toward Basini with that of the narrator toward Törless and his world. An early passage asserts, for example, that the bond of animal spirits among Törless and his friends at the time of the Basini episode constituted a phase, but neither Törless nor his parents could "recognize [in it] the symptoms of a definite psychological [*seelische*] development" (5; 11). Of Törless's entire captivation in "the narrow, winding passages of sensuality," the author writes: "It was all the result not of perversity, but of a psychological [*geistige*] situation in which he had lost his sense of direction" (173; 114). Indeed, the psychological character of the work seemed so pronounced for Musil's readers that Musil had to fight to have its art character acknowledged. Psychology, he wrote, is supposed to serve fiction; you take a wagon to explore a landscape, but you do not look for the landscape in the wagon.[12] The experimental character of Törless's behavior toward Basini is part of the narrator's claim that what Törless wants from Basini is not the sensation of sex or power but psychological knowledge.

I shall not discuss all the other reasons a specialist reader would have for identifying the narrator's values and concerns with those repeatedly affirmed and elaborated in the novels, stories, and essays by the empirical author Robert Musil. Here, though, is just one example of a permanently

Musilian trope, found in the aperçu that concludes *Young Törless*: "Any great flash of understanding is only half completed in the illumined circle of the conscious mind; the other half takes place in the dark loam of our innermost being. It is primarily a state of soul, and uppermost, as it were at the extreme tip of it, there the thought is—poised like a flower" (210–11; 137). Musil is throughout the pupil of the Nietzsche who wrote, "[By assuming] that really words exist only for *superlative* degrees of [inner] events and drives, . . . we misread ourselves in this apparently clearest letter-script of our self [Buchstabenschrift unseres Selbsts]."[13]

In the narrative situation I am proposing, the language with which this narrator (Musil) tells Törless's (Musil's) adventures will have to be Musil's chosen diction. He is responsible for it, and the description and explanation of Törless's motives are Musil's best justification and defense of his own experience—experience that, as the novel repeatedly reminds us, requires justification. But then, if we are not satisfied with this defense, Musil himself (in 1906 and all the days of his life and reputation thereafter) would expose himself to the charge of bad faith: that he has constructed in this novel an exquisite but impotent alibi for his youthful abuse of a certain Basini. Such a response would be intolerable for the author. It would point up his need to substitute fictional representatives for himself at the level of both theme and narrative structure. The complications of the latter, with their inevitable power to inform everything they touch with a profound and inescapable fictionality, are especially evident through striking breaks in narrative perspective, to which I shall soon return.

In the novel the pupil is called "Törless"—with its over-marked connotation of "Türlosigkeit" (the being from which there is no exit)—and not "me" (young Musil).[14] This, of course, is the main index of the substitution of a fictional subject for a real one at the center of the novel. The pattern of substitutions at the order of narration is subtler and more engaging. The author Musil, although he once says "I" early in the novel,[15] in fact conjures a narrator who by no means has to be the empirical personality Musil or even to represent aspects of him. Who then is this "I"? The shifting "I" encourages the attempt to identify personally a speaker even thus minimally embodied.

The narrator, I have suggested, could seem throughout much of the novel to be the fictive Törless grown up.[16] In offering this equation seriously, I do not mean to ignore bits of evidence scattered throughout the novel that contradict any such strict identification. And yet a fictive narrator can be "more or less" uniformly identified and still be meaningfully identified. The narrator of Kafka's *Metamorphosis*, for example, narrates from a perspective congruent with Gregor's own—with the exception of the coda following Gregor's death and with the exception of a minute break or two. Yet, even though in at least one small scene the narrator speaks from a perspective wider than Gregor's own, it will certainly not do to describe the perspective as therefore authorial rather than figurally congruent. What is crucial in such descriptions is a sort of narratologist's tact, which examines breaks in perspective for the importance of the information they convey at the moment they do.[17]

In *Young Törless*, such breaks arise whenever the narrator, putatively the older Törless, describes with confidence the innermost sensibility of someone he cannot have known personally—for example, Beineberg's father—without offering even the suggestion of a "perhaps" or "as it were" ("Only occasionally did his [General Beineberg's] thoughts lose themselves in a twilit state of agreeable melancholy," 19; 19). In another case, he describes events that befall the pupils at academy W. during the time when Törless has run away ("Basini was still paralysed with terror from his experiences of two days earlier, and the solitary confinement in which he was kept . . . was in itself a tremendous relief to him," 205; 133). It is true that a mature Törless writing a history of himself as a younger man could be imagined as having taken pains to find out, but the effect is still of a break in perspective, though unimportant.

Finally, in a very important and controversial passage two-thirds of the way into the novel, the narrator starts out abruptly from a temporal standpoint much in the future of the events narrated. Here he is very likely saying explicitly, and for the first time, that he is not Törless. The passage begins, "Later, when he had got over his adolescent experiences, Törless became a young man whose mind was both [very] subtle and sensitive" (169; 111). While all through this passage it is possible (though farfetched) to suppose that the grown-up Törless is referring to himself even under the alias "Törless," it is implausible, I think, to imagine him describing his own mind as "[very] subtle and sensitive." This would make him an impossible prig. True, the passage goes on to describe the mature Törless as something of an impossible prig, but such a hypothesis, aiming to preserve at all costs the coherence of the fiction that the narrator is Törless, would then also succeed in too radically alienating the reader. Yet the whole purpose of Musil's narrative strategy must be *not* to alienate the reader while continuing to preserve the advantage, of course, of an intimate and hence authoritative perspective. The narrative must maintain an appropriate balance of distance from the character and sympathy with him—though it must not duplicate in its structure that plainly discreditable play of abusive intimacy and intellectual contempt that young Törless maintains for Basini.

Considering these various breaks, one must of course conclude that in the strict sense the narrator is not Törless grown up. But one should not leave this assumption behind before drawing all conceivable profit from it.

That is because the text gives eminent grounds for finding the assumption interesting and valuable. Here are several.

The narrative is a work of art, and it lies well within the thrust of Törless's depicted development that he is to become an imaginative writer.[18] Thus, we hear that if he has not given evidence of literary abilities while a pupil at W., it is only because of the impoverished literary education he receives there: he has not been acquainted with the literary examples ("Goethe, Schiller, Shakespeare") that a student at a gymnasium would have been able to emulate (9; 12). At the same time the pupil Törless is a writer—of letters and psychological notations—and the bliss of writing to his parents at the beginning of his stay at W. is incomparable.

> He wrote letters home almost daily, and he lived only in these letters; everything else he did seemed to him only a shadowy, unmeaning string of events. . . . But when he wrote he felt within himself something that made him distinct, that set him apart; something in him rose, like an island of miraculous suns and flashing colors, out of the ocean of grey sensations that lapped around him, cold and indifferent, day after day. And when by day, at games or in class, he remembered that he would write his letter in the evening, it was as though he were wearing, hidden on his person, fastened to an invisible chain, a golden key with which . . . he would open the gate [*Tor*] leading into marvelous gardens. (3; 8)

The access he thus obtains to these arcane recesses of the "inner life" (170; 111) is "novelistic," because it is the entire project of the novel *Young Törless* to provide such access generally. Furthermore, it is habitual with Törless, when he has to "do some hard thinking about himself . . . to do it with pen and paper" (130; 87), and it can seem that the text we have in front of us is the direct descendent of such spiritual-artistic exercises: "He had worked out, during the course of the day, what it actually was he wanted to make notes about: the whole series of those particular experiences from the evening with Bozena on, culminating in that vague sensual state which had recently been coming over him" (132; 88). Indeed, as he watches Basini during an entire day's vigil in the study hall, Törless "seemed to himself as one elect—like a saint, having heavenly visions. For the intuitions of great artists was something of which he did not know" (137–38; 92). Törless is allowed to think of himself as one of the elect; the moment in which he gazes with muddled lust at Basini constitutes (he thinks) a consecration, an initiation into a religion of sensibility. Are we to criticize the exaltation in this moment? The narrator prefers to read it without irony, as an intuition of the moods of great artists—an intuition he is presumably not denying to himself as the narrator of this work of obvious intellectual power.

There are many different kinds of evidence for the continuity of subject

and narrator. In the important interpolated passage that introduces the mature Törless, he is described as an "aesthetically inclined intellectual" with
"creative talent" (169–70; 111). The suggestion that this very book *Young
Törless* is his own work continues to be appealing. As young Törless glances
at Basini, "something instantly began in him that was like the crazy whirling of a top, immediately compressing Basini's image into the most fantas-
tically dislocated attitudes and then tearing it asunder in incredible distortions, so that he himself grew dizzy. *True, these were only figures of speech
[Vergleiche] that he found for it afterwards*" (my italics) (134; 90). The conclusion reads like a self-reflexive gesture, directed toward the thick abundance of figures of speech ("those obscure metaphors [*Gleichnisse*]," 213;
138) that arise and grow in the narrative in proportion to Törless's increasing preoccupation with Basini.[19] Furthermore, the novel continually thematizes "changes in perspective" (159; 105)—including, especially, the alternation between the sunlit perspective of psychological science and the
"dreamy" perspective; and this prevailing reality, the Törless-reality, re-
emerges in the "behavior" of the narrator, who, in this sense, is iconic with
his subject as a bundle of heterogeneous perspectives. "It was this mental
perspective that . . . [Törless] had experienced, which alternated according
to whether he was considering what was distant or what was nearby; it was
this incomprehensible relation that according to our shifts of standpoint
give happenings and objects sudden values that are quite incommensurable
[*unvergleichlich*] with each other, strange to each other" (216; 139).

Here is another detail helping confirm the association of Törless the suf-
ferer-poet with Törless the narrator-poet. "It was a pet notion of his that
the capacity for enjoyment, and creative talent, and in fact the whole more
highly developed side of the inner life, was a piece of jewelry [*ein Zierat*]
on which one could easily injure oneself" (170; 112). It is hard to understand the sense of "a piece of jewelry on which one could injure oneself,"
but it is much easier and richer to understand if it is read as referring to the
Maeterlinck quote that appears as the epigraph of "Törless's" novel.[20] This
famous passage describes experiences of the inner life—of "the abyss"—as
a kind of diving for jewels. Yet when they are brought to the surface, they
seem like only poor chips of glass. The jewels on which one could injure
onself (lose one's sanity) are all the fascinations of the inner life, which
harm in the sense of their very imperviousness to articulation and use in
the sunlit world: their otherness, their mystery, their lure is an impediment
to good conscience. Nevertheless, says Törless, it is expected of the proud
possessor of such jewels that he will "make exquisite use of them afterwards" (170; 112), and the novel *Young Törless*, requiring courage to publish, is exactly the use Törless has made of them.

Finally, one could note the obsessive imagery of web (79; 57), veil (89;
63), and net (132; 82) that mysteriously cover Törless's vision. But if we

pursue this image over its various appearances, I think we will understand it as a pattern formed from the superimposition of the two modalities of vision—outer and inner, lighter and darker, science and "tensed image."[21] This play of texture—a "bewilderingly close-knit [*verwirrend eng*] mesh" of moments of disjunctive intersection between these orders of word and thing, husk and gleam (90; 64)—could seem to be the very text we have before us. Törless's veiled vision becomes this book. The veil having been fully drawn, the knots situated, there could be a beginning to the legitimate and regulated distinction between disjunct worlds, which is the sense of Törless's final perception: "He now knew how to distinguish between day and night" (216; 140).

In the type of narrative structure I have been discussing, the modalities of intimacy and distance in the attitude of Törless toward Basini tend to shape the attitude of the narrator (Törless) toward Törless, even though, for obvious reasons, it cannot be advantageous for this to happen. The events of Törless's relation to Basini prove to Törless that his sense of adventure can flourish only as he imagines at a contemplative distance from the real Basini what it is to be Basini and be in his predicament. To come too close to his object—to "become" Basini—is to risk an identification that destroys a necessarily imaginary rapture. This set of injunctions could answer well to the program of the narrator, who as Törless 2 intuits the perplexities of a young Törless he no longer strictly resembles, having come the length of the journey on which Törless has just embarked.

But, paradoxically, as the general resemblance of these two stances seems more pronounced, the narrator risks a kind of inculpation. Even as a fictive personality, in appearing to employ Törless's intellectual discovery he assumes the profit of the vanity and cruelty of the young man he was. And if the youthful Törless seems discreditable, despite the narrator's efforts to do everything in his power to secure a good opinion of him, then Törless's older ego stands condemned by a sort of condemnation forward. Would not a young man so precocious at hypocrisy and at the construction of elegant alibis have contaminated the narrator he was to become?[22] They are not a good or reliable pair, this Törless 1 and Törless 2. And this may be why the narrator has to make such lofty claims for the dignity of Törless's sensibility, pleading more and more urgently, as the novel proceeds, for the importance of his adventures to his and indeed any person's development.

So it seems as if the assumption of an only fictive narrator—Törless 2—were not defense enough. As if determined by this flight from a moralizing reading of his novel, Musil must further complicate the narrative position. The narrator keeps all the values of Törless grown up—for who else could report reliably, in mature language, moods of such intimacy? But it no longer becomes obligatory to assume that the narrator is telling a story about himself in order to disburden himself. Earlier, I noted that the narrator describes Törless's evolution into an aesthetically inclined intellectual whose feelings were "[very] subtle and sensitive." This is praise that would be vaunting and indiscreet in the mouth of the mature Törless. Hence the phrase only really seems possible on the lips of an observer not personally involved—one who "knew" the real Törless as a friend or confidant. Musil winds up—in what is essentially the best fictive model of the narration—speaking as "the friend" of the mature Törless who has heard his story [*jemandem, dem er die Geschichte seiner Jugend erzählt hatte*]" (170; 112), even though there cannot be such a friend, with such powers of recall, in real experience. (To refine this impossible model still further: the narrator of *Törless* is retelling the story he overheard Törless telling himself.) Hence, by means of the "friend," the external double, the work takes on the reliability of psychonarration even as it preserves the intimacy and psychological "realism" of the fictive autobiography (one narrated from the third-person perspective)—a fictive autobiography apparently animated by the motive of a sought-after catharsis and exculpation. Moralizing readers are thus disarmed. If, captivated by the pathos of a novelized confession, readers nevertheless refuse their sympathy, they are immediately corrected. After all, the exculpation is being performed by an omniscient narrator who is not Törless and has no discernible axe to grind. Interestingly, the clearest signs (or the most signs) of the case that the narrator cannot be Törless, because he knows more than Törless can know, occur during the late chapters of the work, when the expectation might be highest that the reader will turn in disgust from Törless as not worth saving.

This discussion of the narrative structure of the novel so far aims to articulate just that judgment on Törless that the novel attempts to hide—and reveals through the mechanism of its *Verneinung*.

The exculpatory narrative structure is also involved in the great theme of *Young Törless*—the richness of the "inner life." This follows as a consequence of Musil's chief psychological postulate: the elusiveness of this inner life with respect to verbal representation. One special way of showing its elusiveness is by the complexity with which motives are represented. What is striking, again and again, is the intricate *dis*continuity of the arc leading from motive to expression, from intent to deed. Musil writes, typically: "Even as . . . [Törless] talked he could feel that he had nothing but irrelevant points to bring up, and that his words were without any inner substance, having nothing to do with his real opinion" (62; 47). Of course this is a novel not rich in event but rich in the (elliptical) representation of what underlies event. The novel "proves" the standard claim of *Lebensphilosophie*, especially in its decisive formulation by Dilthey: the deed is a poor thing next to the imagination that gives rise to it. In Dilthey's words,

Through the power of a decisive motive, the act emerges from the fullness of life into one-sidedness. However meditated, it nonetheless expresses only a part of our being. Possibilities which lay in this being are annihilated by it. Thus the act detaches itself from the background of the context of life. And without clarification of the way in which in its circumstances, purpose, means, and life-context are connected, it does not allow a full-sided definition of that inwardness from which it sprang. Quite otherwise the objectivation of experience![23]

("Objectivation," for Dilthey, means, chiefly, artistic expression.)[24]

These passages will make us think of Törless. "An idea wakened him . . . : what in the distance seems so great and mysterious comes up to us always as something plain and undistorted. . . . What . . . approaches from a long way off is like a misty sea full of gigantic, ever-changing forms; what comes right up to any man, and becomes action, and collides with his life, is clear and small, human in its dimensions and human in its outlines" (159–60; 106). It goes without saying that all Törless's actions can be detoxified (exculpated, palliated, deconstructed) by reference to the complex originality of their motives.

This is only a small part of the thematic logic of Törless's justification. The true subject matter of the novel—Törless's felt perplexities—is informed by two apparently conflicting claims. One is moral, though it might be unconvincing; it asserts the value for the hero's development of his experiment in sadistic cruelty. The other claim is epistemological; it is made about moods, asserting that they are valuable for their distinctive cognitive power.[25] Typically, we learn that Törless's pained mood "touched his inmost balance at a much deeper point than any moral consideration could" (158; 105).

On the face of it, these two claims do not have a lot in common. Yet in *Young Törless*, moral and epistemological claims are indeed connected, and their covert linkage shapes the novel in important ways. In a word, Musil's epistemological claim on behalf of moods is as if necessitated by the novel's apologetic, justificatory intent. Because the narrator needs to come to terms with acts of sadistic cruelty, he shifts the moral gravity of interpersonal action onto the penumbra of the mood that accompanies it. The narrator's repeated assertion of the cognitive dignity of moods effectually serves to justify his hero's sadism.

The plainest evidence for this argument is the statement that Törless's sadistic adventure was the necessary product of a time of experiment marked by the cultivation of outré states of minds or moods. In later life, we are told, Törless was to grasp this experience as beneficial, if not indeed redemptive—as heightening and refining his capacity for experience.

Therefore, claims put forward as discrete actually intersect—"unconsciously," one could say, because the idea of their interinvolvement and reciprocal motivation (which is a true idea, in the sense that it is able to organize disparate themes and rhetorical features of the novel) is never explicitly asserted to be the case.[26] At the same time, we find in the novel the expectable effects of the unconscious denial of such motivation—namely, signs, at levels of rhetoric that seem least under control, saying the opposite of what the narrator says most plainly: that Törless, despite and indeed because of his power to experience the world "moodfully," is not different from and not superior to the victim of his sadism. That is because the condition of the experience of moods is a certain passivity.

From the start, Törless is defined through his susceptibility to moods. He gives himself up, with the sense of danger attendant on cultivating passive states of mind, to moods, which are revelatory though they cannot be translated into discursive language. "The more accurately . . . [Törless] circumscribed his feelings with thoughts, and the more familiar they became to him, the stranger and more incomprehensible did they seem to become, in equal measure" (28; 25).

> Törless's taste for certain moods was the first hint of a psychological development that was later to manifest itself as a strong sense of wonder. The fact was that later he was to have—and indeed to be dominated by—a peculiar ability; he could not help frequently experiencing events, people, things, and even himself, in such a way as to feel that in it all there was at once some insoluble enigma and some inexplicable kinship for which he could never produce any evidence. . . . The severity of these struggles [to resolve his feelings into words and ideas] was indicated only by a frequent sudden lassitude, alarming him, as it were, from a long way off, when ever some ambiguous, odd mood . . . brought him to a foreboding of it. Then he would see himself as powerless as a captive, as one who had been abandoned and shut away as much from himself as from others. (28–29; 25)

Afterward we read (just to give a few salient instances) that Törless "was in that state of more psychic than bodily fever which he loved. The mood went on intensifying" (136; 91). He reacts to his having thought something out all too carefully in advance: "It was too unspontaneous, and his mood swiftly lapsed into a dense, gluey boredom" (144; 95, cf. 88).

Törless has a marked consciousness of boundaries and frontiers without being able to map the zones they define; having moods, he escapes consciousness of the disparity between zone and limit. Typically, in the attic, "he saw people in a way he had never seen them before, never felt them before. But he saw them without seeing, without images, without forms, as if only his soul saw them; and yet they were so distinct that he was pierced through and through by their intensity. Only, as though they halted at a threshold they could not cross, they escaped him the moment he sought for words to grasp them with" (76; 55). Moods themselves, like a darkness populated with shapes that hold him fast (65–66; 49), are subliminal or superliminal. At a certain stage they are attractive, and Törless clings to them, because they pass over and erase boundaries, even in their negative modality fusing inner and outer worlds, like that "same dreadful indifference that had been blanketed over the surrounding countryside all that afternoon [and which] now came creeping across the plain." Törless's act of marching along behind Beineberg through the indifferent mist reinscribes a boundary—"and he felt it as though it must be so, as a stony compulsion catching his whole life up and compressing it into this movement—steadily plodding on along this one line" (14; 16). The marking of the boundary line is painful. As for his fascination with Basini, "Shut up!" he cries, in self-defense. "It wasn't me. It was a dream. A mood [*eine Laune*]" (187; 123). Afterwards, "he now knew how to distinguish between day and night; actually he had always known it, and it was only that a monstrous dream had flowed like a tide over those frontiers, blotting them out" (216; 140).

The painful deficit of Törless's openness to moods is the passivity he has identified in Basini and which is literally poisonous. The image of one who administers or takes poison amounts to a link between them. Poison is at first associated negatively with Basini: "He had no power of resisting anything that occurred to him and was always surprised by the consequences. In this he resembled the kind of woman . . . who introduces doses of poison into her husband's food at every meal and then is amazed and horror-struck at the strange, harsh words of the public prosecutor and the death-sentence pronounced on her" (69; 51). Törless's weak target here figures as a subtle and dangerous avenger—author, as well as victim, of a fatal sentence. But when the poison image resurfaces in the later passage to justify Törless's behavior, it is homeopathic. In his case, he alleges, the poison he took became a factor that improved him—"that small admixture of a toxic substance which is needed to rid the soul of its over-confident, complacent healthiness, and to give it instead a sort of health that is more acute, and subtler, and wiser" (171; 112). But the defense is compromised for being spoken, not by the narrator, but by the mature Törless, in his very own words.

The thing the novel needs fundamentally to defend against is not only or chiefly Törless's sadistic experiments with Basini. It is the possibility that even in asserting his superiority to Basini, Törless is essentially like Basini; that even and especially in tormenting his victim, he is exhibiting his identity with him. If it is true that *for Törless* to be a girl is to assume the passivity simultaneously craved and feared, then the preconscious meditation in which he rediscovers his "unspeakable longing to be a little girl" is revealing, for it culminates in the figure of Basini: "Today for the first time he felt something similar again—again that longing, that tingling under the skin . . . and then, last of all, there was only the pleasant warmth that lapped him . . . like a bath and a stirring of the senses . . . but no longer conscious to him as that, only in some utterly unrecognisable but very definite way being linked with Basini" (128–30; 86–87).[27] From the outset, Törless has "yearned to feel . . . definite needs that would distinguish between good and bad, . . . and to know he himself was making the choice, even though wrongly—for even that would be better than being so excessively receptive that he simply soaked up everything" (54; 42). But little better than Basini, in Törless "the moral force of resistance . . . was not yet developed either" (172; 114).[28]

If, now, the young Törless is to escape whipping, then the narrator of *Young Törless* must himself be the moral force. In reproducing Törless's confusions (and illuminations), the narrator must fight clear of identity with Törless the sadist, voyeur, and collector of poisonous moods. Put otherwise, young Törless's fear of being exposed as Basini's accomplice (195; 128) may be supposed to haunt the narrator: he must not be exposed as Törless's accomplice. Only as a disembodied intelligence, and not as a single, envisionable personality, is he certain of being exculpated.[29]

Weight falls on "intelligence." According to the narrator, Basini is principally corrupt, with an immorality linked to his stupidity: "The moral inferiority that was apparent in him and his stupidity both had a single origin" (69; 51). Hence, it is as if the young Törless could not possibly be corrupt since he is so evidently not stupid.[30] Indeed, it is with this very claim to intelligence that the narrator afterward defends Törless's taking of Basini's poison.

> His tastes had become so acutely and one-sidedly focused on matters purely of the mind [*schöngeistig zugeschärft*] that, supposing he had been told a very similar story about some rake's debaucheries, it would certainly never have occurred to him to direct his indignation against the acts themselves. He would have despised such a person not for being a debauchee, but for being nothing more than that; not for his licentiousness, but for the psychological condition that made him do those things; for being stupid. (170; 112)

Suppose, however, we cannot agree that corruption and stupidity must have the common root they allegedly have in Basini. Suppose we believe that despite Törless's intelligence, "the more or less worm-eaten hero" is defective; that as one of "such people [to whom] the things that make demands only on their moral correctitude are of the utmost indifference," he is inexcusable (169; 112). Are we going to be persuaded that this argument is wrong by a narrator chiefly distinguished for his aesthetic intelligence?

Even the disembodied narrator's immunity cannot be achieved, as I have

suggested; the stance he adopts is only Törless's stance vis-à-vis Basini—
and improved. In keeping distance so as to guarantee a rich imagined sense
of the other's inner life, he *repeats* Törless's truth—his great discovery apropos of using Basini, the truth that constitutes him. This is the truth of
the superiority of the aesthetic view of persons to the moral one, the truth
that says that only the detached and cognitively curious identification is
productive.[31] "That kind of knowledge of human nature" is valuable as "a
source of exquisite psychological enjoyment" (7; 11). To the extent that
the stance of the impersonal narrator is any more morally concerned than
Törless 2's, it is only with Musil's special refinement: "From youth on I
have considered aesthetics as ethics."[32] But this position is not much different from that of the "dictator" Reiting: "You've only got to drop the
idea that there's any relationship between us and Basini other than the pleasure we get out of what a rotten swine he is!" (63; 48).

The problem of Musil's narrative authority in *Törless* is the same as
Flaubert's in *Madame Bovary*, with a change of sign. If Flaubert's *aporia* is
how to condemn the novelistic novelistically—how to expose, by means of
a novel, the novelistic contamination of Madame Bovary's desire—Musil's
aporia is how to justify an aesthetic intelligence by means of an aesthetic
intelligence in practice. The narrative stance of *Törless* is sometimes dictated
by science, sometimes by aesthetics ("as ethics"); it is suspended between
lucid analytical modes and effects of elegance, between dictions of episte-
mology and expressiveness, observation and special pleading, the pursuit
of founded psychological truths and moral defenses based on erotic identification.[33] In a way there is the bedazzlement of verbal intelligence in
excess, and in a way too little rigor. Both are suspicious. Hence there remains at the heart of the novel, for all its intricate flights of narrative and
mood, something inexcusable—in a word, scandalous—which assures its
fascination, as it has done for almost a century now.

POSTSCRIPT

Though it is late in the day, I should like to profile my conclusion as to the
status of the narrator of *Young Törless*. "His" position is best situated outside two extreme positions, both of which I discard: they are (1) the model
of identity between the perspective of the author Musil and that of young
Törless and (2) the model of radical disjunction between the author and
his character—a disjunction so absolute that it is alleged also to include the
radical disjunction between the author and the narrator.

The first model of identity is proposed by Gert Mattenklott, who writes,
"It can be shown that the author has no superiority of knowledge over his

hero. . . . Törless's aesthetic mode of perception is not only the theme of a novel about an artist; it actually *determines* the novel's own perspective."[34]

This is clearly indefensible, because it discounts the novel's many moments of enacted disjunction. The narrator knows the direction of Törless's perplexities as Törless himself does not and generalizes them in a theory of necessary development. In many important places the narrator's stance is mediated by the perspective of the grown-up Törless—congruent but not identical with his own, and harder and cleverer than that of young Törless.

As a corrective to Mattenklott, one is inclined to suggest that even the "authorial" narrator of this novel is a fiction constructed by the author. This extreme position is implied in Eckhard Heftrich's account of Törless at work on his autobiography.

> Törless had bought himself a copy-book and now carefully set out his pen and ink. Then, after some hesitation, he wrote on the first page: De natura hominum. The Latin title was, he thought, the philosophic subject's due. Then he drew a large artistic curlicue round the title and leaned back in his chair to wait until it dried. (131; 88)

"This is characteristically the only scene in the book in which the author *has his narrator become entirely ironic.*"[35]

But the implications of this theory are not acceptable, for they put an impassable divide between the empirical author Musil and his narrator. It becomes impossible to say a single certain thing by way of explanation, motivation, and intent about Musil's relation to his novel as a whole. If the narrative is itself a consciously fictive construction, then Musil can be holding it up for our incredulity, too, as only the kind of narrative told by the kind of narrator whose diction and opinions are no better than they are. It is interesting that exponents of this formalist principle (of the fictive authorial narrator) are determined to dignify its product as literature and never to denigrate it as a fabrication, evasion, or contrivance; yet by the latter assumption, which cannot be refuted, the twenty-two-year-old Musil could also have constructed this telling of the tale as an example of perfectly sculptured error. In fact, he could have told it infinitely better or with an entirely different bearing. One can see that this assumption is so instrumentally fruitless as to be false.

I therefore conclude that Musil constructs a narrative position out of a bundle of paradoxical motives. The narrator must speak on his behalf, with intimate knowledge of a special episode—a knowledge that could only have been obtained from personal involvement in that experience and one, therefore, that could only have been in the main experienced by Musil. Yet this intimate knowledge must not involve the risk of legal or any other sort of inculpation.

I would therefore be prepared to accept Howald's interchangeable use of the terms "Musil" and "narrator"[36] except for the fact that this occludes the whole complex of distancing gestures at work in *Törless*—products of the built-in injunction that no reader take the narrator to be Musil. I have argued that the best approximate model for the narrator is a "friend"—of Törless's—and insofar as "Törless" is the alias of a real person, a "friend" of Musil's. This "friend" speaks on behalf of Musil but deflects censure to himself. The author displaces the narrative position from an identifiable position of real speaking, disguising the speaker beyond recovery but in his manner of doing so *becomes* Musil. For the relation of the empirical author to his narrator, my colleague Michael Jennings suggests the phrase "tormented complicity."

NOTES

1. The novel I am dealing with, by the conventions of publication in the United States, is *Young Törless*, an English translation of Robert Musil's *Die Verwirrungen des Zöglings Törless*, trans. Eithne Wilkins and Ernst Kaiser (New York: Pantheon, 1955). I have decided to base my interpretive essay on the English version of Musil's novel, checking every sentence for accuracy, not just the ones quoted. Taking the English-language version as my basic text is, I believe, a more coherent procedure than writing about the German original and then presenting my results as if they were based on illustrative sentences torn out of the Wilkins and Kaiser translation.

2. Musil wrote apropos of *Törless* that "the reality [the subject matter], depicted is always only an excuse [*Vorwand*]." Musil, *Tagebücher, Aphorismen, Essays und Reden*, ed. Adolf Frisé (Reinbeck bei Hamburg: Rowohlt, 1955), 808. There would have been more truth, I think, in the statement "in *Törless*, the mode of depiction is the excuse."

3. Musil, *Young Törless*, 132. Henceforth, all English-language quotations are taken from this version, and page numbers are given in parentheses in the essay. For the reader's convenience, I follow these page numbers with corresponding page numbers from *Die Verwirrungen des Zöglings Törless* (Hamburg: Rowohlt Taschenbuch Verlag, 1959). The quote above is found on 88.

4. No wonder, since "Basini is in fact introduced into the structure of the novel as deputy and precursor of Törless." Stefan Howald, *Ästhetizismus und ästhetische Ideologiekritik: Untersuchungen zum Romanwerk Robert Musils* (Munich: Fink, 1984), 46.

5. More is involved, of course, than an abstract sense of difference. As Martin Swales points out, "In mimetic terms we have a narrator who is clearly, and securely, in possession of the outcome of the tale. . . . And this superior knowledge is allowed to inform the narrative performance at every turn." Swales, "Narrator and Hero: Observations on Robert Musil's Törleß," in *Musil in Focus: Papers from Centenary Symposium*, ed. Lothar Huber and John J. White (London: Institute of Germanic Studies, University of London, 1982), 2.

6. For example, if a part of Thomas Mann's *Joseph* tetralogy is narrated from the explicit standpoint of an angel, it is still not unreasonable to think of this fictive narrator as representing "aspects" of Thomas Mann's "personality."

7. Musil was inclined to deny the literal, autobiographical truth of the scenes and events in *Young Törless*. He said that he had been willing, for one thing, in 1901 "to give the plot away" to a few "naturalistic" writers he knew (*Tagebücher*, 803). Peter Henninger stresses how, for Musil, *Young Törless* did not constitute a deeply autobiographical, deeply private enterprise. A year and a half after writing it, he began a second autobiographical novel, which he elaborated for years, bringing to this project matters that allegedly touched him more intimately than the theme of *Törless*. Henninger, *Der Buchstabe und der Geist: Unbewußte Determinierung im Schreiben Robert Musils* (Frankfurt, Bern, Cirencester, England: Lang, 1980), 145.

The bisexual behavior described in *Young Törless*, wrote Musil, was hardly crucial: other forms of sexual pathology—"sadism, masochism, fetishism," for example— would have served as well (*Tagebücher*, 723). (It is bemusing to think of Musil *opposing* sadism and masochism to the kinds of sexual exploitation described in *Törless*.) See, further, notes 10, 11, and 26 below.

8. The German word for the kind of school Törless is attending is *Konvikt*.

9. Hannah Hickman, *Robert Musil and the Culture of Vienna* (La Salle, Ill.: Open Court, 1984), 28.

10. The back cover of *Young Törless* simply and audaciously describes this novel as "set in a military boarding school" and illustrates the cover with a drawing by Dagmar Frinta of a cadet holding a large boot in his gloved hand. The German-language Rowohlt edition, which has sold almost half a million copies, also shows on the cover a cadet wearing a shako. These are presumptions very likely dictated by considerations of publicity—namely the desire to make intuitively evident the "militaristic" or "fascistic" bearing of the novel's persons and events as precursors of "today's dictators *in nucleo*" (Musil, *Tagebücher*, 441).

11. Volker Schlöndorff's film *Der junge Törless* (1966) depicts the students at W. as cadets, though they do not wear shakos. In an interview he described the venue as a "military academy" (*Kadettenanstalt*), adding that he had never conceived of his project as a faithful film adaptation. Robert Fischer and Joe Hembus, *Der neue deutsche Film, 1960–1980* (Munich: Goldmann, 1981), 29.

What was Musil's view of the fidelity of the novel to his experience? What he said could justify both positions. In a later biographical draft he declared that of the various motives inspiring his work, the confessional never played a role: he was not concerned "to analyze, portray, put to the test, or defend himself or confess, ask for absolution, repent, or plead for pardon. And yet, many people saw . . . [his] first book as a confessional." On the other hand, he is supposed to have said to Klaus Pinkus: "I never invented a single word in *Törless*." See Karl Corino, "Törleß Ignotus: Zu den biographischen Hintergründen von Robert Musils Roman 'Die Verwirrungen des Zöglings Törleß,' " *Text und Kritik* 21–22 (1972): 61. It is noteworthy that in his late autobiographical drafts Musil dwells on the military paraphernalia at the school where he was educated—pike and regimentals and dress boots—but there is hardly a trace of such things in Törless's school at "W."

12. Musil, *Tagebücher*, 776.

13. Friedrich Nietzsche, *Werke in drei Bänden*, ed. Karl Schlechta (Munich: Hanser, 1954–56), 1:1090.

14. *Türlosigkeit—Robert Musils "Törless" in Mikroanalysen mit Ausblicken auf andere Texte des Dichters* is the title of a useful monograph by Lars W. Freij (Stockholm: Almqvist and Wiksell), 1972.

15. "For the object of this longing, the image of his parents, actually ceased to have any place in it at all: I mean that certain plastic, physical memory of a loved person which is not merely remembrance but something speaking to all the senses and preserved in all the senses, so that one cannot do anything without feeling the other person silent and invisible at one's side" (4; 9). This observation was, to my knowledge, first made by Burton Pike in *Robert Musil: An Introduction to His Work* (Ithaca: Cornell University Press, 1961), 45. In *Crisis and Continuity in Modern*

German Fiction: Ten Essays (Ithaca: Cornell University Press, 1969), Henry Hatfield notes: "At one point, apparently inadvertently, the narrator calls himself 'I' " (181). Martin Swales discusses this point: "If Törleß's development . . . can be seen . . . as an assimilation to the narrative perspective, then this explains why the narrative voice is . . . so insistently in the foreground. . . . The urgency of narrative entry here has to do with the constant intimation that . . . the making of this fiction is the only adequate medium for conveying the import of Törleß's experiences" ("Narrator and Hero," 8). This analysis is surely correct, but the narrative structure can also be a reminiscence of the opening (also in a school) of *Madame Bovary*. There, too, the first-person narrative pronoun promptly disappears.

16. In "Narrator and Hero," Swales develops the view that the narrative perspective may be regarded as a projection of the sensibility of the emergent Törless, stressing, too, its apologetic character. It is true that the perspectives of both Törless 1 and Törless 2 appear to fuse. Dorrit Cohn notes the effect of the abundance of similes in Musil's psychonarrative. They "seem to induce a fusion between the narrating and the figural consciousness by blurring the line that separates them." Cohn, *Transparent Minds: Narrative Modes for Presenting Consciousness in Fiction* (Princeton: Princeton University Press, 1978), 43.

17. See Stanley Corngold, *The Fate of the Self: German Writers and French Theory* (New York: Columbia University Press, 1986), 161–79. See further the unpublished essay by Eric Miller, "Breaks in Perspective in Kafka's *Das Schloß*," Princeton University, which affirms the extraordinary paucity of telling information conveyed by breaks in Kafka's narrative perspective in *The Castle*.

18. The first critic known to me to have (rightly) grasped *Young Törless* as a type of *Künstlerroman*—a novel portraying the unfolding of a young artist—is Theodore Ziolkowski, in "James Joyces Epiphanie und die Überwindung der empirischen Welt in der modernen deutschen Prosa," *Deutsche Vierteljahrsschrift* 35 (1961): 594–616.

19. Swales, in "Narrator and Hero," also cites Törless's newfound metaphorical powers as he defends himself before the school investigators: "These words and these figures of speech, which were far beyond what was appropriate to Törless's age, flowed easily and naturally from his lips in his state of vast excitement he was in, in this moment of almost poetic inspiration" (212).

20. From the chapter "La morale des mystiques," in Maeterlinck, *Le trésor des humbles* (1898). For a discussion of this passage, see Elisabeth Stopp, "Musil's 'Törless': Content and Form," *Modern Language Review* 63 (1968): 110.

21. Pike, *Robert Musil*, 43.

22. Törless declares to Beineberg that his intellectual life is a fraud (24).

23. Wilhelm Dilthey, *Gesammelte Schriften* (Leipzig: Teubner; Göttingen: Vandenhoeck and Ruprecht, 1914–77), 7:206. Indeed, it might be possible to characterize the project of turn-of-the-century Austrian literature as a basic complication of the arc leading from inwardness (the motive) to the expression—a complication, especially, of representation and the syntax of the representation. In Hofmannsthal's *Lord Chandos* letter, the arc breaks down entirely. In a story found in Kafka's diary, a kind of dramatized dialogue that begins " 'You,' I said . . . ," the

relationship of motive to expression is distinctly odd. See Stanley Corngold, *Franz Kafka: The Necessity of Form* (Ithaca: Cornell University Press, 1988), 14.

24. Oscar Wilde, too, "depreciated action in favor of imagination because it was 'a thing incomplete in its essence, because limited by accident, and ignorant of its direction, being always at variance with its aim.' " Cited in Geoffrey Hartman, "Looking Back on Paul de Man," in *Reading de Man Reading*, ed. Lindsay Waters and Wlad Godzich (Minneapolis: University of Minnesota Press, 1989), 21.

25. That Törless's moods will strike readers as occasions for powerful revelations emerges partly from the cognitive importance that has been lent to that mental item by authors called existentialist. Many will read *Törless* in the perspective, for example, of Heidegger's remarkable discussion of moods in *Being and Time* (1927) and *What Is Metaphysics?* (1929). A passage in *Being and Time* from the discussion of *Befindlichkeiten* (approximately, "ways of being in the world") defines Heidegger's stance: "The possibilities of disclosure which belong to cognition reach far too short a way compared with the primordial disclosure belonging to moods, in which Dasein is brought before its Being as 'there.' . . . From the existential-ontological point of view, there is not the slightest justification for minimizing what is 'evident' in states-of-mind, by measuring it against the apodictic certainty of a theoretical cognition of something which is purely present-at-hand. However, the phenomena are no less falsified when they are banished to the sanctuary of the irrational." Martin Heidegger, *Being and Time*, trans. John Macquarrie and Edward Robinson (New York: Harper and Row, 1962), 173–75. For Heidegger, the disclosive powers of mood exceed the theoretical knowledge of objects present at hand.

In *Törless*, moods figure as the noetic correlatives of what are called symbols. Symbolic knowledge means felt saturation by the appropriate mood. At the outset of the novel the symbol of parallel railroad tracks conjures, for example, a correlative mood of isolation, of being lost. In his journals, thinking about *Törless*, Musil profiled the crucial constitutive power of moods: "It isn't stated that these things had this or that mood, but they have it. The attitude was in me" (Musil, *Tagebücher*, 132).

26. "Themes"—passivity, sexuality; "rhetorical features"—obsessive images, e.g., poison.

27. See Henninger, *Der Buchstabe*, 115.

28. According to criteria recently proposed by Dominick LaCapra, *Törless* here becomes a work eminently and legitimately deconstructible. Indeed, *Törless* is the very model of the self-deconstructing text. The novel sets about excluding the *scapegoat figure* (Basini) from the human community on the strength of his difference only to show subliminally—on the basis of poison and passivity—that the pillar of the community (Törless) and Basini are the one and the same.

29. Corino, in "Törless Ignotus," acknowledges the risk of inculpation very pointedly. In his view, *Törless* is an autobiographical novel. Presumably without knowing the research by Ernst Kaiser reported in Stopp ("Musil's 'Törless,' " 98), Corino identified the originals of Reiting, Beineberg, and Basini, whose names Musil only very slightly altered. Corino also demystifies Musil's claim to have had nothing real and personal in mind with the plot of *Young Törless* on the grounds

that to have done otherwise would have been to expose himself to juridical charges of character defamation or worse (62).

30. "For as though independently of himself, Törless's intellect lashed out, inexorably, at the sensitive young prince" (8; 12).

31. Howald, in *Ästhetizismus*, notes the "narrator's unequivocal identification with Törless's instrumental stance" in the following passage: "It would be entirely wrong to believe that Basini had aroused in Törless a desire that was—however fleetingly and perplexedly—a thoroughgoing and real one. True, something like passion had been aroused in him, but 'love' was quite certainly only a casual, haphazard term for it, and the boy Basini himself was no more than a substitute, a provisional object of this longing. For although Törless did debase himself with him, his desire was never satisfied by him; on the contrary, it went on growing out beyond Basini, growing out into some new and aimless craving" (65).

32. Musil, *Tagebücher*, 429.

33. Howald's chapter on *Törless* in *Ästhetizismus* correctly puts pressure on the "integrity" of the narrator. Howald is alert to the major strain of special pleading throughout the novel—Musil's way of "solving" the problem of the expressiveness of inner experience by describing the actual resolutions of it made by his hero, even though he "conceives of his hero in strictly dichotomous terms of aesthetic sensibility and rational judgment" (32). Howald notes, for example, that the immature and retrograde character of Törless's "sensuality" is made into a mark of special distinction vis-à-vis the others. Törless has a "depth" that the others do not have. He is superior to his group by virtue of his "refined psychological interest in Basini and the aesthetic pleasure he draws from it" (47). The narrator profiles the aesthetic pleasure arising from the shattering of that human subject caught up in conventional values opposed to sensuality (37); certainly consciousness of the other human subject instrumental in the shattering is repressed (39). On the other hand, this destruction is incorporated as a fact into the narrator's general argument on necessary although transitional phases of moral development. Therefore, if "aestheticism neutralizes the social-critical force of immorality and thus in the end works toward a morality of social conformism," aestheticism also appears to subserve an argument for genuine moral development (40). This is an important and unmastered contradiction.

34. Gert Mattenklott, "Der 'subjektive Faktor' in Musils 'Törless,' " *Robert Musil*, Wege der Forschung 588, ed. Renate von Heydebrand (Darmstadt: Wissenschaftliche Buchgesellschaft, 1982), 258, 275 (emphasis added).

35. Eckhard Heftrich, *Musil—Eine Einführung* (Munich and Zurich: Artemis, 1986), 36 (emphasis added).

36. Howald, *Ästhetizismus*, 22–80.

PART THREE

GENDER, DIFFERENCE, AND

NARRATION

ELEVEN

CROSSING THE GENDER WALL:

NARRATIVE STRATEGIES IN GDR FICTIONS OF

SEXUAL METAMORPHOSIS

Gail Finney

The woman shall not wear that which pertaineth unto a man,
neither shall a man put on a woman's garment: for all that do
so *are* abomination unto the Lord thy God.
—Deuteronomy 22.5

WHILE THE COLLECTION *Bolt from the Blue* (*Blitz aus heiterm Himmel*) as a whole has not received great critical attention in the West, it aroused considerable interest and controversy in East Germany.[1] Published in 1975 as the result of Edith
Anderson's call to a number of GDR writers to create tales about sexual
transformation, the anthology is a far cry from socialist realism. Indeed, if
socialist realism can be somewhat simplistically characterized as "boy meets
tractor" literature, as I have occasionally done in teaching it, the plot of
these fantastic stories might whimsically be summarized as "boy meets self
as girl" (and vice versa).[2] Whereas all the stories in the collection criticize
stereotypical gender differences that support male privilege,[3] the authors
employ a variety of narrative situations to make this statement. On the
most basic level, to depict convincingly the metamorphosis of a "she" into
a "he" or of a male "I" into a female "I" poses particular technical challenges to the storyteller. I would like to examine here three different narrative situations and, concomitantly, three distinct literary modes represented in the anthology. I will focus on the stories best known to an
American and West German audience (because they were published in the
Federal Republic): Günter de Bruyn's "Sex Swap" ("Geschlechtertausch"),
written in the first person and the existential mode; Sarah Kirsch's ironic,
third-person "Bolt from the Blue" ("Blitz aus heiterm Himmel"); and
Christa Wolf's didactic "Self-Experiment: Appendix to a Report" ("Selbstversuch: Traktat zu einem Protokoll"), which verges on a second-person

narrative insofar as a first-person narrator speaks to a second-person addressee.

My choice of texts reflects the fact that person is, as Franz Stanzel describes it, the "most obvious opposition" present among the structurally significant pairs of elements constituting the narrative situation.[4] Yet this opposition acquires special significance in the stories in *Bolt from the Blue*, since the pronouns that signal a difference in person also signal a difference in gender, the central antithesis propelling the anthology. Even though "I" does not carry the evident gender tag that "he" and "she" do, as Jeanette Clausen observes, "the pronoun 'I' . . . becomes gendered simply through being uttered,"[5] and one could make a similar statement about the gendering of second-person pronouns by the addressing speaker. As we shall see, insofar as the tension between the masculine and the feminine, as well as the ease or difficulty of moving from one gender to the other, are manifested in the tension between the pronouns distinguishing person, close analysis of the pronoun relationships in these three paradigmatic narrative situations offers considerable insight into the stories' depictions of the relations between the sexes.

In de Bruyn's "Sex Swap," the protagonist Karl's sexual transformation occurs as the magical result of the wish he and his wife Anna express to achieve complete unity by attaining the opposite gender. However, their formulation of this wish as simply the desire to be "the woman" and "the man" rather than each other specifically leads to an incomplete metamorphosis that manifests itself in a split between the subjective consciousness and the outer person. De Bruyn's first-person narrative graphically underlines the split in Karl, now Karla, between a maintained male inner self and a new female exterior through the grammatical reflexive. Whereas by definition the subject and object of a reflexive construction are the same person, because the externally female Karla still possesses a masculine consciousness, the identity between the perceiving "I" and the perceived "me" (direct object) (along with the related "my," myself," "me" as indirect object, and so forth) is not complete. The ego disorientation occasioned by this split is already announced, for example, as Karla approaches the office on the first workday following her transformation: "Here, where *I* was more at home than anywhere else, I became foreign to *myself*" ("Hier, wo ich wie nirgendwo sonst zu Hause war, wurde *ich mir* selber fremd").[6] Seeing her face in a window in the office, she has the following realization: "First of all, that *I* still saw women, and hence *myself* as well, with the eyes of a man; and secondly, that my awareness of my good looks reassured *me*" ("Daß *ich*, erstens, Frauen, also auch *mich*, noch immer mit den Augen des Mannes sah, und daß *mich*, zweitens, die Gewißheit, gut auszusehen, beruhigte," 201; emphasis added). The image of the mirror serves as a visual analogue for the linguistic use of the reflexive form, yet in both instances

CROSSING THE GENDER WALL 165

the identity between reflector and reflection is only superficial. Similarly, Karla later recounts "that *I* stood for a long time in the evening in front of the mirror and regarded *my* present form with the eyes of my former self" ("daβ *ich* am Abend lange vor dem Spiegel stand und *meine* gegenwärtige Gestalt mit den Augen meiner vergangenen sah," 209; emphasis added).

Because it is this split between a male consciousness and a female exterior that allows for de Bruyn's unmasking of sexist behavior in the workplace, the effectiveness of a first-person narrative in portraying this issue may be evaluated by focusing on the reactions of the "I" to the treatment of the "me." Doing so, we find that Karla's dissatisfaction with her new female status sets in even before she arrives at the office, as men crowd unnecessarily close to her on the streetcar. She reacts with anger at the sarcastic "For you, Madam!" ("Bitte sehr, gnädige Frau!" 204) of a male coworker as he offers her a chair; with embarrassment when a group of male visitors find her loquaciousness and joke-telling inappropriate for a woman; with irritation when her secretary begins to turn the plant watering, coffee-making, and dishwashing tasks she has formerly taken care of over to Karla; with humiliation when her director makes sexual overtures to her, advancing from flirtation to chasing her around his desk; and finally with rage when she is passed over as a discussant at a conference and applauded there not because of her professional expertise but as the "only rose among thorns" ("einzige[n] Rose unter Dornen," 218).

Karla's male "I" perceives, in other words, that as a female her "me" becomes paramount, that she is judged according to externals rather than essences; as she wearily observes, "They found other things more interesting than my professional expertise" ("Man fand anderes interessanter als mein Fachwissen," 211). Accordingly, she begins to undergo a process she calls "superficialization" ("Veräußerlichung," 211) that contradicts her male consciousness: she begins to occupy herself with clothes and cosmetics; to take pride, as we saw above, in her good looks; and to base her sense of self on her attractiveness to men: "I had reached the point where I viewed my effect on men as an indicator of my worth or worthlessness" ("Ich war schon so weit, daβ ich die Frage nach meiner Wirkung auf Männer für eine nach meinem Wert oder Unwert hielt," 209). More fundamentally, she finds her self-confidence ebbing away in the face of her treatment at work. Yet in contrast, for instance, to "Hiller, sitting there smiling and not saying a word" ("der schweigend und lächelnd dasitzenden Hiller," 209), who is fully feminine inside and out and is appreciated as such, Karla continues to shield herself against the encroachments of the feminine on her inner self, a process again highlighted by the use of the grammatical reflexive: "Of course *I* defended *myself* against these revaluations and attempted to get to the bottom of the psychic mechanism at work here" ("Natürlich wehrte *ich mich* gegen diese Umwertungen und versuchte, den hier wirksam werdenden psychischen Mechanismus zu ergründen," 209; emphasis added).

Hence it is perhaps appropriate that it is Karla's male "I" rather than her female "me" that ultimately dominates her and determines her fate. Going to the clinic to meet Anna (now Adam), who has been ill, in order to have their mutual sex change reversed, Karla continues despite all she has experienced as an external woman about the limits of sexual stereotypes to think one-sidedly as a man: she approaches the situation "confident of victory" ("siegessicher," 222); persists in viewing Adam as a "she" despite his clearly masculine appearance; and is oblivious to the nurse's hints about her relationship with Adam. When the nature of this relationship dawns on Karla, as she recounts, "[masculine] pride suppressed [feminine] tears" ("Stolz hielt Tränen zurück," 222). Most revealing of Karla's one-sidedly masculine perceptions—in this case, men's negative views of the feminine—is the nurse's explanation to her of Adam's reason for wanting to remain a man: "The one-sidedness with which you described to Adam your life as a woman disturbed him. Never again could he have been Anna in any carefree and unprejudiced way. . . . Did Adam as Anna ever complain about being a woman?" ("Die Einseitigkeit, mit der Sie Adam Ihr Frauenleben schilderten, hat ihn verstört. Nie mehr hätte er unbekümmert und vorurteilslos Anna sein können. . . . Hat sich denn Adam als Anna jemals darüber beklagt, eine Frau zu sein?" 222–23). Ironically, Karl's original desire for unity with his wife results in the inescapable isolation of Karla's sexual limbo, since she is able neither to return to her male body nor to acquire a female consciousness.

The plot of "Sex Swap" thus resembles that of de Bruyn's earlier novels *Buridan's Jackass* (*Buridans Esel*) and *The Awarding of the Prize* (*Preisverleihung*) as described by Leonore Krenzlin: "New experiences and decisions present the individual with new demands and thereby with the possibility of new modes of behavior. The question is actually to what degree the individual is capable of living up to his newly attained behavioral norm. Not until a character's failure becomes public is the author's satire pointed against him" ("Aus neuem Erleben, neuen Entscheidungssituationen erwachsen dem einzelnen neue Ansprüche und damit die Möglichkeit neuer Verhaltensweisen. Die Frage ist eigentlich, wie weit der einzelne fähig ist, zu seiner neuerworbenen Verhaltensnorm zu stehen. Erst wenn das Versagen einer Figur offenkundig wird, wendet sich die satirische Spitze gegen sie").[7] Yet several features of the text take it beyond the sphere of social satire into a realm that might best be characterized as existential. Stanzel ascribes an existential motivation to all embodied first-person narrators; he observes that "everything that is narrated in the first-person form is somehow existentially relevant for the first-person narrator" and links David Goldknopf's notion of a "confessional increment" with the first-person narrative act (98). One can scarcely imagine a more graphic example than Karla of an embodied first-person narrator, who according to Stanzel "is tied inextricably to a physical body which he cannot discard when it becomes inconvenient" (93–94). The alienation Karla feels as a male consciousness imprisoned, apparently forever, inside a female body is the basis of her existential compulsion to tell her story.

Furthermore, on a substantial level, Karla's state recalls the existential rootlessness of so many of Kafka's protagonists, and indeed de Bruyn's text contains elements that are strikingly reminiscent of Kafka's narratives. "Sex Swap" opens with two such elements, both evoked again at the story's end: a reference to the mysterious sound that accompanied the sexual transformation—"a creaking, almost a cracking—similar to the sound a person's shoulder joints sometimes make when he stretches in the morning" ("ein knirschend beginnendes Knacken, das dem Laut ähnelt, den beim morgendlichen Recken manchmal Schultergelenke verursachen," 198)—as well as the narrator's admission of her inability to recreate the noise—"In vain I keep trying again and again, although I know that even that could not help me" ("Vergeblich versuche ich es wieder und wieder, obwohl ich weiß, daß auch das mir nicht helfen könnte," 223).

The most obvious echo of Kafka is of course the metamorphosis itself. Franz Fühmann, who when Edith Anderson called to ask him to contribute to her collection of sex-change tales, exclaimed in horror, "A woman! Why, that's worse than Kafka! That's much, much worse than waking up as a cockroach!" ("Genesis and Adventures," 3), was evidently not the only writer to note the parallel. Throughout his story de Bruyn uses the word "metamorphosis" ("Verwandlung") to refer to his characters' transformation. A more subtle similarity is that between the male-female "I-me" tension in "Sex Swap" and the split in Kafka's "Metamorphosis" between Gregor Samsa's human consciousness and the insect he perceives himself to be, a split manifested in the reflexive "he-himself" constructions that begin in the novella's famous first sentence: "When Gregor Samsa woke up one morning from unsettling dreams, *he* found *himself* changed in his bed into a monstrous vermin" ("Als Gregor Samsa eines Morgens aus unruhigen Träumen erwachte, fand *er sich* in seinem Bett zu einem ungeheueren Ungeziefer verwandelt").[8] While the narrative form used here is third person, the term coined by Cohn to describe such rendering of "a character's mental discourse in the guise of the narrator's discourse"—narrated monologue[9]—suggests the closeness of this technique to the first person.

In view of the substantive and formal features of "Sex Swap" discussed here—the embodied narrator's existential isolation, emphasized through echoes of Kafka's works, and her first-person compulsion to recount the genesis of this isolation—we can designate the mode of de Bruyn's story as existential. Kirsch's "Bolt from the Blue" is written in a very different mode. Where "Sex Swap" ends with a spotlight on separation, the central motif of Kirsch's contribution to the anthology appears to be togetherness. This theme is announced early in the story, in the phrase "Let's wait to see what happens and keep combining" ("Weitersehen und kombinieren").[10] Although these words are used to describe the female protagonist Katharina's idiosyncratic taste for discerning regular patterns among the colored clothespins and pieces of laundry that she hangs up randomly, with her eyes closed, to dry, the phrase applies to other contexts in the story as well. For instance, the narrator summarizes Katharina's relationship with her boyfriend Albert, a long-distance truck driver, as follows: "They laughed about their mutual obsession and discovered many of the possible combinations" ("Sie lachten über ihre beiderseitige Versessenheit und entdeckten viele der möglichen Kombinationen," 11). But the combination most significant for the interpretation of the story is that which results when Katharina, transformed after three days of sleep into Max, teams up with Albert. Maintaining the focus on the private, domestic sphere evident in the portrayal of Katharina's life, the narrator tells us how Max and Albert now function together: stacking coal that has been dumped in front of the house and taking a shower together afterward; gathering wood together; sharing the tasks of cooking dinner and cleaning up; rearranging the furniture; repairing Albert's truck together; and projecting a utopia without physical labor, border skirmishes, and war.

The thematic emphasis on combinations in "Bolt from the Blue" is paralleled on the syntactic and linguistic levels as well. Both direct speech and quoted monologue of Katharina/Max, for example, are frequently blended into the text as parenthetical insertions, without mediation on the part of the narrator: Katharina's supposition about the water remaining from her wet laundry as she pours it onto the attic floor—"(it won't leak through)" ("[wird schon nich durchkomm]," 7), the words (we assume) she uses with her neighbor to defend her laundry game—"(what do you mean by sloppiness, this is scientific work, Frau Spiller)" ("[von wegen Schlampe, diß is wissenschaftliche Arbeit, Frau Schpiller]," 8), Max's resolution as he winds the alarm clock before bed on the first evening following his metamorphosis—"(I'm not going to sleep for three days straight again)" ("[Drei Tage schlafich nich nochmal]," 17). This deemphasis on narratorial mediation heightens the disembodied quality of the story's authorial third-person narrator.

Linguistically, where de Bruyn's embodied first-person narrator is victimized by the unbridgeable gap between the perceiving male "I" and the perceived female "me," Kirsch's disembodied third-person narrator depicts Katharina's transition from "she" to "he" as smooth and seamless. Although Katharina lets out a manly scream on discovering her metamorphosis, and "although she was sorry about the loss of her curves" ("obwohls ihr um das Holz vorm Haus etwas leid war," 13), she soon comes to terms with her new status; precisely in the third person, where the reader would expect the greatest difficulty in conveying such a change, Kirsch's narrator achieves it through a simple pronoun leap, effected within a single sentence and without commentary: "Whereas *she* had previously aimed the shower spray at her belly first and then proceeded to the other parts, the water now hit *him* between his shoulders" ("Während *sie* vorher die Brause immer zuerst auf den Bauch gerichtet hatte und dann zu anderen Partien übergegangen war, traf *ihn* nun das Wasser zwischen die Schultern," 14; emphasis added). Subsequently, Katharina is Max, apparently without any problem whatsoever: "His fear and anxiety disappeared, and the feeling of well-being with which he had awakened returned" ("Furcht und Beklommenheit verließen ihn, und das Wohlbehagen, mit dem er erwacht war, stellte sich wieder ein," 14).

On closer examination, however, these combinations are not so harmonious and light-hearted as they seem on the surface to be. Stanzel's typological distinction is again illuminating here: "For the third-person narrator . . . there is no existential compulsion to narrate. His motivation is literary-aesthetic rather than existential" (93). As I will show, the precise literary-aesthetic motivation of Kirsch's narrator appears to be irony, so much so that in contrast to the existential mode of "Sex Swap," the mode of "Bolt from the Blue" can be characterized as ironic.

The narrator's semi-unmediated rendering of the speech and thoughts of Katharina and Max, described above, indicates that Max in fact remains Katharina internally. His possession of her consciousness is evident in their common use of dialect, slang, and curse words. Early in the story, we find the following thought about the local birds attributed to Katharina: "(It doesn't pay to feed them in the summer. The hairdresser downstairs says they just shit on the ladies' heads)" ("[Zahlt sich nich aus, im Sommer füttern. Der Frisör unten sacht, die scheißn den Damen noch aufn Kopp]," 11); similarly, Katharina/Max initially reacts to the metamorphosis with the words "Damned outrage, a thing like that will have a whole string of consequences!" ("Verfluchte Untat, das ziehtn Rattenschwanz nach sich; son Ding!" 13), and after his first shave Max thinks, "(I'll be damned, now that everyday. I'm not going to grow sideburns)" ("[Verdammich, das nu jeden Tach. Ich laß mir keine Kottletten waxen]," 18).

In view of the fact that Max maintains Katharina's consciousness, it is ironic that he externally models himself on Albert. Max now watches the sports news and soccer matches on television—even screaming "a loud, long, drawn out 'Yeeees' at the TV screen" ("ein lautes langgezogenes 'Jaaaah!' auf den Bildschirm," 16)—just as he has seen Albert do many times, and considers accompanying Albert in his truck until he finds another job. Moreover, Albert is himself ironized from the beginning of the story by the authorial narrator. We learn that "[Katharina] had regarded this amusing fellow as a convenient temporary solution to tide her over until she found someone serious" ("[Katharina] hatte diesen kurzweiligen Burschen als günstige Übergangslösung betrachtet, bis sie eines Tages einen ernsthaften Menschen gefunden haben würde"; 11). He is first characterized as one of the "disturbances" that interrupt Katharina's housework, since he tends to arrive after an extended driving job, sleep the entire first day he is with her, and leave his tracks with her after he departs: "Mountains of dirty dishes, the marks of his teeth on her arms, and extreme fatigue" ("Berge Geschirrs, die Spuren seiner Zähne auf ihren Armen und große Müdigkeit," 10). The narrator's tendency to communicate often in an unmediated fashion, through meaningful combinations and juxtapositions rather than through direct commentary, is evident in this connection as well. The description of Albert's "picture" in Katharina's apartment is a telling example; it is no typical photograph but rather a skat card—the king of hearts. "It doesn't have to be replaced as often" ("Brauch man nich so oft wechseln," 11), Katharina explains to her boyfriend, yet the appropriateness of this particular card figure for Albert's relationship to his "subject" is clear. The picture's significance is underlined by the narrator's comment that "the king looked at her benevolently with his four eyes" ("Der König sah sie mild aus seinen vier Augen an," 11). Nor is the picture's location—"in the bookcase in front of Stendhal's *On Love* and Charles de Bono's *Learn to Think in Two Weeks*" ("im Bücherregal vor den Werken Stendhal Über die Liebe und Charles de Bono In fünfzehn Tagen Denken lernen," 10)—without irony.

But the greatest ironization of Albert occurs after Katharina's metamorphosis. Arriving from the road, he makes no mention of the change and seems not to notice it, since he never asks where his girlfriend is. He appears to be dominated instead by his creature needs, exclaiming on his arrival that "I have to sleep first!" ("Ich muß erst mal schlafen!" 17); when Max broaches the subject of the transformation—"That was like a bolt from the blue" ("Das war wien Blitz aus heiterm Himmel")—Albert interrupts him with the question, "What is there to eat, I've got to get something into my stomach" ("Was könn wir denn essen, ich muß erst mal was innen Bauch kriegen," 21). He remains unperturbed even during his shower with Max; when Max gets an erection, his response is to imitate it. In retrospect, the "wondrous tales" ("wunderbare Geschichten," 9) that Albert brings back from his driving jobs assume a highly ironic character in the face of his blindness to the truly wondrous thing that has happened to Katharina.

It is thus not surprising that Max, modeling himself on Albert, is also treated ironically. That Katharina's transformation from "she" to "he" is a bit too smooth is especially evident in the narrator's observation soon after the change, " 'What's done is done,' she sang, and went into the bathroom" (" 'Passiert ist passiert,' sang sie und ging ins Badezimmer," 14). The narrator's tone in describing Max's initial thoughts about the ramifications of his metamorphosis for Albert is similarly ironic: "He caught sight of Albert's enormous bathrobe, and his heart burst like an egg in boiling water" ("Sein Blick fiel auf Alberts enormen Bademantel, und sein Herz sprang wie ein Ei im kochenden Wasser," 14). The tone of this introduction prepares us for Max's assumption of a male way of life that borders on caricature in its stereotypicality. Just as Katharina had been trapped, despite her job as a research technician, in the stereotypically feminine tasks of housecleaning and laundry, Max immediately takes on activities and viewpoints that he has perceived as masculine: in addition to watching the sports news and soccer matches, he rubs himself with 4711 cologne as he has seen men do in television commercials; resolves to order a car, to learn skat, and to leave the Democratic Women's League of Germany; decides that the apartment needs tablecloths that are not so brightly colored and more right angles and fewer curves in its furniture arrangements; and makes up riddles that deal with topics like trucks and gasoline instead of love and sex, the subjects of the riddles Katharina had posed.

But perhaps most ironic of all is the new combination of Max and Albert, whose apparent harmony is described near the end of the story: "They were happily making plans, speaking as quickly and just as compatible as always when they were together" ("Sie waren fröhlich am Entwerfen, so schnell in der Rede und so im Einklang miteinander wie immer, wenn sie beieinander waren," 24). Particularly in view of the importance Katharina had attached to sensual pleasure and of Albert's subordination to his drives, the reader cannot help but envision the unsatisfactory results of this sexless partnership. As Wolfgang Emmerich writes of the story's superficially idyllic ending, "Here a disguised criticism of the social status quo of the GDR becomes evident, a country which now as before allows for only *one* means of self-realization at a time—eros *or* solidarity—but not both together" ("Damit wird eine verhüllte Kritik an dem gesellschaftlichen Status quo der DDR erkennbar, die nach wie vor zu einer Zeit nur *eine* der beiden Selbstverwirklichungsmöglichkeiten—Eros *oder* Solidarität—zuläßt, nicht aber beide zugleich").[11]

Ultimately, then, we see that for all the thematic, syntactic, and linguistic combinations evident in "Bolt from the Blue," the story's intention is to demonstrate its characters' failure to achieve the one combination that would bring them happiness—the combination of conventionally masculine and conventionally feminine traits in a single human being. Locked into gender stereotypes, Katharina never thinks to venture into "male" spheres of behavior as a woman, in the same way that Max, imitating Albert, becomes confined to stereotypically male activities and patterns of thinking after his transformation. Just as the superficially lighthearted tone of this story belies its underlying irony, the seemingly harmonious "she" and "he" are in fact as far apart as the male "I" and the female "me" of de Bruyn's narrative.[12]

Wolf's "Self-Experiment" introduces yet a third mode into our analysis. In this "Appendix to a Report," as the story's subtitle designates it, a woman scientist adds to her official report about her sex-change experiment her candid explanation, addressed to the professor whom she secretly loves and who launched the experiment, of why she broke it off before her transformation to a man was complete. In contrast to the masculine-feminine split expressed in de Bruyn's "I-me" and Kirsch's "he-she," the narrative situation of Wolf's "appendix," in which a first-person female speaker addresses a man in the second person, functions as a textual model for the author's synthetic vision of ideal relations between the sexes. The fact that the first pronoun to appear in the text is "Sie"—the professorial "you" to whom the narrator is writing her appendix—announces her awareness of the need to engage the male Other in dialogue (albeit here one-sidedly, since the story does not contain his response).[13] Yet despite what some critics claim,[14] this narrator is not unbrokenly feminine, but is rather the synthetic product of a dialectical process. The story's mention of the myth of Tiresias is far from gratuitous, for like Tiresias this narrator has been "on the other side," has experienced the opposite gender and left it behind.

In relating the genesis of the narrating subject "Self-Experiment," like so much of Wolf's other work, itself demonstrates "the process of becoming a subject" ("das Subjektwerden des Menschen"), the process she believes prose fiction should nurture in the reader.[15] Concomitantly, the story of how the narrating "I" of "Self-Experiment" came into being manifests the author's much-discussed notion of the "difficulty of saying I," thematized in *The Quest for Christa T. (Nachdenken über Christa T.)* and at the heart of her subsequent work. In "Self-Experiment," the difficult story of how the female scientist attained narrative subjectivity is bound up with her sliding gender identity, best grasped through a close analysis of the relationship between herself and the professor, between the "I" and the "you" of the text.

Scrutiny of this relationship reveals that the narrator's sex-change experiment is merely the culmination of wishes and tendencies she has had for some time. We learn that she had already conceived the idea of becoming a man fourteen years before, when the professor had mentioned the possibility of such an experiment during a lecture she was attending, and that she has hoped for the chance ever since. Having subordinated her personal life to her career, she is still single and childless at the age of thirty-three, unlike the "typical" woman. In her appendix she notes to the professor that she was at the outset of the experiment "capable of summoning up masculine courage and manly self-control, each of which would be required in its own time" ("Imstande, männlichen Mut und mannhafte Selbstüberwindung aufzubringen, die beide zu ihrer Zeit gefragt sein würden") and "that I was, in your opinion, the equal of any male scientist" ("daß ich Ihnen jeden männlichen Wissenschaftler ersetze").[16] Hence we find that the narrator's gender identity was blurred even before she undertook the experiment.

As her teacher and the object of her love, the professor is also the narrator's model. Just as Kirsch's Katharina imitates Albert after becoming Max, Wolf's narrator emulates her professor by wanting to become, like him, a male scientist. Thus his story is crucial to an understanding of her sliding gender identity. And close examination discloses that "Self-Experiment" is as much the story of the "you" addressed as of the narrating "I." This feature of the second-person technique has been discussed by Michel Butor, whose novel *La modification* (1957) is one of the most extensive and best-known examples of second-person narrative. Making typological distinctions with regard to person, he writes that "It is here that the use of the second person appears, which in the novel can be characterized as follows: the one to whom one tells one's own story" ("C'est ici qu'intervient l'emploi de la seconde personne que l'on peut caractériser ainsi, dans le roman: celui à qui l'on raconte sa propre histoire").[17] In telling the story of the "you," he explains, the second-person narrative reveals something the "you" is hiding, is unable to narrate for himself. In the process the "you" is taught, and even judged, since the implied first person serves as a kind of conscience for the second. Hence the tone of second-person narrative is didactic. In Butor's words, "It is because there is someone to whom one tells one's own story, something about oneself which is unknown, or which at least has never been verbalized, that there can be a second-person narrative, which will accordingly always be a didactic narrative" ("C'est parce qu'il y a quelqu'un à qui l'on raconte sa propre histoire, quelque chose de lui qu'il ne connaît pas, ou du moins pas encore au niveau du langage, qu'il peut y avoir un récit à la seconde personne, qui sera par conséquent toujours un récit didactique," 941).

Much of what Butor says about the novel applies to short fiction as well, and even though the implied first-person presence of *La modification* is not embodied in any character and the text does not constitute an address, there are nevertheless similarities between his thoroughgoing use of the second person and the narrative situation of "Self-Experiment." For instance, Wolf's second-person forms recount "true narrative action" as defined by Bruce Morrissette: "a single, unique past or present action. (For example, 'You could look out of your window and see . . .' is not narrative 'you.' 'Attracted by a sudden noise outside, you went to the window and saw . . .' *is* narrative 'you'.)"[18] Correspondingly, the narrator's formulation of her real reason for undertaking the sex-change experiment, for wanting to become a man like the professor, recalls Butor's generic description of the second person: "At that point all my good and bad reasons no longer carried any weight compared to the one which was sufficient in itself: that I wanted to find out your secret" (116) ("Da fielen alle meine guten und schlechten Gründe nicht mehr ins Gewicht gegenüber dem einen, der allein ausreichte: daß ich hinter Ihr Geheimnis kommen wollte," 73). Having discovered through her experience as Anders—named, appropriately, by his model the professor—what makes the professor tick, she now teaches her former teacher (and us) what he is unable to admit consciously to himself, unable to bring up to the level of language. Hence the mode of the narrative in which she transmits this secret can aptly be designated didactic.

In teaching the professor what she has learned about him, the narrator constantly judges him, recalling the judgmental quality of the implied first person in *La modification*. She reproaches him for his scientific rigidity, evident in his "superstitious worship of measurable results" (113) ("abergläubischen Anbetung von Meßergebnissen," 68) and his "fanaticism for impartiality" (114) ("Gerechtigkeitsfanatismus," 68); for his impersonal coldness and calculated invulnerability—"You make every effort never to get caught. . . . Either you know all the answers or you're too proud to risk losing face by asking" (113) ("Sie geben sich alle Mühe, niemals ertappt zu werden. . . . Entweder wissen Sie alle Antworten, oder Sie sind zu stolz, sich durch Fragen eine Blöße zu geben," 68); and for his machinelike "always-prepared-for-everything attitude" (124) ("Immer-auf-alles-gefaßt sein," 88): "Since you would never permit the term 'crisis,' we tacitly agreed to use 'turning point' " (126) ("Da Sie den Begriff 'Krise' niemals zulassen würden, einigten wir uns stillschweigend auf 'Peripetie,' " 92). As Anders she comes to believe that these qualities of the professor are typical of men in general: "The partial blindness contracted by almost all men began to attack me as well, for otherwise it is not possible to enjoy unlimited privileges these days" (128) ("Die Teilerblindung, die fast alle Männer sich zuziehen, begann auch mich zu befallen, denn anders ist heute der ungeschmälerte Genuß von Privilegien nicht mehr möglich," 96); in her post-experimental voice she observes that "above all else we prize the pleasure of being known. But to you, this expectation of ours is pure embarassment from which you try to protect yourselves, for all we know, behind your tests and questionnaires" (124) ("Höher als alles schätzen wir die Lust, erkannt zu werden. Euch aber ist unser Anspruch die reine Verlegenheit, vor der ihr euch, wer weiß, hinter euren Tests und Fragebogen verschanzt," 87).

The sliding gender identity evident in the preceding two quotations, in which a masculine "me" alternates with a feminine "we," manifests itself at other points in the narrative as well. The narrator formulates the "secret" of the professor (and of men in general) as follows: "that the activities you immerse yourselves in cannot bring you happiness, and that *we* [women] have a right to resist you when you try to drag us into them" (128) ("daß die Unternehmungen, in die ihr euch verliert, euer Glück nicht sein können, und daß *wir* [Frauen] ein Recht auf Widerstand haben, wenn ihr uns in sie hineinziehen wollt," 96; emphasis added), yet proceeds on the same page to write "*We* men, on the other hand, hoist the world onto our shoulders, almost collapsing under its weight" ("Während *wir* Männer die Weltkugel auf unsere Schultern laden, unter deren Last *wir* fast zusammenbrechen"; emphasis added). A similar pronoun confusion characterizes the narrator's description of the process by which Anders learns to redefine words in keeping with his new gender, here, the word "city": "For him— that is, for me. Anders—it was a tight cluster of inexhaustible opportunities. He—that is, I—felt intoxicated by a city which was ready to teach me that my duty was to make conquests" (122) ("Ihm—also mir, Anders— eine Ballung unausschöpfbarer Gelegenheiten. Er—also ich—war betäubt von einer Stadt, die mich lehren wollte, daß es meine Pflicht war, Eroberungen zu machen," 84). Obviously the technical reason for these instances of pronoun confusion is that the narrator alternates between an "I" that refers to his period as Anders and a postexperimental "I." But as the last example in particular suggests, the effect of such gender blurring is to underline the narrator's decreasing ability, in the course of his weeks as Anders, to identify with the masculine in general and the professor specifically.

As the professor's value as a model for Anders declines, Anders's own sense of identity as a man is steadily eroded. The climax of his education about the professor—the moment when Anders says that he feels "like at the movies" ("Wie im Kino") and the professor responds, "You too?" (130) ("Sie auch?" 99), revealing himself to be one who perceives and lives life only superficially, from a distance—leads Anders to break off the sex-change experiment. Ironically, the single moment of complete identity between the "I" and the "you" of the story represents "the admission of a defect" (130) ("das vertrauliche Eingeständnis eines Defekts," 100)—leading the "I" to the realization "that you cannot love, and know it" (130) ("Daß Sie nicht lieben können und es wissen," 99)—and causes him to move away from the masculine "you" and return to womanhood. Yet only now, through this dialectical progression from femininity to partial masculinity to a state informed by both, has the "I" achieved authentic subjectivity; in learning the truth about the beloved, emulated masculine Other, the narrating subject has come to genuinely know herself, to be able to say "I." Her second-person narrative is the result. Instead of wanting to *be* the "you" of this text, as Anders, her goal is now a dialogue with him. She has progressed from loving the professor to understanding him to judging him to wanting to attempt a realistic mutual love that joins judgment and affection, a goal evident in her observation that "language, you'll be surprised to hear, can help me; our language which grew out of an amazing mentality that could express 'to judge' and 'to love' in one single word: *meinen*, 'to think, have an opinion' " (122) ("Die Sprache, das wird Sie wundern, kann mir helfen, mit ihrer Herkunft aus jenem erstaunlichen Geist, dem 'urteilen' und 'lieben' ein einziges Wort sein konnte: 'meinen,' " 83).

Thus this didactic appendix ends with an emphasis not on gender separation, such as is conveyed by the existential angst of de Bruyn's "I-me" constructions or by the wry irony of Kirsch's "he-she," but with a call for a synthetic reconciliation between the sexes. The story's penultimate sentence sums up the narrator's dialogic program: "Now my experiment lies ahead: the attempt to love" (131) ("Jetzt steht *uns* mein Experiment bevor: der Versuch zu lieben," 100; emphasis added). The first-person plural, blending the female "I" and the male "you" into an androgynous "we," implies that for the narrator sexual love necessitates the dissolution of rigid gender boundaries. With this experiment of love, clearly set up as an alternative to the scientific experiment she has just undergone, the narrator will continue her education of the professor, begun in the appendix she has addressed to him: just as she has ventured into the masculine realm of science and even into the male gender, so must the professor allow the "feminine" activity of loving to encroach upon his imperviously masculine world.

Hence the common designation of "Self-Experiment" as "utopian" cannot refer to the sex-change experiment, which is, more accurately, a "left-brain utopia," as Nancy Lukens calls it; such utopias, she writes, "represent Hybris . . . , since they disregard essential elements of the whole picture of human life. . . . They create the illusion of progress toward perfection and thereby kill the ongoing process of life."[19] It is rather the story's conclusion that is utopian, in its suggestion that the answer is not to privilege one sex (men), and then allow women to "become men," or acquire these privileges too, but instead to encourage both sexes to appropriate features of the other and thereby become more human. To borrow a distinction from Wolf's narrator, the author's goal is "humane" and not "manly" (123) ("menschlich"/"männlich," 86). Thus the second-person technique of "Self-Experiment" is the perfect vehicle for its message, as is again underlined through comparison with Butor: in the opinion of Roland Barthes, "Butor's *vous* sets up a metaphysics of creator-creature full of humanistic, if not religious, meaning."[20]

NOTES

My thanks to Eric Downing for calling my attention to the epigraph to this essay. I would also like to thank Irene Kacandes and David Scrase for their comments on an earlier draft. This essay was completed before the events that followed November 9, 1989.

1. On the anthology's difficult publication history, for example, see Edith Anderson, "Genesis and Adventures of the Anthology *Blitz aus heiterm Himmel*," in *Studies in GDR Culture and Society*, ed. Margy Gerber et al., vol. 4 (Lanham, Md.: University Press of America, 1984), 1–14. Subsequent page references are given parenthetically in the text.

2. For a survey of recent fantastic literature in the GDR, see Sibylle Ehrlich, "Use of the Fantastic in Recent GDR Prose," in Gerber, *Studies in GDR Culture*, vol. 2 (1982), 68–75.

3. See my "Imagining the Other: Sexual Transformation and Social Reality in GDR Literature," *German Life and Letters* (1990).

4. Franz Stanzel, *A Theory of Narrative*, trans. Charlotte Goedsche (1979; reprint, Cambridge: Cambridge University Press, 1984), 80. Subsequently page references are given parenthetically in the text. The close study of person by Stanzel, Dorrit Cohn (*Transparent Minds: Narrative Modes for Presenting Consciousness in Fiction* [Princeton: Princeton University Press, 1978]), and others has successfully refuted Wayne Booth's view of the distinction of person as "overworked"; see Booth, *The Rhetoric of Fiction* (Chicago: University of Chicago Press, 1961), 150.

5. Jeanette Clausen, "The Difficulty of Saying 'I' as Theme and Narrative Technique in the Works of Christa Wolf," *Amsterdamer Beiträge zur neueren Germanistik* 10 (1980): 325.

6. Günter de Bruyn, "Geschlechtertausch," in *Frauen in der DDR: Zwanzig Erzählungen*, ed. Lutz-W. Wolff (Munich: Deutscher Taschenbuch Verlag, 1976), 201; emphasis added. Except where otherwise noted, the translations are mine. Subsequent page references are given parenthetically in the text. For the sake of simplicity my use of pronouns to refer to transformed characters will be determined by their external sex; hence "she"/"her" for Karla despite her male inner self.

7. Leonore Krenzlin, "Wirkungsvorstellung und Werkstruktur bei Hermann Kant und Günter de Bruyn," in *Funktion der Literatur: Aspekte—Probleme—Aufgaben*, ed. Dieter Schlenstedt et al. (Berlin: Akademie-Verlag, 1975), 329–30.

8. Franz Kafka, *The Metamorphosis*, trans. Stanley Corngold (1972; reprint, New York: Bantam, 1986), 3; Franz Kafka, "Die Verwandlung," *Sämtliche Erzählungen*, ed. Paul Raabe (Frankfurt: Fischer, 1969), 56 (emphasis added).

9. Cohn, *Transparent Minds*, 14. See further Cohn, "Narrated Monologue: Definition of a Fictional Style," *Comparative Literature* 18 (1966): 97–112, and *Transparent Minds*, 99–140.

10. Sarah Kirsch, "Blitz aus heiterm Himmel," in *Geschlechtertausch: Drei Geschichten über die Umwandlung der Verhältnisse* by Sarah Kirsch, Irmtraud Morgner,

and Christa Wolf (Darmstadt: Luchterhand, 1980), 8. Subsequent page references are given parenthetically in the text.

11. Wolfgang Emmerich, "Identität und Geschlechtertausch: Notizen zur Selbstdarstellung der Frau in der neueren DDR-Literatur," in *Basis: Jahrbuch für deutsche Gegenwartsliteratur*, ed. Reinhold Grimm and Jost Hermand, vol. 8 (Frankfurt: Suhrkamp, 1978), 142.

12. Sigrid Damm and Jürgen Engler's use of the phrase "heiter-ironische Gelassenheit" to characterize the tone of the stories by de Bruyn and Kirsch overlooks the darkness of the message both works convey in the end; see Damm and Engler, "Notate des Zwiespalts und Allegorien der Vollendung," *Weimarer Beiträge* 21, no. 7 (1975): 57.

13. As Anne Herrmann points out, "In Wolf's text it is not the feminine but the masculine that is 'Anders' (that is, posited as Other)"; Herrmann, "The Transsexual as *Anders* in Christa Wolf's 'Self-Experiment,' " *Genders* 3 (1988): 47. But the narrator's addressee constitutes another masculine Other of importance in Wolf's story.

14. E.g., Jürgen Nieraad, "Subjektivität als Thema und Methode realistischer Schreibweise: Zur gegenwärtigen DDR-Literaturdiskussion am Beispiel Christa Wolf," *Literatur-Wissenschaftliches Jahrbuch* 19 (1978): 300.

15. See Christa Wolf, "Lesen und Schreiben," in Wolf, *Lesen und Schreiben: Aufsätze und Prosastücke* (Darmstadt: Luchterhand, 1972), 220.

16. Christa Wolf, "Self-Experiment: Appendix to a Report," trans. Jeanette Clausen, *New German Critique* 13 (1978): 114, 115; "Selbstversuch: Traktat zu einem Protokoll," in Kirsch, Morgner, and Wolf, *Geschlechtertausch*, 69, 71; ellipsis Wolf's. Subsequent page references are given parenthetically in the text.

17. Michel Butor, "L'usage des pronoms personnels dans le roman," *Les temps modernes* 16, no. 178 (1961): 941; subsequent page references are given parenthetically in the text.

18. Bruce Morrissette, "Narrative 'You' in Contemporary Literature," *Comparative Literature Studies* 2 (1965): 4. Irene Kacandes, to whom I am grateful for the references in this note and the previous one, is currently at work on the first comprehensive, systematic study of second-person narrative.

19. Nancy Lukens, "Future Perfect?: Language and Utopia in Christa Wolf's Chernobyl Narrative," manuscript, 9–10.

20. Morrissette, "Narrative 'You,' " 16.

TWELVE

FEMINIST INTERTEXTUALITY AND THE LAUGH

OF THE MOTHER:

LEONORA CARRINGTON'S *HEARING TRUMPET*

Susan Rubin Suleiman

To write, of course, is to rewrite.
—Chantal Chawaf

Nothing sacred.
—Angela Carter

T O THE FATE of women in poetry has fallen a tremendous share
of parody, in the most serious and formal sense of the word. *Feminine poetry is an unconscious parody of both poetic inventions and re-
membrances.*"[1] Osip Mandelstam, the great Russian poet, made these remarks in 1922. As Svetlana Boym aptly notes, the crucial word here is
"unconscious": "The poetess lacks precisely that authentic artistic subjectivity that would enable her to turn upon the poetic tradition and critically
comment on it."[2]

If we recall how deeply Western notions of subjectivity—in other words,
self-consciousness and agency—are implicated in thinking about the body
as locus and symbol of sexual difference, then the sentences following the
above remarks in Mandelstam's essay take on a particularly suggestive res-
onance: "The majority of Muscovite poetesses have been hit by the metaphor. These poor Isises are doomed to an eternal search for a forever-lost
second part of the simile, which would return to the poetic image Osiris
its primordial unity."

There is hardly a need to name, for a post-Lacanian reader, the missing
part of which Mandelstam's "poor Isises" are forever deprived. It is worth
pointing out, however, that in his evocation of the Egyptian myth, Mandelstam manages to transfer, by means of his own double metaphor, the
marker of lack from the castrated god, Osiris, to his sister-wife and to her
metaphoric substitutes, the Moscow poetesses; and then transfers the
marker back again (*metaphorein*: to carry across, transfer), not to the god

but to *his* metaphoric substitute: the incomplete poetic image produced by women poets.

Which goes to show that there is nothing like a myth to make a point: by appropriating the old story for his own purposes, the poet proves both his argument and his mastery as an innovator in language.

Poetesses too have learned this lesson, especially of late. "Some of the best-known recent poetry by women," wrote Sandra Gilbert and Susan Gubar in 1979, "openly uses . . . parody in the cause of feminism: traditional figures of patriarchal mythology like Circe, Leda, Cassandra, Medusa, Helen, and Persephone have all lately been reinvented in the images of their female creators, and each poem devoted to one of these figures is a reading that reinvents her original story."[3] Alicia Ostriker, in a more recent study, sees such parodic appropriations or revisionist mythmaking as part of "the extraordinary tide of poetry by American women in our own time," whose effect is not only to challenge and transform the history of poetry, but to "change the way we think and feel forever."[4] In a more explicitly theoretical mode, Patricia Yaeger and Mary Russo have sought to demonstrate both the political force and the poetic power of playful uses of tradition by feminist writers and critics.[5]

Obviously, neither the theory nor the practice of parody as a form of critical rereading (and rewriting) of traditional texts and mythologies originated with contemporary feminism. The contemporary feminist critical emphasis on "writing as re-vision" (to use Adrienne Rich's famous phrase) can itself be seen as an appropriation of earlier theoretical and historical work by male, nonfeminist (sometimes even misogynist) critics—most notably of Mikhail Bakhtin's writings on carnival and on the "carnivalesque": the heterogenous, multivoiced, multilingual discourses of medieval and Renaissance popular culture, and their gradual integration into the high-cultural genre of the novel.[6] It was Bakhtin's work that chiefly inspired Julia Kristeva's theory of intertextuality, which subsumes parody as one of its forms. And it was Bakhtin who formulated, in one of his wide-ranging historical discussions of parody, the politically as well as aesthetically suggestive notion that "parodic-travestying forms . . . destroyed the power of myth over language; they freed consciousness from the power of the direct word, destroyed the thick walls that had imprisoned consciousness within its own discourse."[7]

Extrapolating a bit, we arrive at the contemporary—and contemporary feminist—insight that the stories we tell about reality *construe* the real, rather than merely reflect it. Whence the possibility, or the hope, that through the rewriting of old stories and the invention of new forms of language for doing so, it is the world as well as words that will be transformed.[8]

Bakhtin himself had an optimistic view of the emancipatory potential of carnival and carnivalized discourse. This may explain why his model of carnival has been adopted by so many contemporary theorists interested in the adversarial possibilities of literature and other artistic practices in relation to dominant culture. Peter Stallybrass and Allon White have noted that "everywhere in literary and cultural studies today, we see carnival emerging as a model, as an ideal and as an analytic category."[9] They also note, however, that Bakhtin's theory of carnival lends itself to a more conservative interpretation and has been criticized as such, by historians and anthropologists as well as by literary theorists. They quote Terry Eagleton, for example: "Carnival, after all, is a *licensed* affair in every sense, a permissible rupture of hegemony, a contained popular blow-off as disturbing and relatively ineffectual as a revolutionary work of art."[10] If the transgressions of carnival are licensed and "contained" by the dominant culture, then such transgressions are no more than a particularly clever ruse of the law.

Eagleton's political critique of Bakhtin, while it is no doubt a salutary corrective to overly idealized views of carnival as an emancipatory strategy (to use Patricia Yaeger's phrase), is itself too simplistic in its assumption that symbolic modes like carnival—or like "revolutionary works of art"—have no actual, political effects. I am more persuaded by Stallybrass and White's argument that "the politics of carnival cannot be resolved outside of a close historical examination of particular conjunctures: there is no a priori revolutionary vector to carnival and transgression."[11] Neither, I would add, is there an a priori conservative vector. Everything depends on the context, and only a fine-grained analysis of the relations between context and individual event—which is what I take Stallybrass and White to mean by the "historical examination of particular conjunctures"—will reveal the meanings and effects, including the political effects, of (a) carnival, or of a "revolutionary work of art," as action or mode of expression.

It is a fine-grained analysis that I would like to undertake for Leonora Carrington's comic novel, *The Hearing Trumpet*, in the double context of Surrealist experimentation and contemporary feminist experimentation with parodic rewriting. One of the most interesting aspects of Carrington's novel—a feminist parodic rewriting of, among other old stories, the story of the Holy Grail—is that it must be situated historically, as well as formally and ideologically, in this double context. Such a contextual reading can hope to accomplish at least two things: first, to explore the possible alliances as well as the irreducible differences between the work of male avant-garde artists (in this instance, Surrealists) and the "similar but different" work of women; second, to explore the differences that may exist between and among contemporary women avant-garde writers, especially as concerns the broader cultural and political implications of their work.

Carrington, an English painter and writer who has spent most of her life outside England, was closely associated with the Surrealist movement during the late 1930s and early 1940s, and has continued to produce an impressive body of work since then. She is one of the very few women artists who started out in the relatively heroic period of Surrealism before the war and are still working today. And she is the only one of those, to my knowledge, who has identified herself in recent years as a feminist.[12] She wrote *The Hearing Trumpet* in the early 1950s in Mexico City, where she had been living for several years. At that time she was still in close touch with a number of Surrealist artists and poets, including Benjamin Péret and his wife, the painter Remedios Varo, who were also living in Mexico.

By the time the novel was published—first in a French translation, in 1974—Surrealism's principal protagonists were dead. The French feminist movement, however, was flourishing and producing some of its most interesting experiments in rewriting traditional mythologies. Monique Wittig's *Les guérillères*, whose intertextual strategies I have discussed elsewhere, had appeared in 1969, soon to be followed by other works in the same vein (*Le corps lesbien*, 1973; *Brouillon pour un dictionnaire des amantes*, 1976). Hélène Cixous's "Laugh of the Medusa," perhaps the single best known feminist revision of a classical myth and of its orthodox psychoanalytic interpretation, appeared in 1975.[13] Although Carrington's novel (in French, *Le cornet acoustique*) was quite at home in this context, it received almost no attention in Paris.

In English, *The Hearing Trumpet* first appeared in 1976 and was duly if somewhat perfunctorily reviewed in the *Times Literary Supplement* and a few other journals.[14] Here again, the context was right, or almost (several English and American women writers whom we now associate with postmodern feminist revision were just becoming known or were about to start publishing),[15] but Carrington's place in it went unnoticed. She seemed to be caught between nationalities, between languages, between generations.

The renewal of interest in Surrealism, and particularly in the work of women Surrealists, which gathered momentum in the mid-1980s, has finally brought Carrington's work some of the attention it deserves. The recent publication, in English, of two volumes of her stories, originally written in French, English, or Spanish over a period of more than thirty years, should introduce her to a whole new generation of readers.[16]

Among Carrington's works I single out *The Hearing Trumpet* not only because it is brilliant, outrageously inventive, and comically "carnivalesque," occupying a significant place between Surrealism and (feminist) postmodernism; but also because, quite uniquely, Carrington's novel associates the subversive laughter of carnival with the figure—and even more importantly, with the voice—of the mother. This is certainly not the case in Surrealism or in any of the other male avant-garde movements of this century, nor would we expect it to be: the emblematic subject of male avant-garde practice is, I have suggested, a transgressive son who may, in

Roland Barthes's famous words, "play with the body of his mother," but who never imagines (let alone gives voice to) his mother playing.[17] More surprisingly, however, one almost never finds the figure or the voice of the playful (laughing) mother in contemporary feminist experimental writing either—this despite the well-known revalorization of the mother and of the "maternal metaphor" in some of that writing.[18] As for what is at stake, aesthetically and politically, in the figure of the playful mother, that is a question I shall leave for the end of this essay.

II

The Surrealists' predilection for punning and other verbal games, as well as for the humorous, often scatological or otherwise "scandalous" rewriting of traditional texts or images, is well known; so is their predilection for collage and collagelike techniques of juxtaposing heterogeneous elements, which Peter Bürger considers the hallmark of "the avant-gardiste work."[19]

Was all this just child's play, the nose-thumbing antics of boys drawing mustaches on the Mona Lisa? For the Surrealists of the 1920s, graffiti and defacement were more than "just play"—they were a veritable program for liberation. Louis Aragon, prefacing his 1919 collection of poems and prose texts, Le libertinage, in 1924, the year of the first Surrealist Manifesto and of the official founding of the Surrealist movement, could combine a truculent celebration of scandal for scandal's sake ("I have never sought anything but scandal, and have sought it for its own sake") with an impassioned defense of the "spirit of the French Revolution": "I am irreducibly a man of the left, and if that expression makes you laugh, you're nothing but a clown."[20] This was one way of suggesting that the parodic antics of Surrealism were meant to be understood as (among other things) a strategy for radical political and cultural change.

Despite this radical impetus, explicitly antibourgeois and directed against the "Law of the Father," the sexual ideology of Surrealism, like that of other early European avant-gardes, was resolutely phallic. That is why some feminist critics have suggested that contemporary *feminist* versions of antipatriarchal parody and rewriting have little to gain from being associated with the work of male predecessors; indeed, Gayatri Spivak has claimed that they derive all their power from "their *substantive* revision of, rather than their apparent *formal* allegiance to, the European avant-garde."[21]

As my own previous work has made clear, I share Spivak's desire to emphasize the substantive (ideological and existential) differences between feminist avant-garde practice and the practice of male avant-garde artists who, for all their formal innovations, are still deeply implicated in patriarchy. However, I believe that two points need to be made. First, it is not the case that all feminist avant-garde practices are identical in their substantive implications. In some cases, there may be substantive agreement between some feminist writers and their male predecessors, and substantive differences among feminists: attitudes toward the mother are one such case.

To the extent that the mother has been perceived as a defender and an instrument of patriarchy, she has been repudiated by contemporary feminists (most notably by Monique Wittig) as well as by the male avant-garde, including the Surrealists. It is precisely in reaction to this view of the mother as necessarily "on the side of patriarchy" that Hélène Cixous, Luce Irigaray, and other theorists began, in the mid-1970s, to elaborate the maternal metaphor for women's writing *and* women's cultural politics.

Second, the existence of substantive differences should not blind us to the potentially *positive* aspects of a formal allegiance between contemporary feminists and the European avant-garde. One may criticize or point up the ambiguities of male avant-garde sexual or cultural politics, and still recognize the energy, the inventiveness, the explosive humor and sheer proliferating brilliance of much male avant-garde "play."

This double allegiance—on the one hand, to the formal experiments and some of the cultural aspirations of the historical male avant-gardes; on the other hand, to the feminist critique of dominant sexual ideologies, including the ideology of those same avant-gardes—characterizes some of the best contemporary work by women writers and artists.[22] And it also characterizes Carrington's *Hearing Trumpet*.

III

The narrator-heroine of *The Hearing Trumpet* is ninety-two years old and stone deaf. (Carrington was in her thirties when she wrote the novel.) She is toothless, but her sight is still excellent; she has a "short grey beard which conventional people would find repulsive" but which she "personally" finds "rather gallant" (3). Her name is Marian Leatherby. She was born in England but now lives in a country that sounds like Mexico; she lives in the house of her son and his family, in a room overlooking the backyard. Her son's name is Galahad.

The people Marian lives with do not consider her quite human: "The maid, Rosina, is an Indian woman with a morose character and seems generally opposed to the rest of humanity. I do not believe that she puts me in a human category so our relationship is not disagreeable" (2). Her grandson calls her "the monster of Glamis," "a drooling sack of decomposing flesh"; to her daughter-in-law, she is a senile old woman (" 'Remember

Galahad,' added Muriel, 'these old people do not have feelings like you or I,' " 10); to her son, she appears merely as an "inanimate creature"—on which Marian comments: "He may be right, but on the other hand the maguey cactus seems alive to me, so I feel I can also make claims on existence" (9).

As I have tried to suggest by my quotations, the first thing that strikes a reader of this novel is the heroine's voice; in particular, the contradiction between the humorous intelligence of the subject to whom this voice belongs, and the absolute denial of intelligence—indeed, of subjecthood—to which her age, her physical state, and her dependent status reduce her in the eyes of her family. Only by having the old "senile" crone tell her own story is this contradictory effect achieved: Marian's sharp wit counteracts her "decomposing flesh," and her dependent status is belied by her narrative mastery: "All this is a digression and I do not wish anyone to think my mind wanders far, it wanders but never further than I want" (3).

Even more quotations are necessary to show the sustained effect of Marian's narrative voice—an effect that, I suggest, is cumulative, and is made possible because there is a *story*, albeit an increasingly "mad" and fantastical one.

Here, for example, is the beginning of Marian's description of her friend and fellow ancient lady, Carmella, who changes her life by giving her a hearing trumpet to alleviate her deafness:

> She lives in a very small house with her niece who bakes cakes for a Swedish teashop although she is Spanish. Carmella has a very pleasant life and is really very intellectual. She reads books through an elegant lorgnette and hardly ever mumbles to herself as I do. She also knits very clever jumpers but her real pleasure in life is writing letters. Carmella writes letters all over the world to people she has never met and signs them with all sorts of romantic names, never her own. (4)

Carmella's romantic imagination extends not only to names, but to stories: she picks her correspondents' names out of phone directories in faraway places and writes to them after outfitting them with a life story. Monsieur Belvedere Oise Noisis of Paris, for example, she sees as "a rather frail old gentleman, still elegant, with a passion for tropical mushrooms which he grows in an Empire wardrobe. He wears embroidered waistcoats and travels with purple luggage" (6).

Marian tells her she must be more realistic, not try to impose her imagination on people she has never seen. Suppose, for example, that Monsieur Belvedere Oise Noisis "is fat and collects wicker baskets? Suppose he never travels and has no luggage, suppose he is a young man with a nautical yearning?" To which Carmella replies that Marian is too "negative minded." This is a charmingly Lewis Carrollesque way to remind us of the power of imagination and fancy (Marian's "realist" story is no less fanciful than Carmella's romantic one)—but where is the bite? you may ask. Are these two old playful ladies "avant-garde"? Is this novel critical? Radical? Parodic? Antipatriarchal? Surrealist? Postmodern?

Patience. Slow-burning fuses make big blasts.

Not long after Marian receives her hearing trumpet, she discovers—with its help—that her family is planning to ship her off to a home for senile ladies. Although forewarned is forearmed, there is nothing she can do about it. So she says goodbye to her cats and to Carmella (who makes contingency plans to rescue her with a getaway car and a machine gun, should the institution turn out to be too horrible), and lets her daughter-in-law and her son (whose name, recall, is Galahad) take her to the Well of Light Brotherhood old-age home, presided over by one Dr. Gambit.

Marian's entry into this institution—consisting of gardens and courtyards, and buildings in the shape of medieval castles, towers, toadstools, a boot, an Egyptian mummy, and even a few "ordinary bungalows" (24)— is a crossing over the threshold from the (more or less) real world to a world elsewhere. Some years before *The Hearing Trumpet*, Carrington recounted another such crossing, in her autobiographical narrative, *Down Below*, which tells of her temporary internment in an insane asylum in Spain in 1940.[23] Having crossed the border from the south of France, where she had been living with Max Ernst, after Ernst was taken into custody by French police, Carrington suffered a mental breakdown and was diagnosed as "incurably insane" by a Spanish doctor, then shipped off to the asylum with her family's approval. *Down Below*, first published in the American Surrealist journal *VVV* in 1944, recounts in detail the hallucinations and delusions she constructed in her states of madness. It is a harrowing account, not least because the Carrington who is telling the story (about three years after it occurred) refuses to adopt a safely "distant" perspective; she tries, instead, to convey the experience of madness as it was lived, from the inside—as in the following passage:

> The son was the Sun and I the Moon, an essential element of the Trinity, with the microscopic knowledge of the earth, its plants and creatures. I knew that Christ was dead and done for, and that I had to take His place, because the Trinity, minus a woman and microscopic knowledge, had become dry and incomplete. Christ was replaced by the Sun. I was Christ on earth in the person of the Holy Ghost. (195)

The Hearing Trumpet can be read as a self-conscious, artistically controlled transposition and expansion of some of the delusionary constructions described in *Down Below* (including the one I have just quoted), with an accompanying change in mood and color from the tragic to the comic. Marian is not mad, and the old-ladies' home is not an insane asylum: but the male god is displaced by a female, Christian symbols and mythology become mixed up with pagan (above, the Trinity with the Sun and Moon); the world becomes topsy-turvy.

Obviously, this rapprochement between the two works does not provide a complete reading of either one. But it does suggest a certain continuity in Carrington's preoccupations, as well as her ongoing relationship to Surrealism. *Down Below* is a kind of *Nadja*, but told from the point of view of the madwoman, not the male observer. *The Hearing Trumpet* is closer to Surrealist parody in the manner of Aragon, Desnos, or Péret, but again told from a different subject position.[24]

Galahad, in the Arthurian legends, is the knight pure in heart destined to succeed in the quest for the Holy Grail. In Carrington's rewriting, it is not Galahad but his mother who delivers the Grail. The Grail itself becomes a pagan symbol originally associated with the goddess of love (but also of motherhood), Venus, the Christian version being a later usurpation.[25] And so on.

We recognize here the feminist parodic reversal (or, as is often the case, reappropriation) of a sacred text or consecrated myth. In *Les guérillères*, Wittig also alludes briefly to the Grail cycle, which the women read in terms of female symbols. What distinguishes Carrington's feminist parody is not only its meaning, its sly but unmistakable emphasis on the mother;[26] it is also the sustained, narratively and textually complicated ways in which this revised meaning is achieved.[27] Among the latter, I find most interesting Carrington's play with narrative representation and framing—texts within texts within texts, overlapping in curious ways; her "carnivalesque" accumulation of intertexts, ranging from the Bible and the Grail cycle to classical and Celtic mythology, the lives of saints, fairy tales, Goddess lore from various traditions, alchemical doctrines, and Surrealist theories of collage and the hybrid; her use of humor, especially to create instabilities and moments of self-directed irony; and finally, the ways in which she situates this novel both as a prolongation of and as a (feminist) divergence from Surrealist aspirations.

The play with narrative representation and framing begins, quite literally, with a representation in a frame: on her first day at the institution, while Dr. Gambit is explaining to the ladies gathered in the dining room that the purpose of Lightsome Hall is to "follow the inner Meaning of Christianity and comprehend the Original Teaching of the Master," Marian notices a large oil painting, a portrait of a nun, on the wall facing her: "The face of the Nun in the oil painting was so curiously lighted that she seemed to be winking, although that was hardly possible. . . . However the idea that she was winking persisted, she was winking at me with a most disconcerting mixture of mockery and malevolence" (28).

This painting, at which Marian stares at every meal, begins to obsess her:

the leering abbess (as she calls her) becomes the subject of her fantasies. She gives her a name, Dona Rosalinda Alvarez Della Cueva, and begins to invent a story for her: "She was abbess, I imagined, of a huge Baroque convent on a lonely and barren mountain in Castile. The convent was called El Convento de Santa Barbara de Tartarus, the bearded patroness of Limbo said to play with unbaptised children in this nether region. How all these fancies occurred to me I do not know" (43).

As it happens, Marian's fancies will be "objectively" confirmed when one of the other pensioners, a black woman named Christabel Burns, gives her a book written by an eighteenth-century monk and telling the life story of Dona Rosalinda, "Abbess of the Convent of Santa Barbara of Tartarus," who was "canonized in Rome in 1756" (72). Even before that, however, Carmella writes to say she has been having recurrent dreams about "a nun in a tower" with a winking face (52). Another pensioner, Maude Wilkins, tells Marian about a very detailed dream involving Maude's search for a "magic cup" and her eventually stumbling on a woman in a four-poster bed who is winking at her and in whom she recognizes the nun in the painting (58).

By the time Christabel gives Marian the book, then, the nun's story has the ontologically multiple status of pictorial representation, dream, and daydream (fantasy), elaborated independently by four different subjects. The eighteenth-century book adds yet another ontological layer: that of a written account purporting to be "a true and faithful rendering of the life" (72). The effect is that of a multiple *mise en abîme*, with the usual unsettling and destabilizing of "reality" characteristic of such mirrorings.

The book about the painted nun, technically a framed or embedded tale occupying twenty-eight pages (almost one-fifth) of the novel, includes some framed tales of its own, in various languages. The book itself is "translated from the original Latin," with a few Latin passages kept intact; and some of *its* framed tales, in the form of letters by or to the abbess or in the form of scrolls discovered by the monk/author, were translated, we are told by him, from Hebrew or Greek. It is as if Carrington had grafted the Surrealist preoccupation with doubling and with the boundaries between dream-states and reality onto the postmodernist preoccupation with doubling and with boundaries between ontological levels, levels of narration and narrative representation, and levels of transmission or translation[28]— all this as part of a generally dizzying collage of texts and mythologies, of which the name "Santa Barbara de Tartarus," with its anachronistic joining of a Christian virgin martyr to the netherworld of Greek mythology, is but a small example. And all this underpinned, of course, by the primary structure of the feminist revision.

The story that emerges as Dona Rosalinda's life, told by what turns out to be an unsympathetic narrator, is a story of antipatriarchal and anti-

Christian subversion: the good abbess and her homosexual friend, the Bishop of Trêves les Frêles, are devotees of the Goddess, working to destroy the Christian edifice from the inside—which means, to *rewrite* its story. The means for this rewriting is offered to them first by a "precious liquid" or ointment discovered near the mummy of Mary Magdalen, about which Dona Rosalinda writes to her friend:

> The ointment which was found on the left side of the mummy may very well release secrets which would not only discredit all the gospels but which would crown all the arduous work we have shared during recent years. . . . You may imagine the transports of delight which overcame me when I learnt that Magdalen had been a high initiate of the mysteries of the Goddess but had been executed for the sacrilege of selling certain secrets of her cult to Jesus of Nazareth. This of course would explain the miracles which have puzzled us for so long. (75)

By the next twist of the tale, the origin of the magic (aphrodisiac) ointment is pushed even further back, to merge with the rewritten origin of the Grail. This time, it is the bishop who is the narrative source, although he got his own tale from others in a receding series:

> One evening the boy Angus . . . let me understand that the Knight Templars in Ireland were in possession of the Grail. This wonderful cup, as you know, was said to be the original chalice which held the elixir of life and belonged to the Goddess Venus. She is said to have quaffed the magic liquid when she was impregnated with Cupid, whereupon he leapt in the womb and, by absorbing the pneuma, became a God. The story follows that Venus, in her birth pangs, dropped the cup and it came hurtling to earth, where it was buried in a deep cavern, abode of Epona the Horse Goddess.
>
> For some thousands of years the cup was safely in the keeping of the subterranean Goddess, who was known to be bearded and a hermaphrodite. Her name was Barbarus. (91)

Carrington's emphasis on Venus as mother is in keeping with the early Greek meanings of the goddess of love: Aphrodite was thought to be of Asiatic origin, associated with the mother-goddess Ishtar. However, there was a general tendency even by the Greeks to efface Aphrodite's maternal meaning in favor of her erotic meaning (thus confirming the Western prejudice against associating sexuality with motherhood).[29] In Carrington's version, both meanings are maintained: the "magic liquid" is an aphrodisiac, and the child Venus gives birth to is Cupid.

With the mention of the bearded hermaphroditic goddess Barbarus in the bishop's tale, we sense that the narrative, like the serpent of alchemical symbolism, will soon bite its own tail. (Remember that Marian too has a beard.) One of the alchemical meanings of the serpent with its tail in its mouth is metamorphosis; another is the union of opposites or the coupling of contraries, as in hermaphroditism.[30] More generally, this symbol may stand for self-reflexiveness and the crossing of boundaries, whether onto-logical or narratological.

Indeed, Dona Rosalinda's story spills over onto Marian's story, and the Grail sought by Dona Rosalinda (who infiltrates the Templars' castle dis-guised as a "bearded cavalier," has a solitary encounter with the Grail, and eventually gives birth to a "boy, no bigger than a barn owl, luminously white and winged," 99) is the Grail eventually found by Marian and her "army of bees, wolves, six old women, a postman, a Chinaman, a poet, an atom-driven ark, and a werewoman" (157).

How Carrington gets us from there to here is a whole story. Suffice it to say that after Marian reads the life of Dona Rosalinda, life at the institu-tion—and outside it—becomes increasingly strange. Maud Wilkins is poi-soned by two of the pensioners and turns out to have been an old gentle-man, not an old lady; Christabel Burns turns out to be a devotee of the Goddess, and gives Marian three riddles to solve; Carmella arrives for a visit, bearing chocolate biscuits and port wine, and counseling rebellion; Marian and the other ladies dance around the bee pond, invoking Hecate and the Queen Bee,[31] then stage a coup d'état, exiling the poisoners and deposing Dr. Gambit; Carmella returns, a millionaire after digging up a uranium mine in her backyard; a new ice age begins; the earth quakes; Marian solves the riddles and descends under the Tower to the womb of the world, which is also a kitchen—where she meets herself, stirring a broth.

> She looked me up and down from head to foot and then from foot to head, rather critically I thought, and said finally, as if to herself, "Old as Moses, ugly as Seth, tough as a boot and no more sense than a skittle. However meat is scarce so jump in." . . .
>
> I tried to nod and move away at the same time, but my knees were trembling so much that instead of going towards the staircase I shuffled crabwise nearer and nearer the pot. When I was well within range she suddenly jabbed the pointed knife into my back side and with a scream of pain I leapt right into the boiling soup and stiffened in a moment of intense agony with my compan-ions in distress, one carrot and two onions.
>
> A mighty rumbling followed by crashes and there I was standing outside the pot stirring the soup in which I could see my own meat, feet up, boiling away as merrily as any joint of beef. I added a pinch of salt and some pepper-corns then ladled out a measure into my granite dish. The soup was not as good as a bouillabaisse but it was a good ordinary stew, very adequate for the cold weather. (138)

Such is Carrington's homely version of the alchemical broth, in which the self dissolves everything but its own essence. When Marian next looks at herself in a piece of polished obsidian, she sees, in sequence: "the face of the Abbess of Santa Barbara de Tartarus grinning at me sardonically," then the Queen Bee, and finally her own face (138). Glossing this passage, Gloria Orenstein writes:

> Marian, after a series of adventures, has a revelation of her previous incarnations, all of which symbolize aspects of the spirit of the Mother Goddess. . . . The three-faced female is the image of the Triple Goddess or the Triple Muse, who, according to Robert Graves, is woman in her divine character. Each lifetime is revealed to be one step in the karmic cycle, and the conclusion of the process yields a total knowledge of all-time.[32]

Orenstein is no doubt right, but she misses the humor of Carrington's tribute to the Great Mother. Marian, after her vision of the three faces, adds: "This of course might have been an optical illusion." But curiously, her self-deprecating humor does not undercut the force of Carrington's feminist revision: on the contrary, it makes it even stronger—as if one did not need to be ultrasolemn in order to be taken seriously, in order to be heard.

Which does not mean that all playing is alike in its effects or implications, however. The Monty Python version of the story, *Monty Python and the Holy Grail*, which came out roughly at the same time as Carrington's novel in England, is zany and self-reflexive, full of fake blood and non sequiturs, as we would expect from that irreverent crew. (It is noteworthy that Monty Python films are usually characterized as "Surrealistic.") But in the end, all the play is safely put in its place when the police interrupt the shooting (by the camera, in this case) and pack the actors off in a paddy wagon: one of them had chopped off the head of a "famous historian" who narrated part of the story in an earlier sequence. To me, that ending seems to say (not as flatly as this, of course): "Playing is fun, but let's not confuse it with reality. Cut up as many people as you like in fantasy, but remember that in real life murder is punishable by the law. And a good thing, too."

Civilization is there to remind us of what is possible and permissible in the social world; a child can be all the more wildly inventive and anarchic in his play, knowing that the Law of the Father will keep him from going too far. Carrington's version of the Holy Grail does away with that safety rail—without advocating murder, I hasten to say. *The Hearing Trumpet* ends neither in murder nor in a return to reality as usual. It ends, instead, with a victory for the Goddess, to whom is restored her cup full of honey, wrested away from the "Revengeful Father God" (146). And it ends very far indeed from reality as usual, in a quite unique (but still humorous) surreality.

Marian, before she became an old crone, had known the Surrealists, she tells us. And she had had a great friend, Marlborough, a poet, who loved to see Marian laugh, and who "always seemed to be present when I was overtaken by my spasms, which he was pleased to call Marian's maniac laughter. He always enjoyed seeing me making an exhibition of myself" (37). As it happens, Marlborough turns up again after Marian's kitchen scene, while she and her friends (who now include Carmella's Chinese valet, Majong, and the postman Taliessin, a.k.a. the Celtic bard, who already figured in Dona Rosalinda's story) are pondering how to capture the Holy Grail. Marlborough arrives in an atom-powered ark, accompanied by a pack of wolves and his wolf-headed sister, Anubeth—perhaps a cousin of the Egyptian dog-headed god, Anubis? Or of Max Ernst's bird-headed alter ego, Loplop? Anubeth's hybrid form is explained by the fact that she (like her brother) is related to a "Hungarian nobleman whose Mother was a well-known Transylvanian Vampire" (153). Anubeth is a talented artist specializing in (oh, surprise!) collage.

The interior of Marlborough's ark is "like the opium dream of a gypsy"—or like a Surrealist metaphor/object: "Perfume sprays shaped like exotic feathered birds, lamps like praying mantis with moveable eyes, velvet cushions in the form of gigantic fruits, and sofas mounted on prostrate werewomen beautifully sculptured in rare woods and ivory" (152). One of the more famous objects displayed at the 1938 International Surrealist exhibition was Kurt Seligmann's *Ultra-Furniture,* a chair mounted on women's legs, and the praying mantis was a favored Surrealist stand-in for the femme fatale.[33]

Carrington's homage to her friend Max Ernst (with whom she spent a few crucial years of her life) and to the Surrealist aesthetic of parody and collage is unmistakable, though teasing—and apparently without illusions about the place of women in Surrealism.[34]

In the end, Marian's army captures the Grail, which is borne off by bees to a secret part of the cavern they all share; and Marian can write: "This is the end of my tale. I have set it all down faithfully, without exaggeration either poetic or otherwise" (158).

As we might expect from such a truthful statement, Marian's tale is not quite at an end yet. It continues for a few more paragraphs, which tell us that Anubeth, pregnant by the wolf king Pontefact, has given birth to "six young werewolf cubs which improved in appearance after their fur grew"; that Marian is continuing her job as scribe; and that, with the poles shifting, Marian and her crew are now where Lapland used to be—where Marian had always dreamed of going.

Ice ages pass, and although the world is frozen over we suppose someday grass and flowers will grow again. In the meantime I keep a daily record on three wax tablets.

> After I die Anubeth's werecubs will continue the document, till the planet is peopled with cats, werewolves, bees and goats. We all fervently hope that this will be an improvement on humanity, which deliberately renounced the Pneuma of the Goddess. . . .
>
> If the old woman can't go to Lapland, then Lapland must come to the Old Woman. (158)

The seriousness behind Carrington's "maniac laughter" is obvious: it is no small thing to write off the human race.[35] At the same time, the novel's concluding sentence suggests the hope that if the world becomes sufficiently topsy-turvy, even the peaceable desires of old women (of the Old Woman—a mother) may be satisfied.

It is the perennial hope of carnival, is it not?

IV

Why should we imagine the mother playing and laughing? And why are the stakes political (in the broadest sense) as well as aesthetic?

Playing, as Freud and Winnicott (among others) have shown us, is the activity through which the human subject most freely and inventively constitutes herself or himself. To play is to affirm an "I," an autonomous subjectivity that exercises control over a world of possibilities; at the same time, and contrarily, it is in playing that the "I" can experience itself in its most fluid and boundaryless state. Barthes speaks of being "liberated from the binary prison, putting oneself in a state of infinite expansion."[36] Winnicott calls the play experience "one of a non-purposive state, as one might say a sort of ticking over of the unintegrated personality"—and adds a few pages later that "it is only here, in this unintegrated state of the personality, that that which we describe as creative can appear."[37]

To imagine the mother playing is to recognize her most fully as a subject—as autonomous and free, yet (or for that reason?) able to take the risk of "infinite expansion" that goes with creativity. Some feminist critics have expressed worry over the idea of the female subject, mother or not, playing with the boundaries of the self, given the difficulties women in our culture have in attaining a sense of selfhood to begin with. As Nancy K. Miller, who has most forcefully argued this view, has put it, speaking of the signature: "Only those who have it can play with not having it," and women's signatures, even for those who "have" them, are still undervalued. Naomi Schor has argued, in a similar vein, that feminists should not abandon the notion of feminine specificity in favor of "the carnival of plural sexualities."[38]

Although I share Miller's and Schor's desire to hold on to a notion of female selfhood, it still seems important to me to admit the possibility of playing with the boundaries of the self—especially if Winnicott is right in seeing such play as a necessary part of artistic creativity. I believe that women, and women artists in particular, must be strong enough to allow themselves this kind of play; one way to achieve such strength is, I believe, for girls to imagine (or see) their mothers playing. Jessica Benjamin has argued that if the mother were really recognized in our culture as an independent subject, with desires of her own, that would revolutionize not only the psychoanalytic paradigms of "normal" child development (which have always been based on the child's need to be recognized by the mother, not on the idea of *mutual* recognition), but the actual lives of children in this culture as they develop into adults.[39] Could it be that it would change the way we in the West think about the constitution of human subjectivity?

That may be too big a claim, or at least one that would have to be argued more fully than I am doing here. In fact, I will be content with a more modest vision: of boys (later to be men) who actually enjoy seeing their mothers *move* instead of sitting motionless, "a peaceful center" around which the child weaves his play.[40] Of girls (later to be women) who learn that they do not have to grow up to be motionless mothers.

To imagine the mother laughing as she plays brings a touch of lightness to what otherwise could appear as too pious a dream. (There is nothing so self-defeating, or so grim, as the idea of required or regimented play.) And it may allow us to envision a new, lighter—though no less inventive and free—mode of play than the sadistic, narcissistic, angst-ridden games of transgressive children.

Patricia Yaeger quotes Herbert Marcuse paraphrasing Friedrich Schlegel: "Man is free when the 'reality loses its seriousness' and when its necessity 'becomes light.' "[41] As Yaeger points out, this is not a recipe for learning to live with the way things are, but rather one possible recipe for wanting to change them.

NOTES

1. Osip Mandelstam, "Literary Moscow," quoted and translated by Svetlana Boym in *Death in Quotation Marks: Cultural Myths of the Modern Poet* (Cambridge, Mass.: Harvard University Press, 1991), 193. The present essay is a radically shortened version of chapter 7 of my book, *Subversive Intent: Gender, Politics, and the Avant-Garde* (Cambridge, Mass.: Harvard University Press, 1990). Published here by permission of Harvard University Press.

2. Boym, *Death in Quotation Marks,* 194.

3. Sandra Gilbert and Susan Gubar, *The Madwoman in the Attic: The Woman Writer and the Nineteenth-Century Literary Imagination* (New Haven: Yale University Press, 1979), 80.

4. Alicia Ostriker, *Stealing the Language: The Emergence of Women's Poetry in America* (Boston: Beacon Press, 1986), 7.

5. Patricia Yaeger, *Honey-Mad Women: Emancipatory Strategies in Women's Writing* (New York: Columbia University Press, 1988), especially chaps. 7 and 8; Mary Russo, "Female Grotesques: Carnival and Theory," in *Feminist Studies/Critical Studies,* ed. Teresa de Lauretis (Bloomington: Indiana University Press, 1986), 213–29.

6. See, among other works, Mikhail Bakhtin, *Rabelais and His World,* trans. Helene Iswolsky (Cambridge, Mass.: MIT Press, 1968) and *The Dialogic Imagination,* trans. Caryl Emerson and Michael Holquist (Austin: University of Texas Press, 1981). Although Bakhtin maintained that lyric poetry was essentially "monological," not participating in the heteroglossia of the novel, contemporary theorists of intertextuality, starting with Julia Kristeva, who coined that term, have seen no need to uphold that distinction.

7. Bakhtin, *Dialogic Imagination,* 60. Subsequent page references are given parenthetically in the text.

8. The power of stories in shaping people's perceptions and behavior in the world has been recognized for some time, notably by analysts of myth. It is remarkable that the "rewriting of old stories" has not only given impetus to recent fiction and poetry by women, but has also fueled the work of feminist scholars across a wide range of disciplines. Among literary critics, the currently influential notion of revising the canon turns on the question of how to tell the story of a given literature or literary movement; feminist historians, starting with the pioneers Sheila Rowbotham and Joan Kelly Gadol, have obliged us to look again at the story of Western civilization; feminist psychologists like Carol Gilligan and Jessica Benjamin are significantly rewriting the psychoanalytic story of human development. Gilligan's current work on the myth of Psyche, which she proposes as a more benign alternative to the founding myth of psychoanalysis, Oedipus, seems to me especially relevant, for it specifically makes the link between changes in psychoanalytic paradigms and the real lives of adolescent girls. (See her "Oedipus and Psyche: Two Stories about Love," manuscript.)

9. Peter Stallybrass and Allon White, *The Politics and Poetics of Transgression* (Ithaca: Cornell University Press, 1986), 6.

10. Terry Eagleton, *Walter Benjamin: Towards a Revolutionary Criticism* (London: Verso, 1981), 148; quoted in Stallybrass and White, *Politics and Poetics*, 13.

11. Stallybrass and White, *Politics and Poetics*, 16. A similarly nuanced view, relating specifically to parody as an artistic genre, is expressed by Linda Hutcheon in *A Theory of Parody* (New York: Methuen, 1985). Hutcheon argues that parody has a "potentially conservative impulse," since it necessarily affirms the tradition even while parodying it; at the same time, "parody can, like the carnival, also challenge norms in order to renovate, to renew" (76). In her more recent work, *A Poetics of Postmodernism* (New York and London: Routledge, 1988), Hutcheon has emphasized the critical and radical aspect of parody, especially in the work of contemporary feminists, African-Americans, and other minorities.

12. For a brief but up-to-date biographical essay on Carrington, see Marina Warner's introduction to Carrington's recently published collection of stories, *The House of Fear: Notes from Down Below* (New York: E. P. Dutton, 1988). Carrington's life and work figure prominently in Whitney Chadwick, *Women Artists and the Surrealist Movement* (Boston: Little, Brown, 1985).

13. Cixous, "Le rire de la Méduse," *L'arc* 61 (1975): 39–54; trans. Keith Cohen and Paula Cohen, under the title "The Laugh of the Medusa" in *New French Feminisms*, ed. Elaine Marks and Isabelle de Courtivron (New York: Schocken Books, 1981), 245–64.

14. Among the more intelligent reviews were those by Gabriele Annan, *Times Literary Supplement*, 27 May 1977, 644, and Bettina Knapp, *World Literature Today* (Winter 1978): 80–81. I first learned about Carrington's novel from Gloria Orenstein's far-ranging essay, "Reclaiming the Great Mother: A Feminist Journey to Madness and Back in Search of a Goddess Heritage," *Symposium* 36, no. 1 (Spring 1982): 45–70.

15. Among those who had started publishing earlier but gained special prominence only in the 1970s (or even later), I would mention Angela Carter and Christine Brooke-Rose; among the younger writers, who did not begin publishing until the late 1970s or early 1980s, Jeanette Winterson and Kathy Acker.

16. The two volumes are *The House of Fear: Notes from Down Below* and *The Seventh Horse and Other Tales* (New York: Dutton, 1988). In addition to these stories, Carrington has published two novels: *The Stone Door* (New York: St. Martin's Press, 1977), written a few years before *The Hearing Trumpet*; and *The Hearing Trumpet*, published by City Lights Books (San Francisco, 1985). Subsequent page references to this novel are given parenthetically in the text.

17. I have argued this point in some detail in chapters 3 and 4 of *Subversive Intent*.

18. For a critical assessment (with which I do not always agree) of the maternal metaphor in the work of Luce Irigaray, Hélène Cixous, and Julia Kristeva, see Domna Stanton, "Difference on Trial: A Critique of the Maternal Metaphor in Cixous, Irigaray, and Kristeva," in *The Poetics of Gender*, ed. Nancy K. Miller (New York: Columbia University Press, 1986), 157–82.

19. See Peter Bürger, *Theory of the Avant-Garde*, trans. Michael Shaw (Minne-

apolis: University of Minneapolis Press, 1984), 73–82. Bürger calls such techniques of juxtaposition montage rather than collage, and maintains that "a theory of the avant-garde must begin with the concept of montage" (77).

20. Aragon, *Le libertinage* (1924; reprint, Paris: Gallimard, 1983), 274, 271 (my translation).

21. Gayatri Chakravorty Spivak, "French Feminism in an International Frame," *Yale French Studies* 62 (1981): 167; (emphasis Spivak's).

22. Among the writers one could cite here are Angela Carter and Rikki Ducornet, whose affinities with Surrealism are the most evident; Kathy Acker, who alludes frequently in her novels to European male avant-garde writers; and Jeanette Winterson, whose four novels published so far all have Surrealist "echoes."

23. After being published separately (Chicago: Black Swan Press, 1983), *Down Below* is now included, with a 1987 postscript and a note on the text, in *The House of Fear: Notes from Down Below*, 160–214. Subsequent page references to this edition are given parenthetically in the text.

24. The parodic works I have in mind here are Louis Aragon, *Les aventures de Télémaque* (1920), Robert Desnos, *La liberté ou l'amour!* (1927), and Péret's stories collected in *Le gigot, sa vie son oeuvre* (1957).

25. Curiously enough, scholars of the Grail legend seem to agree that the Grail tradition is pre-Christian, probably of Celtic origin. Carrington's "blasphemous" paganization of the Grail thus appears to be a reappropriation rather than a theft. See Roger Sherman Loomis, *The Grail: From Celtic Myth to Christian Symbol* (New York: Columbia University Press, 1963).

26. I say sly because a ninety-two-year-old bearded lady, with a grown son who drops out of her story—and out of the novel—after the first twenty pages is not the most obvious stereotype of the mother; however, in a rewriting of the Grail quest whose heroine is a woman with a son named Galahad, an identification of the heroine with a (the) mother strikes me as unavoidable. It is also significant, as I note below, that Carrington's association of the Grail with Venus emphasizes her role as mother, rather than exclusively as the goddess of erotic love.

27. Gayatri Spivak has noted that there is an unfortunate tendency among academic critics to "restore [avant-garde] texts back to propositional discourse" (Spivak, "French Feminism," 167). She had in mind chiefly the work of male avant-garde writers, but the pitfall is also there—perhaps even more so—in the case of feminist avant-garde works, whose polemical content may tempt one to overlook the way it is framed, and the fact that the framing is part of the content. This is yet another version of the "how to read" question, which I discuss at length in *Subversive Intent*, especially in chaps. 2, 3, and 4.

28. For an analysis of postmodernist fiction in these terms, see Brian McHale, *Postmodernist Fiction* (New York: Methuen, 1987).

29. On the association of Aphrodite with Ishtar, see Edward Tripp, *The Meridian Handbook of Classical Mythology* (New York: New American Library, 1970), 60. For a more detailed analysis, see Paul Friedrich, *The Meaning of Aphrodite* (Chicago: University of Chicago Press, 1978).

30. For a brief discussion of the importance of alchemy in Surrealism, see Inez

Hedges, *Languages of Revolt,* chap. 1; her discussion of the serpent biting its own tail is on 4.

31. Carrington is multiplying her Goddess lore here, since both Hecate and the Queen Bee have ancient associations with matriarchal cults. However, Carrington's allusions to the Goddess always have an element of humor and self-irony, as I suggest below.

32. Orenstein, "Reclaiming the Great Mother," 65.

33. There is a good reproduction of Seligmann's *Ultra-Furniture* in Susan Gubar, "Representing Pornography," *Critical Inquiry* 13, no. 4 (Summer 1987): 716. For a discussion of the praying mantis as an object of fascination for the Surrealists, see Rosalind Krauss, "No More Play," in *The Originality of the Avant-Garde and Other Modernist Myths* (Cambridge, Mass.: MIT Press, 1985), 69–72. Krauss notes that the mantis's fascination was based on a single detail: "The female of the species was known to eat its partner after, or even during, copulation" (70).

34. For an excellent and detailed study of women in Surrealism, see Chadwick, *Women Artists and the Surrealist Movement.* I discuss the question in *Subversive Intent,* chaps. 1 and 5.

35. There are a few indications, at the end of the novel (145, 146), that the earthquake, ice age, and general upheaval are taking place after an atomic war. *The Hearing Trumpet* was written at the height of the cold war, at a time of particular anxiety about a nuclear apocalypse.

36. Roland Barthes, *Roland Barthes par Roland Barthes* (Paris: Editions du Seuil, 1975), 137.

37. D. W. Winnicott, *Playing and Reality* (New York: Basic Books, 1971), 55, 64.

38. Nancy K. Miller, "The Text's Heroine," in Miller, *Subject to Change: Reading Feminist Writing* (New York: Columbia University Press, 1988), 75; Naomi Schor, "Dreaming Dissymetry," in *Men in Feminism,* ed. Alice Jardine and Paul Smith (New York: Methuen, 1987), 109.

39. Jessica Benjamin, *The Bonds of Love: Psychoanalysis, Feminism, and the Problem of Domination* (New York: Pantheon Books, 1988).

40. The metaphor of the mother as a "peaceful center" who makes possible the child's (actually, the son's) freedom to play is Roland Barthes's in *Leçon* (Paris: Editions du Seuil, 1978), 42–43. The image of the fixed mother and mobile child is common in psychoanalytic thought—Winnicott's notion of the child playing "alone in the presence of the mother" is one version of it. However, Winnicott also envisages the mother playing with the child, "playing together in a relationship" (*Playing and Reality,* 48), which I find a lot more appealing.

41. Yaeger, *Honey-Mad Women,* 228.

THIRTEEN

TELLING DIFFERENCES:

PARENTS VS. CHILDREN IN

"THE JUNIPER TREE"

Maria Tatar

> "She is my mother," said Colin complainingly. "I don't see
> why she died. Sometimes I hate her for doing it."
> —Frances Hodgson Burnett, *The Secret Garden*

"THE JUNIPER TREE" has long been recognized as one of the
most powerful of all fairy tales. Its widespread dissemination
across the map of European folklore—one monograph identifies
several hundred versions of the tale—suggests that there must be something especially attractive or at least compelling about the tale. That it remains popular today, though not necessarily as a bedtime story told by
adults to children, means that it must speak to more than one age and
generation. Even the brutal and bloody events enacted in the tale did not
keep an expert like P. L. Travers from referring to it as "most beautiful,"
nor did it prevent Tolkien from writing about it as a story of "beauty and
horror" with an "exquisite and tragic beginning."

"The Juniper Tree" begins with a stirring tableau of death in childbirth,
moves to a distressingly painful depiction of child abuse culminating in
murder by decapitation, and ends with what is probably the most disturb-
ingly savage scene of revenge staged in any fairy tale. So infamous are the
principal events in this particular tale that even the usually sober Aarne/
Thompson index of tale types refers to this story as not only "The Juniper
Tree" (AT 720) but also as "My Mother Slew Me; My Father Ate Me."
The alternate title comes from the hero's lament in a song that summarizes
the tale's events. The version of the song in the Grimm's tale reads as follows:

> My mother, she killed me,
> My father, he ate me.
> My sister Marlene

Gathered up my bones,
Put them in a silken scarf,
Buried them under the juniper tree.
Keewitt, keewitt, what a fine bird am I.

The song leaves out the tale's final event, which shows us the step/mother in a state of alarm, her hair shooting out "like tongues of fire."[1] As she goes outdoors in an attempt to dispel her fears, "Bam! the bird dropped a millstone on her head and crushed her to death!"[2]

What we have here conforms to the classic model of a cautionary tale for adults: those who threaten and abuse children become themselves targets of brute violence. The punishment enacted in the tableau that closes the tale must have been a particularly suggestive one to the Grimms' contemporaries, who were generally better versed in scripture than successive generations of listeners and readers. These are Christ's words on the means for entering heaven: "Whoever receives one such child in my name receives me; but whoever causes one of these little ones who believe in me to sin, it would be better for him to have a great millstone fastened around his neck and to be drowned in the depth of the sea" (Matt. 18:5). The biblical intertext does not correlate perfectly in its details with the Grimms' tale, but the millstone in both is an instrument of revenge that punishes adults for injuring the young and innocent. The biblical passage surely gave the millstone in "The Juniper Tree" added weightiness, just as it lent a certain authority to this canonical fairy tale about getting back at adults who mistreat children.

Like "Hansel and Gretel," "Snow White," "Cinderella," and many other popular fairy tales, "The Juniper Tree" shows us children victimized by adults. The boy slain by his step/mother serves even before his death as the target of unrelenting physical assaults. His sister, despite her heroic efforts to bring her brother back to life, also suffers from the savagery of adults and, as a sign of her victimization, weeps almost incessantly throughout the tale. When the step/mother chops up her stepson and cooks him in a stew, Marlene weeps so hard that her tears provide enough salt to season the stew; she continues crying while watching her father devour the stew and while planting her brother's bones in the garden under the juniper tree. Then her mood suddenly shifts: the child-victim has set in motion the process of retaliation, reversing the effects of her villainous step/mother's deeds and exacting revenge.[3]

When one considers that fairy tales began as adult entertainment and made the transition to children's literature only gradually in the course of the seventeenth and eighteenth centuries, the ending to "The Juniper Tree" seems more than peculiar. Why would adult audiences want to get the kind of message sent by this tale? As Alice Miller has observed (with some polemical exaggeration), our culture has, over the centuries, accepted a pedagogical ideology that leaves parents blameless and makes them eternally right even as it labels children lazy, spoiled, or stubborn.[4] "The Juniper Tree," probably one of the oldest, best-preserved, and most widely disseminated of fairy tales, inverts this ideology by siding at all times with the children in it. The story is by no means unique in the economy of its role-distribution, but the adult agents driving its plot engage in singularly monstrous acts. And instead of mobilizing their superior strength, energy, and wit to battle fairy-tale heroes, they conduct themselves in a way that can only be described as simpleminded or downright childish.[5]

Take first the case of the step/mother. She has two children: a stepson and a biological daughter. "Whenever the woman looked at her daughter, she felt great love for her, but whenever she looked at the little boy, her heart was cut to the quick." More important than her feelings is her actual behavior: "She pushed him from one place to the next, slapped him here and cuffed him there, so that the poor child lived in constant fear." It does not take long for this kind of bullying to escalate into a murderous assault on the boy. When the unsuspecting lad reaches into a chest to get an apple, the step/mother decapitates him by slamming the lid of the chest down on his head. Her attempt to cover up the bloodcurdling crime is unusual—astonishingly so—in its lack of sophistication. Overcome by fear (she shows no signs of remorse), she fetches a kerchief, puts the head back on the boy, ties the kerchief around his neck, and seats the corpse by the door with apple in hand. This is a distinctly childlike way of concealing a crime, but each step of the process is carried out with the utmost gravity.

While it is true that fairy-tale characters are forever violating the conventions of human behavior (the woman in this tale exhibits decidedly anti-maternal qualities toward both stepson and daughter), just as the events recounted in them often fail to obey the laws of nature (slamming the lid of a chest on a person's head is unlikely to result in decapitation), there is a ring of psychological truth to the step/mother's behavior once one sees it as modeled on that of children rather than adults.[6] The assault on her son may stand as an extreme expression of adult anger, resentment, and aggression, but the woman's attempt to escape blame is so artless that it can be attributed only to a child's way of thinking. It may work, but that it does reminds us of the extent to which the world in "The Juniper Tree" obeys laws legislated by a child's view of the world.

The other adult actor in the tale does not display any greater degree of sophistication than his wife. When, for example, the father notices his son's absence and learns that he will be away for six weeks, he expresses annoyance, but only because the boy failed to bid him farewell. This expression of childlike egocentricity finds its match in table manners that are innocently crude and rude. "Give me more," the father declares greedily while

he is devouring the stew cooked by his wife. "I'm not going to share this
with you," he snaps. "Somehow I feel as if it were all mine." While engaging in this cannibalistic feast, he casually tosses one bone after another under the table. The anthropophagous father may come off well by contrast
to his bloodthirsty wife, but he remains less than admirable in both his
indifference to the lot of his children and his single-minded focus on his
own needs.

   These observations about the behavior of step/mother and father explain
in part why it is that children find the grisly events in this tale so hilarious.
Raconteurs report again and again that when the boy's head rolls, when he
is dismembered for the stew, and when the father dines, children respond
with gales of laughter.[7] Interestingly, the laughter is rarely described as
nervous, but as gleeful, in part perhaps because a child's worst fears about
adult aggression are acted out in a wholly childlike way by the very figures
authorized to monitor children and to keep *their* aggressive impulses in
check. Many versions of the tale make a point of capitalizing on the slap-
stick possibilities of the narrative situation. In the Scottish "Pippety Pew,"
the father fishes a foot out of the stew, turns to his wife, and engages in the
following dialogue:

> "Surely that's my Johnnie's foot," said he.
> "Nonsense. It is one of the hare's," said she.
> Then he took up a hand.
> "That's surely my Johnnie's hand," said he.
> "You're talking nonsense, goodman," said she. "That's another of the hare's
> feet."[8]

In the narrated events of "The Juniper Tree," children witness parental aggression and parental indifference in their most extreme forms. The antirealistic effects (from the transformation of boy into bird to the improba-
bly naive behavior of the adults) mobilized throughout to stage the child's
worst fears serve to diminish the anxiety and heighten the pleasure of the
performance. When children hear about adults acting on impulse in extrav-
agantly ghastly ways without any attempt to cover up their deeds, the ta-
bles really are turned for a change. It becomes easy to laugh about what
could arouse intense uneasiness and pain when the discourse is marked
with constant reminders of its safe distance from reality.

   What marks the behavior of the various actors in "The Juniper Tree" as
especially childlike is an inability to differentiate. The father, for example,
may not know that he is indulging in a feast of human flesh and committing an atrocity that represents the most brutish form of self-preservation,
but he still has made the error of not knowing how to distinguish human
from animal flesh. The distinction between "own" and "foreign" is not one
with which he can operate. The daughter too, even as heroine of the tale,

has trouble making distinctions. For her, this takes the form of not being able to tell the difference between dead and alive. When Marlene sees her brother seated by the door, she is frightened but cannot read his condition. He may be "white as a sheet" and unable to speak, yet she does not recognize the meaning of these signs. Even the boy, as innocent victim, falls into the trap of failing to discriminate between good and evil when he accepts the step/mother's invitation to take an apple. This flaw or lack on the part of all three figures is precisely what makes them agreeable and turns them into magnets for our sympathies. Because they do not differentiate and discriminate, they also become aligned with the forces of good.

The step/mother, by contrast, is an expert in the art of making distinctions, and that expertise fuels her evil impulses, allying her repeatedly with that divider par excellence known as the devil. It is he who "takes hold of her" and compels her to treat the hero cruelly, who "takes possession of her" and forces her to snatch the apple from her daughter, and who "prompts" her to slam the lid down on the boy's head. For the step/mother, the question of own/foreign becomes the touchstone of all decisions. The opposition is fully incarnated in her daughter and stepson. That the step/mother differentiates between the two and is forever drawing distinctions between them marks her as a villain and lends to her every act a kind of self-consciousness absent in the actions of other figures. When her stepson returns from school, she speaks to him in honeyed tones, tricking him into taking the apple that means his death. The obverse of a nurturing and protective figure, she mobilizes the semblance of maternal actions to trap her victims. She deludes Marlene into taking responsibility for her brother's death, and she deceives her husband by telling him that his son is paying a visit to a great-uncle when he is in fact being dished up for dinner. The step/mother may act "as innocently as a child" at times, but her behavior is motivated by the need to see differences and to assert preferences.

Other versions of "The Juniper Tree" confirm that deception fueled by differentiation is the key tactic used by the step/mother to attain her goals. Murderous intentions are masked by maternal goodwill in order to lure the tale's heroes/heroines to their death. In the British tale "The Rose-Tree," a stepmother camouflages the anger she harbors toward her step-daughter with maternal tenderness. " 'Come lay your head on my lap that I may comb your hair,' " she gently proposes. The girl rests her head on the woman's lap, unaware that dissimulation is at work. What follows is a sharp reversal, starkly brutal in its depiction of maternal affection sliding into fiendish savageness:

> So the little one laid her head in the woman's lap, who proceeded to comb the yellow silken hair. And when she combed the hair fell over her knees, and rolled right down to the ground.

Then the stepmother hated her more for the beauty of her hair; so she said to her, "I cannot part your hair on my knee, fetch a billet of wood." So she fetched it. Then said the stepmother, "I cannot part your hair with a comb, fetch me an axe." So she fetched it.

"Now," said the wicked woman, "lay your head down on the billet whilst I part your hair."

Well! She laid down her little golden head without fear; and whist! down came the axe, and it was off. So the mother wiped the axe and laughed.[9]

We do not have to look long or far in the Grimms' collection to find other examples of murderous intentions masquerading as maternal good-will. The three attempts on Snow White's life all nearly work because the heroine suspects nothing when an old peddler woman offers to lace her up "properly," to give her hair a "proper" combing, and to share an apple with her. The ruses work each time precisely because they incorporate gestures openly maternal in their aim. The shock comes when these gestures are revealed to be pure artifice, when the compassion and care they imply un-mask themselves as murderous hatred.

Significantly, the first step in the direction of evil is taken when the step/mother offers her stepson an apple. Numerous commentators have insisted on connecting that apple with Eve and the Garden of Eden.[10] But to see, as they do, the step/mother (as Eve) offering the infamous apple to the stepson (as Adam) signifies a failure to recognize differences. The boy's function is not analogous to that of Adam, and, more importantly, the step/mother is not tempting the boy with knowledge, but luring him to his death. Curiosity, original sin, knowledge (the entire complex of asso-ciations connected with the biblical Fall) are absent from the thematics of this particular episode.[11] If we look at variants of the tale, we also find that few others feature apples. In a version collected by Jacob Grimm, but in-cluded neither in the *Nursery and Household Tales* nor in the notes to it, the step/mother orders the boy to get into the chest and to gather up its con-tents.[12] As soon as he climbs in, she slams the lid down on him, and the boy suffocates. Since the apples are, by virtue of their biblical function, so closely linked with temptation and deception, it is not surprising that they were smuggled into some versions—but that does not mean that the entire range of their biblical associations were transported into the text.

What seems more significant than the step/mother's offer of an apple is her method of committing a crime and of destroying the evidence for it. She first severs the boy's head from his body, inflicting a wound that can-not, for all her efforts, be healed. Once she recognizes the irreversibility of her deed, she further mutilates the corpse by "cutting it into pieces."[13] She thus becomes a person who not only makes distinctions, but also divides what should be whole and destroys things by taking them apart. She inflicts on the body precisely those operations that she also carries out in her mind. "Der zerstückelnde Verstand" (literally, reason that cuts things into pieces) was a central metaphor of negativity harnessed by German idealist philosophy in its nostalgia for organic wholeness and unity. As a differentiator, the step/mother creates a rupture in the "natural" order of things, dividing, segmenting, mutilating, and destroying. In this regard, she bears a distinct functional resemblance to Eve, who is also linked to death through division and sin. As the apocryphal *Book of Sirach* puts it: "From a woman was the beginning of sin, and because of her we all die."[14]

While the hero's step/mother is connected with artifice and malice, his birth mother is described in terms that link her with nature and biological rhythms. When it comes to analyzing the "natural" mother and her role in the Grimms' tale, however, a word of caution is in order. The long paragraph that opens "The Juniper Tree" as it appeared in the version printed in the *Nursery and Household Tales* has correctly been viewed as suspect by folklorists. Its florid language, along with its inclusion of a formulaic phrase that appears in few other versions of the tale (the mother wishes for a child "as red as blood and as white as snow"), suggest that certain liberties were taken to produce as poetic a text as possible.[15]

The textual history of the Grimms' version of "The Juniper Tree" is in fact complicated. To begin with, the Grimms cannot really be credited with taking down the words of the tale. The Romantic painter Philipp Otto Runge recorded "The Juniper Tree," along with "The Fisherman and His Wife," as a sign of his willingness to collaborate in a national effort to preserve folk traditions. The tale subsequently found its way into one collection after another. The Grimms' version deviates slightly from Runge's original, yet there are no real substantive changes.[16]

Philipp Otto Runge, a master in the art of ornamental detail and decorative art, gives us a highly stylized version of the tale even as he uses dialect to convey the impression of "artless" narration. He was, no doubt, largely responsible for the expansive narrative tone that dominates the tale's first paragraph. His is the only extant version of the tale that weds the biological mother so closely to nature—once she becomes fertile and conceives, she is turned into a virtual prisoner of nature, subject to its laws of growth and decay. An elaborate narrative duet coordinates the rhythms of the child's gestation period with nature's seasonal changes. Conceived in the dead of winter after a long stretch of barrenness, the child flourishes in the spring, becomes "big and firm" like the fruit on the juniper tree, and is born at some time in the fall, at which point his mother's health declines, and she dies. (Pro)creation and death are wedded here in the conventional mythical thematics common to cults of fertility and agricultural rites.

The text's linking of pregnancy with the rhythms of nature is implicitly part of a larger project that connects mothers with Mother Nature, an association not altogether flattering, as Dorothy Dinnerstein and other feminist writers have emphasized.[17] Here is how Freud, for example, writes about nature and its hostility to the male-gendered notion of civilization, without once, incidentally, acknowledging how close his description fits that of the pre-Oedipal mother.

> There are the elements, which seem to mock at all human control: the earth, which quakes and is torn apart and buries all human life and its works; water, which deluges and drowns everything in turmoil, storms, which blow everything before them; . . . and finally there is the painful riddle of death, against which no medicine has yet been found. . . . With these forces, nature rises against us, *majestic, cruel, and inexorable*; she brings to our mind once more *our weakness and helplessness*, which we thought to escape through the work of civilization.[18]

Though the poignancy of the opening paragraph in "The Juniper Tree" is unsettled by the complexities of the biological mother's associations with nature and death, it still stands in sharp contrast to the horrors of the tale's main events, events engineered largely by the step/mother. Runge (or perhaps his informants) must have had a clear sense of the biological mother as a "natural" foil to the step/mother, a figure who represents self-consciousness and artifice in its most dreaded and dreadful form. His introduction also establishes a pattern in which birth and death become so entwined that one is not present without the other; indeed, the birth of one person spells the death of another in the biological economy of the text. The co-presence of birth and death is inscribed on this first scene and is then doubled and repeated as rebirth and murder in the tale's subsequent syntagmatic units.

"The Juniper Tree" eliminates both stepmother and biological mother in the end, yet it is (if one may coin the word) matricentric from beginning to end. The mothers serve as progenitors of more than the children; they are the ones who, in their affiliation with origins and endings, generate the action that constitutes the plot and who, through their association with nature at one extreme and with artifice at the other, engender a complex chain of signification. The death of the biological mother, central as it is to the narrative, is often omitted both in variants of the tale and in conventional inventories of the tale's stock events. The Aarne/Thompson index of tale types, for example, lists the following episodes as key: "The Murder," "The Transformation," "The Revenge," and "The Second Transformation."[19]

This tabulation has not been corrected or modified by any of the tale's commentators. But a far more satisfying, and also more revealing, list of the chief events in "The Juniper Tree" would take into account the death of the biological mother as it would take note of the way in which murder alternates with transformation. In classic fairy-tale fashion, "The Juniper Tree" begins with a realistic basic situation, then veers off abruptly into a world where supernatural events and violent actions are the order of the day. Think, for example, again of "Hansel and Gretel," where the villain of the tale first appears as a cruel stepmother at home, then as a cannibalistic witch residing in enchanted woods. The portrait of the cruel stepmother in that story may seem almost as unrealistic in its broad contours as that of the wicked witch with her red eyes and keen sense of smell. Yet if one considers the social realities of other cultures, the heartless stepmother is less of a stark deviation from the norm than would appear at first sight. That stepmothers treated the children of their husbands' first marriages badly—in part because they wished to preserve the patrimony for their own children, in part because they resented the idea of becoming enslaved to a previous wife's children—was more or less a fact of life in the era that gave shape to the tales recorded in the Grimms' collection. In "Hansel and Gretel," as in so many other fairy tales, the plausible and realistic traumas of everyday life, as described in the tale's opening paragraphs, are sharply intensified and repeated in the antirealistic nightmare of victimization and retaliation acted out in the remainder of the tale.[20]

"The Juniper Tree" takes as its starting point a scene of birth and death that constituted a part of the life experience of large segments of the population of premodern Europe. As Eugen Weber has observed, "deaths in childbed and after made for high female mortality between the ages of 20 and 39, hence an unusually high proportion of maternal orphans."[21] The version of "The Juniper Tree" recorded by Philipp Otto Runge is exceptionally expansive when it comes to describing the mother's death. Many tales simply state that the mother of one of the two children (usually the boy, but sometimes the girl) has died, and do not make clear the circumstances of her death.[22] The birth of the boy kills the woman, but the text hints that she is not entirely blameless. Greed becomes implicated in the woman's death: "In the seventh month she snatched at the juniper berries and ate them so greedily that she grew sad and became ill." Still, it is the birth that leads directly to the death, and ultimately the boy is the one who must take on the burden of guilt for his mother's death. In the second phase of action, however, the child is an innocent victim more than anything else, for he becomes the target of his step/mother's abuse and homicidal impulses. From his point of view, the first two principal episodes of the tale enact the syntactical inversion of "I killed you" into "you killed me" ("I" representing the boy in the tale, "you" the mother in both her incarnations). The initial situation has been reversed, with the cold-blooded slaying of a child by his stepmother far overshadowing in dramatic intensity the death of a mother owing to the birth of her child.

The version of "The Juniper Tree" in the *Nursery and Household Tales* lends itself to the construction of two alternative, mutually exclusive scenarios. The one registers in exaggerated form a child's very real fears about parental aggression and engulfment. The other—and this reading attests to the possibility that fairy tales give body to both fears of aggression and fantasies of retaliation—can be read as a story responding to the distress felt by a child growing up under the weight of guilt (whether consciously registered or not) produced by the death of a mother during childbirth or even by the symbolic "psychic" death of a mother when she gives birth. As Adrienne Rich pointedly puts it, in childbirth, "the mother's life is exchanged for the child's; her autonomy as a separate being seems fated to conflict with the infant she will bear."[23] The tale moves from a naturalistic episode of birth and death (in which the child figures as "murderer") to a supernatural inversion of this scene (in which the "mother" stands as slayer). Through this inversion, the tale's child-hero is both enshrined as victim and vindicated as murderer. It may appear crude to turn this version of a classic fairy tale into a therapeutic text for children who feel responsible, however remotely, for their mothers' deaths (real or symbolic), but there is more than a hint in the Grimms' "Juniper Tree" that the tale sought to turn morbid guilt into self-righteous innocence.

The naturalistic scene of death in childbirth is reversed and doubled in the most unnatural possible terms. The boy's murder represents a transgression of moral and legal conventions, while his rebirth as a magnificent bird violates the convention of natural laws. The murder itself is so abominable and the song that describes it so haunting and direct that it becomes easy to erase the victim's implication in the death of his mother and to justify his role as a deadly agent of revenge.[24] The retaliatory murder of the step/mother, which ushers in the return and rebirth of the son, also marks the complete eradication of the mother as a threatening physical presence in her incarnation as step/mother and as a guilty memory in her incarnation as biological mother. In the end, the motherless household becomes the happy household: "[The boy] took his father and Marlene by the hand. All three were so very happy and they went into the house, sat down at the table, and ate." Grief tainted with guilt and the fear of malice associated with domestic tyranny have vanished with the deaths of the two mothers.

We have seen how the step/mother, as the exponent of artifice, malice, and self-conscious reasoning, serves as the agent of murderous forces, just as the biological mother, tied to the rhythms of nature, represents life-giving powers. The one seems to function as an agent of death, the other of life. Why then does the tale eliminate both in the end to culminate in the idyll of a motherless family? This is the same ending that we know from "Hansel and Gretel" and from countless other fairy tales. While the paradigmatic dimension of "The Juniper Tree" ostensibly introduces a sharp division between the regime of the biological mother and that of the step/

mother, that opposition is overturned in the course of the narrative. The biological mother, as we have seen, becomes implicated, through her fertility and childbearing, in the cyclical rhythms of nature, which include decay and death. The step/mother, through her murder and dismemberment of the hero, becomes enmeshed in a process marked not only by death and mutilation, but also by birth and (re)creation. The murder and dismemberment of the hero constitute the events that break down the tale's elaborately constructed binary oppositions to produce continuums in which birth slides into death and destruction into creation. Let us take a closer look at this crucial scene.

When faced with the step/mother's grisly act, critics have made it easy for themselves by referring their readers to Greek mythology, in particular to Atreus, who serves his brother a meal made up of the limbs of his sons. But the story of Atreus has little bearing on "The Juniper Tree," for it stages the shocking event of forced cannibalism as the most vicious possible form of premeditated revenge. The step/mother, by contrast, is not out to get the better of her husband or to get even; she seems to be doing little more than trying to get rid of the evidence for a crime committed in a moment of passionate rage—incidentally also passing on the burden of guilt for the murder to her husband. Given the degree to which "The Juniper Tree" focuses on birth, death, and regeneration, it seems more logical to look at her act of dismemberment in connection with various Indo-European myths of creation. Here it is through the ritual murder and dismemberment of a sacrificial victim (Dionysus and Romulus are the two most familiar examples) that the world is renewed and recreated.[25] While it may seem incongruous to link these mythical plots with the domestic drama of "The Juniper Tree," the creation story helps us understand the cosmic elements that slip into several scenes of the fairy tale. The birth of the bird, along with the boy's return home and transformation, are described in terms that are decidedly apocalyptic in tenor. The step/mother fears that the world is coming to an end at the very moment when Marlene and her father feel relieved and experience a joyful sense of renewal. The boy's rebirth marks the advent of a male savior who puts a decisive end to the step/mother's nightmarish reign of artifice and duplicity. However, it is the maternal force (now in her malevolent incarnation) who serves as agent of both death and (re)birth. Like the biological mother, she too must perish in order that the process of (re)birth be accomplished. As in the drama of cosmic renewal staged in the fairy tale told by the poet Klingsohr in Novalis's *Heinrich von Ofterdingen*, mothers must die as the precondition for a golden age of innocence and peace.

The mythical mysteries of birth and renewal through dismemberment may seem to strain the fragile domestic drama of "The Juniper Tree." Yet they help us understand the way in which the text dismantles the very oppositions on which it builds syntagmatic and paradigmatic structures. What makes "The Juniper Tree" an extraordinary text is the way in which it remains relentlessly domestic and parochial even as it is shot through with mythical allusions and reminiscences. In the end, it remains a story about family conflicts, an allegory of development that charts the reorientation of children from their mothers to their fathers, but with a mythical signature that underwrites the tale's "sacred truths."

Let us return to the original question. Why is it that "The Juniper Tree" does away with mothers and leaves us with a tableau in which brother, sister, and father are seated at a table eating? Recent psychoanalytic literature has done much to help us understand the complexities of the mother/child relationship. Its emphasis on the fearsomeness of the Oedipal mother, whose seeming omnipotence and whose role as an agent of prohibition creates a sense of dependence, powerlessness, and resentment in the child, explains to some extent the hostility projected onto a mother by a child. This does not, of course, rule out the possibility that hostility may also be part of a child's real-life experience. In fairy tales, representations of the mother often slide into one of two categories: the omnipotent, hostile witch or the omnipotent, protective mother. "Representations of the father relationship," as Nancy Chodorow has observed, "do not become so internalized and subject to ambivalence, repression, and splitting of good and bad aspects."[26] In fact, the father often becomes, because of the "separate" and "special" status assigned to him by virtue of his traditional absence from early child-rearing, the representative of autonomy and of the public, social world. Development is thus traditionally defined in terms of growing away from the mother, who represents dependence and domesticity, and turning to the father.[27] "The Juniper Tree" enacts this very process in its exclusion of the maternal component from the domestic tableau that closes the tale. The children have successfully negotiated the path from dependence to autonomy by crushing the mother and joining the father.

That the father, daughter, and son sit down to dine remains more than a curious detail in this enigmatic text. This last supper figures as an important contrast to the shocking meal in which the three participated earlier, with the son as the main course. If nothing else, it signals a normalization of family relations and marks a period of banal stability leading out of the cataclysmic upheavals of the past. Yet for all its positive connotations, this image of the motherless family participating self-sufficiently in the very activity normally arranged and orchestrated by the mother remains eerily static by contrast to the unending cycle of birth, death, and rebirth set in motion through the presence of mothers.

We will never know exactly who first told this tale and for whom it was intended. In light of the story's perspective, voice, and worldview, it is tempting to imagine a child as the tale's narrator. But as Otto Rank has observed in the context of a study about myths, heroic plots may focus on childhood experiences, but adults create them "by means of retrograde childhood fantasies"—and, we might add in a gesture that both supplements and revises, through childhood memories.[28] One prominent intertextual reference to "The Juniper Tree" dramatically illustrates the way in which adults continue to identify with children, even in those cases where they have passed from (child) victim into the most extreme possible form of adult oppressor. Goethe's *Faust* shows us Gretchen, imprisoned for the crime of infanticide, pathetically singing to herself:

> My mother, the whore,
> She slew me!
> My father, the rascal,
> He ate me!
> My tiny little sister
> Took my bones
> To a nice cool place;
> I became a beautiful bird;
> Fly away, fly away! (4412–20)[29]

This astonishingly revealing moment in Goethe's drama draws attention to an adult's strong identification with a child's suffering at the same time that it bares the gesture of appropriation that accompanies feelings of empathy. What we discover in its words is that guilty adults can divest themselves of blame for their most reprehensible acts of aggression against children by identifying with the victims, then projecting their transgressions onto other figures, and finally constructing a drama in which the self takes flight as a form of salvation. The complexities of child/parent relationships are presented with audacious simplicity in these few lines.

Adults, who may have lost the innocence and simplicity celebrated in "The Juniper Tree" (not necessarily as drastically as Gretchen), have their own reasons for telling this tale. Nostalgia—the hope of recapturing moments of childhood by reliving its high drama from a child's point of view—may make tales like "The Juniper Tree" attractive to adults. But reflexes less voluntary than nostalgia may also lead to a need to replay these childhood dramas of injured innocence and justified retaliation. Listening to "The Juniper Tree" provides young and old alike the opportunity to see and feel how a helpless victim escapes his persecutor and triumphs in the end against all odds.

Fairy tales often address specific aspects of a child's growing pains. The version of "The Juniper Tree" in the Grimms' *Nursery and Household Tales* may in the past have proved therapeutic to children who felt that they had "murdered" their mothers (literally or symbolically), and it may well still serve that function today. But this tale, like so many tales of family life, also

serves the more general purpose of empowering children, or at least making children feel less inferior to adults. In cultures that consistently play
adult authority and privilege against childish impotence and inadequacy,
these tales have a therapeutic function that should not be underestimated.
They may lack the subversive dimension we associate with stories about
diminutive giant-killers and foxy innocents, but they still appeal to that
part of us that resists the notion of bowing to authority.

That ill will and evil are so often personified in fairy tales as adult female
figures, even in cultures where paternal authority proves weightier than its
female counterpart, raises some serious questions that threaten to invalidate the notion of the therapeutic gains we so eagerly look for in the stories
we read to children. However satisfying the tales may seem from a child's
point of view, however much they may reflect the psychological realities of
developmental paths leading from dependence to autonomy, they still per-
petuate strangely inappropriate notions about what it means to live happily
ever after. "Hansel and Gretel," as noted, implies that happiness comes in
the form of an enduring love triangle consisting of a father and his two
children (who have defeated an evil female). Other collections show us the
same constellation of figures. In Afanasev's celebrated Russian fairy tales,
Vasilisa the Beautiful marries the tsar, but her story does not end until her
father finds his way into his daughter's house. The hero of the Venetian
"Cloven Youth" finds himself living "in harmony" with his wife and her
father. Perrault lets Tom Thumb return "to his father" and purchase sine-
cures for him and his brothers.[30] The joy produced by the union of a
brother, sister, and father in "The Juniper Tree" after the death of the step/
mother is not unique to this one tale type. For this reason, it is important
to bear in mind that versions of this tale and others are sacred only as cultural documents mapping the most heavily traveled developmental routes
of another era. They may also capture the larger contours of patterns pre-
dominant in our own age, but that does not mean that we have to keep
reading the same stories to our children today. The omnipresent, powerful
mother and distant, separate father are still the most common coordinates
in the world of child-rearing, but enough has changed and is changing for
us to produce new cultural stories to read to our own children.

NOTES

1. Since the woman in the story is mother to one child and stepmother to the other, I designate her consistently as the step/mother.

2. "The Juniper Tree" is tale 47 in the *Nursery and Household Tales*, and appears in English in *The Complete Fairy Tales of the Brothers Grimm*, trans. Jack Zipes (Toronto: Bantam, 1978), 171–79. (The verse translation is mine; otherwise I cite Zipes's translation.) Michael Belgrader dicusses tale variants in *Das Märchen von dem Machandelboom (KHM 47)* (Frankfurt: Peter D. Lang, 1980). For a full description of the tale type, see Antti Aarne and Stith Thompson, *The Types of the Folktale: A Classification and Bibliography*, 2d ed. (Helsinki: Academia Scientarum Fennica, 1981), 249–50. Arland Ussher and Carl von Metzradt refer to "The Juniper Tree" as "the greatest of all fairy tales." See *Enter These Enchanted Woods* (Dublin: Dolmen, 1957), 37. P. L. Travers's observations on the story appear in "Only Connect," in *Only Connect: Readings on Children's Literature*, ed. Sheila Egoff, G. T. Stubbs, and L. F. Ashley (Toronto: Oxford University Press, 1969), 183–206. For J.R.R. Tolkien's reference to the tale, see "On Fairy-Stories," in *The Tolkien Reader* (New York: Ballantine, 1966), 31.

3. Heinz Rölleke notes that the tears and helplessness of many fairy-tale heroes elicit assistance in the form of benefactors or gifts. He observes that the infant's experience of feeling needy, crying, and getting help may well be the realistic model for this pattern. See Rölleke, "Nachwort," in Rölleke, *Kinder- und Hausmärchen* (1857; reprint, Stuttgart: Reclam, 1980), 3:614.

4. Alice Miller, *For Your Own Good: Hidden Cruelty in Child-Rearing and the Roots of Violence*, trans. Hildegarde and Hunter Hannum (New York: Farrar, Straus, and Giroux, 1983).

5. In an engaging analysis of Donald Duck's adventures in *Walt Disney's Comics and Stories*, James A. Freeman observes that Donald "consistently exhibits traits which any schoolboy recognizes as defining a parent." For that very reason, the constant assaults to his dignity and his perpetual failures have a special appeal for children. See "Donald Duck: How Children (Mainly Boys) Viewed Their Parents (Mainly Fathers), 1943–1960," *Children's Literature* 6 (1977): 150–64.

6. The version in the *Nursery and Household Tales* naturalizes the decapitation episode to some extent by putting a "big, sharp iron lock" on the chest, though most versions do not.

7. Both Vilma Mönckeberg and Louis L. Snyder discuss the responses of children to fairy-tale readings. See Mönckeberg *Das Märchen und unsere Welt: Erfahrungen und Einsichten* (Düsseldorf: Diederichs, 1972), 14–15, and Snyder, *Roots of German Nationalism* (Bloomington: Indiana University Press, 1978), 49. My own observations bear out their findings.

8. "Pippety Pew," in Norah Montgomerie and William Montgomerie, *The Well at the World's End: Folk Tales of Scotland* (Toronto: Bodley Head, 1956), 56–59.

9. "The Rose-Tree," in Joseph Jacobs, *English Fairy Tales* (London: Bodley Head, 1968), 13–15.

10. Carl-Heinz Mallet, for example, finds that the tale stages the biblical scene of temptation, with the mother as Eve and the boy as Adam. His interpretation does not, however, account for numerous deviant textual details. See his *Kopf ab! Gewalt im Märchen* (Hamburg: Rasch and Röhring, 1985), 214–15.

11. That a connection exists between the apple offered to the boy and the one peeled by the biological mother at the start of the tale is not wholly improbable. Both apples are linked to an act of mutilation: the mother cuts her finger while peeling an apple; the son is decapitated while reaching for an apple. They function as the object of (limited) desire that sets in motion a train of events leading to death. And their colors (red/white is the conventional association with the fruit) harmonize with the "red as blood/white as snow" motif (itself strongly linked with the notion of mortality).

12. "Jacob Grimm: Sechs Märchen," in *Briefe der Brüder Grimm an Savigny*, ed. Ingeborg Schnack and Wilhelm Schoof (Berlin: Erich Schmidt, 1953), 430.

13. Lutz Röhrich points out that dismemberment has a dual function in fairy tales: it stands as a murderous act of violence, but also forms part of a ritual for rejuvenating the weak, ill, or aged. See Röhrich, "Die Grausamkeit im deutschen Märchen," *Rheinisches Jahrbuch für Volkskunde* (Bonn: Ferd. Dümmler, 1955), 176–224.

14. Cited by John A. Phillips, *Eve: The History of an Idea* (San Francisco: Harper and Row, 1984), 49. The association between Eve and death is a common one. Saint Jerome writes, for example, that "death came through Eve, but life has come through Mary." Cited by Julia Kristeva, "Stabat mater," in *The Female Body in Western Culture: Contemporary Perspectives*, ed. Susan Rubin Suleiman (Cambridge: Harvard Univerity Press, 1985), 103.

15. On the opening paragraph, see Belgrader, *Das Märchen von dem Machandelboom*, 330. Of the 495 tale variants examined by Belgrader, only the version in the *Nursery and Household Tales* describes the child's birth in such detail. Reinhold Steig attributes this detail to the "self-conscious artistic intentions" of its author. See his "Zur Entstehungsgeschichte der Märchen und Sagen der Brüder Grimm," *Archiv für das Studium der neueren Sprachen* 107 (1901): 277–301.

16. "The Juniper Tree" made its literary debut in Achim von Arnim's *Journal for Hermits* (*Zeitung für Einsiedler*) some four years before its appearance between the covers of the *Nursery and Household Tales*. Arnim, who had always been generous with the literary property of his friends, gave copies of the tale to the Grimms, who published it in their collection, and to Friedrich Heinrich von der Hagen, who passed it on to Johann Georg Büsching, who in turn published it in 1812 in his own collection of tales, "Von dem Mahandel Bohm," in *Volkssagen, Märchen, und Legenden* (Leipzig: C. H. Reclam, 1812), 245–58. On the varied fortunes of Runge's tale, see especially Steig, "Zur Entstehungsgeschichte der Märchen," 277–84.

17. Dorothy Dinnerstein, *The Mermaid and the Minotaur: Sexual Arrangements and the Human Malaise* (New York: Harper and Row, 1976), 106–14.

18. Sigmund Freud, *The Future of an Illusion*, in *The Standard Edition of the Complete Psychological Works of Sigmund Freud*, trans. and ed. James Strachey (London: Hogarth, 1927), 21:15–16 (emphasis added).

19. Aarne and Thompson, *Types of the Folktale*, 249–50.

20. On this point, see Maria Tatar, *The Hard Facts of the Grimms' Fairy Tales* (Princeton: Princeton University Press, 1987), 179–92.

21. Eugen Weber, "Fairies and Hard Facts: The Reality of Folktales," *Journal of the History of Ideas* 42 (1981): 93–113. For a compelling analysis of the traumatic effect on a child of a mother's death in childbirth, see Carol A. Mossmann, "Targeting the Unspeakable: Stendhal and Figures of Pregnancy," *Nineteenth-Century French Studies* 16 (1988): 257–69.

22. It is important to note here that many versions of "The Juniper Tree" cast a girl in the role of victim; the boy consequently becomes her savior. Belgrader finds that the roles are almost equally distributed between males and females (320), but my own statistical sample reveals a preponderance of male heroes. Belgrader does not cite a single version in which the murderous parent is a father, though Jacques Geninasca asserts the existence of such a variant (without citing it). See his "Conte populaire et identité du cannibalisme," *Nouvelle revue de psychanalyse* 6 (1972): 220.

23. Adrienne Rich, *Of Woman Born: Motherhood as Experience and Institution* (New York: Norton, 1976), 166.

24. In nearly every version of the bird's song, the boy is slain by his mother, not his stepmother. This suggests that the splitting of the mother into a good biological mother and a sinister stepmother came only as a later development in the tale's evolution. Songs are generally held to preserve the original diction and motifs of a folktale more faithfully than the texts in which they are anchored.

25. On this point, see Bruce Lincoln, *Myth, Cosmos, and Society: Indo-European Themes of Creation and Destruction* (Cambridge: Harvard University Press, 1986).

26. Nancy Chodorow, *The Reproduction of Mothering: Psychoanalysis and the Sociology of Gender* (Berkeley and Los Angeles: University of California Press, 1978), 97.

27. Otto Rank, *The Myth of the Birth of the Hero and Other Writings*, ed. Philip Freund (New York: Random House, 1932), 84.

29. The translation is my own, since many translators—unaware of the folktale—dilute the strength of the original German. See, for example, Walter Arndt's version: "My mother, the whore / Who smothered me, / My father, the knave / Who made broth of me! . . ." Goethe, *Faust: A Tragedy*, trans. Walter Arndt, ed. Cyrus Hamlin (New York: Norton, 1976), 112.

30. "Vasilisa the Beautiful," in Alexander Afanasev, *Russian Fairy Tales*, trans. Norbert Guterman (New York: Pantheon Books, 1945), 447; "The Cloven Youth," in *Italian Folktales*, trans. George Martin, comp. Italo Calvino (New York: Pantheon Books, 1980), 102; "Little Tom Thumb," in *Perrault's Complete Fairy Tales*, trans. A. E. Johnson et al. (New York: Dodd, Mead, 1961), 41.

FOURTEEN

NO NO NANA:

THE NOVEL AS FOREPLAY

David Mickelsen

Curiosity sharpened by delay.
—Zola, *Nana*

NANA, Emile Zola's 1880 portrayal of courtesan life during the
Second Empire, is a novel dominated by sustained waiting. Readers of novels, especially nineteenth-century readers and readers of
nineteenth-century novels, have been schooled to seek closure—to overcome gaps, domesticate the unfamiliar, establish connections and coherence, understand motives, and anticipate climax. In *Nana* one can indeed
engage these goals, but only at a relatively general level; the text prevents
a narrower application of that understanding, despite the personal focus
implied by eponymy. For all its proliferation of data, this novel expands
without quite filling out a portrait of Nana herself. Instead, the author
manipulates the reader's access just as the courtesan manipulates the men
who seem to use her. *Nana* begins with the title character's debut in the
premiere of a new play, but these openings are not matched by later clo-
sures.

My point of departure, then, will be an examination of how closure is
forestalled in both *récit* and *narration*[1] of *Nana*: both in what happens to
Nana and in our understanding of why. My goal is not merely to fit the
old naturalist with a postmodern mask, nor to perform familiar deconstructive turns at an unexpected site, though I may do both. More importantly, I want to use this specific example to think about the appeals of
literature and the effect of gender on those appeals.

My analysis will maintain a double optic, migrating between *récit* and
narration, both of which display difficulties of accessibility and control.
What happens in the *narration* parallels what happens in the *récit*—*Nana*
echoes Nana, and readers recapitulate characters. Both suitors and readers
are kept in suspense, in suspension; they are allowed minimal closure in
return for maximal investment.

The concept of foreplay provides a way to read this deferral. This metaphor conveys the explicit sexuality of the novel; less literally, however, I use it to trope both the frustrations and the attractions of Zola's narrative. Thus I emphasize, by turns, the "fore" and the "play": the (always) preclimactic or preludic quality of the narrative and the pleasures that arise from (or despite) that quality.

If foreplay is defined as not yet getting what you want, then *Nana* is thoroughly *ante*climactic. I do not mean to suggest that Zola's novel is without climax, but I will show that Zola quite deliberately forestalls resolution, in part by his very commitment to verisimilitude, especially the narrative stance used to attain it: a selective omniscience that relays visual and aural detail. Ironically, as becomes evident at the conclusion, the center of the novel is precisely what is not portrayed. Nana comes to stand for the inaccessible Other, inaccessible to women as well as to men. One is left, finally, with a portrait that escapes the broad strokes of erotic caricature, opening out instead into a field of play which, however unlikely, might be shared by female as well as male readers. Ultimately, as I will argue, foreplay must be understood not as the anticipation of something else, but as the very raison d'être of the narrative.

To open appropriately with a delay, we might note that the very publication of *Nana* partook of the suspension, the tension that I am calling foreplay.[2] For several months before the start of serial publication in the fall of 1879, *Le Voltaire* spurred reader interest with notices of this kind: "While changing milieux and, this time, taking as its subject not the coarse customs of the common people but those of the more refined classes, the scalpel of the profound analyst has become no less pitiless. *Nana*, we repeat, is destined to cause an enormous sensation." A letter to *Le Voltaire*'s editor, Jules Laffitte, shows Zola's sensitivity to the management of publicity. "You shouldn't start advertising too soon; you have to husband the shocks [*coups*], otherwise you'll exhaust the patience of your public." A week before beginning publication, *Le Voltaire* ran this tendentious notice: "To publish the work of such an audacious writer, a newspaper must itself demonstrate a certain audacity and must count on the courageous attitudes of its readers. . . . Having arrived at the peak of notoriety, M. Zola hasn't retreated an inch in explaining his ideas. . . . The literary friends and enemies of our collaborator hope, with equal ardor, to find in *Nana* either much to admire or much to denigrate. We assert that this dual expectation will not be disappointed." In addition, according to Paul Alexis, the journal "had given itself over to a veritable debauch of publicity, multiplying notices everywhere: in newspapers, on walls, on the chests and backs of a legion of sandwich men, and . . . in every tobacco shop. 'Read Nana! Nana!! Nana!!!' " Finally, with public expectation at its peak, the first installment appeared on 16 October. These efforts produced windfall sales for *Le Voltaire*'s serial publication and later helped exhaust the complete novel's initial printing of fifty-five thousand in a single day.

This sensationalistic orchestration of effects anticipates the similar excitement managed by the novel itself—an excitement crucial to its foreplay. I want to begin my analysis of foreplay by examining how it seems to frustrate this excitement—the fact that it requires the reader to wait for an expected closure. This technique, analyzed as *attente* (anticipation or waiting) by Jacques Dubois, is one of two types of openings used in *Les Rougon-Macquart*.

> The *récit* describes a current of facts whose meaning and direction emerge only very gradually. . . . The narrator [of a realist novel], in principle, does not allow himself to identify, in the fabric of information he offers, that which has the greatest weight or is most influential. The text is seeking its center and raises more questions than answers. . . . The answers will come little by little, but the entry into the material delays or dilutes them arbitrarily. Only apparently, however.[3]

This "fabric of information" constitutes a kind of labyrinth in which, or because of which, the reader is forced to wait until a narrative line establishes itself.[4] In *Nana*, the initial flux of detail within a minimally defined context does indeed create conditions of confusion that heighten the tantalizingly delayed appearance of the title character. I will dwell on this suspended opening chapter since it epitomizes in extreme and explicit fashion the governing principles of the narrative.

Nana begins ex nihilo with an empty theater, a kind of "fore-play," and the note of waiting is already present: "At nine o'clock the auditorium of the Théâtre des Variétés was still virtually empty; a few people were waiting in the dress circle and the stalls."[5] The twenty-nine pages that follow in the Penguin edition firmly situate the reader with the audience to attend the slow unveiling of Nana's debut.

The perspective is located quickly and specifically. The second paragraph introduces two men, one of whom is an outsider and thus a convenient—albeit male—surrogate for the reader. Dubois observes that Zola commonly uses this device. Often, the

> protagonist is the one who is at the edge of the action and who is about to enter it. Now this anticipation-discovery [attente-découverte] is the situation in which the reader finds himself at the start of the novel; for him, the character simulates by an "action," active or passive, the procedure or program of his reading. In this respect the character who anticipates or discovers is, by homology, the reader's intercessor in the realist text, the one who represents in

this text the required mode of reading. . . . The initial character [serves] as a double or simulacrum of the reader . . . [he] possesses a gaze and contemplates, that is, he *reads* a landscape, a decor. He is the vigilant introducer of the realist description. He provides something to see, erects the "real" as a spectacle. . . . Seen from this perspective, the initial situation is a pretext to describe, to set a decor in place. (495)

In *Nana* the two men first introduced serve as *points de repère* while the reader's gaze moves from one clause to another as "naturally" as the narrative focus moves from viewer to viewed: "For a moment they fell silent, gazing up into the darkness of the boxes. But the green wallpaper with which they were decorated made them darker than ever. Down below, under the circle, the ground-floor boxes were lost in pitch darkness. In the boxes in the dress circle there was nobody but a fat lady slumped on the velvet rail. To the right and left, between lofty pillars, the stage-boxes remained empty" (19–20).

By the second sentence, which identifies objects of perception, the gaze has been anchored quite specifically. We no longer look at the men, but with them. Also to be remarked here are the purely visual inventory (with a minimum of dynamic verbs) and the absence of the subjective reactions of the viewers. By confining us to surfaces, Zola has virtually eliminated explicit context, narrative as well as sociohistorical, except that generated by dialogue. He is, we might say, teasing the reader, toying with possible desires for coherence and significance. Peter Brooks, drawing on Roland Barthes, asserts that "what animates us as readers of narrative is *la passion du sens*, which I would want to translate as both the passion *for* meaning and the passion *of* meaning: the active quest of the reader for those shaping ends that, terminating the dynamic process of reading, promise to bestow meaning and significance on the beginning and the middle" (19). *Sens* here is also double: the reader expects *direction* (to be directed/to find a direction) as well as *meaning*. The reader of *Nana*, however, deprived of a Balzacian introductory exposition (deprived of clear directions), is from the outset "suspended" until he or she can assemble the details into a recognizable schema (create his or her own direction) leading to coherent interpretation and meaning.

Soon enough, this expectancy is focused on Nana. Fauchery, one of the two initial observers, tells his companion, "*The Blonde Venus* is going to be the theatrical event of the year. Everyone has been talking about it for the past six months." The youth asks Fauchery if he knows the new star. " 'Oh, dear, here we go again!' cried Fauchery. . . . 'Ever since this morning, everybody has been asking me about Nana. I've met over a score of people, and it's been Nana here and Nana there' " (20).[6] This note of expectation is subsequently enlarged by the narrator: "Nobody knew Nana. Where had Nana come from? And stories and jokes, whispered from ear to ear, went the rounds. . . . A fever of curiosity urged it forward, that Parisian curiosity which is as violent as a fit of brain-fever. Everyone wanted to see Nana" (24).

Sexuality is overt in this prolonged *attente*. Bordenave, the director, is a "notorious exhibitor of women who treat[s] them like a slave-driver" (21), and talent is not an issue for him. "Does a woman need to be able to sing and act?" he asks. "Nana has something else, dammit, and something that takes the place of everything else. I scented it out, and it smells damnably strong in her . . . she'll only have to appear and the whole audience will be hanging out their tongues [tirera la langue]" (22). Ever attentive to "les flairs du mâle," Bordenave has deliberately withheld the premiere until now in order to heighten the fever pitch, but he suggests the fever will not be assuaged ("tirer la langue" means to be thirsty, to desire without obtaining satisfaction). He thus parallels Zola both in the nature of his commodity (female sexuality) and the way in which he purveys it (visual, distant, deferred).

Various members of the audience are introduced, and *The Blonde Venus* itself stretches out in banal scenes. Zola, quite aware of the difficulties such labyrinthine scenes pose for the reader,[7] adeptly uses periodic reminders to sustain expectation through this preliminary section: "Was it Nana at last? This girl was certainly keeping them waiting" (31). "Then followed a scene which seemed interminable. . . . And there was still no sign of Nana! Were they keeping her for the final curtain? Such a long wait had ended up by annoying the audience" (32). Although almost immediately she does finally make her appearance, her own performance is subject to the same withholding tactics encountered earlier. At first she is so inept that audience reactions are largely derisive. They moderate slightly, but the act concludes without exciting. Nonetheless, during the intermission "people were talking about Nana above all else" (34). The second act is better received, and the third act, signaled by terse syntax, finally plunges fairly directly into the long-deferred climax:

> Venus appeared. A shiver went round the house. Nana was naked, flaunting her nakedness with a cool audacity, sure of the sovereign power of her flesh. . . . There was no applause. Nobody laughed any more. The men's faces were tense and serious, their nostrils narrowed, their mouths prickly and parched. A wind seemed to have passed over the audience, a soft wind laden with hidden menace. All of a sudden, in the good-natured child the woman stood revealed, a disturbing woman with all the impulsive madness of her sex, opening the gates of the unknown world of desire. Nana was still smiling, but with the deadly smile of a man-eater. (44–45)

A page later the sexual tension is described even more explicitly:

> Nana had taken possession of the audience, and now every man was under her spell. A wave of lust was flowing from her as from a bitch in heat, and it had spread further and further until it filled the whole house. Now her slightest movements fanned the flame of desire, and with a twitch of her little finger she could stir men's flesh. Backs arched and quivered as if unseen violin-bows had been drawn across their muscles; and on the nape of many a neck the down stirred in the hot, stray breath from some woman's lips. (45–46)

Finally the tension is released: the rest of the paragraph, like a playbill, surveys the principal suitors destined to appear in the forthcoming narrative, another paragraph perfunctorily concludes the play, and the curtain falls "in the midst of thunderous applause and frenzied shouts of 'Nana! Nana!' Then, even before the house was empty, darkness fell. The footlights went out, the chandelier was turned down . . . and the auditorium, lately so full of heat and noise, suddenly fell into a heavy sleep" (47). This postcoital torpor concludes with Countess Muffat, the wife of the man who will become Nana's principal suitor, "very erect and muffled up in furs . . . gaz[ing] into the darkness" (47).

I have quoted extensively, especially from the concluding passages of the chapter, so as to leave no doubt about the massive insistence of Zola's metaphor, though the term "metaphor" may be misleading for a vehicle so little distant from its tenor. Henry James catches the underlying dynamic of the novel when he speaks of the "extraordinary absence of humor, the dryness, the solemnity, the air of tension and effort."[8] Without question the subject is sex, the technique delay. Succeeding sections of the text repeat the same procedures if not the same scene. The action of the second chapter revolves around males kept waiting by Nana, and the wait of Count Muffat extends across the entire narrative (see especially chapter 7). The race at Longchamps, chapter 11, completes the pattern, and again the sexual metaphor is overt.[9] Of course there are in *Nana* moments of resolved tension, climactic moments of thematic release—for example, at the race. But the approach to them is exquisitely drawn out.

Thus far, *Nana* would seem fully to epitomize Peter Brooks's conception of plot, both as general impetus for meaning and as specific theme: "Desire as narrative thematic, desire as narrative motor, and desire as the very intention of narrative language and the act of telling all seem to stand in close interrelation" (54).[10] This account seems to correspond quite closely to the anticipation I have been describing as foreplay in *Nana*. However, *Nana* seems to fit less satisfactorily Brooks's conception of conclusion, the culmination of desire—precisely the moment that Zola, in my view, problematizes. "If the motor of narrative is desire," Brooks argues, "the ultimate determinants of meaning lie *at the end*, and narrative desire is ultimately, inexorably, desire *for* the end" (52). He continues: "One can tell a life only in terms of its limits or margins. The telling is always *in terms of* the impending end." A reading of *Nana* might be mustered to support this view, though perhaps not precisely in the terms suggested by Brooks's language, since its apparent closure is found to be inadequate and even incomplete.

The conclusion of *Nana* is interesting because it is there that foreplay plays itself out in a peculiarly offhand way. Zola has spent the novel carefully detailing Nana's inexorable, albeit destructive, rise to dominance. At the conclusion of the penultimate chapter, Nana is victorious: "She had finished her labour of ruin and death. . . . It was fitting and just. She had avenged the beggars and outcasts of her world" (452–53)—but a few lines later we learn abruptly that "this no longer counted for anything." Shortly after, at the beginning of the final chapter, the character with whom we have spent over 350 pages suddenly disappears. Thus begins the final foreplay, a long delay until Nana's final description in the last paragraph. This last chapter hedges on the thematic as well as the plot level, for significant elements are suddenly added: a sociopolitical context (the Franco-Prussian War), pestilence and death, and Nana's maternal feelings for her son. While men abandon her, women unite—a difference imaged architecturally: the latter gather in Nana's room in the Grand Hôtel while the former stand outside, looking up at the windows, a telling reversal from the novel's initial "male superior" vision. The women, too, are changed—no longer courtesans and competitors but fellow sufferers.[11] The introduction of new angles and new issues necessarily forestalls or complicates resolution. Is female solidarity and noncompetitiveness possible only in death? Is Nana's death the result of "sin"? Is sexual depravity parallel to political and military defeat (the Franco-Prussian War)? Is it a cause? The novel ends before these questions can be explored, thus preserving narrative neutrality but frustrating reader "desire." *Nana* cannot be categorized (appropriated) as either obscene or ultimately moral; it lies in some other (and not necessarily intermediate) terrain.

Foreplay is normally not an end in itself; climax is. But this novel ends with the protagonist "dying," a word now ironically barren of sexual connotation, and this abrupt and unanticipated death reveals that the novel as a whole has been "anteclimactic"—the quality I am trying to convey with the notion of foreplay. Or, to put it in Brooks's terms, the desire of which the last chapter should form the end is not the desire we have just traversed. Can it be foreplay if the play never appears? Has the reader been elaborately teased and then cuckolded by a climax only tenuously related to the preceding narrative?[12]

This frustration of closure on the level of plot has a more pervasive and pertinent correlative: our inability to close on a clear portrait of the protagonist who is always before our eyes. The explanation, I think, lies in Zola's naturalistic program. He exclaims, in a letter to Henry Céard, "I am starving to see things" ("Je suis affamé de choses vues," 26 July 1878 [Zola, *Correspondance*, 3:192]). This impulse transmutes, in *Nana*, to *being seen*— seeing takes precedence over doing or saying, and is the underlying desire that animates the novel. This emphasis is congruent with the familiar Western epistemological bias toward the visual, which reached its zenith in nineteenth-century naturalism. The visual is accessible, shareable, "obvious," and thus lends authority to the narrative. Opening the narrative in a theater reifies this preference, and in addition genders it as a male superior point of view. As Dubois phrases it, "the initial description becomes a protocol for reading. It anticipates the rest of the novel . . . it takes on a metatextual character" (496). Vincent Crapanzano argues much the same point: the "assertion of a fixed vantage point, of an assigned seat . . . must be understood rhetorically. It attests deictically to [the presence of the narrator]. It gives him the authority of the painter before his easel. It enables him to lead his readers into the visualized scene and to convince them (and himself) of its truth."[13]

To be sure, a theatrical milieu raises crucial issues of representation, imitation, illusion. At this point, however, I want to emphasize the way it brings to the fore the audience/reader's relation to play—an essentially voyeuristic one—and the connection between display or exposure and vicariousness. The initial point of view is paradigmatic: located in the audience, seeing (above all, seeing) from a distance, seeing only surface—or, in its auditory cognate, hearing dialogue, the reader is situated solidly on the outside. Narrative voice here is objective, but the authority established by the visual must be seen as "conservative," even minimal—perhaps because it can so easily be shared.

Put another way, the narrator's refusal to develop context and motive means that the reader is in and not in Nana's world. Even in "intimate" chapters, for example chapter 2, the narrator does not comment, interpret, or judge. Instead we get a simple report of what was said and done. If narrative desire ultimately seeks to discover motive, in *Nana* physical description is the obstacle, the means of frustrating that discovery. The work of description is never fully done, and while it is in place one cannot get elsewhere—it blocks and perhaps even misleads.[14]

This effect is nowhere more evident than in the first chapters of *Nana*, which wind through densely populated and closely particularized milieux (a theater, Nana's apartment). In these chapters the detail that lies at the heart of Zola's program produces, if not disorientation, at least deferral. We might observe here that deferral always requires addition; the postponement of one subject requires the presence of something else. Thus both Nana and *Nana* paradoxically resist appropriation by excess generosity, by overabundance. None possess her because she gives herself to many—but she gives only her body. Likewise, the promiscuous detail of the novel gives without yielding.

The insufficiency of narrative authority is most glaringly apparent when Nana disappears at the beginning of the last chapter, glossed as "the impulse of a woman too rich to put up with any annoyance. Besides, she was satisfying an old ambition, for she had long dreamt of visiting the Turkish Empire" (454). This impulse must inevitably seem capricious, at the level of *récit*, because the reader has been imbedded in the present moment (provided minimal temporal context), and especially because Nana's thoughts have been programmatically elided. We become aware, then, of another kind of withholding: not a plot-related withholding from climax, but a character-related withholding from consciousness.

The noted Zola scholar F.W.J. Hemmings claims that Zola's characters "never surprise us,"[15] and Nana does seem eminently predictable. However, the concluding shift makes us conscious that finally one cannot be certain whether Nana is caught up in her role or merely playing it. What animates her? Pleasure, indifference, revenge? The reader is not authorized to say.[16] To be sure, Nana is apparently not a particularly conscious individual, but in any case her consciousness is inaccessible because the omniscient narrative perspective remains, for the most part, rigorously external; there is virtually no exploration of what Nana is thinking.[17] *Nana* contains little or no psychonarration, nor the quoted monologue or narrated monologue found elsewhere in Zola (indirect discourse here mainly reports dialogue). We are troubled not just by deferral but by absence.

Nana's last stage appearance embodies the deceptive hypertrophy of the visual: "only a walking-on part, but it was the great attraction of the show, consisting as it did of three poses representing a silent fairy queen" (454). She is reduced to silence here, an object to be seen ("She didn't say a word . . . they were superfluous. No, not a single word: it was more impressive that way, and she took the audience's breath away by simply showing herself. You wouldn't find another body like that" [459]). But soon she is not even seen; she slips away, to reappear only on her deathbed. The provenance of "factual" details had already become obscured: her life abroad is widely known, "but nobody could cite a precise source of information" (455). The beginning and ending, with Nana the object of male gazes, are thus symbolically asymmetrical. In the final chapter Nana is lost from view, and the men only look up at her windows. Men are not privy to this anticlimactic scene—but neither, finally, are women, and neither are readers. Nana, apparently so "simple," remains unalterably other—a point I will return to shortly.

The novel and its protagonist both circulate in ambiguous territory, and locating that place is not nearly so easy as it might seem—not nearly so easy, certainly, as naturalism's scientific pretensions might claim. It is almost as if Zola were acknowledging Brunetière's early criticism, "Seeing is insufficient" ("Il ne suffit pas de voir").[18] Indeed, Zola helps remind us that even in the classic nineteenth-century novel, a spirit of play is fundamental. We are invited, even required, to play.[19] Zola is still a nineteenth-century novelist, and it would be excessive to claim that this text fully escapes appropriation and closure. But neither can it be brought fully within the sphere of the conventional and fixed.

I have deliberately deferred discussing the attractions of foreplay in order to emphasize its frustrations. But now I want to shift from "goal-oriented" foreplay to a foreplay that highlights process and the concomitant pleasures of speculation, extrapolation, and discovery. The narrative desire driving Brooks's conception of plot is totalizing, moving toward metaphor. But even this move might be seen, at least in *Nana*, as contributing to a reading that turns back from climax toward the anticlimactic narrative just traversed. Brooks claims that the "ultimate determinants of meaning lie *at the end*." Reading "lie" in both senses helps suggest the way a counterdiscursive subtext surfaces forcefully at the conclusion, enlisting a thorough rereading on its own terms. Ambiguity, disjunction, obscurity—these can only be accommodated by going back over the narrative to "justify" the conclusion Zola has imposed. Ultimately, since Zola refuses the reader an easily stabilized target, foreplay may be found necessarily to *be* the play. Instead of being fixed on metaphor, the reader might be conceived as drawn to metonymy, caught up in and by the rush of succession and contiguity.

What, then, is the nature of this play in *Nana*? What are its attractions? I would suggest two broad categories: construction of coherence and flirtation with the other. The first obviously forms part of most readings, to varying degrees, and accounts for the significance of detective fiction in the history and definition of the novel. But I am thinking here not so much of some sort of elementary anticipation or discovery of event as of the knottier divining of thematic pattern and motive (in *Nana* this might involve extracting the pattern of foreplay itself). In a sense, it is a matter of creating the contexts and especially the motives about which Zola's objectivist narrative is silent. That is, most fundamentally, getting beyond the visual surface. This process entails repeated synchronic surveys of the text, departures from diachronic succession in favor of an inventive selectivity. Note that this may result, finally, in a return to metaphor, but a metaphor perhaps not inflected by the conclusion.

Examination of the other attraction operating in this novel requires a slight shift of emphasis in the concept of foreplay, from the activity itself to the reader's relationship to that activity—or, if you will, from its mechanics to its psychology, especially as affected by gender. In the preceding paragraph the reader was presented as engaged directly in the play of investigation and interpretation, but it is important to emphasize that these activities take place at a certain cultural as well as epistemological remove. The voyeurism implicit in the theatrical milieu establishes an erotics of distance; as Hemmings phrases it, in *Nana* "the fiercest concupiscence here is the concupiscence of the eye."[20] Thus foreplay takes on a scopophilic cast; temporal delay (of climax) is ensured by spatial remove. But ultimately, I would guess, that cultural distance is preserved, and the reader retires from the field of foreplay without committing to that other world.

Nearly every character in *Nana* evidences the power of the other and its ultimate denial. All are afflicted with a boredom that propels them from the known toward the unexplored. When respectability becomes boring, relief is sought in the unknown, the unpredictable, the sensational. Even the most proper cannot resist being fascinated by "the unknown world of desire" (45). "Every morning over lunch the kindly Madame Hugon returned to the subject of 'that woman' despite herself, . . . revealing that obsessive fascination which courtesans exert on the worthiest of ladies" (195).

Muffat, Nana's principal suitor, is caught between the outré and the respectable, between Nana and his wife. "Muffat was both the most ardent and the most tortured by novel sensations of desire and fear and anger warring in his anguished heart" (188). He finally chooses Nana over the bland comforts of family and religion, perhaps because she offers the paradoxical appeal of inaccessibility—an appeal as forceful for readers as for characters.

Nana displays the obverse of the same principle. She is a thoroughly antiestablishment figure who seeks pleasures quite foreign to respectability, notably her lesbian liaison with Satin and the sadomasochistic degradation of Muffat. Nonetheless she achieves a status ostensibly equal to her rival and mirror, Countess Muffat, and at times she seems genuinely attracted to respectability. When talking with Muffat on this topic, "she had grown serious, speaking in a hard voice and looking deeply moved, for her stupid longing was causing her real anguish" (299).[21] In short, Nana, like the other characters, is attracted by that which is different.[22]

Childishness offers a compromise, a zone of permitted impropriety or lapsed decorum where taboo is suspended; hence the recurring characterization of Nana's actions as "childish" (for example, the idyll in the country with the young Georges Hugon in chapter 6). But the more common refuges are embodied and linked in Nana herself: the theater and prostitution. *Nana* continually blurs these two worlds. Bordenave insists on calling the Théâtre des Variétés his bordello (that is, a theater of prostitution), and with good reason. He has prostituted the theater by staging sexuality. Both the theater and prostitution might be read in two quite different ways. They propose to entertain by offering the unusual, the unfamiliar, the inaccessible. Yet both are also formalized, delimited, predictable, in some sense safe and tolerated. In either case the relevant radius is drawn from home, which is the locus of boring familiarity as well as familial respectability.

Readers of Nana, like the characters of that novel, are continually drawn to the unfamiliar. The Russian Formalists argued that the hallmark of literature is defamiliarization (ostranenije), a motive as applicable to reading as to writing. We may prize Kafka or García Márquez or Lady Murasaki because they do not give us back ourselves, because they do not allow a reasonable fit. The very distance between a medieval Japanese woman's culture and our own may constitute the attraction. The success of a novel like Nana might well suggest that, rather than requiring "a room of one's own" (a mirror, an automorphic niche), readers may well seek something like its opposite.

The hostile critical reception of Nana and its immense popular success (after La débâcle, it was Zola's most popular and remunerative work) can be read in terms of this impulse. Critical judgments of the time, attempting to enforce conventional (acceptable) values, were rejected by the public in favor of more attractive, forbidden ones. In the competition between acceptable and the taboo, Zola won, because almost by definition a scandale is a succès.

Whatever the commercial success, however, I would underline the limits of that victory. Literature allows "safe" entertainment of different ways of being—and once again we return to a version of foreplay.[23] Note that both the theater and the bordello are literal but only temporary sites of projection. A crucial part of flirtation's appeal is its very lack of risk. Curiosity plays rather than commits.

Gender necessarily affects the nature of this response. As Annette Kolodny, among others, has argued, reading is always sex-coded and gender-inflected.[24] Surely there is some difference between male and female readers watching men watch women. But a close reading of Nana shows that the interplay of displacement, transfer, and empathy in reading is a very complicated issue. Although the attractions of "otherness" I have been discussing need not be defined solely in gender terms (female readers might be attracted by the very strangeness of Nana or by the displacement of looking with males), some critics seem to insist on a "room" for the female reader in the work itself—a place that might be seen as something like a mirror. This imperative would seem to undermine the attractions I am examining under the heading of foreplay, as would Patrocinio Schweikart and Elizabeth Flynn's claim that "a characteristic feature of the masculine mode of reading [is] . . . the inability to entertain or play host to fundamental difference."[25] I have been attributing just such an inclination to male as well as to female readers.

Foreplay, although forestalling full possession, assumes a symbiotic connectedness, a mutually sustained attraction. It involves what might be called a joint "negotiation" and effort. Thus a more apt distinction, I would suggest, is offered by the third of the reading strategies sketched by Flynn, who categorizes readers as dominant, submissive, and a balanced mixture of the two:

> The reader can resist the alien thought or subject and so remain essentially unchanged by the reading experience. In this case the reader dominates the text. Or the reader can allow the alien thought to become such a powerful presence that the self is replaced by the other and so is effaced. In this case the text dominates the reader. . . . [Or] self and other, reader and text, interact in such a way that the reader learns from the experience without losing critical distance; reader and text interact with a degree of mutuality. Foreignness is reduced, though not eliminated. Self and other remain distinct and so create a kind of dialogue.[26]

Although Flynn's essay roughly correlates these categories with gender (the two extremes tending to be male and the balance female), strictly speaking the schema is gender-neutral. In any case, the question remains, what role is inscribed for female readers of *Nana*? What is their relationship to foreplay?

One might easily assume that *Nana*, the tale of a courtesan written by a male, is androcentric. Nana is certainly a commodity valued solely for her appearance. The theater serves as the site of scopophilia, a zone where people from all walks of life join together to watch: "The whole of Paris was there . . . a singularly mixed world" (28). But given the overwhelmingly male tenor of the milieu and point of view, a slight consonantal shift from a "monde singulièrement mêlé" to "un monde singulièrement mâle" distorts little while accurately catching the visual bias discussed above (male observation of [female] surfaces). In general the entire notion of foreplay, as Zola thematizes it over the course of the novel, is a male domain; thus female readers would seem unavoidably co-opted into a male stance. Yet appropriation in terms of gender is also subjected to the foreplayful manipulations of Zola's rhetoric.

I do not wish to claim that Nana is not, in part, a mere object (of foreplay), aligned with spectacle, commodity, and pathology. She fills, even overfills, these traditional and inferior roles, but she does more. This deflection from her object role can best be gauged by examining not just *how* we see in *Nana*—its prevailing narrative stance—but also *what* we see and hear, and *who* that "we" is. In fact, androcentrism is decentered. A counterdiscourse, in fact, is insinuated in a variety of ways: by male dependence and defeat, by privileged "intimate" views of women but not men, and by direct articulations of female independence.[27] The males in the novel are always waiting, always excluded, always on the outside looking in. Even when ostensibly "superior" (social standing, theatrical location, sexual position), males are spectators, on the margins, passive, silent, stationary, malleable, deficient. They are removed from the center where power is staged, a marginalization nowhere more evident than at the conclusion. Even in death, Nana keeps men in the wings (or, to use the more telling British phrase, in the stalls). It is the women who have, unbeknownst to their customers, maintained a secret center of value. In this sense, the novel is not and cannot be rigorously androcentric.

The "other" center, intimated by the glance at Countess Muffat that concludes chapter 1, is stated quite bluntly by Nana when Muffat complains of her infidelities: "Just you get it into your head that I insist on being completely free. When I like the look of a man I go to bed with him" (428). An even clearer articulation of female independence is embodied in Nana's reply to la Faloise's proposal of marriage: "I wouldn't be Nana any more if I saddled myself with a man. . . . Besides it's too foul for words. . . .' And she spat and hiccoughed with disgust, as if she had seen all the filth in the world spreading out beneath her" (438). This exceptional reaction flaunts an intense male-female antagonism already intermittently revealed earlier in the novel.

Already the first chapter had intimated a counterdiscourse undercutting the male view. The theater crowd begins to rush to their seats. "All this eagerness on the part of the public irritated Lucy Stewart. What brutes these people were, pushing women about like that! . . . 'It's not as if these shows of theirs were always amusing!' " (26). The narrator, too, maintains a certain distance by way of negative diction, using such recurrent adjectives as "brutal" and "crude." The suitors rarely have an inkling of this other view; Muffat "ended up by exasperating [Nana] with his stubborn refusal to understand women" (427), and readers may be led to a similar dissatisfaction.

The narration itself favors the women's perspective by spending chapter 2 with Nana in her apartment while never allotting a comparable intimacy to her suitors. Readers in this respect are more privileged than suitors; they are allowed entrance to the site of power. This chapter, in direct counterpoint to the opening, theatrical scene, offers at least in part a female point of view, and one that establishes that male "play" is women's work. Much of the chapter, to be sure, presents Nana as one object among others in the apartment's vulgar furnishings. At other points, however, it reports Nana's views without male mediation, disjoining her role from her desire. Nana returns from an afternoon assignation in a foul mood. "Do you suppose

I've been having a good time?" she asks her maid (63). Soon after she is "cursing the male sex" (65), and when she learns that a man scheduled to spend the night has cancelled, Nana is overjoyed: "What a stroke of luck! She would be free! She heaved a sigh of relief, as if she had been spared the most abominable of tortures" (69). The same sentiment reappears at the end of the chapter. Nana's favors are sought by "a whole mob of men, jabbing at the ivory button" (the doorbell, innuendoes no doubt intentional, 72), but she escapes out the kitchen door. "At least she was free of men and could relax. . . . 'Just imagine, I'm going to sleep all night—yes, a whole night by myself! It's a crazy idea I've had, darling' " (73). These resisting sentiments surely deflate androtropic dominance. They force reassessment and distance, and thus removal from the tunnel vision of foreplay. In this way the novel resists appropriation by "male" readers, and in fact reveals it has all along been harboring something else.

Some critics, relying on empirical studies or on psychoanalytical theory, differentiate between identification in male and female readers.[28] Men, it is argued, want to establish control and distance, while women are more prone to establish a more immediate relationship with the world of the fiction. *Nana*, I would say, offers neither kind of relationship.

When I began this study, I assumed that the act of appropriation, the assertion of control, of interpretive dominance, could be read as "male." Think of our common metaphors of criticism: coming to grips with the text, penetrating its mysteries.[29] This study of *Nana*, however, while using these concepts, suggests a more tentative position.[30] Whether or not both male and female readers share the titillation of seeing behind the veil, a primary pleasure of this work lies not in control but in a relationship better characterized as play, a play that both male and female readers might desire, and which neither can escape. For women, in particular, *Nana* is neither a simple mirror either of oppression or of hope, of silenced objecthood or of unburdened subjectivity. Nana is always deferred sign, the theater always the site of *différance*.

The work of conventional reading often strives to colonize the strange into the service of the familiar, to reclaim deviation for the normal, to make the circle closed, complete—predictable. The concept of foreplay, however, highlights the way novels exploit this urge to connect. Foreplay draws us on, but we never arrive at true closure. That is as true for my speculations about women readers as it is about my reading of *Nana*. That is the play.[31]

NOTES

Special thanks to Shlomith Rimmon-Kenan for her thoughtful reading of an earlier draft.

1. For this and alternative terminology, cf. Wallace Martin, *Recent Theories of Narrative* (Ithaca: Cornell University Press, 1986), 108.

2. The following account is drawn from Albert Salvan, "Introduction biographique," in Emile Zola, *Correspondance*, ed. B. H. Bakker (Montreal: Presses de l'Université de Montréal, 1982), 3:40, and from Zola's letter and Salvan's notes for 15 September 1879 (3:374–75). See also Albert Auriant, *La véritable histoire de "Nana"* (Paris: Mercure de France, 1943).

3. Jacques Dubois, "Surcodage et protocole de lecture dans le roman naturaliste," *Poétique* 16 (1973): 494, 497. Peter Brooks foregrounds and extends the incipience suggested by Dubois's last phrase: "Desire is always there at the start of a narrative, often in a state of initial arousal, often having reached a state of intensity such that movement must be created, action undertaken, change begun. . . . One could no doubt analyze the opening paragraph of most novels and emerge in each case with the image of a desire taking on shape, beginning to seek its objects, beginning to develop a textual energetics." Brooks, *Reading for the Plot: Design and Intention in Narrative* (New York: Vintage, 1984), 38. Subsequent page references are cited parenthetically in the text.

4. Cf. Mario Maurin's discussion of Zola's labyrinths, with his "swarming and teeming" descriptions read as "labyrinthian manifestations of the erotic and the uncanny." "Zola's Labyrinths," *Yale French Studies* 43 (1969): 98.

5. Emile Zola, *Nana*, trans. George Holden (Harmondsworth: Penguin, 1972), 19. Subsequent page references are cited parenthetically in the text. For the original text, consult *Les Rougon-Macquart*, ed. Henri Mitterand (Paris: Pléiade, 1961), vol. 2.

6. Again, one should recall the similar excitement about the novel itself. Cf. Henry Céard's letter: "An enormous curiosity surrounds *Nana*. This name is everywhere on the walls of Paris. It's becoming an obsession and a nightmare" (quoted by Mitterand in Zola, *Les Rougon-Macquart*, 2:1683).

7. "The great difficulty is that this damned book always proceeds by vast scenes, by tableaux where twenty to thirty characters are in motion—premieres, parties, dinners, backstage scenes; and I have to guide all these people, make them act and speak in concert, without ceasing to be clear." Letter to Flaubert (30 November 1878), Zola, *Correspondance*, 3:242.

8. Henry James, "*Nana*," in *Documents of Modern Literary Realism*, ed. George Becker (Princeton: Princeton University Press, 1963), 242.

9. Peter Conroy, in "The Metaphorical Web in Zola's *Nana*," *University of Toronto Quarterly* 47 (1978): 246, details the parallels between Nana and her equine namesake. Georg Lukács, in a singularly obtuse analysis of this scene, wholly ignores the delaying effect, for the reader, of Zola's meticulous detail in "Narrate or

Describe?" in Lukács, *Writer and Critic and Other Essays* (New York: Grosset and Dunlap, 1970), 110ff.

10. Brooks, *Reading for the Plot*. Similarly: "Desire [is] that which is initiatory of narrative, motivates and energizes its reading, and animates the combinatory play of sense-making" (48).

11. The shifts are not entirely unanticipated. Bismarck, for example, is mentioned in chapter 3, but allusions to impending war are oblique and fragmentary. Cf. likewise Nana with the dying Satin (452).

12. In the broader perspective of *Les Rougon-Macquart*, there is yet another disjunction: *Nana*'s near-total isolation from *L'assommoir*, quietly signaled by Anna's transmutation to Nana. References to Nana's history in the earlier novel (for example, Mme. Lerat's passing mention of Nana's parents [55]) are rare.

13. Vincent Crapanzano, "Hermes' Dilemma: The Masking of Subversion in Ethnographic Description," in *Writing Culture: The Poetics and Politics of Ethnography*, ed. James Clifford and George Marcus (Berkeley and Los Angeles: University of California, 1986), 58. He draws on Alexander Gelley, "The Represented World: Toward a Phenomenological Theory of Description in the Novel," *Journal of Aesthetics and Art Criticism* 37 (1979): 415–22. The Dubois passage (495), quoted on pages 3–4, is also pertinent.

14. Cf. Laura Mulvey's claim that women in classical cinema "connote *to-be-looked-at-ness* . . . [their] visual presence tends to work against the development of a story line, to freeze the flow of action in moments of erotic contemplation." "Visual Pleasure and Narrative Cinema," *Screen* 16 (1975): 11. There, too, women remain objectified.

15. F.W.J. Hemmings, *The Age of Realism* (Harmondsworth: Penguin, 1974), 188. For an equally limited view of Zola's characters, see Anna Krakowski, *La condition de la femme dans l'oeuvre d'Emile Zola* (Paris: Nizet, 1974).

16. Notwithstanding, many have attempted to do so. For a sample of the simplifying assays of contemporary critics, see Zola, *Les Rougon-Macquart*, 2:1689.

17. One biographical (rather than programmatic) factor in the externality of Zola's *procès-verbales* might be the fact that he frequented neither the demimonde nor the belle monde, and often turned to others for information.

18. Ferdinand Brunetière, *Le roman naturaliste* (1875; reprint, Paris: Calmann Lévy, 1896), 24.

19. Roland Barthes glimpses this aspect in his brief comments on *Nana*: "Zola sets before us the supposedly universal fact in its historical specificity. And we stop sighing in order to start judging. We better understand, then, the goal of this epic art: in returning the human to History, the artist invites us to become actively conscious of it." Barthes, *Bulletin mensuel*, Lausanne: Guilde du Livre (June 1955): 228. Cf. also Leo Braudy's observations on "the conflicting impulses of detachment and involvement" in Zola, and especially in *Nana* in "Zola on Film: The Ambiguities of Naturalism," *Yale French Studies* 42 (1969): 83.

20. F.W.J. Hemmings, *Emila Zola*, 2d ed. (Oxford: Oxford University Press, 1966), 139.

21. Note, however, that Zola is careful to place this conversation in the context of *playing* a role—in a play significantly entitled *Petite Duchesse*.

22. When Nana tires of her role and retires, her abrupt exit serves to remind us that it has all been a performance. Likewise, respectability is always a role, a facade; the theatrical metaphor still holds.

23. Cf. Clifford Geertz's characterization of anthropology: "The passion to swim in the stream of [another culture's] experience, and the illusion afterward that one somehow has." *Local Knowledge: Further Essays in Interpretive Anthropology* (New York: Basic Books, 1983), 58. In this connection it may be revealing that the two major climax scenes, the theater and the race, are crowd scenes (collective experiences echoing the reading public?), while the anticlimactic conclusion, where the decaying Nana is described in the last paragraph, occurs only after the last person has left the room.

24. Annette Kolodny, "Reply to Commentaries: Women Writers, Literary Historians, and Martian Readers," *New Literary History* 11 (1980): 588.

25. Elizabeth Flynn and Patrocinio Schweickart, eds., introduction to *Gender and Reading: Essays on Readers, Texts, and Contexts* (Baltimore: Johns Hopkins University Press, 1986), xxiv.

26. Elizabeth Flynn, "Gender and Reading," in Flynn and Schweikart, *Gender and Reading*, 268. She continues: "The dominant pole is characterized by detachment, observation from a distance. The reader imposes a previously established structure on the text and in so doing silences it. Memory dominates over experience, past over present. . . . Judgment is based on previously established norms rather than on empathetic engagement with and critical evaluation of the new material. . . . The submissive pole, in contrast, is characterized by too much involvement. The reader is entangled in the events of the story and is unable to step back, to observe with a critical eye. . . . The text is overwhelming, unwilling to yield a consistent pattern of meaning. . . . Comprehension is attained when the reader achieves a balance between empathy and judgment by maintaining a balance of detachment and involvement. Too much detachment often results in too much judgment and hence in domination of the text; too much involvement often results in too much sympathy and hence in domination by the text" (268–70).

27. Another essay would be needed to explore fully the varied means Zola uses to defamiliarize the "familiar": parody, hyperbole, unpredictability (Nana's "caprices"), multiplicity of role and motive. Cf. Chantal Jennings, "Les Trois Visages de Nana," *French Review* 44 (1971): 117–28.

28. See, for example, Flynn and Schweikart, *Gender and Reading*, or the introductory chapter of Mary Ann Doane, *The Desire to Desire: The Woman's Film of the 1940s* (Bloomington: Indiana University Press, 1987).

29. Cf. Dubois on the contrast *attente/marche* (anticipation/development) as feminine/masculine (494).

30. This essay itself may not escape the gender-bound issues it raises—it too, even while describing how *Nana* escapes appropriation, is itself a form of appropriation. (Perhaps metacritical reading itself is "male.") On the other hand, speculation by male critics about women readers could itself be viewed as a (necessary) attempt "to entertain or play host to fundamental difference."

31. Another essay might explore how these observations intersect one of Freud's early, cryptic speculations on literature: "We give the name of an *incentive*

bonus, or a *fore-pleasure* [eine *Verlockungsprämie* oder eine *Vorlust*], to a yield of pleasure such as this, which is offered to us so as to make possible the release of still greater pleasure arising from deeper psychical sources. In my opinion, all the aesthetic pleasure which a creative writer affords us has the character of a fore-pleasure of this kind, and our actual enjoyment of an imaginative work proceeds from a liberation of tensions in our minds." "Creative Writers and Day-Dreaming," in *The Freud Reader*, ed. Peter Gay (New York: Norton, 1989), 443. For the original, see "Der Dichter und das Phantasieren," in *Gesammelte Werke chronologisch geordnet* (1908; reprint, Frankfurt: S. Fisher, 1941), 7:223.

PART FOUR

THE DISCOURSE OF NARRATOLOGY

FIFTEEN

CONTINGENCY

David E. Wellbery

W HAT SORTS OF ISSUES does the concept of contingency
introduce into the enterprise of literacy criticism, in its broadest
sense? Is there a sense in which the objects literary critics study
are characterized by an element of contingency? And, if such is the case,
are they indeed "objects" that could be constituted within a rigorous theoretical program? Or is contingency one of those points where the enterprise of literary criticism touches on its limits, where it takes shape, precisely, as a reflection on the limits of its own epistemological intention?
Such are the questions that the following remarks, essayistically and ten-
tatively, seek to raise. The itinerary of my reflections is as follows. In the
first section, I introduce, in a somewhat informal fashion, what I mean by
"contingency" and endeavor to make the case that that concept is central
to an understanding of what an aesthetic "object"—a work—is. The second section sketches some ramifications of the concept for narrative theory, and the final section addresses itself to matters of historiography, in
particular to the concept of "modernity." Since the question of contingency has not, to my knowledge, been very much treated on a theoretical
plane in literary studies, the contentions I shall put forward are meant to
elicit correction and commentary. For the sake of concreteness I have en-
deavored to adhere as closely as possible to specific textual examples.

Danger: Falling Objects

The contingent is, for Aristotle as well as for Luhmann, that which is possible otherwise, the contradictory of necessity. Thomas Aquinas distinguished three varieties of contingent occurrences: those which are seldom,
those which derive from choice, and those which result from accident (*a
casu vel fortuna*).[1] My concern is with the last of these: the accidental, random, or chance event, or, as some would have it, the event *tout court* as
that which destabilizes and disrupts lawlike regularity.[2] I am certain my
reader knows roughly what I am talking about; you have experienced the
embarrassment that ensues when you are asked: how did you get to be, for

example, a student of literature, or the spouse or partner of that particular person? You can offer no answer to these questions that would derive from a law or necessity, from a plan or project. No, it was a matter of happenstance, of a lucky or not-so-lucky *encounter* at a unique place and time. And we feel this thrust of contingency most acutely when we contemplate those two events that ineluctably mark our singularity: the moments of birth and death, our unthinkable extremes. Exactly this embarrassment of unaccountability, by the way, is what Socrates seeks to provoke in the rhapsode Ion when he points out that the latter's art is not a *techné* obeying a reasoned set of procedures, but rather something uncontrollable, unforeseeable, something that occurs "by lot divine" (534c). Let us hold in reserve this notion that the contingencies of a lottery are in some sense constitutive of the domain of objects attended to by those Socrates calls—and who, in our post-Nietzschean world, can refuse this designation?—interpreters of interpreters.

> But in other situations the idea of chance takes on an essential and no longer merely operational meaning. Such is the case, for instance, in what may be called "absolute coincidences," those, that is to say, which result from the intersection of two totally independent chains of events. Suppose that Dr. Brown sets out on an emergency call to a new patient. In the meantime Jones, the contractor's man, has started making repairs on the roof of a nearby building. As Dr. Brown walks past the building, Jones inadvertently lets go of his hammer, whose (deterministic) trajectory happens to intercept that of the physician, who dies of a fractured skull. We say he was a victim of chance. What other term fits such an event, by its very nature unforeseeable? Chance is obviously the essential thing here, inherent in the complete independence of two causal chains of events whose convergence produces the accident.[3]

This text gives us an account of what contingency looks like. Not that the definition is complete (it leaves unstated the important criterion of relevance in the identification of the contingent event),[4] but it does usefully foreground the central idea of an unforeseen intersection of at least two series, of a "touching together," which is what contingency etymologically means. What I want to call attention to, however, is that at that moment when Monod seeks to convey to us his notion of essential chance he reverts to a narrative-fictional form, as if there were an inherent connection between the phenomenon of accident and the narrative rendering of an individual case or *casus*. What takes place within this scenography of the accident? We have, on the one hand, the teleological project of Brown, whose subjecthood even bears professional certification, and, on the other hand, the inadvertency of the colorless Jones, a mere assistant at one remove from the chief contractor's command. This remove introduces a certain play into the system; it opens up a free space in which the inadvertency—the inattention, the absence of control—asserts itself. Who knows? Perhaps it was a sudden thought of pleasure or some other whimsy that engendered the inadvertency in the mind of the hapless assistant. Or perhaps it was Brown who was careless, diverted by thoughts of his own pleasures and failing to note the sign that warned Danger: Falling Objects. Or maybe the rush of the double emergency (the word occurs twice in our text) simply made it impossible to oversee, control, and command the noise of detail inherent in the situation. The point is that every narrative of an accident must be incomplete, must contain a "black hole," as Musil puts it in the opening chapter of *Man without Qualities*, for the accident is precisely that intersection which cannot be foreseen and which therefore exceeds narrative programicity. The result, however, is clear: the most banal of mechanical tools becomes a free-falling wild card that strikes through the ethical project of the good doctor, reducing his mind and his medical *techné* to the mute facticity of a fractured skull. A nick on the ear would have illustrated the concept just as well, but Monod clearly wanted to achieve more here than mere illustration. He wanted to bring the accident's strike home to his reader, as we say; he wanted a shock effect, and none is greater than that of death, which, in the words of Jankélevitch, "is always improvised in a single blow."[5]

A second example:

Mächtiges Überraschen

Ein Strom entrauscht umwölktem Felsensaale,
Dem Ozean sich eilig zu verbinden;
Was auch sich spiegeln mag von Grund zu Gründen,
Er wandelt unaufhaltsam fort zu Tale.

Dämonisch aber stürzt mit einem Male—
Ihr folgen Berg und Wald in Wirbelwinden—
Sich Oreas, Behagen dort zu finden.
Und hemmt den Lauf, begrenzt die weite Schale.

Die Welle sprüht und staunt zurück und weichet
Und schwillt bergan, sich immer selbst zu trinken;
Gehemmt ist nun zum Vater hin das Streben.

Sie schwankt und ruht, zum See zurückgedeichet;
Gestirne, spiegelnd sich, beschaun das Blinken
Des Wellenschlags am Fels, ein neues Leben.[6]

Immense Astonishment

A river from a cloud-wrapped chamber gone,
Of rock; and roaring to be one with ocean,
Much it reflects from deep to deep, its motion
Never relenting valleyward and on.

But with abrupt demoniacal force,
By forest, mountain, whirling wind pursued,
Oreas tumbles down into quietude,
And there she brims the bowl, impedes the course.

The wave breaks into spray, astonished, back
Uphill it washes, drinking itself always;
Its urge to join the Father hindered, too,

It rolls and rests, is dammed into a lake;
The constellations, mirrored, fix their gaze:
The flash of wave on rock, a life made new.[7]

   As we turn to this example, the initial poem of Goethe's great sonnet sequence of 1807, we discover—despite all the obvious differences in aesthetic stature—a scenography comparable to Monod's lurid anecdote. I shall merely list, without the pretension of an adequate reading, some of the salient features of the text. The accidental intersection here assumes the double form, as in our first text, of a vertical fall, a sudden *Sturz*, and an encounter or *Begegnen*, which word is anagrammatically at work in the second quatrain's series: *Berg* (mountain), *Behagen* (pleasure), and *begrenzt* (limited, bound). The river is the cipher of teleology itself: the purpose present at the beginning and governing development toward an end that here bears the name of the river of rivers, the total river or father *Ozean*. And is it not, in part at least, a looseness or free play within the system that confounds this arc of intention: that is, a jumbling of letters that transforms the paternal telos of *Ozean* into the feminine aberration of *Oreas*? The nymph's plunge obeys no law but that of pleasure, a *Behagen* in which I hear, in addition to the *Begegnen* which will lend the subsequent sonnet its title,[8] a Lucretian *voluptas*,[9] a pleasure principle that actualizes itself precisely in the transgression or crossing of the paternal law and in the containment and inversion—*sich immer selbst zu trinken* (always to drink itself)—of the stream's energetic thrust. A similar play reduces the transcendence-seeking *fort* (away) of the current into the radically localized *dort* (there) of the accident's punctuality,[10] and it alters as well the iambic regularity of *Ein Strom* in the accentual deviation of *dämonisch*, which might be termed the privileged adverb of chance.[11] But what comes forth out of the turbulence or *Wirbelwind* (another Lucretian theme) is something quite different from the blank facticity of Monod's emblematic "skull": it is not a termination, but rather a beginning—*ein neues Leben* (a new life)— as if a birth had taken place. And indeed, what is this *Begegnen* and *Behagen* with its *Sprühen* (spewing), *Schwellen* (swelling), and *Trinken* (drinking) within the enclosure of the wide feminine *Schale* (bowl), if not the poetic inscription of coitus, pregnancy, and birth? At the same time, the text, standing as it does at the head of a sonnet sequence, must be read as a poetological emblem. As it were, Goethe accepts in this text the Socratic definition of rhapsode: what is born here "by lot divine" is the poem itself, an event in and of language; a work, which is to say: the radical emergence of the new and the singular.

Thus we have two variations on the scenography of chance, two possible outcomes, which we can summarize with this statement by Henri Atlan:

> Using noise, i.e., random perturbation, to untighten the constraints at one level produces some heterogeneity, and this goes together with disorder and malfunction because it is done randomly, i.e. with no relationship to the previous state of order, and no finality towards a planned, future state of order. However, up to a certain limit, if this malfunction, which is caused by loosening the constraints, is not enough to kill the whole system, the very same heterogeneity can be seen as a new state of order, having more complexity and less redundancy if it is used at a higher, more integrated level.[12]

These are, in brief, what I referred to above as our unthinkable extremes, and my contention is that the dynamic these two cases illustrate in their remarkable scenographies is one that concerns us as literary historians. Not merely because chance is a sometime theme of literature, but because it inhabits and opens up the literary field. Such would seem to be the poetological implications of Goethe's *Mächtiges Überraschen*, which can therefore be said to embody an aesthetic diametrically opposed to a Hegelian model. For Hegel, the task of art is to render the accidental necessary; that is, to bring the unity of the idea to appearance even within the domain of contingent externality.[13] Goethe's text, on the contrary, suggests that the aesthetic takes place when contingency is enacted, when the work establishes itself—beyond the legitimation of any law or necessity—as a singular event.[14] We might say that the work is that instance that refuses assumption into an overriding order; a unique, unforeseeable, unprogrammable intersection, which vibrates each time we encounter (*begegnen*) it. Something like this vibration, it seems to me, is set into motion even by Monod's little anecdote, which, rather than conceptualizing chance, stages it. Let us call it protoaesthetic, by which I mean that, despite its stereotypic, even hackneyed quality, and despite a certain awkwardness of execution, the anecdote still *strikes* us.[15] It contains a moment, I want to claim, in which the Real—that which for Lacan cannot be represented, be it symbolically or specularly,[16] and which Clement Rosset has specified as an unspeakable *idiocy*[17]—takes place. The work, qua work, is idiotic, a falling object, a divine toss of the dice. On this point, one final quotation:

> The oeuvre provokes us to think of the event. This in turn challenges our attempts to understand luck and chance, to envisage them, to take them in

hand, or to inscribe them within an anticipatory horizon. It is at least because of this fact that they are oeuvres and that they create an event, thereby challenging any program of reception. Oeuvres befall us. They speak about or unveil that which befalls us in its befalling upon us. They overpower us inasmuch as they explain themselves with that which falls from above. The oeuvre is vertical and slightly leaning.[18]

The Utterance and Narrative: Kleist

One sector of literary-critical inquiry to which the question of contingency pertains in what seems to me a pressing way is the area of narrative theory and analysis. It is certainly a matter of some urgency for literary criticism to develop a model of narrative structure and process that does not efface the movement of innovation and event that characterizes at least an important subset of the narratives we are concerned with; and it is likewise a matter of urgency that we as literary historians get some conceptual hold on our own narrative constructions. The most advanced and precise versions of narrative theory available today—I have in mind, for instance, the revised functional model of Barthes, the generative model of Pavel, and the semiotic model of Greimas[19]—are unanimous with regard to one point: that the *evenemential* dimension of narrative can be construed as a large sentence. This theoretical position mirrors a conception of the sentence, common to Augustine and Hegel, for example, as narrative: that is, as the unfolding in time of an internal and simultaneous project that, on completion of the utterance, recognizes itself as having become, in articulate form, what it was at the beginning. The staccato time and space of the utterance—the dimensions in which the event might unforeseeably take place— are gathered within a simultaneity that saturates the utterance with an a priori intelligibility. The narrative is a sentence, the sentence a narrative. What makes this symmetry possible is a shared theoretical move that I would characterize as the positing of the whole as given, a closed and simultaneous set. The movements of transposition within this set are chartable by all the models mentioned, but what gets lost in their mappings is precisely the emergence of the new, the duration/transformation of the whole in its radically innovative and unforeseeable character.[20] All of these models know, as far as I can tell, no accidents, which is at once their strength and their poverty.

I want to sketch here an alternative model of the utterance event that I believe bears important narratological and aesthetic ramifications, and that I find elaborated in the exceedingly canny and slippery text by Kleist, "On the Gradual Production of Thoughts while Speaking."[21] The text is canny because it is a theoretical text consisting almost entirely of a concatenation of anecdotes, as if its territory were the very sphere of indifference between generality and particular case or *casus*; and it is slippery because of its perpetual meander, as if each *Fall* or case it considers occasioned the new. It speaks, as all Kleist's texts do, of the event of speech, an instance of which it is.

The text begins with the advice: when you want to know something and cannot find it out through the inward search of meditation, then speak about it with the next person you "stumble on." Let us note right away that the sort of speech thematized here stands from the beginning in a dual relation: to an Other who exerts a defining pressure on the production of the utterance, and to a certain randomness, an unforeseeable occasion and collision (*aufstößt*). But as important as these factors are, they do not initially occupy the narrator's focus. Instead, he draws attention to a rather paradoxical view of the relation of speech to knowledge. The common view of this relation (which the narrator attributes to his addressee, thereby using the Other as a foil for the articulation of his own position) is that knowledge is the precondition of knowledgeable speech, that one should speak therefore only about that which one understands, that speech should be governed by the foresight of epistemic competence, by a *techné*. This common view, however, does not apply to all situations: "Damals aber sprachst du wahrscheinlich mit dem Vorwitz, *andere*, ich will, daß du aus der verständigen Absicht sprechest, *dich* zu belehren" ("At that time you were probably speaking with the aim of instructing *others*; I am thinking of cases where you speak with the understandable intention of instructing *yourself*"). The claim being made here is precisely that which Husserl nearly a century later in his *Logical Investigations* will dismiss as absurd: that the subject can indicate to itself something it does not antecedently know; that my speech can be, for me as well, the source of the new.[22] This would imply that in my speech there is an element irreducibly heterogeneous to my animating intention, that in speaking I am engaged in a field of interaction that I do not fully oversee; in short, that my utterance *is not properly my utterance*.

However, the absurdity or analytical dead end that Kleist's contention leads us to here is merely a function of the commonsense model of communication within which we evaluate it. If we shift our frame of reference, we get further, and I find a possibility for making such a shift in a little-known article called *Two Models of Communication* by the Soviet semiotician Juri Lotman.[23] As his title indicates, Lotman argues in this piece that there exist two types of communication, which, although always intertwined in concrete transactions, nevertheless have an independent existence and cultural function. The first of these models is what Lotman calls "external" or "I-He" communication. It corresponds to the function Kleist describes as *"andere . . . zu belehren,"* and can be schematized with the canonical diagram established by Roman Jakobson (schema 1):

CONTEXT

MESSAGE

ADDRESSOR--ADDRESSEE

CONTACT

CODE

Schema 1. "I-He" Communication

Lotman's description of "I-He" communication runs as follows: "Given a code, a text is introduced that is encoded in the code's system, transmitted and decoded. Ideally the text coincides at entrance and exit. The code constitutes the constant, the text is the variable" (99). Note that this model renders autocommunication absurd in the Husserlian sense, since the sender knows the message in advance and therefore could not but receive from it, were he or she to occupy the position of receiver, redundant information. In contrast to this canonical version of what communication is (a version linked, of course, in essential ways to the theories of the sentence and the narrative alluded to above), Lotman posits a structure he calls "internal" or "I-I" communication. His definition runs as follows: "Given a text that is encoded in a certain system, another code is introduced and the text is transformed; the code constitutes the variable and the texts differ at entrance and exit. An increase in information occurs in the text due to its interaction with the new code" (100). This structure can be diagrammed as follows:

CONTEXT 1   CONTEXTUAL DISPLACEMENT   CONTEXT 2

I--MESSAGE 1-----   -----MESSAGE 2--I

CODE 1   CODE 2

Schema 2. "I-I" Communication

Here we have a conception that begins to approach Kleist's notion of a language of self-teaching: in both, the process is not fully under the control, command, or *foresight* of the speaking subject; rather, the speech itself acquires, in its *detachment* from the subject, its own productivity in such a way that it alters decisively the situation of the speaker, enhancing his knowledge or information. The message that returns to me is not the same message *I* generated; it is not—and the statement seems a bit less absurd now—*properly speaking my message*.

This happy coincidence between Lotman's and Kleist's positions, however, should not tempt us to an overhasty identification of their views. In fact, essential differences obtain between the two. First of all, according to Lotman (and schema 2 makes this abundantly clear), the change in the status of the text comes about when the text is interpreted in a different context and in terms of a different code than at the point of its original formulation. The innovatory moment does not reside in the speech itself, but rather in the fact that other codes and contexts come to the text from the outside. For Kleist, however, the new codes and contexts—for it is a question, later, of much more than just *Gedanken* or knowledge—emerge in and through the utterance itself. We can put the matter this way: the power of *displacement*, which for Lotman affects only the *finished* text, is located by Kleist within the very process of speech production (*Verfertigung*). In the accomplishment of the utterance, and not merely on its conclusion, that alteration takes place through which something unforeseen, even by the subject producing the speech, occurs. Displacement is a spatiotemporal notion that points to a contingent element in the text: that my text returns to me in a different context, and thus with a different meaning, is something I cannot foresee. The text escapes my intentional control precisely to the degree that it is subject to accidents. What Kleist has done, then, is to introduce chance into the production of speech itself. Contingencies do not merely come to language from the outside but rather are effective, as it were, from the beginning, within the individual utterance. By virtue of this fact (which is the fact of facticity), the utterance can become an event, the site of the emergence of the new.

The name such emergence carries in *Über die allmähliche Verfertigung der Gedanken beim Reden* is *Einfall*: the *Einfall*, I want to claim, is the linguistic variant of *Zufall* (contingency or accident) that is the essay's theme. (The term *Einfall* might be approximated by the English word "occurrence," as a nominalization of "occur" in "It occurs to me.") What must be stressed here is that *Einfall* is not a psychological concept. It does not designate something that precedes speech in order then to be linguistically articulated; rather, it is an event that occurs in and through the utterance itself. And it does so because of the nonimmanence of speech, its spatiotemporal extension, its reach into a domain where contingencies occur. This is why the speaker Kleist describes draws out his utterance: he creates a temporal space, a delay, a gap between intention and realization; he pursues a strategy of postponement that maximizes the opportunities for the fortunate accident or *Einfall* to occur. "Ich mische unartikulierte Töne ein, ziehe die Verbindungwörter in die Länge, gebrauche auch wohl eine Apposition, wo sie nicht nötig wäre, und bediene mich anderer, die Rede ausdehnender, Kunstgriffe, zur Fabrikation meiner Idee auf der Werkstätte der Vernunft, die gehörige Zeit zu gewinnen" ("I mix in inarticulate sounds, draw out the connecting words at length, even use an apposition where it would not be necessary, and employ other devices that draw out speech in order to win the requisite time for the fabrication of my idea in the workshop of reason"). The *Einfall* is the unforeseen event that brings this process to a fortunate conclusion; it is the *turn* that transforms the initial situation of nonknowledge into one of knowledge; and it is the turn of the utterance itself that bends it to its conclusion: "Dergestalt, dass die Erkenntnis, zu meinem Erstaunen, mit der Periode fertig ist" ("In such a fashion that the cognition, to my astonishment, is finished with the period"). (Recall here the "staunt zurück" of Goethe's *Mächtiges Überraschen*.)

The notion of the rhetorical period referred to in this last quotation leads us a bit further into Kleist's conception. Let us define the period as the correlation of two dimensions: on the one hand, the syntactico-semantic dimension of linguistic intelligibility, and on the other, the somatic dimension of breath and pronunciation. It is the *Einfall* that brings these two dimensions into a fortunate alignment with one another, thereby constituting the period as a single whole. There is nothing necessary or automatic in this; the two orders can fail to coincide, submerging or overwhelming the subject in its failure to speak. For Kleist, the period, as a contingent order, is always precarious, is never fully mastered, and the essay contains an interesting reference to a speaker whose periods do not succeed, whose utterances *miscarry*, that is: fail to survive the contingencies of birth:

> Man sieht oft in einer Gesellschaft, wo durch ein lebhaftes Gespräch, eine kontinuierliche Befruchtung der Gemüter mit Ideen im Werk ist, Leute, die sich, weil sie sich der Sprache nicht mächtig fühlen, plötzlich mit einer zuckenden Bewegung, aufflammen, die Sprache an sich reißen und etwas Unverständliches zur Welt bringen.

> One often sees in a social group, in which through lively conversation a continuous insemination of spirits is at work, people who, because they do not feel that they have power over language, suddenly with a jerky movement flame up, tear language to themselves, and bring into the world something unintelligible.

Is this not the situation of the village judge Adam in Kleist's great comedy "The Broken Jug": the stutterer, the speaker in whom the syntactico-semantic and the somatic orders are in constant conflict—whose speech, as it were, is clubfooted? Language for Kleist is a field over which the subject has no command, but which imposes on the subject a complex set of exigencies, claims, and possibilities. Within this field the subject occupies the always limited position of the tactician, that is to say, one who, in his effort to gain momentary mastery of the situation, uses the accidents of the situation. This is why the military register is so prominent in the metaphorics of this text, or the register of wrestling and fighting in the related text "On Reflection." Indeed, it is also the reason that on the level of narrative construction Kleist favors battle or fight situations: the fight is characterized first, by a multiplicity of elements over which no subject has absolute control, second, by a turbulence that sets these elements into motion, and third, by the luck of accident, the unforeseen intersection of two elements or orders that decides the outcome, that selects one eventuality as opposed to another. Indeed, so close is this relationship of accident and battle that the Helgolanders, as Kleist reports on one occasion,[24] have seen fit to replace the contingencies of combat with those of a lottery.

The metaphorical register of military combat introduces a second feature by virtue of which Kleist's concept differs decisively from that of Lotman. In the case of the latter, the "I-I" communication is still considered strictly monologic, that is, without any reference to an addressee; but Kleist insists—as we have seen, from the first sentence on—that the addressee plays a constitutive role in the production of the utterance. To be precise: the addressee introduces the sense of pressing exigency so central to the Kleistian notion of speech; hence it is only when he elaborates on this constitutive role of the Other that Kleist draws on the military register. The inner field of speech, which is possessed, of course, of its own noise of detail, is surrounded by an external, pragmatic-contextual field in which questions of power and desire are being worked out and which itself is characterized by a precarious balance of order and randomness. The speaker becomes a "general," his words are "Truppen, die er ins Feld führt" ("troops that he leads into battle"), and his goal is, in the most extreme case, the "Vernichtung seines Gegners" ("the destruction of his opponent"). The Other is there, in every utterance of the speaker, and his or her actions, themselves unforeseeable and thus a further source of randomness, affect the course of speech. Nowhere is this clearer than in the central example the narrator of *Über die allmähliche Verfertigung der Gedanken beim Reden* adduces in the meander of his argument: the "Donnerkeil" or bolt of lightning with which Mirabeau inaugurated the French Revolution, that *Einfall* from above that altered the course of history and brought forth, out of a situation in which—this is Kleist's point—it could not be foreseen, the radically new. After a detailed discussion of the verbal delays and the play of energy investments that characterized Mirabeau's unheard-of sentence, the narrator offers this speculation: "Vielleicht, daß es auf diese Art zuletzt das Zucken einer Oberlippe war, oder ein zweideutiges Spiel an der Manschette, was in Frankreich den Umsturz der Ordnung der Dinge bewirkte" ("Perhaps in this way it was, finally, the jerking of an upper lip, or an ambiguous play in a lace cuff, which effected in France the toppling of the order of things"). Let us note the constellation: on the one hand, the order of things, the juridico-historical order grounded in the word of the king, and on the other hand, a certain disorder—a random twitching or *Zucken*, a play within the manifold folds of a lace cuff; then the vertical strike of the lightning bolt, the fall or *Sturz* of the old order, and the emergence of the new. The unforeseen message of this speech does not occur, as in Lotman's model, by virtue of displacement to a new context; rather, it produces that new context, and transforms the juridico-historical order by virtue of an operation that conforms to no antecedent program or intention.

We have reached the point where the comparison with Lotman has exhausted its usefulness, where it is necessary to seek support elsewhere for a reading of this marvelous text by Kleist. What is required is a theoretical model concerned with the investments of power and desire in speech, which develops a theory of conflict and tactics, which explores the relationship between discourse and "the order of things." To develop such a model we might move back in time to the extremely delicate conjunction of juridico-political rhetoric and introspective writing of Montaigne's *Essays*. There, in an essay entitled *Of Prompt and Slow Speech* (1:10), of which Kleist's text strikes me as a subtle redaction, we find the statement: "This also happens to me: that I do not find myself in the place where I look; and I find myself more by chance encounter than by searching my judgment."[25] Or we might move forward in time, to the discourse analysis of Michel Foucault, whose work could undoubtedly help us understand why Kleist's essay culminates in a discussion of pedagogical institutions that teach their pupils to answer such questions as: "What is property?" "What is the State?" To be sure, in Foucault's stunning inaugural lecture *L'ordre du discours* we would encounter the assertion that his (that is, Foucault's) research seeks "to introduce into the very roots of thought the notions of chance, discontinuity, and materiality."[26] Located between these two thinkers of the limits of the subject, I am convinced, Kleist's remarkable essay and his work generally would reveal anew their singular fecundity.

I shall leave these comparisons for another occasion and return instead to my point of departure, which was the question of narrativity. My initial observation was that current models of narrative are based on the grammatical conception of the sentence. The discussion of Kleist's account of the utterance event, in which the sentence-grammar emerges, as it were, *après coup*, seems to me to suggest the possibility of an alternative model of narrative structure and process, a model that takes into account the unforeseeable and transformative qualities of the event. Such a model would by no means abandon the inherited conception of narrative, with its "programs" and "projects," its actantial positions, its paradigmatic repertoires, bur rather set that model into a productive tension with its other: the sudden strike of accident, the unforeseeable event, the noise of detail, which constitute, as it were, that dimension of the prenarrative that makes narrative possibile at the same time that it eludes full absorption into any narrative rendering. Every narrative that seeks to close off this domain of contingency, and that therefore denegates its own contingent production, is ideological. The measure of narrative achievement is the degree to which this element of contingency becomes palpable without sliding into the all-too-easy and utterly false rendering of the world as thoroughly random.

Let me try to be a bit more precise about the alternative model of narrative structure I am suggesting. The base component of every available model of narrativity is a sequence whose coherence is guaranteed by the relations of solidarity among its elements—a sequence, in other words, that has the form of a chrono-logic, a temporal unfolding that is the actualization of a set of logical relations. The logical matrix (the semiotic square of Greimas, the logic of problem-solving in Pavel) guarantees the homogeneity of the narrative's temporal movement. My point is that this dimension of narrative structure—the *evenemential* dimension, the dimension of action—cannot be conceived autonomously. To do so is to define narrative circularly: narrative is a sentence, the sentence is a narrative. A noncircular definition of narrative will set the chrono-logic of action sequences into a relation with another order, or more precisely with a nonorder, the anachronic dimension of contingency. Narrative thus appears, as does every semiotic system, as the articulation of two noncoincident, independently organized systems. To phrase the matter differently, narrative order is only possible as limited, limited by a non-narrativity that randomly selects from an array of disjoint possibilities. Contingency is always a selection, an actualization that draws on a reservoir of other, nonactualized possibilities, a throw of the dice, an intersection. Without this selection there would be no events to concatenate in narrative series, but the selection itself—the fact that this, and not something else, happens—belongs to no chronological pattern. The formula Kleist uses in his own narrative experiments for this element of random selection is: "Es traf sich, daß . . ." ("It happened that . . ." or literally translated: "It met [encountered] itself that . . ."). Sentences thus introduced instigate narrative processes without themselves belonging to any narrative order. They mark the anchorage of the narrative in a field of contingency that can never be narratively appropriated, but without which narrative would not be.

Contingency and Modernity: Nietzsche

Literary history is intrinsically tied up with the question of modernity—with the question, that is, of the specificity of the present and the new and of the relationship of that present to a past, be it that of myth, of religion, or of an antecedent literature deemed classical. Indeed, not the least interesting way of considering the history of literature and its theory is to construe it as a series of engagements with the problem of modernity. My argument in this section is that the particular way this problem poses itself to *us* has to do with the issue of contingency, and I want to make this argument by focusing on a writer whose work continues today, perhaps more powerfully than ever before, to delineate what our modernity is. I am referring to Nietzsche, and I should like to begin by highlighting certain features of his second *Unzeitgemäße Betrachtung: Vom Nutzen und Nachteil der Historie für das Leben*.

Two readings of this text have gained widespread attention in recent years. The first, which I shall call the hermeneutic reading, is represented by Gadamer and, to an extent, by Habermas.[27] At issue in Nietzsche's text, according to this reading, is the hermeneutic problem bearing on purportedly "objective" interpretation: Nietzsche's critique is aimed at the historicist endeavor to understand the past "as it really was"—that is, at the objectivist self-understanding of a mode of interpretation that suppresses its own historical boundedness. This reading practices an *epistemological reduction* of Nietzsche's text insofar as it limits the force of his critique to the narrow perimeters of a theoretical debate involving the nature of historical understanding. But in fact Nietzsche's argument does not seek to demonstrate the adequacy or inadequacy of one form of knowing as opposed to another; it is not an epistemological question that guides his inquiry, but rather the broader cultural question of the function of institutionalized knowledge production in the organization of the sociocultural sphere.

A second, and I think more interesting, reading has been elaborated by Paul de Man in *Blindness and Insight*.[28] According to de Man, Nietzsche's text thinks through to its aporetic center the fundamental project of modernism: namely the attempt to capture and bring to consciousness—to live, one might say—the emergent moment of the *New*, the historical *present*, an attempt which, however, can only be carried out in a representational construct that, by its very nature, betrays that moment, condemning it to repetition. This reading contains an element I very much want to preserve: the insight that Nietzsche's text is profoundly concerned with the definition of the modern. The difficulty I see with de Man's reading is that it restricts this definition to an epistemological, or perhaps semiotic, crux; once again, the broader cultural implications of Nietzsche's essay are lost.

My contention is that a reading of *Vom Nutzen und Nachteil der Historie* that stresses the systems-theoretical aspects of the argument can bring into sharper focus the modernist cultural situation that Nietzsche so acutely diagnoses. I shall have to forego here a ramified account of what "systems theory" is and offer instead merely this violently brief definition: systems theory is concerned with the relations between systems and their environments, and the evolution of systems within their environments, which it analyzes in terms of the central problem of complexity and its reduction. The idea is embodied in the following passage from Humberto Maturana's "Biology and Cognition":

> A cognitive system is a system whose organization defines a domain of inter-actions in which it can act with relevance to the maintenance of itself, and the process of cognition is the actual (inductive) acting or behaving in this domain. Living systems are cognitive systems, and living as a process is a process of cognition. This statement is valid for all organisms, with and without a nervous system.[29]

The claim being made here is that the process through which organisms, or living systems, reduce the complexity of their environments, and thereby maintain themselves as systems within those environments, is cognition. Compare this passage with the following fragment by Nietzsche dating from 1887.

> Die Welt, so und so gesehen, empfunden, ausgelegt, daß organisches Leben bei dieser Perspektive von Auslegung sich erhält. Der Mensch ist nicht nur ein Individuum, sondern das Fortlebende Gesamt-Organische in einer bestimmten Linie. Daß er besteht, damit ist bewiesen, daß eine Gattung von Interpretation (wenn auch immer fortgebaut) auch bestanden hat, daß das System der Interpretation nicht gewechselt hat.[30]

> The world, seen in such and such a way, sensed, interpreted, such that organic life maintains itself in this perspective of interpretation. The human being is not only an individual, but the on-living total-organic in a definite line. That the human subsists, therewith it is proven that a species of interpretation (however further developed) has subsisted, that the system of interpretation has not changed.

Nietzsche's generalization of the concept of *interpretation* to cover the entire class of interactions between the organism and its environment has its exact analogue in Maturana's expansion of the notion of cognition. In both cases, the living system is viewed as a unit of interactions with a circumambient world such that the contingent challenges that world offers up to the system can be managed without the system's integrity being disrupted. The way this problem is solved—that is, the way the complexity of the environment is reduced and made operable—is through interpretive/cognitive manipulation: the living system is itself a system of inferences about the world or, as Nietzsche puts it, a *Gattung von Interpretation*. If we recall now that Nietzsche's second *Untimely Meditation* is concerned with the uses and disadvantages of history *for life*, it becomes clear why the hermeneutic reading is indeed a gross simplification. For Nietzsche, the question of interpretation is not primarily an epistemological issue, but rather a question of system constitution. And the living system or species of interpretation he is concerned with in the history essay is what we call culture. His analysis diagnoses, as we shall see, a certain crisis within that system.

For the purposes of my argument, Nietzsche's critique of history can be construed as resting on two basic premises. The first of these is that forgetting, far from being a deficient mode of apprehension, is a positive act requiring the exertion of force or *Kraft*. This *Kraft zu vergessen*, which Nietzsche also terms *das Unhistorische*, is the prerequisite for the maintenance of identity and for the ability to act. *Zu allem Handeln gehört Vergessen*, Nietzsche writes, illustrating the point with the following imaginary case:

> Denkt euch das äusserste Beispiel, einen Menschen, der die Kraft zu vergessen gar nicht besässe, der verurtheilt wäre, überall ein Werden zu sehen: ein Solcher glaubt nicht mehr an sein eigenes Sein, glaubt nicht mehr an sich, sieht alles in bewegte Punkte auseinander fliessen und verliert sich in diesem Strome des Werdens: er wird wie der rechte Schüler Heraklits zuletzt kaum mehr wagen den Finger zu heben. (2:246)

> Imagine the most extreme example, a human being who would not at all possess the power to forget, who would be condemned to see becoming everywhere: such a person no longer believes in his own being, no longer believes in himself, sees everything flowing apart in moving points and loses himself in this stream of becoming: he will be the authentic student of Heraclitus who in the end hardly dares to lift a finger.

The example, which Borges, by the way, exfoliated in his remarkable text *Funes the Memorious*, dramatizes the fundamental systems-theoretical insight that a system, if it is to maintain itself and act within its environment, must reduce the complexity of that environment to a manageable level. Such reduction involves, as Luhmann puts it, a "looking away" or *Absehen* from various features of the context so that some few features can be attended to. This mandatory ignorance or *forgetting* expresses what Luhmann calls the "requisite latency" (*notwendige Latenz*) of certain structures within any system, a latency that stands in harsh conflict with the Enlightenment project of a total illumination of the unthought. Nietzsche too insists on this counter-Enlightenment theme of knowledge *limits*, of a boundedness more fundamental than the limitations of historical perspective, which are merely one of its expressions:

> Die Heiterkeit, das gute Gewissen, die frohe Tat, das Vertrauen auf das Kommende—alles das hängt, bei dem Einzelnen wie bei dem Volke, davon ab, dass es eine Linie gibt, die das Übersehbare, Helle von dem Unaufhellbaren und Dunkeln scheidet. (2:247–48)

> Serenity, good conscience, the joyful deed, trust in what is to come—all that depends, both in individuals and in peoples, on the fact that there is a line that divides the surveyable and illuminated from that which cannot be illuminated and is dark.

This limit is the very condition of possibility of the continuing existence of the system; without forgetting, memory makes no sense.

The second basic premise of Nietzsche's essay bears on the question of *Wissenschaft*, of science, let us say, keeping in mind that this translation is neither entirely right nor entirely wrong. Of course, in retrospect Nietzsche came to view this question as the central one of his *Geburt der Tragödie* as well, the foyer of its originality; but the issue becomes all the more urgent when, in the second *Untimely Meditation*, Nietzsche turns to the contemporary cultural situation. It is here that knowledge has separated itself off from all other functions and becomes an autonomous force, exercised through its own institutions, within the sociocultural system. Nietzsche's insight, in other words, has to do with the functional differentiation of a scientific subsystem within the sociocultural field and with the fact that this subsystem has assumed the task of processing the past. This scientifization of history, indeed of the entire labor of transmitting the cultural heritage, has little to do with the objectivist epistemological premises of historicism; what is at stake, rather, is a fundamental shift in cultural organization.

The question Nietzsche is concerned with in his essay can be formulated as follows: what are the consequences for the culture at large, and in particular for the organization of cultural subjects, of the emergence of *Wissenschaft*; that is, of a specialized sociocultural subsystem for the production of the culture's relationship to its past? Nietzsche's analysis, it should be stressed, is both ramified and subtle, and especially in its metaphorics reveals an interpreter at work who is keenly aware of the manifold interconnections that run between various social subsystems. For example, there is an intriguing strand of argument running through the text that bears on the interrelations of scientifization, commodification, and state power. But I must ignore these features of Nietzsche's text here in order to focus on what I take to be the fundamental systems-theoretical problem his essay is concerned with, which seems to me to be the consequences that the modern reorganization of cultural memory bears for the organization of subjectivity. The following passage states what I take to be Nietzsche's basic finding:

> Jetzt regiert nicht mehr allein das Leben und bändigt das Wissen um die Vergangenheit: sondern alle Grenzpfähle sind umgerissen und alles was einmal war, stürzt auf den Menschen zu. So weit zurück es ein Werden gab, soweit zurück, ins Unendliche hinein sind alle Perspektiven verschoben. Ein solches unüberschaubares Schauspiel sah noch kein Geschlecht, wie es jetzt die Wissenschaft des universalen Werdens, die Historie, zeigt. (2:267–68)

> Now life no longer governs alone and tames the knowledge of the past: rather, all border markers have been torn down and everything that once was rushes in on the human being. As far back as there was a becoming, this far, into the infinite, all perspectives have been displaced. No previous race has ever seen such an unsurveyable spectacle as that which the science of universal becoming, history, displays.

The analysis here is systems-theoretically astute in that it focuses on the *Grenze*, the instituted difference between system and environment, as the key factor in the establishment and maintenance of any system. In order that a system be, there must be a border between system and context, and this border is established through a reduction of complexity, through an interpretive organization of the interrelations between the two. The cultural subsystem *Wissenschaft*, however, has produced a cultural environment that, in its complexity as *unüberschaubares Schauspiel*, can no longer be held within the limits—or *Sinngrenzen* (meaning limits), as Luhmann puts it—of that cultural organization of subjectivity that Nietzsche, in other passages, refers to as *personality (Persönlichkeit)*. The scientifization of the past has rendered impossible a unified style in all expressions of life. The modern is the demise of the personality—that is, of the inherited cultural form of subjectivity that expressed itself particularly in such synecdochally representative figures as the Author and the Intellectual; and it is the demise also of the grand historical narrative through which this personality accounted for its past. The modern subject has no reduced set of meaning selections that could be construed as its own, and no unique history that does not immediately proliferate into a thousand other histories. The subject has become a *Mann ohne Eigenschaften*.

There is a great deal more to be said about Nietzsche's truly prodigious essay, but I must begin my turn toward a conclusion. The single and simple point I am endeavoring to make with regard to *Vom Nutzen und Nachteil der Historie*, I trust, will have begun to profile itself. I want to claim that the systems-theoretical dimension of Nietzsche's text—its cybernetic stratum, if you will—points to an aspect of modern cultural organization that is essentially related to the concept of contingency. At issue here is the *background*, the circumambient field, in which entities, actions, and organizations are situated. This environmental field comes to be viewed as a field of infinite complexity such that any particular organization establishing itself within that field must be seen as an accomplishment of considerable *improbability*, and therefore as *problematic*. To put the matter another way: the background of infinite complexity, or noise, against which structures are profiled renders those structures *contingent* with regard to their existence and *imperiled* with regard to their maintenance. Whatever is, is in part attributable to the selection and institutionalization or replication of chance occurrences. This optic, though of course it renders impossible all teleological accounts of things, all the grand narratives of historical development, nevertheless does not make conceptualization and even prediction impossible. Quite to the contrary: the cultural perception of chance or contingency in human and natural affairs presupposes that mechanisms for the registration of chance have become available on a broad scale. Indeed, this was historically the case: the same nineteenth century that produced the *tychism* of Charles Saunders Peirce and the *Coup de dés* of Mallarmé also developed a probability theory capable of dealing with chance phenomena. As Ian Hacking has shown, the decisive achievements in probability theory with regard to this question of chance occurred at the beginning of the 1870s; in other words, they coincide exactly with the beginning of Nietzsche's writing career.[31] Furthermore, as Hacking has also shown, one precondition for this development of probability theory was the "avalanche of numbers" that overwhelmed European consciousness as governments, starting in the 1830s and then with increasing frequency, took it on themselves to gather statistical data regarding the constitution and behavior of their populations. My hypothesis, then, is that Nietzsche's contemporaneity with us with regard to the systems-theoretical dimension of his thought has to do with the fact that he lived in the same numerically saturated world as we do. The immensity of the data produced and collected has eliminated the possibility of a conceptual synthesis of that data; thus all syntheses—or systemic organizations—appear contingent and susceptible to evolution. In Nietzsche's view, it is not merely the rhapsode whose activity is constituted "by lot divine"; the entire earth, as he says in *Zarathustra*, is "ein Tanzboden für göttliche Zufälle" ("a dance floor for divine accidents"). This realm of contingency is the space of our modernity.

NOTES

1. See "Kontingenz," in *Historisches Wörterbuch der Philosophie*, ed. Joachim Ritter (Basel: Schwabe, 1971–89). See also the brilliant historical sketch of the concept by Hans Blumenberg, "Kontingenz," in *Handwörterbuch für Theologie und Religionswissenschaft* (Tübingen: Mohr, Paul Siebeck, 1959), cols. 1793–94.

2. See Denis Kambouchner, "The Theory of Accidents," *Glyph* 7 (1980): 149–75.

3. Jacques Monod, *Chance and Necessity: An Essay on the Natural Philosophy of Modern Biology*, trans. Austryn Wainhouse (New York: Knopf, 1971), 114.

4. On the criterion of relevance, see Max Weber, "Kritische Studien auf dem Gebiet der kulturwissenschaftlichen Logik," in Weber, *Gesammelte Aufsätze zur Wissenschaftslehre*, 2d ed., expanded, ed. Johannes Winkelmann (Tübingen: Mohr, Paul Siebeck, 1951), 215–90, esp. 215–33.

5. Vladimir Jankélevitch, *La mort* (Paris: Flammarion, 1977), 275. All translations are mine unless otherwise noted.

6. Johann Wolfgang von Goethe, *Werke*, 8th ed., ed. Erich Trunz (Hamburg: Christian Wegner, 1955), 1:294.

7. Johann Wolfgang von Goethe, *Selected Poems*, ed. Christopher Middleton (New York: Suhrkamp, 1983), 177. The translation is by Christopher Middleton.

8. The title of the second sonnet in the sequence is "Freundliches Begegnen" ("Friendly Encounter").

9. See the study of Lucretius by Michel Serres: *La naissance de la physique dans le texte de Lucrèce: Fleuves et turbulences* (Paris: Minuit, 1977), which gives an excellent account of the role of randomness in Lucretius's thought and its relation to such concepts as that of *voluptas*.

10. I have in mind here Roland Barthes's notion of the *punctum* of the photograph. Cf. Barthes, *Camera Lucida: Reflections on Photography*, trans. Richard Howard (New York: Hill and Wang, 1981), esp. 27: "A photograph's *punctum* is that accident which pricks me (but also bruises me, is poignant to me)." For a generalization of Barthes's concept to include other domains of representation, see Jacques Derrida, "Les morts de Roland Barthes," in Derrida, *Psyché: Inventions de l'autre* (Paris: Galilée, 1987), 273–303.

11. On the Greek concept of *daimon*, on which Goethe's own concept was patterned, see Walter Burkert, *Greek Religion*, trans. John Raffan (Cambridge, Mass.: Harvard University Press, 1985), 179–81. Burkert's account reveals the close affinity between the notions of *daimon* and accident.

12. Henri Atlan, "Disorder, Complexity, and Meaning," in *Disorder and Order: Proceedings of the Stanford International Symposium*, ed. Paisley Livingston (Saratoga, Calif.: Anma Libri, 1984), 116.

13. See Dieter Henrich, "Hegels Theorie über den Zufall," in Henrich, *Hegel im Kontext* (Frankfurt: Suhrkamp, 1971), 157–86, esp. 171.

14. See my article, "Theory of Events: Foucault and Literary Criticism," *Revue internationale de philosophie* 41 (1987): 420–32.

15. In addition to the "fall" and the "encounter," the "strike" is one of the standard figures in the scenography of the accident. See, for example, Leibniz's letter to Coste, "On Necessity and Contingency" (1707) in *Die philosophischen Schriften von Gottfried Wilhelm Leibniz*, ed. C. J. Gerhardt (Hildesheim and New York: Georg Olms, 1978), 3:400–404, esp. 402.

16. The Lacanian category of the Real is developed in Lacan, *The Four Fundamental Concepts of Psycho-Analysis*, ed. Jacques-Alain Miller, trans. Alan Sheridan (New York: Norton, 1981), 53–66. The chapter is entitled "Tuché and Automaton," two Aristotelian concepts for accident.

17. Clement Rosset, *Le réel: Traité de l'idiotie* (Paris: Minuit, 1977).

18. Jacques Derrida, "My Chances/*Mes Chances*: A Rendezvous with Some Epicurean Stereophonies," in *Taking Chances: Derrida, Literature, Psychoanalysis*, ed. J. Smith (Baltimore: Johns Hopkins University Press, 1987), 16–17.

19. Roland Barthes, "Introduction to the Structural Analysis of Narrative," in Barthes, *The Semiotic Challenge*, trans. Richard Howard (New York: Hill and Wang, 1988), 95–135; A. J. Greimas and J. Courtes, *Semiotics and Language: An Analytical Dictionary*, trans. L. Crist et al. (Bloomington: University of Indiana Press, 1982); Thomas G. Pavel, *The Poetics of Plot: The Case of English Renaissance Drama* (Minneapolis: University of Minnesota Press, 1985).

20. My argument is influenced here by Gilles Deleuze's Bergson interpretation in Deleuze, *Cinéma I: L'image-mouvement* (Paris: Minuit, 1983).

21. The text is available in Heinrich von Kleist, *Sämtliche Werke und Briefe*, ed. Helmut Sembdner (Munich: Hanser, 1982), 3:319–24. All translations of Kleist are mine.

22. See Jacques Derrida's analysis of this Husserlian argument in Derrida, *La voix et le phénomène* (Paris: Presses universitaires de France, 1967), 45.

23. Available in *Semiotics and Structuralism: Readings from the Soviet Union*, ed. Henryk Baran (White Plains: M. E. Sharpe, 1977), 98–102. Subsequent page references are given parenthetically in the text.

24. Kleist, *Sämtliche Werke und Briefe*, 3:285.

25. *The Complete Essays of Montaigne*, trans. Donald M. Frame (Stanford: Stanford University Press, 1957), 26–27.

26. Michel Foucault, *L'ordre du discours* (Paris: Gallimard, 1971), 61.

27. Hans Georg Gadamer, *Wahrheit und Methode* (Tübingen: Mohr, Paul Siebeck, 1965), 309–12; Jürgen Habermas, *Knowledge and Human Interests*, trans. Jeremy J. Shapiro (Boston: Beacon Press, 1971), 274–300.

28. Paul de Man, "Lyric and Modernity," in de Man, *Blindness and Insight* (Minneapolis: University of Minnesota Press, 1983), 166–86.

29. Humberto R. Maturana and Francisco T. Varela, *Autopoesis and Cognition: The Realization of the Living*, Boston Studies in the Philosophy of Science 42 (Dordrecht, Holland: Reidel, 1980), 17.

30. Friedrich Nietzsche, "Anpassung," in *Sämliche Werke*, critical edition, 15 vols., ed. Giorgio Colli and Mazzino Montinari (Berlin: de Gruyter, 1980), 3:251. Subsequent references to Nietzsche's work are drawn from this edition and are indicated parenthetically by volume and page.

31. Ian Hacking, *Taming Chance*, forthcoming from Cambridge University Press.

SIXTEEN

A NARRATOLOGICAL EXCHANGE

Dorrit Cohn and Gérard Genette

WHAT FOLLOWS is a translation of letters originally published in *Poétique* 61 (February 1985) under the title "Nouveaux nouveaux discours du récit." They were written shortly after the publication of Genette's *Nouveau discours du récit* (Paris: Seuil, 1983), the sequel to his "Discours du récit" in *Figures III* (Paris: Seuil, 1972). Both works are now available in English, under the titles *Narrative Discourse Revisited* (trans. Jane E. Lewin, Ithaca: Cornell University Press, 1988) and *Narrative Discourse* (trans. Jane E. Lewin, Ithaca: Cornell University Press, 1980). Page numbers without further specification refer to the English edition of *Narrative Discourse Revisited*. The translation is by Dorrit Cohn.

May 14, 1984

Dear Gérard Genette,

In view of the generous attention you gave my work in your *Nouveau discours du récit*, I have turned down a couple of requests to review the book: such a discussion would inevitably be self-serving. I prefer instead to send you these more direct and more personal reactions, limiting myself to our principal areas of (diminishing) disagreement. I shall thus leave aside (perhaps for a second round) matters of mutual, but not mutually controversial, concern, such as your dazzling execution of the implied author.

The two issues I shall address are those you treat under "Narrative of Thoughts?" (58–63) and under "Person" (96–113), with the latter extending also into "Narrative Situations" (114–29). On both these matters I am happy to note that your present position (as compared to the one you held in your earlier work) has moved so much closer to my own. But, as you know, growing consensus tends to sharpen remaining disaccord. In this case it ranges—self-defensively and otherwise—from a matter as small as nomenclature to the one you call "this far-reaching difference [cette vaste querelle]" (60) concerning the distinction of person in fiction.

I. Narrative of Thoughts

1. I am not surprised that you declined to adopt my terminology in *Transparent Minds: Narrative Modes for Presenting Consciousness in Fiction* (Princeton: Princeton University Press, 1978), but why are you surprised that I did not adopt yours? My terms are by no means a "modification [remaniement]" (59) of those you coined in your *Discourse* of 1972. Note that I first proposed "narrated monologue" in 1966! My term "psychonarration," to be sure, was coined at a later date; but how could I have adopted your "narrativized discourse" for a technique that designates primarily the *non*discursive psychic life of fictional characters—precisely a mode you now concede (60–61) having disregarded in your earlier work—and which, incidentally, continues to remain nameless in your system?

2. As for the reason why I altered your "order" (59): I quite simply followed a dialectical, rather than an incremental, ordering principle. My reasons for placing the narrated monologue in final position were didactic—the concept was not yet generally known in anglophone criticism at the time—as well as substantive—it combines aspects of narration *and* quotation. In this respect you misrepresent me when you write "by definition, quoted monologue and narrated monologue treat thought as speech, *in her work as in mine*" (60, my emphasis); more on this below.

3. Even as I applaud the closer attention you now give to free indirect style (52–55)—especially your acknowledgment of its affinity to internal focalization—I am puzzled by your renewed insistence on the presumed parity of its use for rendering speech and thought (54–55). How could this style have become so central a device in modern narrative—as well as so central a subject for the poetics of narrative—if it were no more than just another quotational technique? All the significance and problematics of the free indirect seem to me related to the fact that, *when applied to silent thought*, it can never be understood *simply* as a quotational device. It is only here, for example, that fusions and confusions with focalized narration can come into play, resulting in potentially insoluble problems of interpretation—as in fantastic tales.

4. On this account I cannot accept either of your two "blunt dichotomies" (61–62). In my view, free indirect style can soften (equivocate) both these dichotomies when it applies to thoughts rather than to spoken words. Don't you in fact yourself reveal the softness of your horizontal dichotomy (in the table, 62) when you admit to an initial hesitation as to where to place "transposed speech," and then decide on its *double* assignation? I suspect that, if this "transposition" had referred merely to free indirection in the rendering of *dialogue*, you would simply, without a moment's hesitation, have assigned it to the "character" column; the hesi-

tation, precisely, arises for the free indirect rendering of thought (monologue): is it the narrator's language (and thus narration) or the character's
(and thus quotation)?

5. As you may have divined by now, I intend to counter your stingy
"one-sixth" concession (61) for nonverbalized consciousness with a claim
for fully half my system. Having declared the narrated monologue equivocal in respect to rendering nonverbal thought, I can let you have ("let us
arbitrarily figure") half that. However, since indirect quotation is no more
than a marginal aspect of psychonarration (see *Transparent Minds*, 38), I
must claim this mode in its entirety.—Joking aside: even your amended
presentation of the techniques still seems to me to overestimate considerably the identity of psychic life and mental language. I don't mean this—
needless to say—in regard to some abstract psychological norm or order,
but in regard to the actual state of affairs in the narrative canon to which
we ordinarily refer; and I won't be so unfair even as to take *A la recherche*
as my norm, where—your synthetic sentences notwithstanding—you will
surely grant that quotational presentation of the psyche is the exception
rather than the rule!

6. What probably chagrined me most in this section is the "peculiarity
[bizarrerie] of distribution" (60) that you attribute to me in assigning the
autonomous monologue to first-person forms. The fact is that this is exactly in accord with your own earlier discussion of this form (under the
name "immediate speech"): "When the monologue blends with the whole
of the narrative, as in the *Lauriers* . . . , the higher . . . instance is annulled,
and we are again in the presence of a narrative in the present tense and 'in
the first person' " (*Narrative Discourse*, 175). And just above this you say:
"As the example of Molly Bloom's monologue in *Ulysses* shows . . . , the
monologue does not have to be coextensive with the complete work to be
accepted as 'immediate' " (*Narrative Discourse*, 174), etc. Whence my puz-
zlement over the passage beginning: "I have particular difficulty understanding why Dorrit Cohn . . ." (60). Molly's monologue, you say here, is
no more a first-person text than any monologue quoted within traditional
third-person novels, since it is itself part of a third-person novel. But you
would surely agree that the heterodiegetic narrator of the rest of *Ulysses* in
no way infringes on the *internal* structure of "Penelope," which is therefore
in every sense identical to the structure of independently published autonomous monologues like *Les lauriers, amants, heureux amants*, and others.

Would you now also refuse to classify *Les lauriers* or *Martereau* as homodiegetic fictions (and note that I don't say "homodiegetic *narratives*")? If
so, how are we to understand what you say further on in *Narrative Discourse Revisited* about homodiegetic texts written in the present tense: that
in them "the narrative recedes before the discourse and at every moment
seems to be tipping over into 'interior monologue' "—whereupon you re-

fer the reader to the chapter of *Transparent Minds* entitled "Fron Narration to Monologue" (82)?

No, on careful reflection, there is only one way I can explain to myself your insistence that the autonomous monologue belongs to hetero- rather than to homodiegetic fictional forms. Just as my view of this matter is, in your view, "due to a misplaced desire to *divide up*—that is, to an *over*valuation of the criterion of person" (60, my emphasis), your view of this matter is, in my view, due to a misplaced desire to *join together*—that is, to an *under*valuation of the criterion of person. Which opens directly on to my second group of problems.

II. Person

1. Concerning the boundary between hetero- and homodiegetic types of narration (103–5): my reservation about "Stanzel's gradualism" concerns only the figural, not (as you seem to believe) the authorial side of this boundary (see "The Encirclement of Narrative: On Franz Stanzel's *Theorie des Erzählens*," *Poetics Today* 2, no. 2 [Winter 1981]: 165–66). So I welcome your accord with Stanzel concerning homo-heterodiegetic transitions of the type found in *The Brothers Karamazov* or *Madame Bovary*.

But I still firmly insist (against Stanzel, and now apparently against you as well) on the discontinuity between homo- and heterodiegetic forms on the *figural* side. All the cases of alternating person-reference you mention here—with the single exception of *La route des Flandres*—are clearly "true" homodiegetic narratives with "fake" third-person reference (*Henry Esmond*, *Stiller*, the Borges stories). By contrast, the Simon novel and numerous other modernist novels just as clearly play with this effacement of person in a self-consciously transgressive manner—transgressive of what is (as I hope you will agree) the fundamental logic of pronominal reference. You seem in fact to reaffirm the boundary on the next page, when you refer (after Lejeune) to autobiography in the third person as a "figure of enunciating" (106). What you say here of real autobiographies must surely also hold for homodiegetic novels that imitate this form (*Henry Esmond*, etc.).

2. Concerning transvocalization: you are mistaken about the case of *Crime and Punishment*. Fairly extensive fragments in homodiegetic form have been preserved and published (one of about forty pages); see *The Notebooks for Crime and Punishment*, edited and translated by Edward Wasiolek (Chicago: University of Chicago Press, 1967). What is more, these notebooks also demonstrate Dostoevsky's hesitations and reflections about narrative voice. Here are some samples: "The plot's structure is such, *the story must be narrated by the author and not by the hero*." "If a confession, then in parts it will not be chaste and it will be difficult to imagine why it was written." "Narration from the point of view of the author, sort of in-

visible but omniscient being, who doesn't leave his hero for a moment" (*Notebooks*, 52–53).

As for the case of *The Castle*: Your comments here are evidently based on my brief mention of this transvocalization in *Transparent Minds* (169–71), not on my earlier article (to which I there refer the interested reader): "K. enters *The Castle*: On the Change of Person in Kafka's Manuscript," *Euphorion* 62 (1968). In the latter—which you list in your bibliography but have clearly not read—I go into much greater detail and indeed provide what you call for when you say "One therefore expects to see here an account of the advantages of Kafka's final decision; but Cohn immediately takes refuge in the circular argument of the infallibility of the author's choice" (111). Since Kafka (unlike Dostoevsky) never explained his reasons for transvocalizing his first version, a cautious critic cannot go beyond conjectures (whence "the phrases that express doubt or evasion" you highlight in my text [112]). But my detailed examination of Kafka's manuscript led me to pin down very strong arguments concerning the "modal advantages" of his transvocalization and I am not at all doubtful or evasive concerning its theoretical implications. Please look up my article and judge for yourself.

Would a recasting of *The Castle* (or *Crime and Punishment* or *The Ambassadors*) in first-person form constitute (for me) "such a catastrophe" (112)? Did I ever suggest it would? All I maintain is that it would constitute a different work, and one that would create a different effect on the reader. The "Ur-Castle" (as I call the homodiegetic first version of the early chapters of Kafka's novel) would actually have constituted a new narrative mode, in fact the one you seek yourself to create with your spectral "empty box " (121)—on which more below. Kafka *seems* to have preferred reverting to a (slightly) more traditional mode, one that (as you yourself concede) is "*able*, naturally and without any transgression, to do more than homodiegetic narrating can do" (113).

Finally, at the risk of ridicule for taking your final word on "Person" (113) seriously: to attribute the choice of person to a writer's momentary whim does not greatly disturb me—provided only it is not therefore taken to be a less weighty choice than all the others he makes in matters of narrative form. If anything, I would maintain that—since it is usually the *first* choice he makes (on the level of discourse)—it is *more* weighty than others; perhaps even (dare I say this?) more weighty than the choice of focalization, since focalization can vary from scene to scene, even sentence to sentence, whereas person is for the most part (in conventional narrative) maintained stable from start to finish.

3. Now for the "empty box" (121ff.). (I leave aside your alignment of "external" focalization with the other types of focalization. This has never seemed plausible to me. In this respect—if not in all others—I agree with

Mieke Bal's critique.) I agree with you that homodiegetic narration without presentation of the narrator's past inner life is conceivable in theory and that it can be approached in practice. I would however maintain that this form of narration calls—better: *yells*—for interpretation. More precisely, it forces the reader to seek a plausible motivation in the psyche of the narrator: macho hard-boiledness in the case of Hammett or Hemingway, pathological removal of affect in the case of *L'Etranger*, mental vacancy in the case of Benjy. In this respect your sixth type of narrative situation stands in clear contrast with your fifth type: no educated reader will seek a psychorealistic interpretation for the narrator's barring of inside views in *The Killers*—though he may of course feel the need to seek the author's *aesthetic* motivation.

As you suggest yourself, none of the examples you propose for external focalization in homodiegetic texts (121–24) is entirely satisfying, since we can't be sure that there *is* a mental life eclipsed in them: "Meursault . . . does not say (not: *what he thinks about it*, but:) *whether he thinks about it*" (124). This is where I want to propose the "Ur-Castle" for your consideration, particularly the quotations you will find in section 3 (35–38) of my *Euphorion* article. As you will see there, this Kafka text even includes sentences of the type Barthes declares anomalous in first-person form and that you conjecture as perhaps acceptable "tomorrow under the pressure of stylistic innovation" (126). Whether or not you agree with my overall argument in that essay—I wrote it over twenty years ago and am not sure I myself still agree with everything I say in it—I think the textual passages themselves point up the major differences effected by grammatical persons in narratives of this sort. From which I conclude that your sixth type, if it exists, far from demonstrating the parity (symmetry, similitude) between third- and first-person narration, once again confirms the basic differential between them—*especially* where the rendering of a protagonist's inner life is concerned.

Well, my thoroughly hardened position is now plainly in view. Need I say that nothing would please me more than the prospect of these remarks triggering a *Nouveau nouveau discours du récit*?

Dorrit Cohn

July 10, 1984

Dear Dorrit Cohn,

No, there will be no *Nouveau nouveau* . . . —beyond this one. Even the worst things come to an end; and if, on occasion, I am to return to narratology, I don't want it to be on a perennial mode of self-criticism or self-satisfaction. But your letter puts its finger on such neuralgic points that I'd like to answer it, if only briefly, following roughly the sequence of your remarks.

I. 1. and 2. Since your terminology is, at least in part, anterior to mine, the word "modification [remaniement]" was clearly inappropriate. Nor do I in any sense wish to impose on you the use of the term "discourse" to designate a mode that you regard, on principle, as nondiscursive. But I persist in preferring the participial triad *narratized/transposed/reported*, which clearly indicates the degree of the narrator's intervention on the material, discursive or not—even as I understand the reasons for your dialectical presentation in the form of *psychonarration/quoted monologue/narrated monologue*.

I. 3. and 4. Concerning the free indirect, our disagreement seems to me circumscribed but irreducible. I see no reason to limit its potential for creating ambiguity to silent thought: my manufactured example in chapter 9, note 10 (55) could quite as easily, and without loss of interest, be cast in terms of dialogue: "I announced to Maman my intention to marry Albertine: I was definitely in love with her." Which justifies my double inscription of free indirect discourse: even in this case one does not know "who speaks"—which, in this specific instance, means that one does not know whether or not Marcel (the hero) pronounced the second phrase.

I. 5. Less irreducible perhaps, even if one abandons (it's done!) the battle of numbers, but clearly central: our disagreement concerning the more or less verbal nature of psychic life in literature. Since you disarm me by objecting to my Proust (though one could argue that the grand meditation of *Temps retrouvé* presents itself in its entirety as a vast monologue more or less directly reported—substantially improving my score), I feel strongly inclined to disarm you by objecting to your Joyce—setting the stage for my next move.

I. 6. Having arrived at the interior monologue, it seems to me that here you misunderstand my criticism. My point is not that it belongs to heterorather than to homodiegesis; I simply refuse to "assign" it to either, i.e., to say that it belongs to one form rather than to the other. My reason for this is simple and it was well described (and illustrated) by Joyce himself; you should be the last to underestimate it, since you were the one to draw the correct terminological consequence: its *autonomy*. Granted that, by definition, an autonomous monologue (like any character's discourse) *is* cast in first-person form. But this tells us nothing about the narrative situation of the work in which it occurs and to which, again by definition, nothing (no quotation signal or introduction) attaches it formally. This surrounding narrative can be heterodiegetic, like *Ulysses* in respect to Molly's monologue, or it can be homodiegetic—far more rarely, it would seem, but my "Joycean *hapax*" in the *Recherche* (*Narrative Discourse* 180) offers an example. It can also be neither/nor, when it is missing: the case of *Les lauriers sont coupés*, where the monologue is not only autonomous (i.e., unquoted and unintroduced), but also isolated, and thus fully independent, capable of constituting a narrative in its own right, cast in first-person/present tense. Autonomous or independent, *Penelope* or *Lauriers*, its *own* first-person form in no way *places* it *in* a first-person narrative. In fact the nature of the surrounding narrative situation (homodiegetic, heterodiegetic, or non-existent) is not pertinent for its description. And this is why, to my mind, it is no more appropriate to discuss it in a study of "first-person narration" than in a study of "third-person narration." One must either situate it altogether outside this dichotomy, or else stop regarding this dichotomy as a fundamental principle for a narrative typology. As you know, I have opted for the latter, for this and a number of other reasons.

II. 1. Regarding the boundary between these two types, I am pleased to see that we agree on effacing half of it: its authorial side. On the figural side, one would no doubt have to examine patiently each of the disputed examples we invoke; but the crux of the debate clearly lies in the role one here accords to the *grammatical person*, which for you remains the criterion, or rather the essential *fact*, while for me it is merely one linguistic trait among others—variously pertinent in different idioms, periods, and situations. To give you a simplistic idea of my feeling on this matter: if a family member (Mimi or grandpa) referred to herself or himself constantly in the third person, we would soon realize that their discourse is nonetheless fully autodiegetic. You describe in grammatical terms, I describe in terms of narrative relationships, and there will inevitably be cases where these two descriptions will no longer be equivalent and interchangeable.

II. 2. and 3. I capitulate completely when it comes to the homodiegetic versions of *Crime and Punishment* and *The Castle*; the mounting disarray of our Parisian libraries is a poor excuse for the bibliographic carelessness with which I treated these texts. The justifications offered by Dostoevsky strike me as no more weighty than those offered by James. But the sentences from Kafka quoted in your article delight me: some of them are indeed, as you say, perfect examples for external focalization in homodiegetic narration. And the incontestably paradoxical nature of this narrative situation may readily and sufficiently explain, as you do, why Kafka finally decided in favor of his transvocalization. But to explain is not to justify: in his case, as in others, his practice (in writing the first version of *The Castle*) was ahead of his critical consciousness; it is on account of the latter that, on rereading, he took fright at such sentences as: "*apparently* on account of my tiredness I hesitated to leave the road." In short, I regret—a bit childishly, perhaps—the initial, "slighty *less* traditional" version. At the same time I maintain that the vocal choice—even if it comes "first"—is not necessarily the most important, since in this instance it did not prevent a writer as exacting as Kafka from pairing it, at least for a time, with a reputedly incompatible modal choice (and you will have to admit that the latter was apparently more important to him). In short, the drafts of *The Castle* bring me (by your auspices) two confirmations on two decisive, and clearly interrelated, points: the relative independence of mode and voice, and the possibility of external focalization in homodiegetic narration. A paradoxical possibility, to be sure, but, all things considered, not more so than the inverse possibility—the problematical crux of the psychorealist novel since Flaubert and Kafka—which demands of the reader an equal dose of cooperation or (as Coleridge would say) of complaisance. That the former (the more recent) of these paradoxical forms calls out more loudly (as you put it) for interpretation than the simple external focalization in heterodiegesis is perhaps a proof of its greater expressive power. I would simply say that it surprises the reader more, that it increases his perplexity, or his malaise. It's up to him, at that point, to decide whether interpretation (as in the case of the fantastic) is his only way out.

A final word on this matter: once again, to assert that the vocal choice does not inevitably determine the modal choice (and vice versa, as the Jamesians have said and shown many times over) is not to diminish the importance of this vocal choice. I am even inclined to say that it augments its importance by restoring its autonomy. I do not choose a certain voice *for its modal effects*, but *for itself*: is this not the proudest homage? As one of Goldoni's characters says: "If I love you, it is not for profit."

Trying now to pin down precisely what continues to separate us, I would define it as follows: (1) an evident (though purely quantitative) difference concerning the importance we attribute to the verbal in psychic life (within fiction, that is); (2) a curious misunderstanding, or cross-purpose, concerning the importance of voice, which you are intent on justifying functionally on the grounds of its modal effects, and which for me is so self-evident that it needs no justification whatever (I overstate!) and no function; (3) the common feature of these two disagreements? No doubt the opposition between what I would describe in you—somewhat unjustly (but it does explain your disdain for external focalization)—as a remnant of psychologism, and what you could describe in me—somewhat justly— as a predisposition in favor of formalism and/or behaviorism (I reserve the right to choose between macho hard-boiledness, pathological removal of affect, and mental vacancy). In sum, a slight disagreement about the importance (or the interest) of the "inner life"—I mean, of course, in literature.

Gérard Genette

INDEX

Aarne, Antti, 213, 215

Acker, Kathy, 197

Ackroyd, Peter, *Chatterton*, 59, 61; *T. S. Eliot*, 59, 61

Adams, Robert M., 113, 122

Adams, Timothy Dow, 69

Adorno, Theodor W., 38, 44

Aeneid, The. See Virgil

Afanasev, Alexander, 212

Alexis, Paul, 217

Altman, Janet Gurkin, 81–82, 86

Ambassadors, The, 262. *See also* James, Henry

Ancien Regime et la Revolution, L'. See Tocqueville, Alexis de

Anderson, Edith, 163, 177; "Genesis and Adventures," 167

Anderson, Sherwood, 113; "Hands," 112

Andrew, Dudley, 14

Annan, Gabriele, 196

Apuleius, 51

Aquinas, Thomas, 237

Arabian Nights, The, 40

Aragon, Louis, 187; *Aventures de Télémaque, Les*, 197; *Libertinage, Le*, 183, 197

Aristotle, 8, 24, 29, 30, 37, 41, 237

Arndt, Walter, 215

Arneth, Alfred von, 71, 75, 85

Arnim, Achim von, 214

Arthur, Chester G., 125, 135

As I Lay Dying. See Faulkner, William

Assmann, Aleida, 35, 43

Assommoir, L'. See Zola, Émile

Atlan, Henri, 241, 256

Augustine, Saint, 242

Aurelius, Marcus, *Meditations*, 51

Auriant, Albert, 231

Auto de Fé. See Canetti, Elias

Aventures de Télémaque, Les. See Aragon, Louis

Awarding of the Prize, The. See Günter de Bruyn

Bachmann, Ingeborg, 36

Bakhtin, Mikhail, 9, 10, 12, 180, 181, 195

Bal, Mieke, 5, 6, 263

Balzac, Honoré de, *Human Comedy, The*, 17, 28

Barthes, Roland, 5, 8, 10, 11, 13, 38, 44, 176, 183, 193, 198, 219, 232, 242, 256, 257

Baumgartner, Hans Michael, 41

Belgrader, Michael, 213–215

Bell, Pearl, 62, 69

Being and Time. See Heidegger, Martin

Benjamin, Jessica, 194, 195, 198

Benjamin, Walter, 32, 42

Benn, Gottfried, 32

Bernhard, Thomas, 36

Bernier, Olivier, 85; *Secrets of Marie Antoinette*, 72

Bible, The, 12, 18

Birth of Tragedy. See Nietzsche, Friedrich

Bleikasten, André, 106, 111

Blöcker, Günter, 95

Bloom, Harold, 47, 60

Blumenberg, Hans, 256

Böll, Heinrich, 32

"Bolt from the Blue." *See* Kirsch, Sarah

Bonheim, Helmut, 122

Booth, Wayne C., 3, 33, 43, 126, 135, 177

Bordwell, David, 14

Borges, Jorge Luis, 261; "Funes the Memorious," 252

Borst, Arno, 31, 41

Boswell, James, 62

Boym, Svetlana, 179, 195

Braudy, Leo, 232

Breton, André, *Nadja*, 187

Broch, Hermann, 32, 36

Broken Jug, The. See Kleist, Heinrich von

Brontë, Emily, 53

Brooke-Rose, Christine, 196

Brooks, Peter, 219, 221, 222, 225, 231, 232

Brothers Karamazov, The. See Dostoevsky, Fyodor

Brouillon pour un dictionnaire des amants. See Wittig, Monique

Browne, Sir Thomas, 53

Brunetière, Ferdinand, 225, 232

Bürger, Peter, 183, 196
Buridan's Jackass. See de Bruyn, Günter
Burke, Kenneth, 33, 43, 135
Burkert, Walter, 256
Burkhardt, Jakob, 18
Butor, Michel, 176, 178; *Le Modification*, 173, 174

Camus, Albert, *Etranger, L'*, 263
Canetti, Elias, *Auto da Fé*, 36
Carrington, Leonora, 12, 181–198; *Down Below*, 186, 187, 197; *Hearing Trumpet, The*, 12, 181–187, 191, 196, 198; *Stone Door, The*, 196
Carroll, Lewis, 112; *Alice's Adventures in Wonderland* and *Through the Looking Glass*, 122
Carroll, Philip, 69
Carter, Angela, 196, 197
Castle, The. See Kafka, Franz
Cervantes, Miguel de, *Don Quixote*, 22
Chadwick, Whitney, 198
Chase, Richard, 106, 111
Chatman, Seymour, 11, 42
Chatterton. See Ackroyd, Peter
Chekov, Anton, 113, 121
Child in the House, The. See Pater, Walter
Chodorow, Nancy, 210, 215
Cicero, 35
"Cinderella," 200
Cixous, Hélène, 10, 184, 196; "Laugh of the Medusa," 182, 196
Clausen, Jeanette, 164, 177
Cohn, Dorrit, 4–9, 13, 17, 19–22, 26–28, 32, 34, 42, 43, 45, 58–60, 102–104, 107, 108, 111, 114–116, 120, 122, 123, 135, 136, 157, 167, 177, 263
Coleridge, Samuel Taylor, 266
Collingwood, R. G., 18, 36, 43, 44
Commedia. See Späth, Gerold
Confessions, The. See Rousseau, Jean-Jacques
Confessions of Felix Krull. See Mann, Thomas
Conrad, Joseph, 112
Conroy, Peter, 231
Constant, Benjamin, 25
Corino, Karl, 156, 158
Corneille, Pierre, 23
Corngold, Stanley, 7, 157, 158
Corps lesbien, Le. See Wittig, Monique
"Coup de dés." *See* Mallarmé, Stéphane
Courtes, J., 257

Courtney, William L., 11, 14
Crapanzano, Vincent, 223, 232
Crime and Punishment. See Dostoevsky, Fyodor
Croce, Benedetto, 18
Culler, Jonathan, 32, 42, 101, 111

Daiches, David, 135
Damm, Sigrid, 178
Dangerous Liaisons. See Laclos, Choderlos de
Danto, Arthur C., 31, 37, 41, 44
"Dead, The." *See* Joyce, James
Death in Venice. See Mann, Thomas
Débâcle, La. See Zola, Émile
de Bruyn, Günter, 163–178; *Awarding of the Prize*, 166; *Buridan's Jackass*, 166; "Sex Swap," 163–168
Decline and Fall of the Roman Empire. See Gibbon, Edward
Defoe, Daniel, 53; *Moll Flanders*, 21
Degenfelder, Pauline E., 111
Deleuze, Gilles, 257
de Man, Paul, 21, 28, 250–251, 257
Demandt, Alexander, 34, 43
De Quincey, Thomas, 53
Derrida, Jacques, 11, 14, 256–257
Desnos, Robert, 187; *Liberté ou l'amour!, La*, 197
Diengott, Nilli, 5, 6, 13
Dilthey, Wilhelm, 18, 26, 147, 148, 157
Dinnerstein, Dorothy, 206, 214
Doane, Mary Ann, 233
Döblin, Alfred, 32
Doctor Faustus. See Mann, Thomas
Dos Passos, John, 32
Dostoevsky, Fyodor, *Brothers Karamazov, The*, 261; *Crime and Punishment*, 261, 262, 265; *Notes from the Underground*, 22
Down Below. See Carrington, Leonora
Dray, William H., 35, 43
Dubliners. See Joyce, James
Dubois, Jacques, 218, 223, 231–233
Duby, Georges, 41
Ducornet, Rikki, 197
Dujardin, Eduard, *Les Lauriers sont coupés*, 260, 264–265
Dumont, Louis, 28
Durrani, Osman, 69

Eagleton, Terry, 38, 44, 181, 196
Eckermann, Johann Peter, 90

Eco, Umberto, 33, 42
Edel, Leon, 52, 59, 61, 62
Edwin Mullhouse: The Life and Death of an American Writer. See Millhauser, Steven
Ehrlich, Sybille, 177
Einstein, Carl, 32
Eliot, T. S. See Ackroyd, Peter
Ellmann, Richard, 59, 61, 135
"Emerald Uthwart." *See* Pater, Walter
Emerson, Caryl, 195
Emmerich, Wolfgang, 171, 178
Engler, Jürgen, 178
Ethics. See Spinoza, Baruch
Etranger, L'. See Camus, Albert
Eusebius, 51

Faulkner, William, *As I Lay Dying*, 102–111; *Sound and the Fury, The*, 107
Faust: A Tragedy. See Goethe, Johann Wolfgang von
Fielding, Henry, *Tom Jones*, 125
Finney, Gail, 11
First Circle. See Solzhenitsyn, Aleksander
Fish, Stanley, 33, 42
Flaubert, Gustave, 23, 25, 28, 124, 266; *Madame Bovary*, 152, 261
Fletcher, Lain, 60
Fliess, Wilhelm, 83
Flynn, Elizabeth, 227, 228, 233
Forster, E. M., 3, 43, 112
Foucault, Michel, 9, 37, 44, 74, 76, 81, 85, 86, 248, 257
Freeman, James A., 213
Freud, Sigmund, 21, 83, 86, 193, 206, 214, 233
Friedemann, Käte, 13
Friedman, Alan, 112, 113, 122
Friedrich, Paul, 197
Frisch, Max, 36; *Stiller*, 261
Frye, Northrop, 43
Fühmann, Franz, 167
"Funes the Memorious." *See* Borges, Jorge Luis
Furet, François, 41

Gadamer, Hans-Georg, 12, 250; *Truth and Method*, 257
Gadol, Joan Kelly, 195
García Márquez, Gabriel, 227
Gay, Peter, 42, 234
Geertz, Clifford, 233

Geffroy, M. A., 71, 85
Gelley, Alexander, 232
Genette, Gérard, 3–6, 13, 32, 42, 258
Geninasca, Jacques, 25
Gerlach, John, 122
Gibbon, Edward, *Decline and Fall of the Roman Empire, The*, 18
Gide, André, 32; *Immoralist, The*, 20, 22
Gilbert, Sandra, 180, 195
Gilligan, Carol, 195
Girard, Georges, 71, 75, 85, 86
Goethe, Johann Wolfgang von, 89, 90, 92, 95, 97, 144, 256; *Faust: A Tragedy*, 211, 215; "Immense Astonishment," 239–241, 246; *Sorrows of Young Werther, The*, 80
Goldknopf, David, 166
Golob, Eugene, 35, 43
Gooch, G. P., 71, 85
Gosman, Lionel, 28
Gottsched, Johann Christoph, 29
Grass, Günter, 32; *Tin Drum, The*, 38
Greimas, A. J., 13, 242, 249, 257
Grimm, Reinhold, 32, 41
Gubar, Susan, 180, 195, 198
Guerillères, Les. See Wittig, Monique
Guizot, François, 18

Habermas, Jürgen, 250, 257
Hacking, Ian, 255, 257
Hamburger, Käte, 5, 8, 9, 13, 19, 32, 34, 35, 42, 43, 49, 56, 61
Hammett, Dashiel, 263
Handke, Peter, 32, 36; *Langsame Heimkehr*, 32
"Hands." *See* Anderson, Sherwood
"Hansel and Gretel," 200, 207, 208, 212
Hardy, Thomas, 112
Harshav, Benjamin, 4
Hartman, Geoffrey, 158
Hatfield, Henry, 157
Hearing Trumpet, The. See Carrington, Leonora
Hedges, Inez, 197, 198
Heftrich, Eckhard, 153, 159
Hegel, G.W.F., 18, 23, 26, 37, 241, 242
Heidegger, Martin, *Being and Time*, 158; *What is Metaphysics?*, 158
Heinrich von Ofterdingen. See Novalis
Hemingway, Ernest, 113, 121, 263
Hemmings, F.W.J., 224, 226, 232

Henninger, Peter, 155, 158
Henrich, Dieter, 256
Henry Esmond, 261. *See also* Thackeray, William Makepeace
Hermotimus, or the Rival Philosophies. See Lucian
Hernadi, Paul, 67–69
Herrmann, Anne, 178
Hesiod, 18
Hickman, Hannah, 156
Hildesheimer, Wolfgang, *Marbot: A Biography*, 8, 45, 47, 49, 53, 57–61, 87–97
History of the French Revolution. See Michelet, Jules
Hoberman, Ruth, 63, 69
Hochhuth, Rolf, 38
Hofmannsthal, Hugo von, *Lord Chandos Letter*, 157
Hölderlin, Friedrich, *Hyperion*, 126, 135
Holquist, Michael, 195
Homer, 18, 23, 51
House of Fear, The. See Carrington, Leonora
Howald, Stefan, 153, 155, 159
Human Comedy, The. See Balzac, Honoré de
Husserl, Edmund, 244; *Logical Investigations*, 243
Hutcheon, Linda, 196
Hyperion. See Hölderlin, Friedrich

Iliad, The. See Homer
Imaginary Conversations. See Landor, Walter Savage
Imaginary Portraits. See Pater, Walter
"Immense Astonishment." *See* Goethe, Johann Wolfgang von
Immoralist, The. See Gide, André
Ingarden, Roman, 7
Ion. See Plato
Irigaray, Luce, 10, 184, 196
Iser, Wolfgang, 7, 33, 43

Jacobs, Joseph, 213
Jakobson, Roman, 244
James, Henry, 21, 124, 221, 231, 265; *Ambassadors, The*, 262
Jameson, Frederic, 38, 44
Jankélovitch, Vladimir, 239, 256
Jauss, Hans Robert, 39, 41, 44
Jennings, Chantal, 233
Jennings, Michael, 154
Johnson, Uwe, 32

Jost, François, 80–82, 86
Joyce, James, 26, 32, 113, 121, 124, 126, 133; "Dead, The," 114–123; *Dubliners*, 117, 123; *Portrait of the Artist as a Young Man*, 7, 115–117, 124–129, 132, 135, 136; *Stephen Hero*, 126, 135; *Ulysses*, 126, 260, 264
"Juniper Tree, The," 10, 199–215

Kafka, Franz, 22, 227, 263; *Castle, The*, 6, 157, 262, 265–266; *Metamorphosis, The*, 142, 167, 177; *Trial, The*, 7, 120, 123
Kahler, Erich, 28
Kambouchner, Denis, 256
Kant, Hermann, 32
Kant, Immanuel, 26
Kayser, Wolfgang, 32, 41
Kenner, Hugh, 128, 133, 135–137
Kermode, Frank, 112, 113
Killers, The. See Hemingway, Ernest
King Lear. See Shakespeare, William
Kipphart, Heinar, 39
Kirsch, Sarah, 11; "Bolt from the Blue," 167–178
Kleist, Heinrich von, 242–249, 257; *Broken Jug, The*, 247; *On the Gradual Production of Thoughts While Speaking*, 242–249; *On Reflection*, 247
Klotz, Volker, 39, 44
Knapp, Bettina, 196
Kolodny, Annette, 227, 233
Korte, Barbara, 122
Kosellek, Reinhart, 29, 31, 41, 43
Krakowski, Anna, 232
Krauss, Rosalind, 198
Krenzlin, Leonore, 166, 177
Kristeva, Julia, 10, 180, 195, 196, 214
Kühn, Dieter, 36

Lacan, Jacques, 10, 241, 257
LaCapra, Dominick, 35, 43, 158
Laclos, Choderlos de, *Dangerous Liaisons*, 21, 80, 81
Lafayette, Mme de, 23–24; *La Princesse de Clèves*, 28
Lämmert, Eberhard, 13, 32, 42
Landor, Walter Savage, *Imaginary Conversations*, 51, 52
Langsame Heimkehr. See Handke, Peter
Lanser, Susan S., 12, 14
Lardreau, Guy, 41

"Laugh of the Medusa." *See* Cixous, Hélène
Lauriers sont coupés, Les. See Dujardin, Eduard
Lawrence, D. H., 112
LeGoff, Jacques, 41
Leibniz, Gottfried Wilhelm von, 256
Lentricchia, Frank, 10, 14
"Lesen und Schreiben." *See* Wolf, Christa
Lessing, Gotthold Ephraim, 29
Lesskow, Nicolai, 32
Lévi-Strauss, Claude, 10, 13
Liberté ou l'amour, La. See Desnos, Robert
Libertinage, La. See Aragon, Louis
Lincoln, Bruce, 215
"Little Tom Thumb." *See* Perrault, Charles
Locke, John, 78, 85
Logical Investigations. See Husserl, Edmund
Loomis, Roger Sherman, 197
Lord Chandos Letter. See Hofmannsthal, Hugo von
Lotman, Juri, 243–248
Lotte in Weimar. See Mann, Thomas
Lubbock, Percy, 3
Lucian, Hermotinus, or the Rival Philosophies, 51, 52
Ludwig, Emil, 19
Luhmann, Niklas, 237, 252
Lukacs, John, 44
Lukács, Georg, 37, 231, 232
Lukens, Nancy, 176, 178
Lützeler, Paul Michael, 8, 9

Macaulay, Thomas Babington, 53
McHale, Brian, 4, 197
Madame Bovary. See Flaubert, Gustave
Madelénat, Daniel, 52, 61
Maeterlinck, Maurice, 145, 157
Mallarmé, Stéphane, "Coupe de dés," 255
Mallet, Carl-Heinz, 214
Mandelbaum, Maurice, 35, 43
Mandelstam, Osip, 179, 195
Mann, Thomas, 63, 136; *Confessions of Felix Krull, Confidence Man,* 22; *Death in Venice,* 7, 114–123; *Diaries,* 69; *Doctor Faustus,* 62–69, 95; *Lotte in Weimar* (The Beloved Returns), 92; *Joseph and his Brothers,* 155; *Story of a Novel: The Genesis of Doctor Faustus,* 65, 69; "Tonio Kröger," 7, 124, 125, 129–132, 135, 136
Mansfield, Katherine, 113, 121
Man Without Qualities. See Musil, Robert

Marbot: A Biography. See Hildesheimer, Wolfgang
Marcuse, Herbert, 194
Maria Theresa, 9, 70–86
Marie Antoinette, 9, 70–86
Marius the Epicurean: His Sensations and Ideas. See Pater, Walter
Martens, Lorna, 28
Martereau. See Sarraute, Nathalie
Martial, 51
Martin, Wallace, 231
Marx, Karl, 26, 37
Mattenklott, Gert, 152, 153, 159
Matthews, John T., 111
Maturana, Humberto R., 251, 257
Maurin, Mario, 231
Meditations. See Aurelius, Marcus
Meier, Christian, 41
"Metamorphosis, The." *See* Kafka, Franz
Metzradt, Carl von, 213
Michelet, Jules, *History of the French Revolution, The,* 33–34
Mickelsen, David, 11, 12, 216
Mill, John Stuart, 83
Miller, Alice, 200, 213
Miller, Eric, 157
Miller, Nancy K., 193, 198
Millhauser, Steven, *Edwin Mullhouse: The Life and Death of an American Writer,* 62–69
Mink, Louis O., 42
Minow-Pinkney, Makiko, 61
Mrs. Dalloway. See Woolf, Virginia
Modification, La. See Butor, Michel
Mönckeberg, Vilma, 213
Monod, Jacques, 238–241, 256
Montaigne, Michel de, "Of Prompt and Slow Speech," 248; *Essay,* 257
Montgomerie, Norah, 213
Montgomerie, William, 213
Morrisette, Bruce, 173, 178
Mossmann, Carol A., 215
Mulvey, Laura, 232
Munz, Peter, 33, 42
Muraski, Lady, 227
Musil, Robert, 32; *Diaries,* 159; *Man without Qualities, The,* 36, 239; *Young Törless,* 7, 125, 138–159

Nabokov, Vladimir, *Pale Fire,* 62
Nadja. See Breton, André

Nana. See Zola, Émile
Nausea. See Sartre, Jean-Paul
Neubauer, John, 7
Neutsch, Erik, 32
Nicolson, Harold, *Some People*, 45, 46, 52
Nicolson, Nigel, 52
Nierrad, Jürgen, 178
Nietzsche, Friedrich, 37, 142, 156, 257; *Birth of Tragedy, The*, 253; "On the Uses and Disadvantages of History for Life," 250–255; *Thus Spoke Zarathustra*, 255
Nora, Pierre, 41
Notebooks of Malte Laurids Briggs, The. See Rilke, Rainer Maria
Notes from the Underground. See Dostoevsky, Fyodor
Novalis, *Heinrich von Ofterdingen*, 209

"Of Prompt and Slow Speech." *See* Montaigne, Michel de
"On the Gradual Production of Thoughts while Speaking." *See* Kleist, Heinrich von
"On Reflection." *See* Kleist, Heinrich von
"On the Uses and Disadvantages of History for Life." *See* Nietzsche, Friedrich
Orenstein, Gloria, 191, 196, 198
Orlando: A Biography. See Woolf, Virginia
Ortheil, Hanns-Joseph, 42
Ostriker, Alicia, 180, 195
Ovid, 51

Pale Fire. See Nabokov, Vladimir
Pamela. See Richardson, Samuel
Pater, Walter, 46–53, 58–61; "Child in the House, The," 46; "Emerald Uthwart," 47; *Imaginary Portraits*, 46–48, 60; *Marius the Epicurean: His Sensations and Ideas*, 46–52, 57–59, 61; "Sebastian von Storck," 47, 51, 52; *Studies in the History of the Renaissance*, 46–48
Pavel, Thomas, 8, 9, 242, 249, 257
Peirce, Charles Saunders, 255
Péret, Benjamin, 187, 197
Perrault, Charles, "Little Tom Thumb", 215
Petrie, Dennis, 65, 69
Phillips, John A., 214
Pike, Burton, 156, 157
Plato, 29, 37, 51; *Ion*, 238
Plutarch, 23
Porath, Hans-Jörg, 44

Porter, Carolyn, 14
Portrait of the Artist as a Young Man, A. See Joyce, James
Portugese Letters, 71
Prince, Gerald, 33, 42
Princesse de Clèves, La. See Lafayette, Mme de
Proust, Marcel, *Remembrance of Things Past*, 18, 20, 260, 264

Quest for Christa T., The. See Wolf, Christa

Racine, Jean, 23
Rank, Otto, 210, 215
Ranke, Leopold von, 18, 36, 43
Red and the Black, The. See Stendhal
Rich, Adrienne, 180, 208, 215
Richardson, Samuel, *Pamela*, 80
Ricoeur, Paul, 31, 41
Rieckmann, Jens, 8
Rifaterre, Michael, 33, 42
Rilke, Rainer Maria, *Notebooks of Malte Laurids Brigge, The*, 32, 42
Rimmon-Kenan, Shlomith, 4–6, 10, 14
Riquelme, John Paul, 126–128, 135, 136
Robbe-Grillet, Alain, 32, 42
Röhrich, Lutz, 214
Rölleke, Heinz, 213
Ron, Moshe, 6
Ross, Stephen M., 110, 111
Rosset, Clement, 241, 257
Rougon-Macquart, Les. See Zola, Émile
Rousseau, Jean-Jacques, *Confessions, The*, 18, 21
Rousset, Jean, 80, 82
Route des Flandres, La. See Simon, Claude
Rowbotham, Sheila, 195
Rüsen, Jörn, 31, 41, 44
Ruskin, John, 58
Russo, Mary, 180, 195
Ryan, Judith, 8, 14

Sackville-West, Vita, 52, 57, 58
Salvan, Albert, 231
Sarraute, Nathalie, *Martereau*, 260
Sartre, Jean-Paul, *Nausea*, 113
Schieder, Theodor, 43, 44
Schiffer, Werner, 41
Schiller, Friedrich, 144
Schlegel, Friedrich, 35, 43
Schlöndorff, Volker, 141, 156

Schnädelbach, Herbert, 28
Scholes, Robert, 3, 13
Schor, Naomi, 193, 198
Schorer, Mark, 135
Schweickart, Patrocinio, 227, 233
Scott, Walter, 17, 53
"Sebastian van Storck." *See* Pater, Walter
Secrets of Marie Antoinette. See Bernier, Olivier
Seeba, Hinrich C., 44
"Self-Experiment." *See* Wolf, Christa
Serres, Michel, 256
Seventh Horse and Other Tales, The. See Carrington, Leonora
Sévigné, Mme de, 82, 83, 86
"Sex Swap." *See* de Bruyn, Günter
Shakespeare, William, 53, 144; *King Lear,* 26, 101
Simon, Claude, *Route des Flandres,* 261
Small, Ian, 52, 61
Smith, Barbara Herrnstein, 113, 122
"Snow White," 200
Snyder, Louise, 213
Solzhenitsyn, Aleksander, *First Circle,* 18
Some People. See Nicolson, Harold
Sound and the Fury, The. See Faulkner, William
Späth, Gerold, *Commedia,* 32, 42
Spinoza, Baruch, 51, 52; *Ethics,* 48
Spivak, Gayatri, 183, 197
Stallybrass, Peter, 181, 196
Stanton, Domna, 196
Stanzel, Franz K., 4–6, 13, 14, 32, 164, 166, 167, 169, 177, 261
Starr, G. A., 28
Steig, Reinhold, 214
Stein, Gertrude, 112
Steiner, George, 38–39, 44
Steinmetz, Horst, 41
Stendhal, 28; *Red and the Black, The,* 24
Stephen, Leslie, 46
Stephen Hero. See Joyce, James
Sternberg, Meir, 4
Sterne, Laurence, 53
Stiller. See Frisch, Max
Stone, Lawrence, 31, 41
Stone Door, The. See Carrington, Leonora
Stopp, Elisabeth, 157
Story of a Novel, The: The Genesis of Doctor Faustus. See Mann, Thomas
Strachey, Lytton, 45, 59

Strauss, Botho, 32
Studies in the History of the Renaissance. See Pater, Walter
Suleiman, Susan Rubin, 12, 14
Swales, Martin, 155, 157
Szondi, Peter, 30, 41

Tatar, Maria, 10, 14, 28, 215
Thackeray, William Makepeace, *Henry Esmond,* 261
Thompson, Kristin, 14
Thompson, Stith, 213, 215
Thucydides, 23
Thus Spoke Zarathustra. See Nietzsche, Friedrich
Tibullus, 50, 51
Tindall, William York, 135
Tin Drum, The. See Grass, Günter
To the Lighthouse. See Woolf, Virginia
Tocqueville, Alexis de, *Ancien Régime et la Révolution, L',* 34
Todorov, Tzvetan, 13, 81, 82, 86, 101, 111
Tolkien, J.R.R., 199, 213
Tolstoy, Leo, 23, 25; "Death of Ivan Ilych, The," 23, 28; *War and Peace,* 92
Tom Jones. See Fielding, Henry
"Tonio Kröger." *See* Mann, Thomas
Travers, P. L., 199
Trial, The. See Kafka, Franz
Tripp, Edward, 197

Ulysses. See Joyce, James
Ussher, Arland, 213

Varela, Francisco T., 257
Veyne, Paul, 41
Virgil, 51; *Aeneid, The,* 23
Voltaire, Le, 217, 218

Walser, Martin, 32
Walzel, Oskar, 122
War and Peace. See Tolstoy, Leo
Warhol, Robyn, 11, 14
Warner, Marina, 196
Watt, Ian, 28
Weber, Eugen, 207, 215
Weber, Max, 256
Weigand, Hermann, 69
Weinrich, Harold, 41
Weiss, Peter, 38
Weisstein, Ulrich, 122

Wellbery, David E., 12
What is Metaphysics? See Heidegger, Martin
White, Allon, 181, 196
White, Hayden, 9, 33–35, 42, 43
Winnicott, D. W., 193, 198
Winterson, Jeanette, 196, 197
Wittig, Monique, 184; *Brouillon pour un dictionnaire des amants*, 182; *Corps lesbien, Le*, 182; *Guerrières, Les*, 182, 187
Wolf, Christa, 32, 36; "Lesen und Schreiben," 178; "Self-Experiment: Appendix to a Report," 163, 172, 173, 176, 178; *Quest for Christa T., The*, 172
Wolff, Larry, 9

Wölfflin, Heinrich, 113, 122
Woolf, Virginia, 8, 26, 32, 45–47, 52–61, 83, 124; *Diary*, 61; *Mrs. Dalloway*, 135; *Orlando: A Biography*, 47, 52–59, 61
Wordsworth, William, 50

Yacobi, Tamar, 4
Yaeger, Patricia, 180, 181, 194, 195, 198
Young Törless. See Musil, Robert

Zola, Émile, *Assommoir, L'*, 232; *Débacle, La*, 227; *Nana*, 11, 216–234; *Rougon-Macquart, Les*, 218, 231, 232
Zweig, Stefan, 71, 85